BURNT CORK AND TAMBOURINES

BURNT CORK AND TAMBOURINES

A Source Book of Negro Minstrelsy

CLIPPER STUDIES IN THE THEATRE
ISSN 0748-237X * Number Eleven

Edited by

Edited by William L. Slout

**The Borgo Press
An Imprint of Wildside Press**

MMVII

Copyright © 2007 by William L. Slout

All rights reserved.
No part of this book may be reproduced in any form
without the expressed written consent
of the author and publisher.
Printed in the United States of America

Library of Congress Cataloging in Publication Data:

Burnt cork and tambourines : a source book of Negro minstrelsy / edited
by William L. Slout.
    p. cm. — (Clipper studies in the theatre, ISSN 0748-237X ; no. 11)
    Includes index.
    ISBN 0-89370-358-3. — ISBN 0-89370-458-X (pbk.)
    1. Minstrel shows—History. I. Slout, William L. (William
Lawrence). II. Title. III. Series.
PN3195.B87 2007   95-3717
791'.12'0973—dc20   CIP

FIRST EDITION

CONTENTS

Dan Bryant

INTRODUCTION

The *New York Clipper*, in its support of popular amusements, made a monumental contribution to historians of popular culture. This is particularly true in the area of negro minstrelsy. The paper carried a weekly column of minstrel activities almost from its inception. Biographical sketches of burnt cork performers were frequently included. And there were innumerable reminiscences and chronicles of minstrels and minstrelsy contributed by men who were a part of that colorful profession. This interest continued as long as the *Clipper* and minstrelsy were functioning institutions. During the 19th century the *Clipper* was the only house organ for the hundreds of burnt corkers performing in every part of America, and was looked to for reliable reporting in an era when theatrical puffery predominated.

This volume is representative of the *Clipper's* contributions to minstrel history. With but one exception, all of the material has been compiled from its pages. Col. T. Allston Brown's "Early History of Negro Minstrelsy," a painstaking documentation of its "rise and progress in the United States," was carried in fifty-nine installments, beginning with the anniversary issue on February 17, 1912, and continuing intermittently through March 8, 1914. The work is the most complete record of the genre ever assembled.

T. Allston Brown (1836-1918) is often underrated as an amusement historian, perhaps because he lacks an eloquence of style. He possesses neither the fluidity of William Dunlap, the quaintness of Joseph Ireland, nor the whimsy of George C. D. Odell. But where other 19th century amusement chroniclers were primarily interested in the "higher drama," Brown concerned himself with a broader theatre; where they identified themselves with their immediate theatrical provinces, Brown kept no provincial borders. In announcing the beginning of Brown's *Clipper* series on the "History of the American Theatres." (March 10, 1888), the editor stated:

> We speak advisedly when we say that it is the most complete---indeed, the only complete---history of the kind that has ever been written.... He has been more than thirty-two years collecting the material for this stupendous work. In all that time his researches have been thorough, patient, and intelligent. No historian of our stage has labored with greater enthusiasm; none who have chronicled the rise and progress of the drama in America have approached their task with a more sympathetic appreciation of its manifold perplexities and its vast possibilities.

Brown's varied experiences in the theatrical profession as literary correspondent, publisher, editor, business agent, advance man, circus treasurer, theatre manager, and talent agent supplied him with an intimate understanding of the business and its people. The mobility required by the nature of his various employments

History of the American Stage (1870) and *A History of the New York Stage from the First Performance in 1732 to 1901*, three volumes (1903), are still in use, but his other material, his prolific contributions to the *New York Clipper*, are not easily available to the general researcher. They have been buried on dusty archival shelves for over one hundred years. And the microfilm copies of the paper, with its small type and hazy images, make for laborious reading. It is the intent of the editor, therefore, to create a greater accessibility to Brown's "Early History of Negro Minstrelsy" as compiled in *Burnt Cork and Tambourines*.

To this end, Brown's work, which originally resembled a "scrapbook," almost randomly assembled, has been freely tampered with. The material has been rearranged and edited into a more orderly format so as to enhance its usefulness as a source book of minstrelsy.

To make the volume more complete, additional material has been added, separated from Brown's efforts through the Burnt Cork Supplement, a collection of articles written by men who were closely involved with the blackface entertainment. The selections were originally published over a period from 1860 to 1915. They augment Brown's history by giving a more personal view of minstrelsy and minstrel people.

Charles White (1821-1891), author of "Negro Minstrelsy: Its Starting Place Traced Back Over Sixty Years," is one of the earliest of minstrel performers. His recollections on the origin of minstrelsy add another piece to that controversial pie. He was said to have kept a diary of all that transpired in the profession; and, we are assured by the *Clipper*, he "is always found to be correct in his summing up." A biographical sketch of this famed minstrel can be found on pages 186, 187, and 188.

Frank Dumont's "The Golden Days of Minstrelsy" and "The Younger Generation in Minstrelsy and Reminiscences of the Past" are supported by the authority of the writer's long career as a minstrel and manager of minstrel companies. He was perhaps a more prolific composer of songs, jokes, and afterpieces than anyone in the field. As manager, his record of continuous engagement at the Eleventh Street Opera House, Philadelphia, with the Dumont Minstrels, has never been surpassed. Dumont came from Utica, NY, the home town of minstrels Billy Birch, Sam Hague, Tom Prendergast and others. He began with George Christy as a boy singer at 585 Broadway and worked with a number of troupes before joining the Carncross party in Philadelphia in 1882. When Carncross retired in 1893, Dumont became the manager, a position he held until 1911, when the final curtain rang down on May 13 to the strains of "Auld Lang Syne."

Ralph Olmstead Keeler's (1840-1873) charming account of his experiences in "Three Years as a Negro Minstrel" was carried in three parts by the *Clipper* from August 1 through August 15, 1874. Orphaned at eight, he followed a path of self-reliance, which led him to brief stays at various schools including Karl-Rupert University at Heidelberg; and, along the way, a three year stint as a minstrel. As a journalist, Keeler contributed articles to various periodicals, including *Atlantic Monthly*, *Alta California*, *Golden Era*, *Every Saturday*, etc. What is considered his best work, *Vagabond Adventures*, an autobiographical account of his life, appeared in 1870.

On November 25, 1873, he left for Cuba as a special correspondent for the *New York Tribune*. He served the *Tribune* in Santiago during the excitement over the *Virginius* massacre---the execution of 53 men aboard a U. S. ship by the Spanish in 1873 because the vessel was carrying arms to Cuba. On the night of December 17, 1873, while en route from Santiago to Havana on his return to New York, he either fell or was thrown overboard and disappeared into the sea---dead at but thirty-three years of age. The article included herein was published after his demise.

Al G. Field (1850-1921), one of the last of the great cork artists and managers, relates in "Minstrelsy" his pleasing recollections of the great Dan Emmett. Field, whose real name was Alfred Griffith Hatfield, began as a ballad singer at the age of fifteen with Sharpley, Sheridan, Mack & Day's Minstrels. In 1886 he formed his own minstrel troupe, which he operated successfully until his death in 1921---during which time, so he claimed, he never had a losing season----and became a wealthy man, known as the "Millionaire Minstrel," from his successful managerial activities in that line of business. He was considered a good minstrel performer, remembered for his monologues. His training in management came from working with the Sells Bros.' Circus and with Duprez & Benedict's Minstrels, both outfits being noted for their advertising practices. It is said that Field was the first minstrel manager to carry entire stage settings and scenery and the first to use a special train of cars for transporting his troupe. He was a devoted family man and fond of dogs and horses. Indeed, he carried a fine pair of horses with the show to drive about in the cities he visited. His permanent residence was in Columbus, OH, where he owned considerable real estate, which included his "Maple Villa" Farm, located in the Olentangy Valley near the city, on which he bred blooded horses, pedigreed cattle, game fowl, and hogs. By 1909, he was director of the Central National Bank of Columbus, the Columbus Casualty Co., and had an interest in the street railway system there. And he was the author of the book *Watch Yourself Go By*.

Birkit "Kit" Clarke (1845-1918), the author of "Some Cork and Sawdust Thinks of the Past," was for many years an advance agent for a variety of traveling amusements. He was connected with Satterlee & Bell's Circus at the early age of thirteen. Within a few years he took up the study of photography in Chicago. However, he was back in the business with VanAmburgh's Menagerie, 1864-67, during which time the circus visited Europe. Throughout the 1870s he was director of press work for Adam Forepaugh's Circus for nine years, being one of the first agents to use alliterative advertising. Aside from circus work, he occupied himself, among other things, by managing Prof. Hartz and Zera, magicians; conducting the business affairs of M B. Leavitt's musical troupe, "The Rentz Company"; and accompanying Haverly's Minstrels to London. He had the distinction of being a friend and fishing companion of Grover Cleveland and Joseph Jefferson. After devoting much time in retirement to the writing of short stories and other items, several of which appeared in the *Clipper*, he died at his home in Flatbush, NY, at age 86.

The final inclusion in the Supplement, Brander Matthews' (James Brander Matthews, 1852-1929) "The Rise and Fall of Negro Minstrelsy," is the only selection not taken from the *New York Clipper*, it being from *Scribner's Magazine* of June,

1915. The piece represents an intelligent assessment of minstrelsy from the perspective of the 20th century by a man well qualified to make it. Matthews' credentials hardly need explanation. As a respected man of literature, he mingled with the elite writers of his age. He was part of a group who founded the Authors' Club, the American Copyright League, the Dunlap Society, the Kinsmen, and the Players. He was a prolific writer on theatrical matters, the list of books, articles and plays being too long to mention. As a professor of literature at Columbia University he became the first man to hold the Chair of Dramatic Literature at a United States university. He has been called the "last of the gentlemanly school of critics and essayists that distinguished American literature in the last half of the nineteenth century."

William L. Slout

BIOGRAPHICAL SKETCH OF COL. T. ALLSTON BROWN

Col. T. Allston Brown was born in Newburyport, MA., January 16, 1836. His grandfather was the Reverend Charles William Milton, who preached in one church in that town forty-two years. In 1852 Brown removed to Philadelphia and in September, 1855, became the Philadelphia correspondent of the *Clipper*. In April, 1858, he founded a dramatic paper called *The Tattler*, which subsequently changed its name to *The Philadelphian*. Shortly after this he was connected with the dramatic department of Col. Fitzgerald's *City Item*. In December, 1858, he commenced the compilation of a "History of the American Stage," which included biographies of every actor and actress who had appeared on the American stage from 1752 to 1858; also a complete history of every theatre that had been opened in America during that time. In 1859 the *Clipper* commenced to publish this work, and continued it for a long time. In January, 1860, he first entered the theatrical business, going in advance of the Cooper English Opera Co. In May of that year he began the publication of a series of dramatic articles for *The New York Programme*. By December he was treasurer for the Gardner & Madigan Circus. In January, 1862, he was the business manager for Isabella Cubas, Spanish *danseuse* and pantomimist. In the summer of 1862 he was with Dan Rice, afterward with Tom King's Circus in Baltimore and Washington. When James M. Nixon opened the Cremorne Gardens that year on Fourteenth Street in New York City. Brown was engaged as business manager. The Garden closing October 9, when the circus part of the show went to Washington for the winter and Brown accompanied it. In February, 1863, he went in advance of Hart & Simmons' Minstrels. During the summer of 1863 he was writer for Thayer & Noyes' Circus, and in the fall became dramatic editor of the *New York Clipper*, resigning in April, 1870, to establish a dramatic agency. He was manager of the Theatre Comique, Broadway near Spring Street, when he retired temporarily from the agency business in March, 1877, transferring his interest to his brother, J. Alexander Brown. He next went on the road with Boucicault's "Shaugbraun," but returned to the agency business in January, 1878. In September, 1882, he was manager for Hanlon Brothers in "*Le Voyage En Suisse*," he having engaged them in Europe for an American tour of three years. His next tour was as manager for Marie Aimee, then a tour with Mrs. Gen. Tom Thumb, and next with Charles Arnold in "Hans the Boatman." Brown died in Philadelphia, April 2, 1918.

William "Billy" Birch

EARLY HISTORY OF MINSTRELSY

by
Col. T. Allston Brown

Col. T. Allston Brown

BROWN'S BURNT CORK HISTORY

Ethiopian minstrelsy, with its accompaniments of wit and drollery, became one of the standard amusements because of the strong appeal it made to the masses, who were touched by its simple melodies and its effusions of genuine wit. In its proper place we confess to a tender admiration for burnt cork and we believe that one of the moral uses of colored minstrels is to give increased amusement to the fagged public. We admire the middle man. We respect the quiet and simple dignity with which he endures the jests and ignorance of those frivolous creatures, the end men. We reverence, too, the vast intellectual acquirements he displays when applied to for information by those witless waifs, and his unlimited capacity for propounding conundrums and correcting the errors in grammar and pronunciation of "brudder bones" and "tambo." He is the minstrel mentor to a brace of African Telemachuses, but he labors under the disadvantage that so many great minds labor under, of being dwarfed by the circumstances by which he is compelled to remain surrounded. He is continually letting himself down to the capacities of the rest of the troupe, now making smooth a piece of disjointed syntax, now letting in light upon some scientific misconception, now ploddingly endeavoring to understand the tangled anecdote that one of his associates is telling, and now the victim of a heartless jest that one of them has perpetuated; but always the same genial, gentlemanly, unruffled creature, surveying the end men---those silly black butterflies at either terminus of the footlights---with the smiling forbearance which comes of innate superiority. Probably without a possibility of doubt we can safely say that William Bernard, of the San Francisco Minstrels, had no living equal as an interlocutor or middle man.

The community owes much to these representatives of the Negro who, by talent and industry, divested the black face entertainment of the coarseness and vulgarity that once characterized it; for amusements have an influence as well as other popular demonstrations; and when that influence tends only to the production of fun and harmony, no sensible or feeling mind can object to the popularity of an entertainment that can certainly do no harm and which will at times help to drive care from the aching heart or tend to divert the musical taste in a channel that is correct, simple and pure.

Many people wonder why minstrel music has so broad a hold on the public taste and why the cork opera, with its threadbare smartness and everlasting repetitions, so stubbornly defies the ordinary revolutions of the public taste. But the explanation is furnished on the one side by the talent and ever-springing "animal" wit of such men as Billy Birch and Charley Backus, while, on the other hand, the genius of Tom Moore---denied by artists any lofty place in music---is the unseen shrine at which, through these touching minstrel tunes, the millions of our race on both sides of the Atlantic who love music solely for its melody, bow down and worship. Nothing could remain heavy or be stale when handled by such men as Birch and Backus. The merest commonplace, under their grotesque touch, became at once imbued with their overflowing fun and every thought received a form so ludicrous that it could not fail to electrify an audience.

It is this singular faculty of diversifying sameness which we have designated animal wit; not because it is groveling and low, but because, instead of depending upon idea or upon verbal turn, it consists mainly of a certain indescribable magnetism of manner, which is usually involuntary with the actor, but which surprises and irresistibly captures the risible of every looker on. A dull story, which in ordinary hands would send every listener yawning to his bed, would, when told by one of those comedians, fairly split the sides of the gravest of his audience. Those who look on everything with a serious face will find, in the popularity of negro minstrelsy among the educated classes, a singular illustration of the close connection that exists between Puritanism and extreme frivolity. Scores of persons who would think it wicked to see the highest work of dramatic art, performed by the finest company in the world, will, with the utmost complacency, spend a long evening with the minstrels.

When negro minstrelsy was in its infancy, the opening part was always the great feature of the evening's entertainment; the simple yet beautiful ballads touched the great heart of the masses, while the well-told jokes and conundrums of the end men leavened the whole with a spice of life and joyousness which sent the audience to their homes in a delightful frame of mind. In those days the members of the troupe appeared in the first part dressed as humble laborers or slave hands of the Southern plantations, and afterwards as dandy darkies of the North. Many changes have since taken place. Negro minstrelsy of the present time is quite a different amusement to that given in the olden times. If our minstrel managers would give simple, touching melodies more real negro minstrelsy instead of so much tomfoolery and lavish scenic display and wardrobe, it would engender a more healthful tone and prove more attractive and beneficial in the end.

When and why should genuine negro minstrelsy be refined? Was there anything coarse and vulgar about the sports and songs of a group of field hands who enjoyed themselves on the lawn and amused the planter and his friends and family on the verandah? Never! What might be considered vulgar in minstrelsy has been introduced by performers who prefer the boisterous guffaws of the gallery to the more subdued and dignified plaudits of the orchestra.

ORIGINS OF NEGRO MINSTRELSY:

For nearly seventy years negro minstrelsy has been one of our public amusements. Ever since 1843 it has been steadily improving. The plantation darkie who sang about the ham fat and danced the essence is a thing of the past and "Old Black Joe" traveling back to Dixie is an absurdity and an anomaly in the present day. Much has been said and written of this popular branch of amusement---as to where it had its origin, who were its originators, etc. As early as 1799, a Mr. Grawpner blacked up and appeared at the old Federal Street Theatre, Boston, and sang a song of a Negro in character, in the part of the poor African slave in the play of "Orinoko; or, the Royal Slave." This was on the 30th of December of that year.

Lewis Hallam the younger was the original Mungo in America. Mungo is a stage Negro, and Mr. Hallam did it at the John Street Theatre, New York, May 29, 1769.

"Potpie" Herbert blackened his face and publicly sang a song on the stage at the Albany (N.Y.) Theatre in 1815. When the curtain rose the immense audience were astonished to see appear before them, dressed and blacked-up, a man the perfect representation of a full blooded African. When he commenced singing to an original air, the excitement was great. The following is the song. It was called "Siege of Plattsburgh."

Back side Albany, stan' Lake Champlain,
One little pond, haf full o' water,
Plat-tes-burg dare too, close 'pon de main,
Town so small--he grow bigger dough hererter.
On Lake Champlain
Uncle Sam set he boat,
And Massa M'Donough he sail 'em;
While Gen'ral M'Comb
Make Plat-tes-burg he home,
Wid de army, whose courage nebber fail 'em.
On 'lebenth day of Sep-tem-ber,
In eighteen hund'ed an' fourteen,
Gubbener Probose, an' he British soger,
Come to Plat-tes-burg a tea party courtin';
An' he boat come too
Arter Uncle Sam boat,
Massa 'Donough da look sharp out de winder---
Dem Gen'ral M'Comb,
(Ah! He always a'home.)
Catch fire too, jiss like a tinder.
Bang! bang! bang! der de cannons gin to roar
In Plat-tes-burg, an' all 'bout dat quarter;
Gubbener Probose try he hand 'pon de shore
While he boat take he luck 'pon de water---
But Massa M'Donough
Kneck he boat in he head,
Break he hart, broke he shin, 'tore he caffin in,
An' Gen'ral M'Comb
Start ole Probose home---
Tot me soul den, I must' die a'laffin'.
Probose scare so, he lef all behine,
Powder ball, cannon, tea-pot an' kittle---

> Some day he cotch a cole---trouble in he mine,
> 'Cause he eat so much raw an' cole vittle---
> Uncle Sam berry sorry,
> To be sure, for he pain;
> Wish he wuss heself up well an' harty---
> For Gen'ral M'Comb
> An' Massa M'Donough home,
> When he notion for anudder tea party.

As the song proceeded in detail with the incidents of the battle and final success of the American Army, the excitement increased to the highest intensity and the enthusiasm became uncontrollable. The curtain was again rung up and the song again sung and this was continued until the manager was compelled to apologize for the exhaustion of the singer. So great was its success that "Pot-pie" Herbert was engaged to open at the Park Theatre, New York. The tune in which it was sung was the most musical and characteristic of the rich African melody ever heard and the verse was flowing and disclosed poetic talent.

George Nichols, the clown, attached many years to Purdy Brown's Theatre and Circus of the South and West, was also among the first of burnt cork gentry. Nichols was a man of no education, yet he was the author of many anecdotes, stories, verses, etc. He was original. He would compose the verses for his comic songs within ten minutes of the time of his appearance before the audience. His "flights of fancy" and "flashes of wit" were truly astonishing and highly amusing. Nichols first sang "Jim Crow" as clown in 1834, afterwards as a Negro. He first conceived the idea from a French darkie, a banjo player, known from New Orleans to Cincinnati as Picayune Butler---a copper colored gentleman, who gathered many a picayune by singing "Picayune Butler is Going Away," accompanying himself on his four-stringed banjo. An old darkie of New Orleans, known as "Old Corn Meal," furnished Nichols with many airs, which he turned to account. This old Negro sold Indian meal for a living. He might be seen from morning till night with his cart and horse. He frequently stopped before Bishop's celebrated hotel and sang a number of Negro melodies. He possessed a fine falsetto and baritone voice. Corn Meal picked up many bits and pieces for his singing.

A brother to Arch Madden, the clown, sang Negro songs on a raised platform at the old Vauxhall Garden in New York in 1828, one refrain of his songs reading,

> Come, brudder, let us go off to Hayti.
> There we be as grand as Gen. Lafayette.

He also sang Negro songs at the Military Garden, kept by Gen. Storms, on the southwest corner of Broadway and Prince Street, New York.

Bob Farrell, an actor, sang "Zip Coon," composed by Nichols. Lewis Hyel, of Brown's Company, sang "Roley Boley" by Nichols. Nichols first sang "Clar de Kitchen." This song he arranged from hearing it sung by the Negro firemen on the

Mississippi River. The tune of "Zip Coon" was taken from a rough jig dance, called "Natchez Under the Hill," where the boatmen, river pirates, gamblers and courtesans congregated for the enjoyment of a regular hoe-down in the old time. Sam Tatnall, the equestrian, sang "Back Side of Albany." John and Frank Whittaker sang "Coal Black Rose" in 1830. Bill Keller, a low comedian of Philadelphia, was the original "Coal Black Rose." John Clements, leader of the orchestra for Duffy & Forrest, composed the music. George Washington Dixon created a furor by singing this song; also "Long-Tailed Blue," "Lubla Rosa," and other plantation songs at the Chatham Theatre, New York, under the management of Flynn in 1829, when Sloman commenced singing buffo songs. Dixon commenced singing buffo at the Albany Theatre in 1830. In July, 1830, he was at the Park Theatre, New York, announced as "The celebrated American buffo singer," and continued to get his name at the head of the bills. The *New York Mirror* of August 7, 1840, said:

> We do not exactly understand on what he founds his claim, unless it be impudence; and we are strongly urged to this conclusion by a comparison between the gentleman and Mr. Placide, whose name is to be found the same night Dixon appears, in small letters, while Dixon's is in capitals. Dixon swings about his limbs with the same vile motion which Mr. Sloman used to rejoice in; but he has neither Sloman's voice nor humor, and in his imitations of African character he is far inferior to Blakely.

Mr. Dixon first appeared in Philadelphia at the Arch Street Theatre, June 19, 1834, and sang his prize extravaganza of "Zip Coon" for the benefit of Andrew J. Allen.

When the cholera broke out in Philadelphia, he published a "Cholera Gazette," giving, day by day, the exact state of the city's health. Just at mid-day each day, there assembled in front of the Health Office a crowd, dense enough to breed a cholera, to listen to the report of the Board of Health on the cases and deaths of the previous twenty-four hours. And as true as the bell struck twelve, so true would Dixon come forth and from the elevated step announce the calamities of the time. But the cholera left and so did Dixon. In May, 1836, he visited Boston; and what his reception was there we refer to the following, which we extract from the Boston *Courier* of that date:

> This fellow, the notorious "buffer singer" and humbug, who has been vagabonding about the country for many years, is at last likely to obtain a steady home and something useful to do. He has been arrested for forgery and lodged in jail. The stupendous amount of thirty dollars is what he is "in for." He will be remembered by many of our citizens as the competitor of Mons. Chabert in the fire-eating business and for the ignominious manner in which he retreated from his dangerous victuals when the glowing meal was placed before him. He succeeded no better in his attempt to take poison for a living. He is the most miserable apology for a vocalist that ever bored the public ear.

Any hearer of taste would much prefer a dose of ipecacuanha to hearing him sing.

In 1830 we find him in New York, publishing a paper called the *Polyanthus*, which dealt in personal abuse. He suffered six months' imprisonment for an alleged libel on the Rev. Dr. Hawks, rector of St. Thomas' Church. In 1852 he was living in New Orleans. He is said to have been the cause of the death of Miss Missouri by publishing a filthy article against her in his notorious sheet. Dixon died at the Charity Hospital, New Orleans, March, 1861.

Barney Burns, known from Quebec to New Orleans as a job actor, first sang "Long-Tail Blue" and "Sich a Getting Up Stair," written and composed by Joe Blackburn. Burns was very eccentric and talented and originated many of the best "gags" still popular with his successors. He was famous as a clown in the circus. He was the first clown to sing "Jim Crow" in a circus, the song having at that time just been popularized by Daddy Rice.

Joe Blackburn was originally trained for the Roman Catholic priesthood but proved a great favorite as a circus clown. He was the first American clown to visit England. He died at Memphis.

The first to do "Lucy Long" were Dan Gardner, Barney Williams and S. S. Sanford. The first black "clown" was William Donaldson. He had been a minstrel performer. He first appeared in the circus ring in Philadelphia. The first song ever sung on any stage by a band of minstrels was "The Boatman's Dance" by R. W. Pelham.

De boteman dance, de boteman sing,
De boteman's up tu eberyting,
Wen de boteman gets on shore
He spends his monne den work, fo mo.
Chorus:
Dance de boteman dance,
Dance de boteman dance,
Dance all nite till broad dalite,
Den go hum wid de gals in the mornin.
Hi ro, de boteman ro,
Flotin' doun the riber, de Ohio.
Hi ro, de boteman ro,
Flotin doun de riber, de Ohio.

I went on board de oder da,
Tu here wat de boteman had tu sa,
Wen I lef mi pashun lose
Dey kramm'd me in de kalabuse.
I kum dis time an kum no mor,
Lef me luse and I'll go on shor;
Dey tole dey was a bulli krew,

Wid a hooser mate an capten too.
Wen yu go tu de boteman's ball
Dance wid mi wife or don't dance at all,
Sky blu jacket and tarpaulin hat,
Look out niggers fo de nine-tale kat.
De boteman he is a lucky man,
Nun can do as de boteman kan,
I neber sor a pritte gal in my life
But dat she was sum boteman's wife.

In 1835 a miscellaneous entertainment was given at the Patriot House in Chatham Square, New York. Dan Gardner was the wench dancer and William Whitlock made his first appearance on the stage here in the Negro sketch of "Oh, Hush." A young man by the name of Lester first composed and sang a song called "Sitting on a Pail;" also another he called "Gumbo Chaff." This was about the year 1836. In 1836, P. T. Barnum traveled with Aaron Turner's Circus and in consequence of some of the Negro performers of the company having left at Camden, S. C., Barnum blacked himself thoroughly and sang the songs, "Zip Coon," "Gittin' Up Stairs" and "The Raccoon Hunt; or, Sitting on a Pail." T. D. Rice accumulated quite a fortune by singing the song of "Jim Crow" and "Long-Tail Blue."

In 1837 an entertainment consisting of equestrianism and minstrels was given at the Lion Theatre, Boston, commencing on February 22. A burlesque Ethiopian opera was given. "Oh, Hush!" was performed with Harper (the original representative) as Gumbo Cuff, alias Jim Brown. Hall appeared as Sambo Johnson, Reeve as Peat Williams, Ruggles as Clem Green, Churchill as Col. Ben, Knapp as Joe Harris, Robinson as Pompey, and Mr. Nathan as Miss Dinah.

"Daddy" Rice appeared at the Chatham Theatre, New York, in November, 1843, in the farce of "The Foreign Prince; or, Nigger Assurance," also in "Bone Squash Diable."

During the year of 1838, E. P. Christy, Dick Sliter, John Daniels and John Perkins (a Negro jig dancer who played on the jawbone) were giving entertainments in Child's Alley (now Pine Street), Rochester, N. Y. They charged three cents each admission. They all blacked up and had bones, tambourine, banjo (made out of a gourd), fiddle, jawbone (horse's), and triangle. The bones used were horse rib fifteen inches long. E. P. Christy was the originator and manager.

In 1838, James Sanford played the "Black Doorkeeper" at the Franklin Theatre, New York. Charles Jenkins and G. W. Pelham appeared at the Museum, New York, in January, 1842. The same month Frank Diamond, Billy Whitlock and Tom Booth appeared at the Arcade Garden, 255 Bleecker Street, New York. At the same time, Dick Pelham, Master Chestnut, Dick Van Bremen and Joe Sweeney performed at the Bowery Amphitheatre, New York. In April of the same year, Frank Diamond and Whitlock were at the Chatham Theatre, New York.

In the Spring of 1839, John Diamond was dancing jigs at the Franklin Theatre, New York; and in the fall of 1839 he went to the New Chatham Theatre, where, in addition to dancing, he became an actor, playing Black Ike in "Shabby Genteel" and appearing in extravaganzas with Barney Williams, William Whitlock, John Smith, and Master Coleman. When Diamond danced, Barney Williams used to keep time. In those days, Barney Williams was a dancer and on one occasion he was announced to dance the "'Cawchoaker," a burlesque of Fanny Elssler's "Cachuca."

While P. T. Barnum was managing Vauxhall Garden, New York City, he brought out John Diamond, the jig dancer. Negro delineations had become a popular amusement with the public. Having some trouble with Diamond, he let him go.

Diamond was accidentally discovered about the wharves of New York by Barnum. Barnum was then as poor as Job's turkey; but having an eye to business, conceived the idea (i.e., gag) to write a life of Master Diamond. A greater amount of nonsense is seldom if ever put together---but it took! Barnum reaped a harvest. He cleared $1,500 the first night at the St. Charles Theatre, New Orleans, on Sunday evening. The types said it was a grand match dance for $2,000. Barnum, finding that the Diamond excitement was played out and the dancer was an uncontrollable and vicious youth, dropped the burnt cork speculation and left for New York.

Diamond was of a revengeful and passionate disposition. He narrowly escaped with his life in Mexico. Having enlisted in the American army, he made an attack on his superior officer. For this he was sentenced to be shot, but fortunately for Diamond the treaty of peace saved his life.

He danced for many years with Jim Sanford. They both lived fast, dressed in the height of flashy extravagance. They both died in Blockley Alms House, Philadelphia. Diamond died October 29, 1857, aged thirty-four years. Diamond was brought from the Alms House and buried from the domicile of Mr. Grear, in Sansom Street, a man of good heart and full of philanthropy and kindness.

Jim Sanford was a Baltimorean. His correct name was Blandford. He dressed in the height of fashion, with never a hair on his head out of place. He commanded a large salary, lived fast, and died one of the most miserable objects at the Alms House that human eyes ever beheld.

The original Diamond and Dick Pelham were rivals. They had a match dance at the Chatham Theatre, New York; on February 13, 1840, for $500 a side, and Diamond was declared the winner.

Shortly after Barnum lost the original Diamond, he drummed up an opposition "Diamond," whose right name was Frank Lynch. He was a jig dancer. We would here state that there have been two Jubas and three Master Diamonds. Every night was Vauxhall Garden crowded to witness Diamond's antics by anxious spectators who suffered themselves to be inveigled into an excitement which formerly could have been conjured up at the old Haymarket by the production of half a score of thoroughbred darkies, eager to dance themselves to death's door to acquire the paltry trophy of a string of eels. There was also another Diamond (No. 3), but he never amounted to much as a performer. The last we heard of him was in Philadelphia, where he danced a trial jig at Jayne's Hall, December 7, 1857.

The original Juba, whose real name was William Henry Lane, was a colored boy. He was the greatest jig dancer ever seen. He was a great attraction wherever he appeared. He danced a match with Diamond, the original, at the Bowery Amphitheatre, New York, on July 8, 1844, for $200. Juba's father and mother were both living at this time. His step-father's name was Zachary Reed, well known in those days as a frequenter of Pete Williams' dance house.

In 1849, Tom Briggs, the banjo player, and Gilbert Ward Pell, brother of Richard Pell (Pelham), took Juba to England, where he became quite a card. He was married there to a white woman, lived a fast life, dissipated freely, and died miserably during the season of 1851-52. It has been stated that his skeleton was on exhibition at the Surrey Music Hall, Sheffield, England.

For the benefit of John Smith at the Bowery Amphitheatre, New York, in June, 1842, T. Coleman, Chestnut, Hoffman and Smith put on burnt cork and appeared.

On November 14, 1842, the Franklin Theatre, New York, was re-opened with a variety entertainment. Dan Emmett, Frank Brower and Master Pierce were billed as the "Southern Gentlemen," Master Pierce being specially called "The Little Darkie Ariel." At the same time, Tom Backus, Masters Gil W. and R. W. Pelham were playing at the Franklin Theatre. Brower shortly after withdrew, while Emmett and Pierce alternated their performances between the Franklin and the "Amphitheatre of the Republic" (the Bowery Circus), 37 Bowery. Pelham withdrew from the Franklin and Frank Kent took his place. Tom Backus, called the "Negro Paganini," was the violinist.

At the Amphitheatre (now the Arch Street Theatre) was announced a performance of Negro singing, etc., by Frank Whittaker, Bob Williams, Master Bob Edwards and Tom Vaughn, on January 4, 1843. But this was not a minstrel performance. They used bones and banjo.

On January 16, 1843, Dick Pelham took a benefit, when he appeared in sixteen songs and dances as a Negro clown and [in] the Ethiopian opera of "Negro Assurance." Leaving the Amphitheatre, Pelham went to the Chatham, where he took a benefit on January 31. It was at this time that "the original 1842 band" were using the stage of the Chatham during the day, rehearsing for their early public debut.

THE FIRST MINSTREL BAND:

Much has been said and written as to the first regular band of minstrels as we came to know them. That Billy Whitlock was the originator no one will deny. One day in July, 1842, Whitlock, who happened to be with Dan Emmett at his (the latter's) boarding house in New York, suggested to Emmett the practicing with him of the banjo and the fiddle. After practicing several times at the boarding house (in Catharine Street), Frank Brower (who happened to call in) was added to the party and played the bones. In a few days Dick Pelham joined the party and played the tambourine. They continued to practice until the winter of 1842 fairly set in. One day they all happened to meet at the North American Hotel in the Bowery and, while chatting together, Whitlock proposed going across to the Bowery Circus and serenade the manager, Nat Howes; which they did, the result of which was an offer of an engagement to the party, provided they could sing together. When asked if they could sing, Dan Emmett vocalized "Old Dan Tucker," etc.

Dick Pelham, who was playing an engagement at the Chatham Theatre, took a benefit January 31, 1843, and the party played for him. They styled themselves The Virginia Minstrels. Frank Brower played the bones; Dan Emmett, the violin; Billy Whitlock, the banjo; and R. W. Pelham, the tambourine. This was the first time a regularly organized minstrel band ever played in America.

The party continued their rehearsals at Bartlett's billiard room in the Branch Hotel, a leading sporting house on the East Side, opposite the Bowery Amphitheatre and at one time kept by Tom Hyer, the pugilist.

Emmett, Whitlock, Pelham and Brower were engaged by the management of the Bowery Amphitheatre; and, as The Virginia Minstrels, they opened at that house February 6, 1843, and repeated their performance given at the Pelham benefit. This was the first regular engagement of this party (their first performance having been a complimentary one) and it was at this house that they got their first real recognition from the press, which probably accounts for the fact that the date of February 6, 1843, has so long erroneously been recognized as the birthday of minstrelsy. They met with such success that they were at once secured by Welch & Rockwell (then managers of the Park Theatre, New York), and appeared there for two weeks in conjunction with the original Diamond. Then they went to Boston and for six weeks they played to large audiences at the Tremont Temple. Returning to New York, they appeared at the Park Theatre three nights for manager Simpson. They were making great additions to their entertainment. The quartette were gradually improving in their performances, which consisted of "songs composed expressly for the minstrels by their leader, old Dan Emmett," banjo solos, jig, reel and trial dancing, "Dinah's Serenade" and "Locomotive Lecture."

The party had met with so much success that they concluded to take a trip to Europe. They took a benefit at the Park Theatre and sailed for England in the packet ship *New York*, under the direction of George Wooldridge (afterwards known as "Tom Quick"), who had accompanied them on their Boston trip as agent.

They sailed on April 23, 1843, and arrived in Liverpool on May 21. The entire capital of the party when they started was five dollars. On the voyage a frivolous quarrel caused a separation, Brower and Emmett sticking together, while Whitlock clung to Pelham; but Emmett's song of "Dandy Jim" was the means of speedily bringing the four into harmony again. During the voyage, a German with a fondness for poker had an hour's sitting with Pelham, who won all his money; and, relying upon this unexpectedly acquired wealth, the party were in no hurry to begin operations after reaching Liverpool, especially as all had heavy colds. They put up at the Bear Tavern, where (unknown to Whitlock, Brower and Emmett) a German from Charleston, S. C., beat Pelham out of all his winnings from the Teuton aboard ship. This forced the minstrels to go to work and they opened at Concert Hall, Concert Street, Liverpool, on May 25, 1843. This was the first "minstrel" entertainment ever given in Europe.

They then went to Manchester, where they gave six entertainments at Sloan's Theatre. The following week they appeared at the Queen's Theatre, same city. Thence they went to London, appearing at the Adelphi Theatre in conjunction with the well known wizard, Anderson. The following is a copy of an advertisement from one of the newspapers of the day:

NEW AND NOVEL ENTERTAINMENT!!!
Grand Ethiopian concerts by the four highly celebrated
VIRGINIA MINSTRELS FROM AMERICA
who will appear in London on
MONDAY, JUNE 19, 1843.
TO THE CITIZENS OF LONDON AND WESTMINSTER:

The Virginia Minstrels would, with great respect, say that, in their delineations of the sports and pastimes of the Southern slave race of America, they offer an exhibition that is both new and original, which they illustrate through the medium of songs, refrains, lectures and dances, accompanying themselves on instruments of a peculiar nature, which, in their hands, discourse most exquisite music. Their melodies have all been produced at great toil and expense, from among the sable inhabitants of the Southern States in America, the subject of each ascribing the manner in which the slaves celebrate their holidays, which commence at the gathering-in of the sugar and cotton crops; and they flatter themselves that, from the great success which attended their efforts in their own country, to introduce not only a chaste and pleasing school of Negroism, but also a true copy of Ethiopian life, that they can not fail to please all who will honor them with their patronage, their exhibition being void of any objectionable feature, either in word, look, or motion, which could offend the most fastidious.

On the appearance of the "band" upon the stage, the reception they met with was anything but encouraging. An officer in the first tier of boxes saluted them with:
"Go home! You d----d humbugs! Go home, I say!"
While the disconcerted minstrels were debating as to whether they should "go home" or begin their entertainment, a white-haired old gentleman arose to their relief:
"Gentlemen, Americans, go on with your performance. There is but one fool in this house. He sits up there with a soldier's coat on."
The father of the officer had lost money through Pennsylvania's act of repudiation. The officer essayed to retort. The old gentleman began to hiss him. The whole house joined in. The officer was ejected and there was no further interruption throughout the minstrels' engagement in London, the terms of which were that they were to share equally with Prof. Anderson after deducting £10 for expenses. But the house was filled nightly with orders; so that during their four weeks' engagement the Americans did not get enough to pay their board.

Their London engagement having terminated, Billy Whitlock and Wooldridge returned to America. Frank Brower, with Joe Sweeney, went traveling with Cooke's Circus through Scotland. Emmett and Pelham went to Astley's in London, where they performed eight weeks. While at this theatre, the stage manager annoyed Emmett in every conceivable manner. He would not permit him to tune his banjo in his dressing room. When Emmett first attempted to tune it, he was asked by the stage manager:

"Can you play the 104th Psalm?"

"Yes!" was the quick answer. "My daddy played it for yours in 1812. If I mistake not, it goes like this." And the banjoist thrummed "Yankee Doodle." Whenever he related this incident, Emmett added: "Broadfoot, the stage manager was such a fool that he couldn't see the point."

Leaving Astley's, Emmett went on a traveling tour with June & Sands' American Circus, finishing out the summer of 1843. In the following spring (1844), Whitlock opened (April 22) at the Theatre Royal, Dublin, with Brower, Emmett and Joe Sweeney for four weeks, the party having joined fortunes once more. From Dublin the party went to Belfast, Cork, Glasgow, Edinburgh, and a return visit to Glasgow. The party then broke up. Brower and Sweeney returned to America. Dan Emmett joined Cooke's Circus for a few weeks, after which he returned to America.

Soon after Whitlock's arrival in America he met Barney Williams, who persuaded him to accept an engagement at the Chatham Theatre. Barney Williams in those days was an ambitious performer. He was anxious to become a minstrel. One night he would play the bones, the tambourine the next, or anything they chose to put him at. He played at the Vauxhall Garden in 1838 with Sam Johnson, Jerry Bryant and Tom Booth. His great specialty was "Dandy Jim," Irish stories and "Fox Hunter's Jig." It was while at the Chatham that Whitlock sang for the first time (in America) "Dandy Jim."

Thackeray, the great British novelist, thus spoke of negro minstrelsy, (A more comprehensive criticism on the "black art" than is here rendered never emanated from man.).

I heard a humorous balladist, a minstrel with wool on his head, and an ultra Ethiopian complexion, who performed a negro ballad that I confess moistened these spectacles in the most unexpected manner. They have gazed at dozens of tragedy queens dying on the stage and expiring in appropriate blank verse, and I never wanted to wipe them. They have looked up, with deep respect, be it said, at many scores of clergymen in pulpits without being dimmed; and behold! a minstrel with a corked face and a banjo sings a little song, strikes a wild note, which sets the whole heart thrilling with a happy piety. Humor! Humor is the mistress of tears; she knows the way to the *fons lachrymatorium*, strikes in dry and rugged places with her enchanting wand, and bids the fountain gush and sparkle. She has refreshed myriads more from her natural springs than ever tragedy has watered from her pompous old urn.

THE BANJO:
When minstrelsy was in its infancy, the banjo was the favorite instrument. It was a simply made instrument and its invention was not due to the Negro. J. G. Wilkinson, in his work on the ancient Egyptians, shows a picture of the Egyptian lyre that, in every vital respect, is a modern banjo. It has an oblong hoop, a neck and head, with pegs and strings running from the head across the skin, stretched over the hoop. There were no places for stopping the four strings, and hence only four notes could be made.

The "tack-head" banjo, made in the old minstrel days, was the one that possessed beauties of its own. The calfskin head was wet and stretched over the rim as tightly as possible and then tacked down around the edge. James Buckley, father of the Buckley Brothers, made the first important improvement on the instrument, which was tightly fitting a narrow iron ring over the outside of the skin at the top of the hoop, so that pulling the ring downward all around would tighten the skin on top. Brackets were fixed to the side of the hoop in the middle of the outside and pierced for screws, which ran upward into the iron ring. A key worked the screws and pulled the iron ring that stretched the hide to the desired tension. Joe Sweeney made the innovation of adding the short, fine catgut string beside the wire string, making the banjo a five string instrument.

David Jacobs was the first banjo manufacturer. He had a little store on Grand Street, New York. In 1858, a German named Harless commenced the manufacture of banjos at from $3 to $5 each. In less than ten years he returned to Germany with $20,000.

The first time the banjo was ever used in the orchestra of a regular dramatic establishment was at Wallacks Theatre, New York. Charles E. Dobson was engaged by Thomas Baker, the musical director, and was one of the features every evening of the week, commencing March 4, 1867.

THE FIRST MINSTREL ENTERTAINMENT UNDER CANVAS:
This was in 1843 under the management of Hugh Lindsay, familiarly known as Old Hontz, the clown. Dan Rice, Dan Minnich, Master Frank Rosston, Hen Nagle, and S. S. Sanford comprised the company. Sanford was then known as the champion dancer. Hugh Lindsay, through his connection with the show business, acquired a widespread popularity and acquaintance and, in his day, by his natural born talent and wit, probably contributed as much to the hilarity, mirth and amusement of mankind as any man living. He was born in Philadelphia in April, 1804. At the age of fifteen years he engaged himself as an apprentice to the show business with J. H. Myers and Lewis Mestayer, who kept a sort of show room in Market Street, above Fourth, in Philadelphia, consisting of gymnastic performances, wire walking, jugglery, etc. Subsequently, he became connected with the traveling circus and menagerie of John Miller (the pioneer of the business) of Allentown. While with Miller he attended to the door, acted clown and drove the camels. Subsequently, he engaged with Weyman's traveling company. This was in 1832-34. After

this he re-engaged with Miller's company, then under the management of Rufus Welch.

In 1825, Mr. Miller sold out his menagerie to Mr. Crosby of New York for $4,000, and Lindsay engaged under the new proprietor. The performances in those days consisted of ground and lofty tumbling, slack rope vaulting and tight rope dancing, still vaulting on a spring board over men and horses, and, in fact, nearly all kinds of acting that you see now in the circus, except riding in the ring. They had a spotted horse who was well trained and performed many tricks of sagacity. He introduced to the public S. S. Sanford, a son of his sister. A few years prior to his death he left the profession and went to tavern keeping in Northumberland County, Pa., and afterwards moved to Bucks County, where he died.

MINSTRELSY WELL ADVERTISED:

From the days of Edwin P. Christy down to date, the minstrel managers have been good advertisers. Christy, like some of the ambitious politicians, "claimed everything in sight." Very naturally, the early minstrel managers, shrewd and observant, patterned after the circus in the method of advertising, especially in poster billing and press work and later on as to the street parade. To begin with, the pioneers of minstrelsy did not employ the posters to any great extent, for the reason that the placing of the pictures on the walls was limited, the billposting business still being in its infancy. The billposter was most instances the janitor of the hall and "the hall" was bare of scenery and the stage but little more than a platform.

Probably William W. Newcomb was the first minstrel manager to appreciate the poster at its full value. Over the routes which he played, he caused to be placed and maintained at his own expense a number of small stands, which on each recurring visit were covered with his pictorial work. During the interim, the billposter was permitted to use the boards, but in no case to be used by any rival minstrel organization.

Three-quarter sheets, printed on both sides, came into use and they were usually illustrated in the highest style of the then crude art of wood engraving.

Some of the minstrel managers were ready writers. Such was W. W. Newcomb, accounted for by his advantage of education and superior intelligence. Sam Sharpley also wrote a good bill and knew his English, as did Charley Morris, M. T. Skiff, J. A. Raynor and William Foote, originator of J. H. Haverly's Masto-dons and the ever-to-be remembered "Forty, Count 'em Forty." Charles Duprez could get up a stunner of a bill, piling adjective upon adjective, paying no regard to Webster's Dictionary or Lindley Murray. And some of the brilliant advance men took their first lessons in practical show advertising in passing 'round the quarter-sheets. I have been there myself and know how it was.

Morris Bros., Pell and Trowbridge used stands of posters in plain black. Alington had an effective bill. It was a large half-sheet printed in red and bearing two attractive illustrations.

James W. Morse was the discoverer of pine wood engraving. Not many years ago he was still alive and in good health, at the age of eighty-six. He resided on

West Twelfth Street, New York. Before pine wood was used, cuts were made on mahogany and only block printing could be done. After experimenting a great deal, he found that he could use soft wood on the side grain and that a picture could be cut on pine as well as mahogany and that show bills could be printed in many colors and at a much lower cost. The first posters of this kind were made for Seth B. Howes, the circus man, who took them to England, where they were regarded as a great novelty. He never took out a patent, although he kept his discovery a secret for six years. Mr. Morse was related to the great telegraph inventor.

The first lithograph ever used was in the spring of 1871. It was a twenty sheet stand, made by Mears of Buffalo, N. Y., for Johnny Thompson's "On Hand" Co. It cost 12 cents a sheet of plain black. The subject was a large hand with the word "On" in the center.

CHALLENGE DANCING:

In 1850, Dick Sliter, who billed himself as the "champion dancer," challenged the world to produce a white man or boy to dance a trial dance with him for a sum of $50 to $1,000, he to dance his original rattlesnake jig, Tar River dance, and Lucy Long. For his masterly dancing on the morning of December 12, a public presentation of a champion belt was made to Mr. Sliter by the citizens of Cincinnati, with the word "Champion" engraved thereon in silver letters.

A match dance took place at the Melodeon, Boston, on March 16, 1859, between Mickey Warren and Hank Mason. They danced two jigs, a reel, and a walk around. Mickey was declared the winner. A. Ronne, banjoist, played for both.

It was in 1862 that the match dance controversy was started among the friends of R. M. Carroll, who was at the Canterbury, and Tommy Peel of Bryant's. Many other dancers laid claim to being the best, or chanpion dancer. After much talk, a "match" was made between Carroll and Peel for $250 a side and the championship. The trial took place at Wallack's Theatre, Broadway, near Broome Street, New York, on Wednesday afternoon, April 16, 1862, at about 4 p.m. Tommy had the first put in, Frank Converse furnishing the music on his old cremona. Carroll followed, with William Ross as his "musicianer." The result was Peel was decided the victor. The amount of stakes (said to he $500) was deposited in the hands of a Mr. VanTine, who was chosen stakeholder. The attendance at the theatre was large. A short variety entertainment preceded the dance. Robert Hart, judge for Carroll, announced that the audience would keep quiet and no applause indulged in. In tossing for choice, Carroll was the winner and Peel was sent on to dance first. He was attired in pink striped shirt, dark blue velvet knee breeches, white stockings and black pumps. Converse took his seat upon the upper part of the stage with one banjo by his side and another in his hands. All being ready, Converse struck up and Peel stepped out to the sound of the music.

During the dancing a dog was very thoughtlessly permitted to make his way upon the stage and walk towards the dancer. The canine was called off and again made his appearance. At the expiration of 10 minutes 4 seconds from the time the first step was taken, the last movement of the wind-up was given and Peel retired amid a perfect storm of applause. Once during the dance and while Peel was executing a very fine step the people applauded and that was the only time while the contest was in progress. Peel and Converse then made their exit and Mr. Carroll appeared with his banjo player, Mr. Ross. Carroll wore a dark blue shirt, trimmed, with lapels and collar thrown open, disclosing a white shirt underneath; trousers of bright red, reaching to the ankle, around which they were tight, but somewhat loose upwards; white stockings and black pumps. Early in the dance he made one very bad break. As he progressed he executed some difficult steps. He appeared to labor more than Peel and was apparently more distressed. Towards the latter portion of the dance he revived by performing a side-step, going clear around the stage, moving the feet sideways, in and out. This was a sort of rest for him and enabled him to make a most capital wind-up, in which he performed some of the most novel, attractive and difficult steps of the match, surpassing in execution the most difficult exhibited by Peel. Like his predecessor, he was loudly applauded at the finish, the time occupied by him in actual dancing being 11 minutes 16 seconds, a minute and more longer than Peel. Bob Hart then stated that the judges and referee would retire and render a verdict in five minutes. It seemed to be a conceded thing, however, that there could be no difficulty in declaring in Peel's favor; when the judges appeared at the expiration of ten or fifteen minutes and announced that it would be impossible to give a decision. There and then much dissatisfaction was expressed and a good many asserted that it was a "set thing," and that the crowd was sold; but upon Hart explaining the difficulties under which the judges labored in arriving at the true facts of the case, a better feeling prevailed. He said that there were points in dancing which the casual observer might not be able to detect but which the judges and referee had been very particular in noting,. It was stated that the decision should be made known on the morrow and the audience dispersed. In about half an hour after, the judges and referee having been closeted that length of time, a decision was arrived at, which was that Peel was the winner of the match and the money. As both judges agreed that Peel was the winner, the referee was not appealed to. Robert Hart was judge for Carroll, Mr. Tousey judge for Peel, and John Landers referee. There was much dissatisfaction on the part of Carroll and he published a card offering to dance Peel a jig in private for $1,000, the best dancer to win the money; the most difficult steps and best time constituting the best dancer; and each party to select twelve friends to witness the contest. Peel replied to this and agreed to make the match. A meeting was held at the *Clipper* office, May 12, but after much talk nothing was arrived at owing to a difference of opinion in reference to the points on which a jig dance should be decided. Carroll wanted style left out, while Peel wanted it included. The affair was finally settled by spreading themselves before a basket of wine. After this, sundry challenges and counter challenges were issued but no more matches were made and Tommy was fully recognized as the champion jig dancer of America.

A match dance between Hank Mason and Alex Ross took place in March, 1863, at the Bowery Theatre, St. Louis, Mo., for $100 a side. Mason danced 79 steps and Ross danced twenty-eight. Charles Vorce was judge for Mason and Mr. Morris for Ross.

A match dance for the championship between Otto Burbank, Tommy Peel, and Billy Sheppard came off at the Metropolitan Theatre, San Francisco, Cal., August 12, 1864. Ben Cotton played for Tommy Peel. William Bernard for Otto Burbank, and Charley Rhodes for Sheppard. The judges were selected from the audience, who, when the dancing was over, adjourned to a private room to write their decision, and they decided in favor of Burbank, and the champion jig belt of California was given to Otto Burbank. The belt was a magnificent silver one, with three old stars attached and used as slides, with the name of each of the contestants in the center of the stars.

A match clog hornpipe for $250 a side and the receipts of the house after expenses, between Tommy Peel and John R. Mason, took place August 24, 1864, at the American Theatre, San Francisco, Cal. Mason was backed by Leslie Blackburn and Peel by himself. Peel proved the victor. Peel: 35 steps; time, 6 minutes, 30 seconds. Mason: 27 steps; time, 5 minutes, 30 seconds.

A championship dance for the "belt" of California took place at Maguire's Opera House, San Francisco, Cal., December 15, 1864, between Tommy Peel and Otto Burbank, the former having challenged the latter for superiority in jig dancing. Peel danced seven minutes and Burbank five and a half minutes. The heel-and-toe business was so nearly balanced between the parties that the judges were unable to decide and the match was repeated on December 17 at the same house. The judges were selected by Maguire, who disagreed, and it was left to the audience. Seven judges finally volunteered from the audience and settled the question by ballot---one going for Burbank and six for Peel.

FIRSTS AND ODDITIES:

Nelson Kneass took a benefit at Palmo's Opera House, New York, in 1845, on which occasion a burlesque on "The Bohemian Girl," written by Mr. Kneass and called "The Virginia Gal," was produced in black. Joe Kavanaugh, the basso, appeared; also Mrs. Sharp, Mrs. Phillips, Clara Bruce, Nelson Kneass, Joe Murphy, James Lynch, Ned Huntley, and George Holman (manager of the New Holman Opera Troupe). This was the first operatic burlesque ever "negroized" in this or any other country. So great was its success that Palmo at once engaged the party to run it. Success ruined the company, as they all became possessed of too much cash. After a tour South and West, they returned to Palmo's Opera House June 16, 1845; but their continued success they could not stand. All wanted to be managers and so they disagreed and disbanded.

The Dumbolton Serenaders is referred to by the old burnt corkites as one of the great landmarks in the history of negro minstrelsy and the old band is referred to with pride and pleasure. It was in England where this party first introduced white coats and vests and black pants for an introduction performance. The London public was in ecstasy over this troupe. The public was made familiar with the true Negro life and the laugh, the wild gestures and strange dialect with which they were regaled by the end men, who produced such a novel mixture of wonder and delight that they fairly worshipped them. At first a few endeavored to stem the popularity of the company by declaring that the artists were real blacks. Far from wishing to pass themselves off for veritable niggers, they lost no time in publishing portraits of themselves with the white faces bestowed upon them by nature, in addition to others in which they wore the sable hue of their profession. They set a fashion in the strictest sense of the word. The highest personages in the land patronized their performances. An ingenious young gentleman who could play on the banjo and sing "Lucy Neal" or "Buffalo Gals" was a welcome guest in the most aristocratic drawing rooms; and if four amateurs clubbed together and imitated the entire performance of the professors, they were regarded as benefactors to their species. Let the music books of 1846 be turned over and it will be found what an enormous influence the company had over the social pianoforte performances of the day.

"Coal Oil Johnny" became a phenomenon identified with the negro minstrelsy. We will give a brief account of him. His right name was John W. Steele. Some four miles above Oil City, directly on the line of the Oil Creek and Allegheny River Railway, lies a tract once celebrated as the "Widow McClintock Farm." Here for some years, ignorant of the boundless wealth beneath their feet, the McClintocks, in common with the other natives of that little more than half civilized region, plodded along, day after day. No children came to cheer the solitude and eat the flapjacks of the worthy matron---probably a wise dispensation of Providence, as the products of the farm were not extensive enough to fill many mouths with any degree of certainty. At last, however, as old age came creeping in their direction, thoughts regarding the disposal of their valuable property began to trouble them and the conclusion was at last reached to adopt some healthy boy and make him sole heir. But a short distance from the McClintocks lived a man by the name of Steele; and as the barrenness of the land had not extended to his wife, he found himself the father of a numerous progeny, and often was sorely puzzled about plans for keeping the wolf from the door. To him due application was made, and without hesitation he gave them the pick of the flock, remarking that he had ten or twelve more to dispose on the same terms. As the most promising one, "Johnny" was selected and thereafter he was trained up in the way he ought to have gone.

In the fullness of time came the discovery of petroleum and the accompanying army of seekers after the greasy fluid. One eruption after another swept across the McClintock farm, literally tramping out the expected harvest; and at the age of three score and ten, the old man saw starvation staring him in the face. Besides this, he was continually pestered by offers for the purchase of the old homestead until finally his ancient body succumbed and he was gathered to his fathers.

For a long time the old lady refused to have anything to do with the outside barbarians; but at last, in sheer despair, she leased a portion of the farm, every portion of which afterward proved wonderfully productive. Being forever ruined for agricultural purposes, the venerable widow now employed some household assistance and spent her days in cording up bonds and greenbacks in the cellar, though she was afterward induced to purchase a safe, as being more secure. In this pleasant pastime she might have passed the remaining period of her useful life, had she not attempted to make the fire burn one morning by pouring on it a bucketful of crude oil. In an incredibly short space of time she was in a country where petroleum is supposed to be unknown; and from that date began the career of her heir, soon known far and wide as "Coal Oil Johnny."

After the mortal remains of the old lady had cooled and been properly interred, Steele, who up to this time had been busily engaged in hauling oil, took $75,000 from the safe, and, with three or four teamsters, started out on a cruise into that outside world of which they had heard strange rumors. These companions were soon shaken off, however, and their places seized by a number of parasites, who clung to the young man as long as he had a penny left. Prominent among these was one Seth Slocum, who installed himself as "financial agent," and, afterward inseparable, the two then plunged into the wildest species of excess. Spending the greater portion of the time in Philadelphia and New York, one may hear there yet the stories of their extravagance and wild orgies. Doubtless many of these tales are exaggerated, but enough is known to mark Slocum down as a most successful swindler and Steele as the most consummate fool of the present generation. The chief aim of the latter's life appeared to be to literally throw away his fortune as rapidly as possible, and he succeeded so well that he squandered nearly two million dollars in less than twelve months. His methods of doing this were very peculiar and perhaps original. Gifts of five and ten thousand dollars, sets of diamonds to his male and female friends were matters of every day occurrence, while to vary the monotony he would sally into the street, purchase the finest barouche and span he could find, take a short ride and give the turnout to the driver. Another favorite freak was to lease the hotels where he might be stopping and allow none of the guests to pay bills during his administration; while his losses at faro were heavy and continuous, John Morrissey's bank having won $50,000 in one night. But what, perhaps, gave him as much notoriety as anything else, was the organization of SKIFF & GAYLORD'S MINSTRELS.

He gave two members of the company a diamond pin and ring and to each member of the company a complete wardrobe; and they started on their way rejoicing. He purchased an interest in a large hotel in Meadville for $45,000, and getting a little hard up one day sold it back for $10,000; while other property in and around the same place was bought and sold in about the same proportion.

Through the medium of these and other devices, success crowned his efforts, and the wells gave out and the bottom of the old safe was reached at last. The McClintock farm was sold to satisfy a little hotel bill of $32,000, incurred at the Girard House, Philadelphia, while enough other mortgages were placed on record to cover the old place a foot deep. Steele, "Coal Oil Johnny" no more, now disappeared for a season from the scenes of his triumphs, but some time afterward came to the surface in the position of doorkeeper for the minstrel troupe of which he was the founder. We next heard of him trying to keep a seven by nine tavern in Franklin, but he was not so successful as in his previous efforts to play Boniface. In the present instance he was willing to take pay from his patrons. At last, however, "Johnny" found his level again, and he was seen daily in the neighborhood of his old home, guiding an ancient pair of equines attached to a dilapidated wagon. Sitting perched above his half-dozen barrels of oil, he was a picture of greasy contentment. Must not the man be happy who can so gracefully adapt himself to circumstances?

It may be a source of satisfaction to some who read this sketch to learn that Slocum, who was responsible more than all others for Steele's course, died in jail at Erie, where he had been for some months incarcerated, being unable to obtain one hundred dollars bail. This Slocum should not be confused with the late E. V. Slocum, who was also associated at that period with Steele.

The Bamford and Norman shooting affair took place an the afternoon of July 26, 1867. Bamford and Norman, soprano and balladist of Newcomb Minstrels, had previously been warm friends, but through some misunderstanding a coolness had sprung up between them. They became jealous of each other and several altercations had occurred between them, when they finally met in a drinking saloon on the above mentioned date and again renewed their wordy quarrel, during which Norman laid violent hands on Bamford, who did not attempt to retaliate immediately, but in the course of a few minutes slipped out and borrowed of an acquaintance a small sized, four barreled Sharp's pistol with revolving hammer. Norman refusing to take back what he said, Bamford drew his pistol, cocked, and aimed it at Norman's breast. He took a deliberate aim as he said:

"Take it back, I'll give it to you if you don't take it back by the time I count three. One---two---three!"

With the "three" came the sharp report of a pistol and the ball went straight into Norman's body above and to the left of the navel. The victim threw up his hands with a yell of fright and pain and with the words, "Oh God, I'm killed," sank back into the arms of a barkeeper, with a stream of blood spouting out from his wound. Bamford walked to the station house and surrendered himself.

In a few weeks Norman recovered and, refusing to make a charge against Bamford, he (Bamford) was discharged. On August 19 both Norman and Bamford made their re-appearance with the company. The quick recovery of Mr. Norman and the release of Mr. Bamford was the wonder of all. It was truly a remarkable case (the release of Bamford). Mr. Newcomb exerted all the influence he could bring to bear to procure his release, and this, aided by Mr. Norman declining to appear as prosecutor if Mr. Bamford would abide by such decrees as he would give and made valid and binding by legal authority; set him at liberty.

In December, 1867, Edwin Leon shot Sam Sharpe. The particulars of this sad affair are as follows. It occurred on the afternoon of December 11, 1867, at the close of the matinee of the Fifth Avenue Opera House, on Twenty-fourth Street near Broadway. When Kelly and Leon came to New York and leased Hope Chapel as a place of amusement, they met with every opposition from those in the same business in this city and were looked upon with naught but jealousy; but thinking there was room enough for all, they went to work attending to their own business. During the summer of 1867 they appeared in Boston at the Theatre Comique; and Sam Sharpley with his minstrel band appeared at the Howard Athenaeum in the same city. Quite a rivalry was kept up between the two bands and the merits of each were pretty freely canvassed by the public. The ill feeling existing toward the Kelly & Leon party grew stronger when it was known that Add Ryman, the end man with the Sharpley party, had engaged with Kelly & Leon for one year, to commence with their re-opening in New York; and to make the matter still worse, Delehanty and Hengler also went over to the Kelly & Leon party to open with them in New York. From the day the two companies re-appeared in New York up to the day of this sad occurrence, quite an ill feeling existed between the two managers, occasioned by someone repeating to Sharpley that Leon had prejudiced Delehanty and Hengler against him (Sharpley) by saying he (Sharpley) was an irresponsible party and that all his property in New York was mortgaged, which Leon afterwards denied ever having said. On the afternoon mentioned, Kelly and Leon visited the Fifth Avenue Theatre to see the performance. Sharpley also attended the performance. At the close and while the audience were dispersing, Sharpley stepped up to Leon, tapped him on the shoulder, and told him he had heard he had been talking about him and that he was a d----d liar. A quarrel soon followed and Kelly joined in the melee. Suddenly Tom Sharpley (brother of Sam Sharpley) showed up, when a general fight took place. Kelly drew a revolver, fired at Tom Sharpley, and he fell dead. Sam Sharpley then drew his revolver, fired at Kelly, and was about to fire again when an officer seized his hand and arrested him. The pistol was discharged, the ball going through Sharpley's own hand. The first shot from Sharpley's pistol struck Kelly on the head, between the eyes and ear, from the effects of which wound he laid in the station house some days, the writer of this spending much time with him. As soon as Kelly got better he was discharged, as Sharpley refused to make any charge against him or appear. Kelly also refused to appear against Sharpley. At midnight of the 13th, Sharpley was discharged on his own recognizance and Leon entirely discharged. On the morning of the 14th, bail was accepted for Kelly to the amount of $5,000. Nothing of its kind that has ever transpired in this city caused so much excitement as this. While Sharpley had hosts of friends calling upon and sympathizing with him in his misfortune, the station house was besieged by the friends of Kelly and Leon, including a delegation of the Jesuit priests of this city.

The trial of Edwin Kelly came up in the General Sessions on April 24, 1868. After swearing three jurymen, one was obtained who had not expressed an opinion, after which the court was adjourned until April 28, when the trial commenced and lasted all that day. Then the court adjourned until the 30th, when the case was resumed. All the evidence went to show that Kelly was wholly unacquainted with Tom Sharpley and throughout he acted on motives of purely self-defense, as he anticipated another attack. Recorder Hackett, in charging, said the accused could not be convicted of murder in the first degree, nor could he be convicted of manslaughter in the second degree. The jury, after being out fifteen minutes, rendered a verdict of "Not Guilty." Seldom has there been more unmistakable demonstrations exhibited in a court of justice of approval and gratification with the verdict of a jury than that which greeted the acquittal of Edwin Kelly.

The well known circus proprietors, Dr. Spalding and Charles Rogers, had the steamboat *Banjo* built expressly for Ned Davis' Ohio Minstrels, which were organized in Cincinnati, Ohio, in October, 1855, for the purpose of visiting the river towns of the West and South. They gave their first show at Lawrenceburg, Ind. The boat was a stern wheeler. A regular stage and scenery occupied nearly two-thirds of the forward part of the saloon deck, while behind the stage were the state rooms for the "boys," who ate and slept on board. The balcony of the saloon was fitted up in regular hall fashion, with seats, etc. Performances were given every afternoon and evening (and Sunday in the South), and frequently in the morning.

BROWN'S BURNT CORK ACTIVITY

ABELL'S (BOB) MINSTRELS: were started from Pawtucket, R. I., and gave their first show at Providence, May 1, 1867. Charles Greene, bones; Charles Coggeshall, tambo; and Bob Abell, interlocutor.

AEOLIAN MINSTRELS: under J. W. Allinson's management, and consisting off T. Gettings, A. S. Remington, E. West, J. Norrie, N. Kelly, W. Parsons, F. Schaffer, T. Deverell, O. P. Perry, H. Schindler, J. Arnold, J. Van Muse and P. Cary, were playing in New Orleans up to February 25, 1865, when they sailed for Ship Island and opened there March 2 for two nights. They went thence to Mobile Bay and performed under canvas at Navy Cove. The soldiers cut and slashed the tent nearly to pieces. That night they proceeded to sea, arriving at Warrington Navy Yard, Pensacola Bay, where they performed in Temperance Hall to crowded audiences, they being the first show there during the war. On March 27, they sailed for Matamoras, Mexico.

AEOLIAN STAR TROUPE: was organized in Albany, N.Y., June 26, 1860, with D. H. Johnson, William Gaveline, E. S. Near, L. Norton, J. Harris, S. Falline, Master Edward, T. Batchellor, Master Rourck and William Rogers.

AEOLIANS: organized in Philadelphia in the fall of 1867 for a traveling tour. The party consisted of: J. N. Reber, A. K. Harding (afterwards known as Add Collins), J. W. Reber, A. S. Whiteman, Master Hughey, jig; Mike McGraw, G. W. Lollor, and J. Collins, agent. They closed in New Brunswick, N. J., April 24, 1869.

AFRICAN MINSTRELS: was the title of a band of minstrels performing at the Bowery Theatre, New York, in April, 1843.

ALABAMA MINSTRELS AND NIGHTINGALE SERENADERS: was organized in Hartford, Conn., in October, 1859. M. B. Leavitt, bones; G. W. Florence, banjo; C. Peer, violin; J. Neal, guitar; Frank Smith, tambo; W. T. Wright, H. Irving and Master L. Levi.

ALABAMA MINSTRELS: a colored troupe under the direction of A. R. Garrison, commenced a tour on November 13, 1876. Toddy Hedden, tambo; George Brookes, banjo; and Ferd Hight, director.

ALABAMA MINSTRELS: traveled through the East a brief time and disbanded in Boston in September, 1859.

ALABAMA SERENADERS: started. from Buffalo, N. Y., February 21, 1876, for a trip through Canada. Ike Booth, Billy Mack, Charles Harcourt, Charles Belden, Fred Sharpley, Chauncey Olcott, J. P. Welbert, John Hanley, Dixon and Udell. This company only lasted three days.

ALABAMA SLAVES: See MOCKING BIRD MINSTRELS.

ALBINO MINSTRELS: [formerly the SKIFF & GAYLORD party] In February, 1871, the company appeared in the first part in white clothes, white faces and blonde wigs. Harry Talbott, Johnny Stiles, Tyrrell, Bideaux, Girard, and Andy McKee. The Skiff & Gaylord title was resumed for the next season and the company consisted of Low Gaylord, director; Prof. Olney, musical director; A. Holmes, stage manager; John Stiles, James Dalton, Frank Carroll, Joe Mairs, Add Collins, Willie Gaylord and Sam Lang. They made an extensive tour through the West and the South. The next season the company consisted of: Frank Carroll, John Stiles, Al Holmes, Low Gaylord, J. E. Green, Dan Gilfoil, the Morris Bros., Willie Gaylord. Low Gaylord was sole proprietor. In 1874 Gaylord's health began to fail and his troupe suspended operations, except for a short time when they visited small towns of Pennsylvania. They closed April 1. 1876, but reorganized and started from Columbia, Pa., August 14 and collapsed in two weeks.

ALHAMBRA MINSTRELS: was a new party made up by Thomas Maguire to open at the Alhambra Theatre, San Francisco, when Simmons and Slocum had closed their engagement there. Rickey, Add Ryman, Cool Burgess, Sweatnam, Bob Hart, M. Ainsley Scott, Charles Sutton, J. G. Russell, Delehanty, and Hengler were in the party who opened August 5, 1872. Emerson having sold out his interest in the place to Maguire, the band was called Maguire's California Minstrels until December, 1872, when the old name of Emerson's Minstrels was used, Billy Emerson having returned and opened November 25. On December 9 the Worrell Sisters and Lillie Hall appeared in burlesque and Jenny Worrell in song and dance. The season closed January 19, 1873, and the party went traveling. They re-appeared at the Alhambra February 3, 1873. Add Ryman closed March 19. Charles Vivian opened April 7, followed by Kelly and Leon and Master Barney, who appeared May 5. Emerson disposed of his interest in the theatre in May, when Maguire became sole proprietor and the band was called MAGUIRE'S CALIFORNIA MINSTRELS. In June, 1873, a company was made up from this party and sent into the interior for a tour. In the troupe were Sam Rickey, Bob Hart, Little Mack, Master Barney, Justin Robinson, and J. G. Russell. Frank Morgan and Billy Manning opened June 30 with the company in San Francisco; and the party that had been out traveling returned and opened the same date. Billy Sweatnam opened July 28, 1873. Owing to bad business the season closed September 7 and the party started on a tour, opening in Sacramento, September 8 with Kelly, Leon, Manning, Sweatnam, Little Mac, Welch, and Rice in the party. They re-appeared at the Alhambra October 20 with Sweatnam, Little Mack, Manning, Robert Frazer, John Robinson, Charles Reed, Welch, Rice, J. G. Russell, W. F. Bake, B. Montague, D. I. Sherwood, Esther Williams, and orchestra. On February 23, 1874, they opened Maguire's Opera House, San Francisco. In April, Manning seceded from the company, who went traveling. They re-appeared in San Francisco, May 11, at the Opera House. Bobby Newcomb opened May 18. Canfield and Booker opened January 18, 1875. Their season closed April 17. They opened at Hooley's Opera House, Chicago, May 3 with Arlington, Cotton, Billy Rice, Emerson, Little Mac, John Oberist, Kemble, J. G. Russell, Norcross (Norrie), Con Murphy, and others. This party opened in New York at the Park Theatre, May 31, 1875. On September 25 they appeared in Chicago. Tilla, Mackin, Wilson, and James Morrison left on that date and Charles Sutton, Marrchette, Jennings, Charles Henry,

C. S. Fredericks and John Oberist opened. The company then split up and a portion went to Detroit, opening on September 30. This company, then under the management of J. H. Haverly, closed in Chicago, January 1, 1876, and went traveling. They reappeared in Chicago at Hooley's Opera House, June 24. Pat Rooney, Schoolcraft, George Coes, and Charles Howard joined on the opening night. On August 21, 1876, this party opened at Haverly's (previously known as Hooley's) Opera House. Emerson, Schoolcraft, Coes, Ben Cotton, Sanford, Wilson, Scanlon, Cronin, J. G. Russell, Ernest Linden, W. H. Tilla, C. S. Fredericks, R. Tyrrell, Oberist, and James Morrison. A re-organization was made in November for a Western tour under the management of Haverly and Maguire. Beaumont, Read, Savori, and others were added. They opened in Milwaukee, November 20. They closed the traveling season at Washington, D. C., December 13, 1876. A new company was then organized, which opened in Ottawa, Ill., February 26, 1877 with Fredericks, Oberist, Heywood, Morton, Lester and Williams. Billy Emerson, Karl Steele, Fredericks, Nat Horner, and Wash Norton left Chicago April 15 for San Francisco and opened at the Opera House, Bush Street, April 23. Arlington left the company October 16 for a lecturing tour. The band appeared in New York, January 14, 1878, at the Olympic Theatre. Emerson, Schoolcraft, Coes, Charles Heywood, J. Mack, Quilter, Goldrich and others. Their stay there was a very short one and a new party was organized, which started out February 25 under the business direction of J. Mack. Emerson, Smith, Waldron, Morton, Martin (the Big Four), and C. Heywood. The season closed in Buffalo, June 15. On August 26 they appeared in Philadelphia with R. Abecco in the party.

ALLEN & PETTENGILL'S MINSTRELS: [formerly ALLEN, PETTENGILL, DELEHANTY & HENGLER'S] opened in New York at Bryant's Opera House, Fourteenth Street, June 6, 1870. There were thirteen in the first part---four end men consisting of Johnny Allen and Fayette Welch, tambos; Walter Bray and George Edwards, bones. Frank Girard was middleman. Gustave Bideaux, R. T. Tyrrell and Cox were in the party. In consequence of illness, Charley Pettengill did not appear. They closed there June 18.

ALLEN, HART & RYMAN: with a minstrel organization under their manage-ment, consisting of Johnny Allen, Add Ryman, John Hart, Abecco, Sanford, Wilson, Lester and others, opened April 6, 1874, at Tony Pastor's Opera House, New York. They closed May 2 and the firm dissolved.

ALLEN, PETTENGILL, DELEHANTY & HENGLER'S MINSTRELS: open-ed September 22, 1869, in Brooklyn, N. Y. George M. Bassett was middleman, and Charles Church, tenor. C. B. Griste started with the company as advance agent, but in consequence of a reduction of salaries Mr. Griste left and his place was taken by H. J. Sargent. This company opened in New York at the Waverly Theatre (formerly Kelly & Leon's) November 29, 1869. Gustave Bideaux was in the party then. They closed there January 1, 1870, and opened at the Tammany Music Hall, New York, giving a "first part" January 3 in the burlesque of "Bad Dickey." They remained there four weeks, closing January 29 and opening in Boston January 31 at

Olympic Theatre, where they closed February 12. Then Delehanty and Hengler withdrew and the company was called ALLEN & PETTENGILL'S.

ALLEN'S (HARRY) MINSTRELS: opened December 9, 1872, in Milwaukee, Wis. Harry Allen, George Burgess, Billy Welch, Johnny Rice, Chris Mathews, John Larkeller, Charles De Von, S. H. Montgomery, and Charles de St. Clair.

AMAZONS: See FOSTER'S MINSTRELS.

ANDERSON'S MINSTRELS: were organized for a tour through the East while the Melodeon in Boston was being fitted up for them. They started on October 12, 1859. After a few weeks tour they laid up, the Melodeon not being ready. On December 12, they opened the Melodeon with Frank Brower, E. Bowers, Donniker, Bideaux, Warren White, G. Kelly, Unsworth, Hen Smith, Master Peel, Master James Sanford, Herr Endes, J. Stratton, J. S. Budworth and Max Irwin. The Melodeon was situated on Washington Street adjoining the Boston Theatre. After performing at the Melodeon five weeks and four days, they disbanded. Most of the company came to New York and a portion of them re-opened the hall January 20; but on the opening night no performance was given, as several of the party refused to play and the audience were dismissed. There was too much style about this party to last. Anderson, like Sniffen, was "in the hands of his friends" and he promised too high salaries for his or their own good.

AREND, LEVI & THOMPSON'S AMERICAN OPERA TROUPE: was organized in Albany, Ga., in January, 1860, and made a South American tour. George Schultz, Matt Thompson, William Dunn, Francis Williams, Thomas Arend, and O. W. Harris.

ARLINGTON & DONNIKER'S MINSTRELS: organized in July, 1862, with the following: William Arlington and J. B. Donniker, proprietors; Master Leon, Edwin Kelly, S. Price, W. H. Brockway, C. Newton, H. Butler, J. H. Dale, O. H. Carter, Master Frank Dumont, V. B. Bummell, and Charles Wood, business manager. After traveling for a while, they concluded to locate in Chicago; and, after going to an expense of about $300 fitting up Kingsbury Hall, collapsed (owing to a disagreement in the company) in November.

ARLINGTON, COTTON & KEMBLE'S: See ARLINGTON'S MINSTRELS.

ARLINGTON, LEON & DONNIKER'S: Edwin Kelly, Jones, Leon, Arlington, and Donniker were the managers. The party consisted of Arlington, Donniker, Leon, Kelly, Albert Jones, Sam Gardner, William Spalding, Sam Price, Frank Cardella, Frank Shorer, and James Granville. They opened in Cincinnati at Smith & Ditson's Hall, December, 1862. After a lengthy stay in Chicago, Ill., they closed in July, 1863, and their hall was rejuvenated. They made a short traveling tour and then returned to Chicago and opened November 16, at Metropolitan Hall. In December, 1863, they took possession of a new hall located on Washington Street, between Clark and Dearborn, Chicago, which they opened December 21. George Wrightman was added to the company. On November 20, 1864, Arlington sold out his interest in the firm and withdrew from the company. Kelly & Leon then became managers, and continued in Chicago until March, 1865, when they made a brief tour. They shortly after returned to Chicago, where they once more located for some time. Arlington returned to this party shortly after and the company was once more known as ARLINGTON, LEON & CO. But in October, 1865, Arlington again suddenly withdrew. The party continued under the title of Kelly & Leon's Minstrels, and remained in Cincinnati, Ohio, at the Academy of Music (situated on Fourth Street, between Elm and Plum Streets), which was destroyed by fire January 12, 1866.

ARLINGTON'S MINSTRELS: was a new band that opened in Chicago on April 23, 1867, at a hall on Washington Street, between Clark and La Salle Streets, opposite the Court House. Arlington and C. Pettengill were the end men; with W. A. Johnson, interlocutor; J. Barsby, J. W. Hilton, H. Voss, C. Norrie, R. Snyder, J. Mack, M. Lewis, Master George, J. Ricci, Billy Barry, J. Augustus, F. Freeburg, and E. Warden. On July 15 they left for a brief traveling tour, with McAndrews and Arlington on the ends; Johnson, middle man; Jackson, Hilton, Ricci, and Barsby as the quartette. They re-opened in Chicago under the management of J. Haverly, September 6, 1867, with Johnny Booker, Samuel Gardner, N. D. W. Ainsworth, R. J. Tooke, Billy Barry, W. C. Emmons, H. Fuller, Thomas Roberts, Voss, T. Warhurst, H. Stuart, Barsby, Charles Koehl, G. W. Jackson, J. R. Russey, J. Bagar, C. H. Simpson, J. Bunnell, J. T. Clayton, and Arlington. They closed November 30 and went traveling. Haverly then secured Witowski's Hall, corner of Clark and Monroe Streets, Chicago, and commenced fitting it up as a minstrel hall in April, 1868, which he opened with Arlington's Minstrels, May 12. Arlington, Cool Burgess, Charley Reynolds, O. P. Sweet, C. S. Fredericks, Otis Carter, Sig. Brandisi, Blakely, Russy, Voss, Kalis, Stanton, Ainsworth Brooks, Eugene Florence (wench), and Mike Kannane. On July 7 they went to Wood's Museum, Chicago. Delehanty and Hengler joined the party and Sam Price took the bone end. J. Haverly sold out his interest in Arlington Hall to Sam Sharpley in October, 1868. The company closed November 7 and Haverly withdrew from the company. Arlington reorganized and opened December 4 with Sam Price as bones; Arlington, tambo; T. L. Estrange, D. L. Morris, and others. Ed Gooding joined the party April 26, 1869. They closed their season traveling, June 3. 1869, and commenced the next season on November 22, 1869, at Lincoln, Neb. Johnny Booker joined them January 28, 1870. Billy Arlington, whose right name was Burnell, was a first class comedian and made funny speeches.

ARLINGTON'S MINSTRELS: was a new organization that opened the West Side Opera House, Chicago, Ill. (formerly known as Rice & Jackson's Hall), November 27, 1871, under the management of Sam Myers. In the company were: Billy Arlington, Billy Reeves, Sam Price, Clark Gibbs, Johnny Booker, G. W. Mills, Morton, Manning, William Scott, A. W. Hamilton, John Stout, Walter Phillips, Horace Bontwell, and John Buel. This party was shortly after known as ARLINGTON, COTTON & KEMBLE'S. Harrigan and Hart appeared with this party in April, 1872. This party inaugurated Myer's New Opera House on Monroe Street, between State and Dearborn Streets, Chicago, on September 23, 1872. Arlington, Cotton, Kemble, Surridge, E. M. Kane; J. A. Lang, Hunneman, and C. Fostelle were in the party. The season closed May 3, 1873, and they went traveling. They commenced their next season in Chicago on August 25, 1873, with Sam Myers as manager.

Kemble, Cotton, Arlington, Billy Rice, E. M. Kane, Surridge, John Lacy, R. T. Tyr-rell, Mackin, Wilson, Bobby Newcomb, C. S. Fredericks, John Davis, Ernest Linden, and Master G. Davenport. The season closed May 16, 1874, and they traveled.

ASSOCIATED ARTISTS: made up from Kelly & Leon's Minstrel Band, went through the West in September, 1866. The end men were Price and Williams; W. H. Brockway, middle man; and Dan Collins was of the party.

AUSTIN'S (CHARLES) MINSTRELS: started on the road March 4, 1870, and consisted of Tyrilla, female gymnast; Charles Austin, J. G. H. Shorey, Charles La Forrest, Thomas Presho, E. S. Austin, Fred Hoffmeister, Harry Norton, Albert Nix, J. S. Norton, Oliver White. and Harry Metcalf.

BACKUS' (CHARLEY) ORIGINAL MINSTRELS: organized in San Francisco, Cal., in the summer of 1854 and appeared at San Francisco Hall, Washington Street, between Montgomery and Kearney Streets with C. D. Abbott, musical director; O. N. Burbank, stage manager; H. Donnelly, D. F. Boley, Backus, J. N. White, Morgan. They took a trip to Australia in 1855. Prior to their departure, a benefit was given them by the San Francisco Minstrels, August 3, at the Metropolitan Theatre. Mitchell and Burbank, the rival dancers, appeared. There appeared in the first part S. C. Campbell, Jerry Bryant, Stadtfeld, D. F. Boley, Eph Horn, and W. M. Barker, besides the instrumentalists, in the second part J. Collins, George Coes, C. Backus and Mrs. Julia Collins (Julia Gould). In July, 1856, the party returned to San Francisco and opened at San Francisco Hall, Sunday evening, July 6, 1856, a portion of the San Francisco Minstrels being added to the party, which then consisted of Billy Birch, E. Deaves, Max Zorer, Charles Henry, Napier Lothian, Sam Wells, M. Lewis, George Coes, S. C. Campbell, Charles Backus, W. D. Corrister, and Jerry Bryant. They continued there for some time very successfully and afterwards went to Maguire's New Opera House, where in January, 1857, Hiram W. Franklin, the gym-nast, joined them. In March, 1858, they made a tour of the mountain towns with Zorer, Mitchell, Wells, Campbell, C. Henry, Coes and Kelly. On February 28, 1864, Backus joined the EUREKA MINSTRELS. He became manager of BIRCH, WAM-BOLD & BACKUS' MINSTRELS, who opened in Eureka Hall, September 15, 1864, and shortly after went to the Academy of Music, San Francisco, and continued there until March, 1865. Then Backus, Birch, Wambold and W. H. Bernard sailed for New York and arrived April 5. The San Francisco Minstrels, organized by these gentlemen, opened at 585 Broadway, formerly Buckley's Hall, opposite Niblo's Garden. The place had been called the New Olympic Theatre (F. S. Chanfrau, manager), the Academy of the Drama, the Metropolitan Music Hall, Hooley & Campbell's Minstrel Hall, the German Theatre, the Canterbury, Palace of Mirrors, the Broadway Theatre, St. Nicholas Hall, Heller's Salon Diabolique, and finally, this unlucky house was called San Francisco Minstrels' Hall. The company consisted of Billy Birch, Charley Backus, W. H. Bernard, David S. Wambold, Cooper and Fields, W. S. Mullaly, Richard Sands, E. Haslam, Hays, Shattuck, W. H. Rice, J. B. Donni-ker, Ainsley Scott, and Templeton. They opened here May 8, 1865, and the first season closed July 7, 1866. The second season commenced August 12, 1867, and closed June 27, 1868. Their next season commenced August 31, 1668, and closed

June 12, 1869. Their next season opened August 30, 1869, and closed May 14, 1870. Bobby Newcomb, Lew Brimmer, Joe Brown, Harry Raynor, Billy Emmett, John Queen, Ira Paine, William West, Leggett and Allen, Henry Norman (first appearance in America), Rollin Howard, and Master Fink at different times appeared. The "boys" next appeared at Apollo Hall, North side of Twenty-eighth Street (now a portion of the Fifth Avenue Theatre). It was also known as the St. James Theatre. Bernard had withdrawn from the firm when they closed at 585 Broadway. They opened here August 26, 1872. They closed March 1, 1873, and went on the road for the summer. A large billiard hall in the Gilsey Building, on the west side of Broadway, between Twenty-eighth and Twenty-ninth Streets, was re-constructed for the San Francisco Minstrels and they opened September 3, 1874, and called it The San Francisco Hall. They continued here for six years, closing April 4, 1880. Wambold retired from the company the closing night. Birch put his money into Wall Street and lost it all. During the summer of 1882, Backus visited Europe and performed with MOORE & BURGESS' MINSTRELS.

BARLOW BROS.' MINSTRELS: organized. in Cincinnati, Ohio, and opened in Cynthiana, Ky., on April 10, 1877. Archie White and Charles W. Young were the principal cards of the company.

BARLOW, WILSON, PRIMROSE & WEST'S MINSTRELS: gave their first public entertainment at Wilmington, Del., August 20, 1877. The company consisted of Milt G. Barlow, manager and end man; George Wilson, end; James W. Lamont, stage manager; Gus Herwig, leader; Carl Rudolph, vocal director; George H. Primrose and William H. West, song and dance and clog; E. M. Hall, banjoist; Harry Percy, Frank E. Jamison, Lamont, Stout and Rudolph, the quintette; an orchestra and brass band. Charles B. Griste, advance agent. In May, 1878, Eddie Fox joined. The season closed June 8. They reorganized and opened August 12, 1878, at Reading, Pa., with Edwin French, Eddie Fox, Jacob Koenig, D. R. Hawkins, Edwin Harley, Frank Howard and W. H. Hunt, with the four proprietors and an orchestra.

BELER, POSTLETHWAITE & CO.'S CAMPBELLS: was organized in 1859 for a tour in the West. Pell, Talbot, Durant, Beler and Haywood were in the party. They were afterwards known as FRANK BELER'S CAMPBELL'S, and in June, 1859, were traveling in Iowa, with Harry Peel, C. Haynes, banjo; W. F. Durant, J. V. Chadduck, A. J. Talbot, and P. Hayward. They closed their season in August, 1859, but soon after reorganized under the name of BELER'S CAMPBELL'S; but shortly after they were known as DURANT & HAYWOOD'S CAMPBELLS, with A. J. Talbot, Fred J. Henneman, E. J. Melville, Frank Howard, W. F. Durant, W. Hayward, and Master Willie. They started from St. Louis, Mo., in April and disbanded July 19 at Michigan City. They reorganized September 12 and opened at Witkowsky Hall, Chicago. In April, 1861, this party was called POSTLE-THWAITE'S MINSTRELS and traveled West. John Boyce, J. W. Postlethwaite, Chadduck, Herr Kellerman; Charlie Petrie, bones; E. D. Gooding, Victor Mauger, A. Hoffman, P. Osterman, Master Willie, and Mons. Pepples.

BELER'S CAMPBELL'S: See BELER, POSTLETHWAITE & CO.'S CAMPBELLS.

BELFAST ETHIOPIANS: were organized in Belfast, Me., in March, 1861, where they opened March 31. J. H. Harmer, J. H. Trussell, Ned Lindsey, Master J. Wheeler, J. O'Connell, and George Dyer.

BELROY'S ETHIOPIANS: [formerly WOOD'S ETHIOPIAN TROUPE] opened March 6, 1861, in Hempstead, L. I., with J. Lewis, J. Belroy, tambo; W. Zeville, middle man; Master Ward, Ferdinand Wallace, William Colson Burgess, R. B. Donnique, B. E. Wood, C. A. Edwards, C. Clifton, George Dodge and A. B. Sanders.

BELROY'S ETHIOPIANS: See WOOD'S ETHIOPIAN TROUPE.

BENEDICT'S (LEW) MINSTRELS: started out under the management of Joseph E. Jackson of Philadelphia and gave their first performance September 21, 1876. In the company were Lew Benedict and Charles Lord, end men; Theodore Jackson, interlocutor; J. A. Barney, John Stout, T. B. Dixon, Charles E. Dobson, John Hogan, Adams, and Lee. They closed December 30, 1876. Lew Benedict was a good end man. His pathetic ballads in the olio were a feature of his entertainment.

BENJAMIN'S NEW ORLEANS MINSTRELS: consisting of Hank Goodman, Tom O'Neil, W. Converse, Mayette, Manning, L. P. Benjamin, J. Gaston, Maude Stanley, Walter Wentworth, and Mrs. Gaston, pianist. They opened in Kansas City, May 4, 1868. In May, 1869, they disbanded during the warm weather and reorganized August, 1869. Another re-organization was made in November, 1871, and the party consisted of J. Rainey, Frank West, Miss Maude Stanley, Hank Goodman, Johnny Keegan, Tommy O'Neil, and Nellie Gaston, pianist.

BENJAMIN'S NEW ORLEANS MINSTRELS: started early in April, 1874, on a traveling tour with N. B. Shimer, F. B. Church, Maud Stanley, Nellie Gaston, Charles King, Joe Gaston, Henry Pfaff, Walter Wentworth, F. P. Benjamin, Sheridan, and George W. Stuart. They closed the season October 17, 1874; but reorganized the following week and started on a tour through the East. In January, 1876, this company was under the management of J. H. Haverly with William Foote as business manager. Ben Brown, Hank Goodman, Frank West, N. B. Shimer, Joe Gorton, L. P. Benjamin, Otis H. Carter and others were in the company.

BERNARD & LAMONT: formed a minstrel party in Chicago, Ill., in October, 1865, for a trip down the Mississippi River. In the party were Marie Stella, Louise Harris, Louis Lamont, W. H. Hardenberg, and Master Willie Morris.

BIRCH, BOWERS & CO.'S MINSTRELS: were organized in New York February, 1859, and went traveling, opening in New Haven, Conn., February 21. Billy Birch, E. Bowers, Ned Davis, and J. B. Donniker were in the party. A difficulty occurring, Bowers withdrew in April and returned to New York. A reorganization took place and the party was made up from the Birch & Brower and Sniffen's party, who had just closed at 444 Broadway, New York. They started on a tour through Canada under the title of BIRCH & DONNIKER'S MINSTRELS.

BIRCH, BOWERS & FOX'S MINSTRELS: organized for a traveling tour in 1857 and John T. Boyce was one of the party. Later, they opened in St. Louis, Mo., at the Museum, September 6, 1858, where they located with Billy Birch, E. Bowers, C. H. Fox, J. T. Boyce, E. D. Gooding, G. Charles, J. Ritter, H. Fenton, R. Moore and J. V. Chadduck. They commenced a brief tour but soon returned to St. Louis, then disbanded Christmas night.

BIRCH & COTTON'S PARTY: were performing at Maguire's Opera House, San Francisco, Cal., in June, 1862, with a party who also gave Sunday night performances at Hayes' Park, that city. In July, Maguire's party, with Birch, Backus, Joe Murphy, Ben Cotton, and others, went to Sacramento. They soon after made a trip through the country, returning to San Francisco in September and appeared at Maguire's Opera House. During the same month, Birch, Cotton, George Coes, and others, left; and, October 4, Birch and Cotton opened in Sacramento, after which they made a tour of the country towns---Cotton, Birch, O'Neil, Peel, Sam Wells, and Abecco in the party. Returning to San Francisco, they appeared at Maguire's Opera House, when Jenny and Alicia Mandeville and Harry Courtaine joined them. They closed at Maguire's in March, 1863, and went traveling. W. M. Barker, F. H. Oldfield, A. Watterman, and W. Wasburg were added to the party. They re-opened in San Francisco on June 1, 1863, at the Eureka Theatre under Maguire's management. Backus' Minstrels, having returned to San Francisco from Hong Kong, China, June 14, 1863, appeared at the Eureka June 29 with the Birch and Cotton party, now called the SAN FRANCISCO MINSTRELS, for the benefit of Ben Cotton. Frank Hussey organized a party in San Francisco in September, 1862, consisting of Miss Lotta, Jake Wallace, A. P. Durand, and Ella Cadez, and made a trip to Oregon. BIRCH & COTTON, with Bideaux, Abecco, Ainsley, Scott, J. Bradshaw, M. Riley, T. J. Peel, C. Goodwin, M. Barker, Alf Parry, and C. V. Hand (agent) was a party made up in New York in April, 1862, for a trip to Australia; but the whole speculation was knocked in the head in consequence of some of the boys demanding advance money. A rupture followed and the company dissolved. Birch and Cotton sailed for California on May 24, 1862.

BIRCH & DONNIKER'S MINSTRELS: [See BIRCH, BOWERS & CO.'S MINSTRELS.] went to St. Louis, where a new opera house was built for them on the corner of Market and Fourth Streets, which they opened with J. Ritter, jig; Ben Cotton, J. B. Donniker, L. Conduit, J. T. Boyce, Master Boyce, J. Stratton and Pete Morris. The party soon after closed and Billy Birch and wife sailed for California, August 5, 1859.

BIRCH & MURPHY'S MINSTRELS: organized in San Francisco to travel through the state in February, 1860, with W. Birch, Joe Murphy, Sam Wells, Frank Medina, W. H. Smith, P. Sterling, and H. Williams.

BIRCH & SHARPLEY'S MINSTRELS: were organized in November, 1860. Billy Birch arrived home from California, July 16, 1860. The party consisted of Frank Brower, Billy Birch, Sam Sharpley, Morris Edmonds, Eugene Thiodon, William Villiers, Charles, Dupont, Williams, J. D. Payne, and William D. Spalding. They opened at Jayne's Hall, Chestnut Street, Philadelphia, on November 19 and closed January 2, 1861. They then went traveling and opened in Reading, Pa., the same week. James Gaynor, Johnny Pierce, Dan Collins, Sam Sharpley, Thiodon, John Williams, James Lamoux, and Villiers were in the traveling party. They were known as SHARPLEY'S MINSTRELS when on this tour.

BIRCH & WELLS' MINSTRELS: organized in San Francisco in March, 1860, and after traveling through the interior for six weeks opened at Maguire's Opera House, San Francisco.

BIRCH'S MINSTRELS: traveled West and opened in Chicago in February, 1858. They shortly after located in St. Louis for a season with Billy Birch, W. Penn Lehr, S. Gardner, J. Williams, J. Mairs, Ben Mallory, J. T. Boyce, M. D. Edmonds, J. Cochran, K. Moore, Chet Moore, and G. M. Hill. They closed in St. Louis, May 22, 1858, and proceeded on board of Spalding & Rogers' steamer, *Banjo*, up the Mississippi River to St. Paul, Minn., and thence to New Orleans. In July they took to the road through Missouri. J. A. Leonard, tragedian, appeared in a scene from "Damon and Pythias" to Birch's Lucullus. They were playing to good business at the Forrest Theatre, San Francisco, Cal., in October, 1859. On the last night of their appearance they were all arrested for giving a performance on Sunday. They afterwards appeared at the Opera House under Maguire. Billy Birch, Sam Wells, George Coes, H. Donnelly, Charles Henry, J. W. Charles, E. Deaves, C. C. Keene, G. H. Edmunds, Mike Mitchell and Corrister were in the party. After taking a trip through the mountains, they returned to San Francisco in December. Under the direction of Billy Birch, they opened at the Athenaeum, San Francisco, April 22, 1860, with William Bernard, Frank Hussey, Frank Medina, Pete Sterling, W. H. Smith, E. H. Harvey, H. Williams, W. D. Corrister, E. Deaves, T. Bond, and P. Sterling. Late in May they started for a trip through the interior.

BISHOP & FLORENCE'S MINSTRELS: consisting of Mons. Movecio, Navoni, John Murphy, Henry Healy, E. P. Horoling, H. H. Baker, J. G. H. Shorey, George Williams, M. B. Leavitt, George Bishop, J. W. Horoling, Frank Dayton, Henry Florence, J. Myers, Frank Talbot, W. Clark, Henry S. Livingston, Charles Hewitt, James Stewart, R. A. Lindley, Billy Porter, and H. W. Springsteen were on the road in September, 1865. Leavitt and Porter had the ends. In October, 1865, Cooper & Decker became managers and reorganized for the winter.

BLACK BRIGADE, THE: was the title of a party organized in New York and opened April 4, 1864, at Poughkeepsie, N.Y. Dr. William P. Valentine and Erastus Conklin were proprietors.

BLACK HUTCHINSON FAMILY, THE: consisted of five male and three female vocal and instrumental performers. They appeared in New York on January 30, 1845, in chants, refrains, songs, choruses, glees, melodies and parodies.

BLAIR'S BAND: was a party that performed on a barge at the foot of Steamboat Wharf, Troy, N.Y., in June, 1854. They gave performances morning, afternoon and evening and, in addition to a minstrel performance, Old Grizzly Adams' Menagerie was an attraction. In the company were Billy Blair (manager), E. A. Perrine, P. B. Hammond, Tom Vaughn, C. O. Neil, Mons. Covelli, W. Birch, and Mons. Valatin.

BLAKE & MALLORY'S MINSTRELS: with Augusta Blake, Maggie Nichols, Cora Chase, Emma Wadsworth, Dan Shelby, Charles Mallory, Miles O'Riley, Jim Riley, Frank Wild, Prof. Davenport, Cole, and Johnny Blake commenced a tour of

New York State December 12, 1864. G. W. Mallory was manager. This party was combined with Haverly's Minstrels late in December.

BOLEY'S MINSTRELS: were organized by D. F. Boley and left Australia in January, 1862, on a visit to the Maritius Islands. After a not very successful engagement they embarked for the Cape of Good Hope, but were wrecked off Cape St. Mary late in 1862. Mr. and Mrs. Boley and the children were lost, as was the entire troupe---a Mr. Robson being the only one saved from drowning. George W. Demerest, Charles L. Grew, W. White Lee, W. Robson, and Totten Arent were in the company.

BOOKER & CLAYTON'S GEORGIA MINSTRELS: real Negroes, opened October 9, 1865, in Detroit, Mich. Clayton, Thomas & Co., proprietors; Charles B. Hicks, manager. In November they were in the East. They commenced their second season September 3, 1866, at Chicago, Ill., with John W. Wilson, Willie Clarke, Helon Johnson, J. Manning, C. Warsaw, J. E. Booker; H. Fields, bones; Tom Slater, tambo; and Jake Hamilton. Booker & Hicks were proprietors.

BOOKER & EVARTS' MINSTRELS: consisted of Johnny Booker, Dick Sliter, Robert Lane, G. L. Hall, A. C. Stone, Harry Evarts, S. S. Purdy, Thomas Jefferson, G. H. Warre, and Herr Heck. They organized in November, 1860, and made a tour through New England. In January, 1861, they were on a Mississippi River floating palace. In February, Harry Evarts left the company, having been stricken with paralysis and losing the use of his left arm. They took to the road in April with Johnny Booker, Thomas H. Jefferson, George H. Hall, C. A. Shattuck, R. Lane, Dick Sliter, A. C. Stone, J. E. Hartel, Herr Heck and O. N. Hart.

BOOKER (JOHNNY) & FRANK HOWARD'S MINSTRELS: traveled with Lent's Circus in the West in the summer of 1865 with Johnny Booker, Frank Howard, George Charles, Robert Ellingham, Master Robert, Prof. Holmer, and Frank Wyant.

BOOKER'S MINSTRELS: were on a traveling tour in Ohio in September, 1862, with John E. Hartel, Glendenning, Moran, Billy Vaughn, O'Neal, James Owens, Master J. Bech and others. They soon closed. Later, BOOKER'S MINSTRELS were organized by Johnny Booker, after a rest on his farm in Adrian, Mich. (having recovered from the wound he received some time previous). They opened in Toledo, Ohio, October 22, 1865. Johnny Booker was dangerously wounded by a ball from a pistol entering the left breast, just below the collar bone, passing through the lung and lodging somewhere in that locality, in Dayton, Ohio, in October, 1864, while he was traveling with Bailey's Circus. Early in 1877 he arrived in Philadelphia after a long tour through the East Indies.

BOSTLEWAITE & SHADDOCK'S MINSTRELS: See ROSS, SPRUNG, SMITH & CHADDUCK'S MINSTRELS.

BOSTON HARONISTS: organized in Palmyra, N.Y., in 1850 and made a traveling tour. G. W. H. Griffin made his debut with them, he being the manager.

BOWERS & PRENDERGAST: made up a band in New York and opened January 3, 1864, in Newark with E. Bowers, T. B. Prendergast, S. S. Purdy, James Budworth,

N. Gould, T. Simpson, Nevilles, Trige, Fagan and others. In June, 1864, they reorganized and were known as the AEOLIANS.

BOWERS' ETHIOPIAN SERENADERS: organized in Troy, N.Y., in March 1855, with J. Bowers as manager; E. Pierce, tambo; Dick Berthelon; J. Warren, bones; Bob Smith, J. Hogan; and E. Warren, wench. They traveled North, but closed in two weeks.

BOWERY MINSTRELS, THE: were organized in St. Louis, Mo., in January, 1858, by J. E. Esher and played there over a year. Fattie Stewart, tambo; Frank Lynch, violin; Charles Petrie, bones; Matt Thompson, jig; Tommy Pell, Ben Wheeler, Tom Allen, Paul Kraft, Major Flinn and Miss Leslie were in the company.

BOYCE & MUDGE'S MINSTRELS: consisted of J. T. Boyce, W. Holding, E. Kirwin, E. S. Wilson, George L. Hall, F. Logan, H. Llalande, H. T. Mudge, J. Herrell, J. Burgess, A. Glynn, J. T. Herbert, P. Nortrand, H. Bloodgood, M. Dedanoti, P. Grattle, N. C. Dumaille, Prof. De Rauff, E. K. Ceine and Sig. Vayo. They reorganized in New York and started early in May, 1866, for a tour East. They collapsed at Dover, N. H., June 12.

BOYCE'S MINSTRELS: were organized in Baltimore, Md., where they opened August 13, 1866, with W. S. Budworth, John K. Campbell, Frank Leslie, J. Tannenbaum, Frank Campbell, Joseph Garatagui, and George and Willie Guy.

BOYNTON'S EXCELSIOR MINSTRELS: composed of W. J. Boynton, Frank Wyant, John Pettit, Walter Walsh, and G. F. Macarty, organized and traveled through New York State in September, 1858.

BREMOND'S (E. L.) MINSTRELS: organized in Galveston, Tex., January 5, 1874, and started out on a traveling tour. In the company were Milt G. Barlow, Prof. C. Schmidt, Wash Norton, Sprague, Mack, and a brass band. They closed their season on March 14, the same year; but reorganized and took to the road under the title of the BREMOND & NORTON MINSTRELS and traveled through the Far West, closing up July 4, 1874, at Denver.

BRIMMER, GAYNOR, WHITING & CLARK'S MINSTRELS: were traveling through New York State in November, 1865.

BROADWAY MINSTRELS, THE: in January, 1858, appeared at the Melodeon, Boston. Shortly after they reorganized and made a traveling tour West and were known as the METROPOLITAN BURLESQUE OPERA TROUPE, with L. W. Myers as manager; C. Frank West, bones; Harry Blanchard, banjo; William B. Brown, tambo; John C. Woodworth, accordion; Harry Barton, violin; Joe Mairs, wench; Billy Bray (the Albany rattler), and C. Dockstader, basso.

BROWN, JONES & WOODRUFF'S MINSTREL PARTY: were traveling in 1850 under the management of Joe Brown and Tim Woodruff.

BROWN'S (JOE) CHRISTY'S: consisted of W. P. Collins, Joe Brown, C. W. Rayner, Harry Herbert, W. H. Castor, Ted Saunders and N. La Fenillade. They sailed from Southampton, England, September 27, 1863, under the management of J. W. Smith, on their way to India to oppose the Nish party, then in Australia. They visited Gibraltar, Malta, Alexandria, Cairo, Suez and Aden, reaching Bombay on October

29 and giving their first concert on November 2 in the Grand Road Theatre to a house doubly rammed and jammed, with prices as follows: reserved seats, six rupees (about three dollars); parquet, five rs.; gallery, three rs.; pit, two rs. They remained one month and gave sixteen concerts, the last two in the Town Hall and one private entertainment for Sir Jamsetiee Jeejeebahoy. They left many kind friends who assembled to see them off about the 7th of November, for Madras, via Point de Jalle. There they gave two concerts in the Military Theatre while awaiting the arrival of the English mail steamer to take the company to Madras. Every favor was shown them in this hospitable city. The use of the banqueting hall in the government house and the patronage of His Excellency the Governor was obtained. A perfect furor awaited the company here, and ten concerts were given to crowded and delighted audiences. The boys, having time and wishing to see the interior, went to Bangalore in the mountains some two hundred and fifty miles, proceeding two hundred by rail and fifty by "donk." Here they gave two concerts and paid expenses, returning to Madras and, four days after, arrived in Calcutta. And here, in five weeks, they gave twenty concerts to good business. The first night was 3,900 rs. Prices---reserved, 5 rs.; second class, 3 rs. The remaining concerts were very good, notwithstanding the city and India generally was in mourning for Lord Elgin, the late Governor-General. The arrival of Sir John Lawrence (the present viceroy) acted bad for them, in consequence of the numerous balls and parties that took place. However, on the whole, they did in four months what would be considered at home comfortable returns for a year. The boys left Calcutta on the steamer *Persia*, February 15, for Rangoon, in the Burmese Empire, proceeding thence to Ava to play for His Majesty, the King; his wives and children. The Nish party reached Sydney December 9, 1863, and opened Boxing Night (in December), where they made a lengthy stay.

BROWN'S (JOE) MINSTRELS: organized and started from Chicago, September, 1856, and went traveling.

BRYANT & MALLORY'S: Dan Bryant and Ben Mallory organized a party in 1855 and visited the East. Dave Wambold was in the company. They played in New York at the Chinese Buildings, Broadway, where they closed on August 23, 1856. In October they appeared at Concert Hall, Philadelphia, when Eph Horn joined them. Mallory left and Jerry and Neil Bryant joined. They shortly after disbanded in New York.

BRYANT'S CAMPBELL'S: were at the Chinese Rooms on Broadway, New York, in 1856, with Dan Bryant as manager.

BRYANT'S DIXIE MINSTRELS: organized in Savannah, Ga., where they opened April 15, 1861.

BRYANT'S MINSTRELS: were organized and opened February 23, 1857, by Jerry, Dan and Neil Bryant at Mechanics' Hall, 472 Broadway (formerly occupied by the original Christy's), New York: Jerry, bones; Dan, tambo; Neil Bryant, accordion; T. B. Prendergast, Dick Carroll, Charles Fox, W. Penn Lehr, John H. Savori, S. Howard, B. Mallory, E. H. Winchell, M. Lewis, and Harry Leslie (the rope walker), versatile performer. October, 1857, Frank Moran, banjo; George S. Fowler and W. Percival appeared. After a brief absence, Prendergast re-appeared December,

1857. Unsworth opened in January, 1858, and in April J. T. Huntley commenced and B. Mallory re-appeared. Fred Wilson, the clog dancer, was added to the company October 18, 1858. In September, James Carroll took Mr. Howard's place as interlocutor. David Wambold, who returned from England, opened here December 6. Unsworth (who had been with the Campbells) also reappeared December 6. Wambold, after a brief absence, re-appeared during the season of 1859 and remained eight months. Dick Sands made his first appearance on the stage in January, 1859. George Coes opened in June. After a tour, they re-opened in New York August 1, 1859, with G. S. Fowler, Dan Emmett, G. W. Charles, W. Hobbs, James Carroll, Unsworth, Donniker, Savori, F. Hobbs, S. S. Crosby and P. T. Mitchell. In September, G. H. Warren (ballads) opened. On March 26, 1860, Eph Horn took the position of Dan Bryant (who had sailed for Europe to see the Heenan and Sayers fight) and remained there until the season closed on July 14. Dan Bryant arrived home May 19 and opened on the 28th. The party then made a tour and re-opened in New York August 6, 1860, with Wambold, Paul Berger, P. B. Isaacs, James Carroll, George Charles, J. H. Savori, W. L. Hobbs, N. W. Gould, M. Ainsley Scott, Dan Emmett, T. J. Pell, G. S. Fowler and Aynsley Cook. Tim Norton retired. Prendergast left them. Charles Backus opened October 15. T. B. Prendergast left New York for the South with the 71st Regiment, April 22, 1861, and was one of the first to set foot on Alexandria, Va., ground when that city was captured by the U. S. Forces. In June, 1861, he made a flying visit to New York on business and appeared with the Bryants (for that night only), June 13, and sang *"Vive la America."* He was presented with a beautiful gold medal by Dan on behalf of the company. On May 6, Eph Horn relieved Norton and remained until July 5. In the company were N. W. Gould, Eph Horn, Aynsley Cook, J. W. Hilton, Dan Bryant, P. B. Isaacs, Norton, T. J. Peel, Dan Emmett, Japanese Tommy, Fowler and D. W. Chitton. The season closed July 13, 1861, after giving performances for nearly one year, with the exception of a week's cessation on account of the death of Jerry. They opened in Boston at the Museum July 22, when Eph Horn and S. C. Campbell joined them. Returning to New York, they re-opened August 5 with Eph Horn, Dan and Neil Bryant, S. C. Campbell, T. J. Peel, Frank Leslie, James Morrison, J. Garratagua, J. H. Savori, Hobbs, G. S. Fowler, Dan Emmett, Japanese Tommy, Gettings, and J. W. Hilton. After having been absent a while, Dan Emmett re-appeared in March, 1862. The season closed July 5, 1862. Their next season opened August 25 and the company was about the same as the past season. W. W. Newcomb, having returned from Europe, opened November 24, taking Nelse Seymour's place, and remained until April 4, 1863. The Bryants opened their next season August 10, 1863, and closed January 9, 1864. Nelse Seymour was on one end. Dave Reed, Green, and Hilton (middle man) were added to the forces for a few nights in January. S. A. Wells, basso, opened January 11. The next season commenced September 12, 1864, and lasted until July 8, 1865. During the season, C. C. Templeton, J. W. Hilton, D. C. Winans, A. Ross, W. Mellins, B. W. Buchanan, Dave Reed, Nelse Seymour, J. Morrison, J. H. Savori and Dan Emmett were in the company. On May 1, Frank Moran and Mickey Warren opened. Dan and Eph Horn sailed for Europe May 3, 1865. The season of 1865-66 commenced September 11 and the company was about the same as before, excepting Eph Horn, who took Dan's place, he (Dan) having opened in Irish comedy. Little Mac appeared November 27; Charles Henry and Garratagua, January 1, 1866; Rollin Howard, January 10; J. W. Rayner, January 15; followed by Master Ryan, Hogan, Collins and Ira Paine. The season closed June 2, which was their final performance in Mechanics' Hall, 472 Broadway. The Bryants' Minstrels did not again appear in New York until May 18, 1868, when they opened their new hall in the lower part of Tammany Hall, east side of Fourteenth Street, between Third Avenue and Irving Place. The party consisted of Dan Bryant, Eph Horn, Nelse Seymour, James Unsworth, Eugene, Monroe, Dempster, W. P. Grier, Charles Henry, J. Hogan, R. Hughes, G. W. Rockefeller, J. H. Ross, G. B. Ross, Garratagua, G. H. Schott, James Morrison, G. Trunkett, and Francis Bracht. In June, J. K. Emmett opened. During the season, Warren White, F. St. Clair, Raphael de Solla (tenor) opened, also Neil Bryant, who made his appearance February 1 for the first time in three years. The season closed April 17, 1869, and they went traveling. They returned and opened at the same hall May 10. William Dwyer, Little Mac, Dave Reed, and G. W. H. Griffin appearing soon after. The season closed July 24, 1869, and re-opened September 13 with Dave Reed, Unsworth, Eugene, Grier, J. G. Russell, T. Brandisi, Dempster, Rockefeller, Delehanty and Hengler, Jasper H. Ross, Garratagua and J. H. Savori. The season closed June 4, 1870. On the opening night at this hall, over one thousand persons were turned away before eight o'clock. The receipts for the first six performances amounted to $4,296.25. The season closed April 24, 1869, and they went traveling. They re-opened in New York, May 10, 1869, at reduced prices of admission. Dave Reed joined them and on May 24 William Dwyer appeared. Nelse Seymour closed June 12 and sailed for Europe on the 16th. Little Mac appeared June 28 in the "Essence." They closed the season July 24, 1869, and went to Philadelphia; but returned to New York, September 13, 1869, and opened with the following company: T. Brandisi, J. G. Russell, Delehanty, Hengler, Unsworth (bones), G. W. H. Griffin (middle), Rockefeller, W. P. Grier, Monroe, Dempster, Dan Bryant (tambo); Eugene, William Dwyer, Dave Reed, J. W. Ross, J. Morrison, J. Garatagua and J. H. Savori. Delehanty and Hengler appeared in the celebrated "Shoo Fly, Don't Bother Me." Delehanty's stay was short, however, for on the 16th he left in consequence of the death of his father. Dan Bryant and Dave Reed afterwards dressed the song and dance to suit their own tastes and gave it to their patrons in an amended form on October 11. On January 1, Little Mac put in an appearance and was engaged for the rest of the season. R. M. Carroll opened for a short season on the 3d. February 23 was a gala day with the valiant Dan, for on it he celebrated the thirteenth anniversary of the establishment of his minstrel band in this city and danced "The Essence," which was one of the principal rounds in the ladder that led him up to fame. The house was closed the night of June 2 as Dan Bryant had a benefit at the Academy of Music. The season closed June 4, 1870. The following are the receipts of the hall excepting the last month: September, $3,722; October, $7,317; November, $11,400; December, $10,904; January, $9,925; February, $9,453; March, $8,303; April, $7,340; May, $5,500. On November 23, 1870, they opened their new Opera House on West Twenty-third Street (north side), a few doors west of Sixth Avenue. In the company was Dave Reed, Nelse Seymour, Little Mac, Hughey Dougherty, George Warren, S. C. Crosby, James Morrison, H. Norman, W. P. Grier, J. Brandisi, Garatagua, Martin Setz, J. H. Schott, Monroe Dempster, Thomas Sully, W. H. Brockway, William F. Stanley, J. d'Alberte, Dan and Neil Bryant, D. W. Carre, J. H. Savori, Master Warren, E. W. Mitchell, T. H. Monroe. The season closed July 1, 1871. Their second season here commenced September 4, 1871, with James A. Barney, R. Kohler, Morrisey, Emerson, Nelse Seymour, McAndrews, W. F. Stanley, Savori, Charles Karoll, G. H. Weston, Little Mac, Dave Reed, Monroe Dempster, Charles d'Alberte, James Morrisey, Martin Setz, C. H. Foster, and Dan Bryant. They traveled during the summer. W. W. Newcomb opened with this company on November 13, 1871. On January 1, "Shoo Fly" was revived. The season closed April 20 and the party traveled. They re-opened in New York August 26, 1872. Kelly and Leon were in the company, but they closed on November 16. McAndrews appeared December 2. Master Barney appeared March 31, 1873. On May 29, Thomas Lynch was announced to make his first appearance on the stage and sing a ballad for Brockway and Donniker's benefit. The season closed June 25. Dan Bryant and Eph Horn arrived home from Europe August 31, 1873. They commenced their next season September 4, 1873. Dave Reed, Nelse Seymour, Eugene, Unsworth, Bob Hart, Con T. Murphy, Brockway, Donniker, Savori, J. J. Joell, Harry Stanwood, James Morrisey, Karl Steele, Templeton, Dwyer, Lamont and others were in the company. On December 1, A. H. Clarke, basso, first appeared. Theo Jackson, bass singer, appeared May 4, 1874, under the assumed name of T. Merchant. The season closed June 24, 1874. On June 27 the hall was re-opened for a benefit to Nelse Seymour and Bob Hart, when, in addition to all of the company, Eph Horn, Charley White and George F. Brown appeared. They re-opened the hall for the season August 31 with Bob Hart, Seymour, Dave Reed, Brockway, Fred Walz, J. J. Kelly, Joseph Norrie, W. Raymond, Templeton, J. Robinson, F. Emerson, J. P. Hogan, W. Henry Rice, Donniker, J. H. Ross, Savori, James Morrison and others in the company. James S. Maffitt opened January 25, 1870, in burlesque. The Bryants' Minstrels continued to occupy this house until April 10, 1875.

BRYANT'S (NEIL) MINSTRELS: at Mechanics' Hall often reached a yearly profit of $40,000. The only week business was poor was when Fort Sumter was fired upon. That week the profits were only $27. On May 3, 1875, Neil Bryant organized a band for the road, opening in Boston. They appeared for one night only at the Academy of Music, New York, on May 29. Neil Bryant appeared and performed a solo upon the flutina, being his first appearance in ten years. On September 20, 1875, Neil Bryant reorganized and opened in Bridgeport, Conn., with the following company: Will A. Morton, Albert Welling, Lew Benedict, Billy Gray, Tierney, Cronin, Welling Bros., Harry Stanwood, Bernardo, and J. W. Freeth. Another re-organization took place in December, 1875. Neil Bryant was proprietor; S. F. Stevens, manager; D. B. Hodge was agent. In the company were: Lew Benedict, T. M. Hengler, Goss, Fox, Billy Bryant, Flem Adams, Lee, the California Quartette (consisting of the three Welling Bros. and J. W. Freeth) and orchestra. They closed May 8, 1876. On September 10,

1877. Neil Bryant opened a season with a company at the Globe Theatre, Broadway, New York, with Cool White, Prof. Corner, W. H. Hamilton, Little Mac, Charles Banks, Justin Robinson, Seamon, Somers, Adams, Lee, Dave Reed and others. They closed December 8 and went on a traveling tour. Another party was formed which opened at the Howard Athenaeum, Boston, February 25, 1878. Hughey Dougherty, Dave Reed, Joseph Norrie, Billy Bryant, Little Mac, and G. W. Harley. They closed on the road June 1, but reorganized, they opened at the Grand Opera House, New York, June 17: Ernest Linden, Dougherty, Little Mac, Eddie Fox, Harley, Fayette Welch, Dave Reed, Billy Bryant, Joseph Norrie, Neil Bryant and others. In September, 1878, with Neil Bryant organized another company which started on a few weeks' tour under the financial management of John P. Smith. They opened September 23 and closed in five weeks, the business being very bad. The company consisted of Neil Bryant, Dave Reed, W. Quilter, Pete Goldrich, Billy Bryant, W. Henry Rice, J. M. Norrie; Charles Storms, Henry Percy, Albert Welling, Gustave Johnson, Adolph Nichols and orchestra. While Bryant's Minstrels were performing in Buffalo, N.Y., in April, 1878, a suit was brought against Neil Bryant on a claim against him of $1,000. It was an old claim of Lew Benedict, the minstrel. The Messrs. Meech became bondsmen for Neil Bryant and he and his troupe continued their travels. Shortly after, a referee having decided in favor of the plaintiff and Mr. Bryant, having no property, his prosecutors proposed to get out an execution upon his body as a preliminary to making his bondsmen forfeit if Mr. B. could not be found within the legal fifteen days; and his prosecutors had no idea that he would permit himself to be found. But just here Neil's sense of honor fooled the judgment creditors. Within one hour after the bodily execution was issued, the subject of it was in Buffalo, where he presented himself in court; and being neither willing nor able to repay the $1,000, he was committed to the Erie County jail, where he remained until December 30, when he was released by Judge Daniels in consequence of a technical error having been discovered in the prosecutor's proceedings. Neil was in jail just forty-nine days.

BUCKEYE MINSTRELS: were organized in the winter of 1861 by Billy Manning for a winter tour in the West.

BUCKLEY & SHARPLEY: (G. Swayne Buckley and Sam Sharpley) started out on a tour with a party September 3, 1872. They made a tour of the East and West and opened in New York at the San Francisco Minstrel Hall (St. James Theatre), March 3, 1873. The first part minstrel scene was abolished and the performance commenced with a protean farce, followed by an olio. They closed March 22.

BUCKLEY'S MINSTRELS: opened at the Tabernacle, the present site of the Howard Athenaeum, Boston, in October, 1843. G. W. Hoyte, banjo; Linton, tambo; Buckley, violin; Brewer, bones; Neagle, violin. Among their selections were "Gumbo, Sound Your Horn," "De Re My True Love," "De Piper's Son," "Dandy Jim of South Carolina" (announced as the first time it was ever sung), by Hoyt and chorus, "Gib Us Chew Tobacco," "Old Dan Tucker," "Dance de Boatmen," "Old Aunt Sally," "Come Day, Go Day," "Work Jaw Bone," "Jenny, Come Along," and "Come Sally with the Booties On" (first time in this country). Twelve and a half cents was the only price of admission. After their first season in Boston they traveled through the

East by means of their own teams. They first appeared in New York, January 8, 1845, at the Park Theatre with J. Law Buckley, Little Ole Bull, George Swain Buckley (announced as Sweeney Buckley), and Mr. King in the party.

BUCKLEY'S MINSTRELS: was the title given to a party that opened in Newark, N. J., June 6, 1868, and closed June 5, 1869. J. K. Buckley, J. W. Crayton, Mons. De Burton, Frank Allison, Harry Walters, Ed Holden, G. Williams, C. W. Edwards, W. Payne and Clara Le Brun (trapeze) were in the company.

BUCKLEYS' MINSTRELS: was a party traveling in the South in February, 1860. They were in no way connected with the Original Buckleys.

BUCKLEY'S SERENADERS: formerly NEW ORLEANS MINSTRELS, John Mulligan joined them and Julia Gould appeared in burlesque opera in November, 1858. Dave Reed, S. Swaine, Bishop, T. Waddleton, J. W. Palmer and G. Clarence in the company. Dave Reed was doing his "Sally, Come Up." Allston Hall was located on Tremont Street, nearly opposite the Park Church. It was afterwards occupied as a theatre, first managed by Mrs. Jane English, and subsequently called the Tremont Theatre, being managed by various persons but without financial success. It was converted afterwards into a carpet store. In July, 1859, they re-opened in New York at 585 Broadway. On March 21, 1860, they sailed from Boston for Europe; and their success in all the provincial towns throughout Great Britain and in London was very flattering and encouraging in the highest degree. But, unfortunately, after spending large sums of money in decorating and re-fitting numerous halls and theatres for the production of their burlesque operas, managers of different theatres became jealous of their popularity and called up against them an almost forgotten statute in the law, relative to the performance of operas, and which excluded from license all but the regular Royal Opera. They appealed against it but without success. The obsolete statute was enforced against them and the Buckleys were compelled to abandon their enterprise and return to America, arriving here in 1861. They then visited many of the principal cities in the North and finally settled down in Boston in June, 1863. Previous to this, however, they opened in Boston, October 13, 1862 (being their first appearance there in four years), at Allston Hall. They opened in New York December 22, 1862, at the Palace of Music, Fourteenth Street, near Sixth Avenue, under the solo management of J. G. Collins. The writer of this was the business manager of the Cremoine Gardens, the Palace of Music being one of the many attractions of the place. James E. Nixon was the manager. The company consisted of R. Bishop and G. Swaine Buckley, Dave Read, J. A. Palmer, August Asche, Julia Gould, G. Lonsdale, H. Leake, J. J. Mullen, G. Clarence, and J. Smith. They closed here January 3, 1863, and opened Stuyvesant Institute January 5, which they closed January 31 and went traveling. They opened their new hall on the corner Sumner and Chauncey Streets, Boston, June 15, 1863. Charles Pettengill, F. F. Saurin, Walter Birch, C. C. Pratt and others were in the party. J. K. Campbell opened June 18. Owing to bad business, the Buckleys closed in Boston and started for a traveling tour April 9, 1866, but they closed their season June 23. In August this party dwindled down to a small concern and they were traveling through Massachusetts, giving concerts in white and black face. They took a vacation in

December, 1866 and continued until February 10, when they again started on a tour with L. M. W. Steere as agent. G. Swaine Buckley started a band from Boston, July 8, 1867, consisting of himself, H. Burchard, Jake Budd and two pupils, J. J. Roberts and C. Pickett; L. M. W. Steere as agent. He organized in Boston and started out September 1, 1868, opening at Fitchburg, Mass. In the party were George Swaine Buckley and Jake Budd (on the ends), J. J. Roberts (middle man), the Empire Boys, J. H. Stout, C. D. Bassett and others. This band opened the season at Newport, R. I., on August 31, 1869. G. Swaine Buckley, J. H. Murphy, Jake Budd, J. Waterman, Pete Lee, Charles Heywood, Hogan and Hughes, and O. P. Sweet in the party; Medora Becker, prima donna; H. E. Parmelee, agent. Joseph Norrie joined them December 15. They appeared in New York (first time in ten years) July 11, 1870, at their old standpoint (the San Francisco Minstrel Hall, 585 Broadway) and closed there August 13 and went on a tour. The Buckley family, professionally speaking, consisted of James Buckley, R. Bishop Buckley, George Swaine Buckley and Frederick Buckley---George Swaine first light and eccentric comedian, also banjoist; R. Bishop, low comedian, buffo, etc.; Frederick, leader of orchestra, violin soloist, composer and arranger of all the melodies and operatic music given by the troupe. The cause of S. S. Sanford changing the name of the Buckleys when he took them to Europe was because they were fugitives from England. They were announced as James Burke, Swaine, Rainer and Master Ole Bull. There never was such another family as the Buckleys. Everyone was a master musician. In this combination was an orchestra of soloists, a quartette, as well as a brace of comedians. Who will forget the burlesque operas as played by them---"Cinderella and That Pie," "Bohomian Girl," "Fra Diavolo," "La Buy a Deer," "La Sonam Bull Oh!," etc.

BUCKMINSTER MINSTRELS: were organized in Maine in May, 1860, and traveled through New York State. John Norton, Pete Lee, Frank Cilley, E. S. Gray, D. P. Kincaine, F. Clifford, James Franks, C. E. Mirrell, and B. S. Miller comprised the company.

BUDWORTH & CAMPBELL'S: were organized in New Jersey in February, 1861, with J. H. Budworth, W. S. Budworth, M. C. Campbell, G. Raynor, Frank Spear, Billy Allen, A. H. Wood, Master Yates, M. J. Solomon, and Master M. Lewis. In March, E. Byron Christy, Charles Melville, Matt Thompson, W. Howard, and M. Corwan were in the party.

BUDWORTH'S MINSTRELS: consisted of C. Henry, G. F. Fowler, J. Savori, J. Garatagua, Dan Emmett, W. P. Grier, G. F. Clarendon, H. Budworth, Dick Sands, P. Abbott, W. W. Hodgkins, G. W. H. Griffin, W. S. Budworth, and Willie and George Guy; they opened at the Fifth Avenue Theatre (formerly George Christy's), August 27, 1866. Quite a change in the company was made January 15, 1867. James H. and William Budworth retired from the party and on the 16th George Christy took the bone end and Mr. Hodgkins the tambo. The party was now called GRIFFIN & CHRISTY'S.

BUDWORTH'S MINSTRELS: were organized in New York, and opened in the Olympic Opera House, Sixteenth Street and Eighth Avenue, in March, 1858

BUDWORTH'S MINSTRELS: See WOOD'S MINSTRELS.

BUDWORTH'S MINSTRELS: was a new organization that opened at the Academy of Music, Chicago, July 3, 1865.

BUNNELL'S MINSTRELS: consisting of D. W. Reeves, Billy Drew, Billy Hart, J. H. Taylor, Frank Lum and others accompanied the R. Sands Circus during the summer of 1863.

BURCH, CHRISTIE & CO.'S MINSTRELS: consisting of Tim Woodruff, Leon Berger, George Wallace, Hank Goodman, Ned Foster, Rodney Maguire, F. M. Rhinehart, Hernandez, and Foster's Pantomime Troupe. They traveled West in December, 1863.

BURGESS AND SCOTT: opened with a band at the Theatre Comique, Cincinnati: O., June 3, 1867, James A. Oates being lessee and manager. In the party were M. Ainsley Scott, Cool Burgess, W. S. Budworth, Billy Allen, and the Reynolds Bros. This party collapsed during the same month.

BURGESS' (COOL) MINSTRELS: consisted of: Cool Burgess, bones and second tenor; W. J. Gibson, tambo; George B. Radcliffe, middle man; H. Mortimer, Will H. Coleman, Harry Causland, Mileson Smith, Joe H. Banks, Alex Robertson, Arthur Mortimer, Frank Beaver, and Johnny Burdell. They made a tour of Canada, commencing September 17, 1868. They collapsed in Cincinnati, Ohio, early in January, 1869, but reorganized in February with Mike Foley, Charles Atkins, Joe Banks, Ed African, H. Causland, Billy Coleman, Bobby Price, and Walter Davis in the party. Joe Chenet was agent. They closed their season at Bath, Me., June 16, 1869.

BURGESS, PRENDERGAST, HUGHES & DONNIKER'S MINSTRELS: organized in New York in September, 1865, and started through the East under the management of John A. Dingess. They opened September 11, at Bridgeport, Conn., with Cool Burgess, Archie Hughes, Prendergast, J. B. Donniker, Rollin Dana, A. C. Stone, M. Ainsley Scott, C. A. Boyd, Joseph Bailey, R. Thompson, Charles Elliott, J. Wilson, E. French, Frank Trainer, T. Morris, and Masters George and Charles Reynolds. Frank B. Cilley was agent. In May, 1866, Charley Gardner, O. P. Sweet and W. Alonzo Owen joined the party. In March 1866, Charles B. Griste joined this party as advance agent. J. B. Donniker withdrew from the management early in 1866 and the party was then known as BURGESS, LA RUE, PRENDERGAST & HUGHES' MINSTRELS. In a few months Prendergast withdrew, and in November, 1866, the party was called BURGESS & LA RUE'S MINSTRELS and consisted of Cool Burgess, S. S. Purdy, O. P. Sweet, C. S. Fredericks, Frank Bowles, Harry French, Ned West, Charles Church, Mike Kannane, D. C. La Rue, W. Fowler, T. Simmons, A. C. Stone, Sig. Brandisi, Marcello Tornisi, George and Charles Reynolds, Ned Kneeland, Lewis Kazaran, Dick Thompson, Joe Timpson J. H. Slawson, N. Bernard, and H. A. Stanley, agent. In December, Burgess withdrew and the party was called LA RUE'S CARNIVALS. They opened in Canada in February, 1867. Billy Manning and H. W. Eagan were on the ends; O. P. Sweet, Fredericks, Brandisi, Kannane, West, Frank Bowles, Oscar Kress, Wheaton and C. B. Griste, agent, comprised the party. After a hard struggle they closed at Lafayette, Ind., July 22, 1868, and reorganized November 21, 1868. In August, 1870, they were in St.

Paul, Minn., with Billy Reeves and Ned West on the ends, and Ricardo as prima donna. They disbanded at Petersburg, Va., February 9, 1871, owing to bad business.

BURKLY & COLLARD'S MINSTRELS: were traveling through Ohio in June, 1866. The party consisted of William Butler, J. F. Dunnie, E. Kelly, Charles Shelly, J. W. McAndrews, George Collard, Johnny Judge, J. Arthur, F. Spearl, H. Weber, F. Burkly and others.

BUSWORTH'S MINSTRELS: were traveling through New Jersey in September, 1859.

CALIFORNIA COMBINATION, THE: was a party that was performing on the Pacific Slope in June, 1876, under the management of D. Murray, John Jenkins, Prof. Lobe; Billy Taylor, bones; John Bortell, tambo; T. A. Medina, and Prof. Williams, a deaf and dumb magician.

CALIFORNIA MINSTRELS: were the first minstrels ever organized in California. They were under the management of William H. Bernard, of the well known Birch, Wambold, Backus and Bernard party. They opened in August, 1849, in the Parker House, San Francisco, at $5 a ticket. They next hired Alfred Green's Hall, over the Aguila d'Oro. In the winter they went to the Sandwich Islands and the party was known as the NEW YORK SERENADERS.

CALIFORNIA MINSTRELS: were organized under the management of Mr. Grant, and in the party were Henry Irving (later known as Phil H. Irving), Sam Raymond, Mons. Alexander, Jake Wallace, John De Angelis. This was in the fall of 1858. A re-organization was made for a trip to Honolulu, Sandwich Islands, and the party consisted of Mike Mitchell, Joe and Harry Taylor; C. C. Keene, accordion; Tom King, tambo; Charles Nickerson, wench; Lew Rattler, Joe Murphy, Charles Henry, C. D. Abbott and others. They returned to San Francisco in January, 1859. The season proved disastrous on account of failure of the whale fisheries in the Arctic Ocean that season. Another company calling themselves the California Minstrels organized in 1859 and opened under the What Cheer House, Sacramento Street, San Francisco. Lotta, Louisa, Pauline and Charley Morrell and others were in the party.

CALIFORNIA MINSTRELS: was the title of a party that was organized by W. H. Smith and Mr. Honts, and they opened the New Alhambra Theatre on the south side of Bush Street, between Montgomery and Kearney Streets, San Francisco, May 22, 1868. In the party were: Harry Norman, Johnny Mack, J. De Angelis, Harry Raynor, Fred Spring, T. Bree, G. Smith, Dick Sands, H. Bamford, and William Ashcroft. George Coes soon after joined them. On July 13 they started on a traveling tour. Their receipts from May 22 to July 1 are said to have been $19,415.50.

CALIFORNIA MINSTRELS: was a party organized by Phil H. Irving and started from San Francisco, June 20, 1868. They played all the mining towns in northern California, remaining out four months. Charley Rhoades, Frank Medina, Jake Wallace, Harry Williams, Tommy Farren (of Baker & Farren), George Lynne, Frank Casey and Phil Irving. Phil H, Irving, professionally known twenty years ago as

Harry Irving, first appeared as tenor vocalist in San Francisco, Cal., in October, 1857.

CALIFORNIA MINSTRELS: organized in Cincinnati, O., in July, 1874, and went on a traveling tour. Harry Cadova, Jeff Howard, Dick Durand, Ned Reed, Charles Armstrong and J. H. Casper were in the company. They reorganized at Massillon, Ohio, March 10, 1877, and collapsed Sept. 11, 1877.

CALIFORNIA MINSTRELS: was the title of a party that opened at Bryant's Hall, Twenty-third Street near Sixth Avenue, New York, under the management of William H. Smith, February 7, 1876. The company consisted of Frank Moran, Johnny Allen, Little Mac, Sanford, Wilson, Brockway, William Dwyer, J. Williams, J. Crosher, D. Baron, H. C. Tare, C. Howard, F. Williams, S. Hall, S. Lester, S. Stanton, James Lamont, E. A. Voos and orchestra. Johnny Allen left the first week. Billy Pastor assumed the management February 21, but withdrew March 11. William H. Smith resumed the management March 13 with W. W. Newcomb as stage manager, and a variety performance was given.

CALLENDER'S GEORGIA'S: as they had been called for some time, appeared at Robinson Hall, New York, March 8, 1875, and remained three weeks. This party was next called MAHARA'S GEORGIA'S.

CALLENDER'S JUBILEE MINSTRELS: were organized by C. Callender and started November 12, 1874, under the business management of Gus Frohman. John Uston, D. Porter, S. Tilman, R. Freeman, C. Benson, R. Keenan, J. Johnson, T. Murray, F. Bicks; F. Anderson, F. Jones, P. Zabriskie, Hazzard, and J. Anderson.

CAMPBELL & HOPPIL'S BAND: with Brigham Bishop and Tom Downs, proprietors, was started for a campaign among the soldier boys stationed at Chattanooga, Tenn., where they opened April 25, 1864, under canvas with George Wallace, J. Davidson, Add Ryman, J. Murphy, George and Brigham Bishop, D. Derago, Tom Downs and Master Charley.

CAMPBELL, CARLEY & MILES' MINSTRELS: were traveling in Massachusetts in February, 1861. G. McDewell, Frank Carley, Ned Miles, Dan Campbell, and Dan Ashley were in the party.

CAMPBELL SABLES: organized and made a tour of New England in May, 1859. Frank Wells was in the party.

CAMPBELL'S MINSTRELS: of the many minstrel companies with the name of Campbell attached, this was one of them in 1853. Eph Horn was one of the attractions, also William W. Newcomb. They continued until the fall of 1856, when they were re-christened by H. Rumsey as RUMSEY & NEWCOMB'S MINSTRELS.

CAMPBELL'S MINSTRELS: C. A. Morningstar, manager, and consisting of S. S. Purdy, Joe Mairs, J. W. Smith, J. H. Stout, Frank and Sig. Angelo, Dan M. Holt, J. R. Passerelli, W. H. Griffin, W. C. Manning, Con Murphy, Frank Berger, Charles Sanford, Richard Arnold, Alph Bishop, Sig. Surboni and Miss Frank Christie, were traveling early in 1862 in the South and Southwest. When they reached Louisville, Ky., trouble entered the managerial camp and there was a split in the party in November. Morningstar left with some of the company for Memphis. Dan Holt took charge of those who remained in Louisville and continued to play there. Morningstar organized and traveled South with the following people: W. E. Manning, Stout, Dan W. Collins, Mairs, J. C. Murphy, Mons. Hager, Dan M. Holt, Clark Gibbs, Frank D. and Sig. Angelo, Master Harry, and Miss Christie. George H. Bentley, who had been with this party as advance agent, retired from the profession in March, 1863, and opened a saloon in Memphis. This party Morningstar called the EXCELSIORS.

CAMPBELL'S MINSTRELS: was organized in April, 1859, by Edward M. and Daniel Campbell. They traveled East with William Mayne, violin; W. H. Blood, banjo; Frank Curley, guitar; G. B. Hartfield, accordion, and Plummer.

CAMPBELL'S MINSTRELS: was a party consisting of: G. W. Moore, Dick Melville, M. C. Campbell, J. Kelly, R. M. Ferguson, Master Tommy, J. F. Hall, R. H. Escott, George Reynolds, G. Coes, W. J. Campbell, T. Arlington, Mat Cannon, Harry Seymour, and H. Kelly, with Charles Melville as agent. They took to the road in September, 1868.

CAMPBELL'S MINSTRELS: A. Campbell, proprietor, started from New York, and opened March 7, 1866, at New Brunswick, N. J. A. H. Bennett, William H. Bagley, A. Campbell, T. A. Bennett, H. Buhmier, P. Jones, J. Moffett, A. Williams, J. B. Vinah, John Heath, and George W. Knight.

CAMPBELL'S MINSTRELS: M. C. Campbell leased the Palace of Music, Sixth Avenue and Fourteenth Street, New York, made the necessary alterations, and opened with a minstrel band November 10, 1862, consisting of Ned Davis, George Gray, J. H. Clifford, Raynor, Eddie, Solomon, Mead, Hill, Gibbs, M. C. Campbell, Gripe, Livingston, Rozzi, Weitzer, and Johnson. Rumsey having lately arrived from England, opened November 24, and soon after Pic Butler, T. Waddee and Master Eddie appeared. They closed December 6 and went to Chicago, where the company appeared with great success. They remained there nearly three months, when they took to the road, opening in Baltimore, in March. J. H. Budworth, Johnny Booker, J. W. Hilton were added. Late in March, Dick Sands and Tim Hayes joined them. In July, 1863, Campbell opened at the New Bowery Theatre, New York, with the following people: Davis, Booker, Clifford, E. N. Slocum, Hilton, George Gray, N. W. Gould, T. Waddee, M. C. Campbell, Tannenbaum, Master Eddie, J. Ruig, .Sig. Ette, G. Hill, L. Bonny, E. Green and A. Sawyer. In May, 1864, he leased 199 and 201 Bowery (afterwards Tony Pastor's Opera House), opposite Spring Street, New York, which he fitted up and opened June 27, with W. S. Budworth, A. Macaire, Gould, W. Hodgkins, J. Livingston, Ned Davis, Frank Leslie, J. T. Gulick, Robert Nichols, August Eben, John Whiting, Ainsley Scott, Adolph Nichols, Joseph Bailey, and Master Collins. J. M. Clifford opened August 8; Lew Myers, November 7; W. McManus, November 13; Johnny Booker, December 12. On January 16, 1865, R. M. Hooley became associated in the management with Mr. Campbell, when Cool Burgess, Hilton, Hayes and Hank Mudge appeared. In February, Mickey Warren, Master Reynolds, Donniker and T. B. Prendergast opened. The destruction by fire of Hooley's Opera House, Brooklyn, caused J. H. Budworth, Griffin, Frank Hussey, Fred Abbott, George Clinton, George Parkinson and J. Stanwood to open here May 16. The season closed May 27, 1865.

CAMPBELL'S MINSTRELS: consisting of: Frank Wood, Harry Seymour, J. J. Kelly, Johnny Murray, W. J. Campbell, Ed Sweet, Thomas Arlington, J. H. Moore, J. F. Hall, Charles Coerg, George Hamilton, Mat Cannon, Tommy Pell, Dick Ferguson, Charles Melville, Johnny Booker, Dick Carroll, M. C. Campbell, the Reynolds Bros., formerly called the Utica Boys, James Kirkland, R. P. Ferguson, as agent, made a tour through Kentucky, in November, 1867.

CAMPBELL'S MINSTRELS: was a party organized in September, 1859, and traveled South. D. Gordon, W. W. Pierce, W. C. Mead, W. H. Campbell, Master Leon, J. H. Treifle, A. V. Hartley, L. M. Reese, G. H. Campbell, A. Nicholls, J. H. Nicholls, J. Bishop, W. H. Herman, E. Wilkson, F. Wheeler, C. Melville, and Renard were in the company.

CAMPBELL'S MINSTRELS: were organized in January, 1866, and gave their first show January 11 at Yonkers, N. Y. J. M. Hunter was manager. In the party were: M. C. Campbell, J. M. Hunter, Dick Bertheton, J. H. Sadler, R. W. Ferrier, C. B. Freeman, Master Jimmy, Joe Buckley, J. B. Bishop, Dick Willis, W. P. Melvin, Master Ned Campbell, H. B. Castle, and J. W. White.

CAMPBELLS, THE: This party was one of the many "Campbells" traveling. They visited Philadelphia in January, 1857. Jerry and Dan Bryant and Ben Cotton were in the party.

CANTERBURY MINSTRELS: consisting of Sam Sharpley, tambo; Max Irwin, bones; A. M. Hernandez, Paul Berger, T. Lamont, R. Abecco, E. Byron Christy, Frank Spear and W. Ross. This party opened at the Canterbury Music Hall, Broadway, New York, June 1, 1861. This was Sam Sharpley's debut in New York.

CANTERBURY MINSTRELS: was a band that opened at Canterbury Music Hall, St. Louis, in September, 1861, and consisted of S. S. Purdy, bones; J. T. Boyce, tambo; A. Slocum, middle man; H. Freborthyser, E. W. Story, J. L. Davis, Ed Berry, and Charles Davis.

CANTERBURY MINSTRELS: was a first class minstrel party, engaged in March, 1862, at Canterbury Music Hall, Broadway, New York. They comprised: R. M. Carroll, E. Byron Christy, Billy Birch, Ben Cotton, J. A. Herman, W. Ross, Harry Wilson, and George Germaine.

CARNCROSS & DIXEY'S MINSTRELS: were organized in Philadelphia and consisted of J. L. Carncross, E. F. Dixey, Frank Moran, Charles Villiers, Charles Gibbons, George L. Hall, Edmunds, Ira Paine, James Lamont, P. Ambrosi, A. H. Rackett, P. Deverill, William Ziegler, T. a'Beckett Jr., R. F. Simpson, with Moran and Dixey on the ends. They opened at Sanford's Old Opera House, Eleventh, near Market Street, April 14, 1862. In the summer they went on a traveling tour and re-opened in Philadelphia on August 10, 1863. In May, 1864, Frank Moran left and the season closed in June, 1864, when they went on the road. They re-opened in Philadelphia on August 15, 1864. Lew Simmons was added to the company, also M. Bryan and C. C. Villiers, wench. One week after opening, the Buffalo Boys opened and the season closed on June 17, 1865. They re-opened on August 21, 1865, with the following company: Lew Simmons, Harry Lehr, E. N. Slocum, J. Laurent, W. L.

Hobbs, J. A. Palmer, the Buffalo Boys, Charles Villiers, E. Kerwin, Charles Gibbons, J. Brech, Carncross, Dixey, J. Holden, J. Paul, Thomas a'Beckett and Charles Stevens. The season closed June 9, 1866, and they went traveling. They re-opened in Philadelphia August 20. The house was closed on the evenings of May 27 and 28, 1867, in consequence of the death of Mr. Carncross' father. The season closed June, 1867, and re-opened August 26, 1867, with J. E. Green added to the party. The season closed on June 13, 1868, and they went on a tour. During the following season Harry Lehr, Lew Simmons, Dixey, Slocum, George Charles, J. W. Lamont, T. J. Prestinch, and Master Eddie were in the party. They commenced the season of 1869-70 on August 23. In the first part were fifteen performers, who appeared in white pants and vests and black coats. The instrumental part was strong, as it consisted of two cornets, double bass, clarinet, harp, three guitars, two banjos, two violins, flute, bones and tambo. J. A. Barney, baritone; Carncross, tenor; Lamont, basso; and Charles Stevens, alto; E. N. Slocum, interlocutor; Lew Simmons, tambo; Dixey, bones; the Buffalo Boys, W. H. Rice, Harry Lehr, Charles Gibbons, and Masters Joseph and Eddie were in the company. In March, 1870, Simmons and Slocum withdrew. The season closed May 28, 1870, and they went on a tour. They commenced the next season on August 22, 1870, with Frank Moran, Harry Lehr, Bobby Newcomb, George H. Coes, Frank Arnold, Dixey, Carncross, J. H. Ross, John Armstrong, W. L. Hobbs, J. Cheever, E. Kennedy, George Charles, Charles Gibbons, Lamont, Charles Stevens, Prestinch, Holden, Bech, J. S. Paul, Samuel Hosfield, J. A. Barney, and Charles Mears in the company. The season closed April 18, 1871, and the troupe traveled for the summer. At the termination of the season, Carncross and Robert J. Simpson retired from the firm and the business and the party was then called DIXEY & MORAN'S MINSTRELS.

CARNCROSS & DIXEY: after dissolving partnership with Moran, organized a band in Philadelphia in November, 1872, and started from that city November 25. Carncross and Dixey were managers. In the party were A. J. Talbot, E. F. Dixey, Harry Talbot, John L. Carncross, J. A. Barney, Carl Rudolph, Harry Percy, Con Murphy, Tommy and Willie Daly, George Charles, and R. H. Stratford. Rudolph and Barney left in January, 1873. The company disbanded April 10, but reorganized and opened at the Arch Street Theatre, Philadelphia, May 26, 1873, for one week. They re-opened the Eleventh Street Opera House, Philadelphia, August 25, 1873, with Harry Talbot and Dixey on the ends. Cheever and Kennedy were in the company. On January 22, 1874, four end men (A. J. Talbot, J. H. Budworth, Dixey and Frank Moran) appeared for Carncross' benefit. The season closed February 28, 1874, and they traveled. They opened their next season in Philadelphia on September 7, 1874, with Carncross, Dixey, Harry Lehr, Matt Wheeler, J. H. Budworth, Robert Frazer, Bobby Newcomb, Johnson, Powers, Charles Henry, Harry Percy, James Lamont, and James Quinn. Frank Moran appeared October 12, and Dixey opened the same date for the first time this season. The season closed February 27, 1875, and they went traveling. They commenced their next season in Philadelphia on August 30, 1875, with Carncross, Dixey, Harry Lehr, Matt Wheeler, Bobby Newcomb, Hernandez Foster, James Quinn, A. J. Talbot, Fred Walz, C. R. Clinton, Harry Percy, the Daly

50

Bros., George Charles, L. C. Mettler, G. Frothingham, John and George Armstrong, George Hosfeld, R. Buckholtz, H. and S. Hosfeld, W. Streland, H. Parme, C. Kaufman, D. Bradford, and John Till. Hughey Dougherty appeared November 8. The season closed March 1876, and the company went to Baltimore, Md., for a short stay, but returned to Philadelphia, re-opened at their Opera House, and finally closed the season June 3, 1876. On September 4 they commenced their next season in Philadelphia with Cheevers, Kennedy, Weslyn, Casey, Hughey Dougherty, Matt Wheeler, Eugene, Templeton and others. Matt Wheeler left early in February, 1877, and Charles Sutton opened. They closed the season March 20, and they traveled. They re-opened at the Eleventh Street Opera House, Philadelphia, September 3, 1877, with Eugene, Wheeler, A. J. Talbot, George H. Edwards, Quinn, Casey, Weslyn, Rice, Griffin, J. C. Lacey, C. Templeton, George Frothingham, Carncross, Dixey and others. The season closed March 16, 1878, and they went traveling until May 11, when they returned to Philalelphia. The partnership existing between Carncross and Dixey was dissolved on September 24, and the minstrel band was afterward known as CARNCROSS' MINSTRELS.

CARNCROSS & SHARPLEY'S MINSTRELS: gave their first performance August 22, 1860, at the Continental Theatre, Philadelphia, with Thomas Simpson, Frank Moran, Morris Edwards, Thomas A. Beckett, O. P. Perry, John Conrad, J. O. Fenrie, J. B. Pond, F. M. Fulton, J. L. Carncross, Sam Sharpley and Frank Brower. They closed in Philadelphia, October 20.

CARNCROSS' MINSTRELS: opened for the season September 2, 1878, with Slocum, Eugene, Matt Wheeler, Hughey Dougherty, Quinn, George Charles, E. M. Hall, Griffin, Rice, Weslyn, and Casey in the party. In the summer of 1896 Carncross retired to private life and was succeeded by Frank Dumont. He died in Philadelphia, November 13, 1911. Dumont was the next manager, with George W. Barber as lessee. He continued until April 17, 1909, when the house closed forever. In the company were Charles Turner, Jerry Cunningham, Ben Franklin, Gilbert Losee, Hughey Dougherty, Vaughn, Comfort, Matt Wheeler, Edwin Goldrick and J. R. Dempsey. Richard Lilly was musical director. In a few weeks the house was torn down.

CARROLL & EMMETT'S MINSTRELS: commenced a summer season at De Bar's Opera House, St. Louis, Mo., June 1, 1868. R. M. Carroll was manager.

CARSON & BROWN: David Carson and Tom Brown organized a company for India and left Australia in August, 1861. They arrived in due time in Calcutta, where they astonished the Hindus and Mohamedans not a little with their representations of the sports and pastimes of the Ethiopian race in the United States of America. After performing a season at Calcutta with satisfaction to themselves and the public, they left the "City of Palaces" for a tour through Hindustan. The boys gave their entertainments all through the country, including Benares, the Holy City of the Hindus, Allahabad, Lucknow (where they performed in one of the King of Oude's palaces), Cawnpore (where the terrible massacre occurred in 1857), Agra (formerly the resident of one of the "Great Moguls), Meerut (where the mutiny of '57, which came near costing England her magnificent Eastern Empire, first made its appearance), Delhi, in the absence of whose king, who was enjoying, for the benefit of his health, the balmy breezes of Rangoon, Carson did himself the honor of seating himself on the celebrated "Peacock Throne." From Delhi to Umbala, Loodiankah, Anarkulle and Lahore, all in the Punjab, thence to Cashmere, where Dave was presented by the Rajah with a beautiful cashmere shawl. From Cashmere our traveler took his company to Simla in the Himalayan Mountains, a beautiful sanitarium, situated at about a height of 8,000 feet above the level of the sea. From Simla the company went back to Calcutta, showing on their return at nearly all the places they had visited before. After a second successful season at Calcutta, Carson went to Madras and from thence through to the Malabar country, touching at Goa, an ancient Portuguese settlement; so on to Bombay, the emporium of Western India, where their audiences, consisting of Pharisees, Europeans, Hindus, Musselmen, and a host of natives from all parts of Asia, greeted them at each performance with delight and hard silver, there being no greenbacks in that country. The company remained in India over five years, all the time as the San Francisco Minstrels, and there to not the slightest doubt that, owing to the facility with which Carson attained Hindistanese, the language of the country, and the manner in which he mimicked and caricatured a certain class of the native people, the great success with which the company met with was obtained. In May, 1866, the boys dissolved partnership, owing to the desire to see their native land once more.

CARTON, SPAULDING & MORTIMER'S ORIGINAL AMERICAN VOCALISTS: commenced a traveling season East in June, 1860. J. Mortimer, G. S. Carton, W. B. Spaulding, S. E. Wells, R. T. Hardy, A. I. Boswells (bones); E. Niles, I. S. Kent, and H. Channing were in the party.

CENTENNIAL MINSTRELS: See SIMMONS & SLOCUM'S MINSTRELS.

CHALLENGE MINSTRELS: was the title of a band that opened in Philadelphia at Sanford's New Opera House in January, 1865, under the management of Collins & Co., but their life was but a brief one.

ILLUSTRATION: Frank Brower

CHASE & HOWARD: organized a party in September, 1866. Pete Lee, Barney Williams, George Francis, Johnny Milton, George C. Franklin, Fred E. Mortimer, Allen Reynolds, Charles Bassett, William Briggs and Herr Shutter were in the party.

CHASE, PURDY, MURPHY & BUCKLEY: organized a band in New York in July, 1867, for the purpose of playing the small towns in the vicinity of New York. They gave their first entertainment July 18 in New York with S. S. Purdy, Charles Buckley, J. B. Murphy, George Leslie, R. Chase, Prof. Asche and a full brass band.

CHASE'S MINSTRELS: opened at the hall, corner of Eighth Avenue and Thirty-fourth Street, New York, May 13, 1867, Horace A. Chase, manager and director. In the company were Hughey Dougherty, C. C. Templeton, S. S. Purdy, W. L. Hobbs, George H. Coes, J. Buckley, J. W. Hilton, J. W. Clark, Dave Reed, Charles Church, A. Nichols, W. Robertson, W. P. Grier, W. Fields, Charley Fox, M. Riley, R. H. Buchard, J. Wright, J. Wallace, John Savori, and H. Melville. They closed in two months and went traveling.

S. C. Campbell

CHRISTY'S (GEORGE) MINSTRELS: in May, 1858, R. M. Hooley engaged George Christy (who had just retired from Wood's Minstrels), Eugene, G. W. H. Griffin, M. Lewis, and Master Gus Howard---then members of Christy & Wood's Minstrels---and with S. C. Campbell sailed for San Francisco to join the San Francisco Minstrels under Thomas Maguire's management. They arrived there May 27 and opened at Maguire's Opera House June 7. Lothian, Barker, George Coes, Abbott, and E. Deaves were in the party. Soon after they opened, Sam Wells appeared on one of the ends. As a compliment to George Christy, Mr. Hooley called them the GEORGE CHRISTY'S. In September, 1858, they made a tour of the interior and in October returned to San Francisco and re-appeared at Maguire's. In January, 1859, a split took place in the party in consequence of a difficulty between Christy and Wells. After a stay of ten months on the Pacific Coast, George returned East with a band in partnership with R. M. Hooley; among whom were George Coes, Lothian, Eugene, and others. They went to New Orleans and opened at Odd Fellows Hall. They then came North and were in Cincinnati, April 25, 1859. E. Bowers, Eugene, S. C. Campbell, J. Herman, Master Gus Howard, Griffin, Koppitz, and Christerine. They were then known as HOOLEY & CHRISTY'S.

CHRISTY'S MINSTRELS: under the management of W. A. Christy, was organized in Chicago, Ill., November, 1859, and made a tour of the West. In the company were A. D. Groding, F. G. Fitch, George Florence, George Blish, Frank Sinclair, Jo Blish Jr., Old Ducrow, and Charles Moss. In June, 1861, W. A. Christy left the company at Toronto, Canada It then consisted of C. Lewis, George Tracy, A. Silberberg, L. C. Brimmer, Andy E. Morris, Charles Carples, Frank Kyle, W. McCracken, Harry Lawrence, E. Florence, and George Chilcoat. After Christy withdrew, the party was called FARR & THOMPSON'S.

CHRISTY'S (WILLIAM A.) MINSTRELS: organized in New York in 1861 and opened July 4, in Brooklyn. James H. Budworth, William A. Christy, Thomas McAnally were in the party. They made a tour through the West and closed in May, 1862.

CHRISTY'S MINSTRELS: W. A. Christy, manager, was a party that opened in Brooklyn, at the Opera House, corner of Court and Remsen Streets, early in September, 1862. Herman, Christy, Gray, Raynor, Wilson, Eastmead, Campbell, Schrans, Briesberg, Wood, Waddleton, Oldfield, Converse, Master Eddie, Little Bobby and Japanese Tommy. They very soon closed.

CHRISTY'S MINSTRELS: with W. A. Christy, manager, consisted of Harry Howard, W. A. Christy, Frank Howard, J. Rainer, Alphonso Carter, J. Hallman, and Master George. They opened at Christy's Opera House (late Metropolitan Hall), corner of Randolph and LaSalle Streets, Chicago, in March, 1862.

CHRISTY'S MINSTRELS: under the management of James Christy, commenced a tour in August, 1864. John Thayer, F. Seymour, H. Stevens, Fred Thayer, Billy West, and G. Stevens.

CHRISTY'S (E. P.) MINSTRELS: were organized in New York and opened October 5, 1865, at Hudson, N. Y. In the party were J. H. Clifford, J. H. Taylor, M. Walsh, T. Waddee, George Germain, Charles Dunning, H. McFarland, R. Horn, G.

Goff, W. Bishop, A. Gimber, W. Schwab and M. Lockwood. E. Byron Christy was manager.

CINCINNATI MINSTRELS: were organized in June, 1860, and opened in Cincinnati, Ohio, with J. G. Hathaway, Isaac Glascoe, Joseph A. Schloss, Dr. White, Gov. Wise, Mons. DeLand, Master Joseph Wise, Signor Julius Watson, John Brown, Elias Howard, and Will Williams.

CINCINNATUS MINSTRELS: were organized in Cincinnati, Ohio, in May, 1873, under the management of "Cincinnatus" (right name Mike O'Connor) and Harry Wilton, and gave their first performance May 5, 1873, at Xenia, Ohio.

CLARK & BRUNDAGE'S MINSTRELS: organized in Winona, Minn., in August, 1861, for a tour with Jimmy Clark, Alf Brundage, Thomas Williamson, William Strong, G. W. Hall, Walter Berry, F. Churchill, Lon Myers, R. Darby, and Joseph Cushion.

COES, PURDY & CONVERSE'S PARTY: organized In New York in March, 1867, with S. S. Purdy, George Coes, A. L. Bamford, Louis Nevers, Ned Davis, A. Silberberg, J. B. Hartley, Harry Norman, Henry Isaacs, T. D. Schultz, G. R. Frazier, Sig. Bellini, and J. W. Somers. They opened at Harlem March 19.

COLE, SLATER & HART'S MINSTRELS: started out October 11, 1869, and the party consisted of Charles Ball, Lew Cole, Billy Slater, Jimmy Hart, Joe Gallo, A. Prince, C. Young, Alex Gray, Lottie Lee, and Ada Garland. S. Sylvester was agent.

COLEMAN & WARD'S MINSTRELS: were organized in Fayette, Mich., where they opened July 20, 1874, with Tom Coleman, Harry Ward, John Nelson, W. A. Barron, E. B. Landon and C. M. Mendel..

COLLINS & HULMES' MINSTRELS: opened in Philadelphia on November 20, 1871, at Friendship Hall, after which they went on a tour with the following company: S. S. Sanford, Add Collins, A. Hulmes, Paul Berger, Ed Achuff, Frank Solomon, and Jimmy Daly. Collins and Sanford were the end men.

COMBATIVE MINSTRELS, THE: was the name of a party organized by Hodge Chase, who opened July 12, 1864, with Charley Fox and Dave Reed on the ends and Savori, Hilton, Hobbs and others of Bryant's Minstrels.

COMBINATION MINSTRELS: organized by Jack Haverly in the summer of 1864 for a tour through Michigan and the far West. Cool Burgess left the party in November and at the same time Sallie and Eliza Duval joined the party. In December the party consisted of Sallie and Eliza Duval, Nelly Haywood, Eva Blanchard, Nora Pyne, Edna Willis, L. J. Mayo, Carl Strauss, George Fields, J. Jones, Tom Whiting, Johnny Judge, Frank B. Wise, O. P. Sweet, Edward Mayo, Hugh Hamall, Harry Causland, Bobby Judge, M. Blessinger, Arthur Ferguson, and R. H. Armstrong, agent. Late in December, 1864, a partnership was formed by Haverly with J. W. Mallory, of Mallory's Minstrels, and the two companies combined. They were then called HAVERLY & MALLORY'S MINSTRELS.

COMBINATION TROUPE: was the title of a party that started from New York, December, 1865, under the management of H. A. Fuller, for a tour through New

Hampshire and Vermont. Frank George, M. J. Kerrigan, William McAllister, Mullins, Lewis, Clark, Sturgis and Allen comprised the company.

COMIQUE IRON CLADS: was a party that started out from Haverhill, Mass., on November 4, 1869.

COMMONWEALTH MINSTRELS: announced on May 1, 1876, that they would on that date commence their third season, although we can find no previous account of their existence. They traveled by wagons and the company in 1876 consisted of A. J. Bancroft, A. Benham, the Richardson Bros. (Tony and Charley), A. C. Knoll, A. D. Gates, R. W. Scoville, C. B. Leek and others. They reorganized in Ashtabula, Ohio, September, 1876, and made an extensive tour. On March 26, 1877, they commenced a tour through Ohio under the direction of Ame Lampman, opening at Rock Creek. Phillips, Richardson, Alf J. Bancroft, A. Benham, Fred A. Phelps, Scoville, Leek, Will E. Keeves, and the Richardson Bros.

CONGO MELODISTS: came into existence in 1842. And for a while were very popular. James Buckley, father of the Buckley Brothers, was the proprietor. This is said to be the first band to harmonize Negro melodies, operatic choruses, etc. R. Bishop, G.. Swain, and Frederick, the three sons, were the chief features and they made their debut at the Tremont Theatre, Boston, George Buckley being the principal tenor singer and comedian. Shortly after this (1844) they took the name of BUCKLEY'S MINSTRELS.

CONVERSE'S (FRANK) CAMPBELLS: See ORIGINAL MATT PEEL'S MINSTRELS.

CONWAY'S (WALTER) MINSTRELS: were organized in Baltimore Md., and opened December 19, 1866, at Manchester, Md. They consisted of Walter Conway, Nelse Conway, Harry Weston, Frank Clarkson, Harry Warfield, A. L. Hanline, P. Reinhardt, C. P. Fleming, J. H. Kaiser, P. Holbrook, M. Hamilton, F. Holbrook, and J. Lindall.

COOK'S (JOE) SABLE HARMONISTS: started from Boston for a tour West in November, 1860. Joe Cook, Mme. Joe Cook, Louise Webster, W. Barry, D. Wyatt, Master Willie, N. Rogers, W. F. Sparks, H. Cline, T. H. Brady, Sarah Price, and Frank Meekes.

COSMOPOLITAN MINSTRELS: were organized in May, 1860, and traveled through New Jersey and Pennsylvania with Johnny Pierce, J. Quinn, Johnny Neil, J. H. Collins, Henry Wilks, J. W. Hilton, D. Harper, George Wilks, J. Keith, Herr Van Lathr, L. M. Ford, Original Young America, and William A. Christy. Beasley & Smith were proprietors.

COTTON & REED'S NEW YORK MINSTRELS: were organized by John Simpson (treasurer for Bryant's Minstrels for many years), Ben Cotton and Dave Reed. They opened at Bryant's Opera House, Twenty-third Street, near Sixth Avenue, New York, August 23, 1875. In the company were A. E. Voos, Bob Hart, J. W. Lamont, J. J. Kelly, Dave Reed, Charles Templeton, Ben Cotton, Brockway, W. Raymond, E. M. Hall, Morton, Bernardo, Clark, Pearce, and Bideaux. Eugene appeared

September 13; October 23, Bob Hart left; Eugene withdrew October 30; and the season closed very unsuccessfully on November 13.

COTTON, MURPHY AND SMITH'S CALIFORNIA MINSTRELS: were organized in New York in February, 1865, and gave their first show at Newport, R. I., February 25. Ben Cotton and Joe Murphy were on the ends. J. Tannenbaum, W. H. Lewis (William Henry Rice), Frank Campbell, R. Tyrrell, J. Crosher, J. Murphy, W. H. Smith, F. Blum, George Clarendon, H. Barker, H. Koehler, and George Ross. In July, 1865, they took a rest, after which they reorganized and started out, giving their first show September 2, 1865, at Pawtucket, Mass. They closed up in July, 1866, then reorganized and opened September 1, 1866. Ben Cotton, Master Bennie (Cotton), Jake Budd, Charles H. Atkinson, George Monk, Thomas McNally, Joe Norrie, Frank Campbell, Harry Walters, Thomas Sears, Erastus Clapp, Ned Clapp, Fred King, C. N. Cotton and the "Empire Boys," Johnny and Willie Budd (Welch and Rice). H. E. Parmelee was agent. J. Tannenbaum joined early in September. Smith shortly after withdrew from the company and proceeded to San Francisco, Cal., where he married, September 24, 1866, Clara Sager, the youngest of the three Sager Sisters. Murphy also withdrew a few weeks after Smith and he also went to San Francisco. Ben Cotton continued with the party on the road.

COTTON'S (BEN) COMPANY: organized a band and opened January 19, 1867, at Norwich, Conn. The company consisted of Frank Campbell, Jake Budd, Empire Boys, Charley Atkinson, Joe Norrie, Master Bennie Cotton and Ben Cotton. H. E. Parmelee started with them as agent but E. P. Kendall (without exception the best advance agent ever seen in America) joined them in March. The party closed December 26, 1867, in Kalamazoo, Mich., in consequence of bad business. They reorganized a short time after, but closed in June, 1868.

COURTNEY & SANFORD'S MINSTRELS: was a party made up in New York to travel with Courtney & Sanford's Circus in South America. They consisted of: Billy Watson, Dave Wilson, J. K. Campbell, John F. Oberist, Carl Rudolph, J. B. Carter, Harry Percy, J. G. Rampone and orchestra. They sailed from New York July 23, 1873.

CROSS, BOSSARDET & DUMONT'S ORIGINAL PONTOONS: organized and opened in Portsmouth, N. H., December 14, 1866, and consisted of John C. Cross, tambo; Frank Bossardet, bones; Hen Willey, interlocutor; W. H. Parks, John Morgan, William Carlin, Dickey Simmons, Charles J. Howard, Harry Andrews, Ned Parks, Jerry Dashington, Billy Morris, H. Bloodgood, Master Dixie, Alfred Dumont and Harry Robinson.

CROSS, FAY & MCALLISTER'S MINSTRELS: gave their initial show December 7, 1865, at Troy, N. Y., Billy McAllister and Jimmy Fay on the ends. Prof. Alder, C. P. Blake, J. C. Converse, W. L. Wilson, Henry Moore, Frank Ripley, James Fay, J. K. Whitcomb, J. B. Griffin, E. E. Jones, W. H. De Forrest, Henry Wildman and J. H. Pierce. J. C. Cross was manager. J. McAndrews and George Winship, who had but just arrived from California, opened with this party November 14, 1864. The season closing in May, Campbell disposed of his interest to Mr. Hooley, who became sole proprietor and manager.

DASHINGTON & KLING'S AEOLIANS: consisted of: Jerry Dashington, Master Wagner, Harry Hambrighter, Billy Morris, Fred Williams, Frank Dumont, J. B. Carter, Thomas Yates, and Masters Willie and Charley. They started for an Eastern tour in March, 1869.

DAVIS & CO.'S "CHRISTY'S" MINSTRELS: started from Toledo, Ohio, and gave their first show September 24, 1873, with Christy, Hooley, Richardson Bros., Lew Hallett, J. T. Cook, and Prof. Smith.

DAVIS' (NED) OHIO MINSTRELS: were organized in Cincinnati, Ohio, in October, 1855, by Dr. Spalding and Charles Rogers. The steamboat *Banjo* was built expressly for this band by Dr. Spalding for the purpose of visiting the river towns of the West and South. They gave their first show at Lawrenceburg, Ind. The company consisted of Ned Davis and Silas Weed on the ends, E. N. Slocum, C. B. Griste (then a musician), Levi Brown, Master J. W. Adams, W. Penn Lehr, William Plato, J. Woodruff and Charles Sidestriker. Joel E. Warner was agent.

DAVIS' (NED) TROUPE: organized a band in New York, in May, 1867. They consisted of Ned Davis, Harry Robinson, L. M. Reese, Billy Blair, J. D. Roome, Frank Dumont, T. Buckley, J. Lerche, John Allen, and J. Dixon.

DINGESS & GREEN'S MINSTRELS: organized in Chicago, Ill., and opened in Champaign, Ill., November 18, 1866, with Delehanty, Harry Stanwood, J. E. Green and Young Hengler. John A. Dingess was manager and L. M. W. Steere was advance agent.

DIXEY & MORAN'S MINSTRELS: was formerly CARNCROSS & DIXEY'S MINSTRELS. Moran and Dixey opened the season in Philadelphia on October 2, 1871, with Theodore Jackson, James Walters, J. C. Lacy, J. G. Russell, Harry Stanwood, G. W. Charles, A. J. Talbot, Turner, Hogan, Moran, Dixey, J. H. Ross, W. L. Hobbs, Joseph Walters, J. A. Armstrong, S. Hosfield, J. O. Weisenborn, J. Bech, S. A. Meyer, H. Cummings, O. Braun, D. Wild, C. Weeks, and W. Brown. McAndrews was there the first week. G. W. H. Griffin appeared December 11. The season closed May 25, 1872, and the company made a traveling tour. While on this traveling trip, Carncross entered into co-partnership with Moran and Dixey and traveled with them as the tenor. The spring of 1871, Carncross left minstrelsy and entered the mercantile business. The party opened in Philadelphia August 26, 1872, with Japanese Tommy, the Buffalo Boys, J. J. Kelly, and Fred Walz added to the forces; also William Hamilton, baritone. During the week commencing September 9 and the following week, the troupe, except the end men, appeared in white faces and Lou Brimmer was engaged. A dissolution of partnership took place September 24, Moran becoming sole proprietor and the troupe was then known as FRANK MORAN'S MINSTRELS.

DIXEY'S MINSTRELS: composed entirely of home talent, organized in Piqua, Ohio, in May, 1861, and visited the neighboring towns. They traveled on a packet called the *Dixey*. Billy Manning was the bones, and it was with this party that he made his first appearance before the public. Jack Smith was tambo. They gave their first show at Tippecanoe, after which they visited all the towns along the canal.

They returned to Piqua in a few weeks, reorganized and made a tour of the West, starting September 1. Very soon after starting the treasurer decamped with all the funds, which caused the party to collapse.

DOBSON'S SERENADERS: organized and made a tour through the West in August, 1858, for a few weeks only. C. E. Dobson was one of them.

DONALDSON'S ETHIOPS: in 1853, William B. Donaldson had a band at Hope Chapel, 718-720 Broadway, New York. David Wambold was in the company. On January 15, 1855, he had Wambold, Baker, Malvin Turner, Atherton, Miss Celestine and Adelaide (dancers), Billy Quinn and Emmett, afterward known as Harry Huntington. In the summer he went on a traveling tour, returning to New York and opening at the Academy (Stuyvesant) Hall, 663 Broadway, opposite Bond Street, with Perrine, G. W. Moore, Sinclair, J. W. Byer, Langdon, W. N. Smith, Sam Wells and Billy Quinn.

DOUGHERTY (HUGHEY), JOHNNY WILD, MASTER BARNEY & LITTLE MAC'S MINSTRELS: were organized in Boston for a traveling tour and opened in Lowell, Mass., July 17, 1869; and they closed their season September 25, when they joined Morris Brothers in Boston, September 27.

DOUGHERTY (HUGHEY), LESLIE & BRAHAM: were managers of a minstrel band traveling in South Africa in November, 1873. In the party were: Dougherty, W. S. Leslie, Braham, Cox, Turner and Harvey. Dougherty arrived in London, England from Cape of Good Hope on November 25, 1874.

DOUGHERTY'S (HUGHEY) COMPANY: opened the Alhambra Palace, Philadelphia, June 18, 1877, with a minstrel party consisting of George Thatcher, George Harley, Fred Walz, J. G. Russell, J. J. Kelly, Charles Stevens, C. F. Shattuck and Prof. Hosfeld. A variety entertainment followed the minstrel performance.

DUMBOLTON'S SERENADERS: S. A. Wells and Jerry Bryant in the party, the latter taking the place made vacant by Pell (bones). They played the St. James Theatre, London, one year and eight months.

DUPREZ AND BENEDICT'S MINSTRELS: See SHOREY, CARLE, DUPREZ & GREEN'S MINSTRELS. They closed their fourteenth annual tour at St. Catherines, Canada, in July, 1867. The party then took a vacation, being announced as the first one in five years. This party opened in Philadelphia at the Seventh Street Opera House (Seventh Street, below Arch) on October 25, 1869. L. E. Hicks, Lew Benedict, J. L. Woolsey, G. Bishop, Charles Reynolds, Frank Dumont, Charles Gleason, Frank Pankhurst, Lewis Collins, W. Richards, J. Robinson, G. Wilkes, Calixa Lavallee, and Frank Kent. The last appearance (save one) in public of "Uncle" Frank Brower was with this company on December 18, 1869. He played Ginger Blue in "Virginia Mummy." They closed in Philadelphia, May 7, 1870, and went traveling. One of their novelties was four end men: Dougherty and Benedict, tambo; and Reynolds and Gleason, bones. They opened in San Francisco at the California Theatre, August 8, 1870. After a successful season on the Pacific Slope, they returned East and opened at the Seventh Street Opera House, Philadelphia, November 19, 1870. Arlington joined them November 28 and on December 17 they closed in Philadelphia and went traveling. For the season of 1873-74, the company consisted of C. H. Duprez, Lew Benedict, Frank Dumont, George H. Edwards, Frank Kent, Joseph T. Gulick, W. W. Herman, George J. Lennox, Ferd Heinrich, C. C. Palmer, Fox, Ward, T. B. Dixon, D. H. Smith, B. Kreich, and L. N. Van Horn. The season closed July 4 and the next season was commenced September 7, 1874, with Benedict, Joseph Fox, Frank Kent, Dixon, Heinrich, W. F. Toomey, Killian Willis, John Whitcomb, Joseph T. Gulick, Dumont, Palmer and others. On August 17, 1875, Duprez became sole manager and proprietor, having that day bought all of Benedict's interest. George E. Edwards, Sam Price, J. T. Gulick, D. H. Smith, Frank Kent, John Latour, Heinrich, Fox, Ward, W. M. Hogan, Frank Dumont, and others made up the company at that time. They closed the season June 5, 1876, a continuous one of twenty-two months. They started out again in September. Wash Norton appeared on the bone end at the latter part of the season. Duprez again started September 11, 1876, with George H. Edwards and Joseph Fox, tambo; Billy West and Ward, bones; J. T. Gulick, interlocutor; Andrew Vail and Frank Dumont, tenor; Dunk H. Smith, balladist. They closed the season June 16, 1877. The next season opened September 17, 1877, with Dumont, W. F. Tithill, Heinrich, Gulick, John Harris, Joseph Fox, Archie White, William Ward, John B. Murphy, J. Reese, Harry Pierson, William Haynes, Billy Ayres and others in the company.

DURANT & HAYWOOD'S CAMPBELLS: was under the management of N. F. and W. Hayward, formerly of the NEW ENGLAND BANDS. They organized in April, 1859: W. F.. Durant, basso; A. J. Talbot, bones; Master McAnally, jig and wench; W. Hayward, tenor; E. J. Melville, guitar. They disbanded December 17, 1859, in Chicago.

EDWARDS & SHOREY'S MINSTRELS: was an organization traveling through Pennsylvania in April, 1863, consisting of Bob Edwards, J. G. H. Shorey, J. Purcell, H. Wharfe, E. H. Young, Charles Rivers, A. Jardula, T. Moore, and J. Carl.

EDWARDS' (BOB) COMBINATION: was a musical party organized in New Jersey in April, 1865, and opened on the 19th at Trenton, N.J., with Bob Edwards, Dan Howard, Bill Barker, Harry Hoyt, Joe Cook, Willie Budd (Billy Welch), Jake Budd, G. Bechle, Frank Solomon, T. H. Kellogg, Johnny Rice, and Julia Edwards.

ELDRIDGE'S MINSTRELS: was a company organized in Eastport, Me., August 1, 1865, by James Eldridge for a tour through Maine. Eldridge was middle man; Joe Folsom, bones; George Patterson, tambo; Henry Harrington, George Clark, Samuel Patterson, George Sweet, Frank Gleason, Walter Bradish, George Knox, and Dick Welsh.

EMERSON & MANNING'S MINSTRELS: formerly EMERSON, ALLEN & MANNING'S, re-appeared in Cincinnati, at Wood's Theatre, May 31. They located at the Dearborn Street Theatre, situated on Dearborn Street, between Madison and Washington, Chicago, Ill., in September, 1869, with the following company: Emerson, Manning, Bob Hart, J. R. Kemble, Rollin Howard, Lew Brimmer, Mike Kannane, C. S. Fredericks, G. W. Jackson, Harry Norman, J. F. Dunnie, J. J. Kirby, Charles Hunnneman, Frank Bowles, Jules Seidel, H. Anson, J. Pfeifer, W. Ross, and

W. Hathaway. Emerson withdrew late in January, 1870, and the company was then known as MANNING'S MINSTRELS..

EMERSON, ALLEN & MANNING'S MINSTRELS: gave their first show at Williamsburg, L. I., early in June, 1868. In the organization were Emerson, Manning, bones; Johnny Allen, tambo; Dr. J. Hanmer, E. S. Rosenthal, C. Wheaton, G. H. Clark, Edwin Holmes, C. A. Boyd, Frank Bowles, Harry French, Richard Willis, Harry Kelly, Charles Holly, William King, P. Hanratler, Henry Elliott, Martin Setz, and Master Eddie Manning. They opened at Tony Pastor's Opera House, on the Bowery, New York, June 29, 1868. On July 20, George F. McDonald, the actor, made his bow in burnt cork. They opened in Cincinnati, August 3, at Pike's Music Hall. They then made a tour of the country, opening at the Fourth Street Theatre, Cincinnati, Ohio, October 26, 1868, and then made another traveling trip. They returned to Cincinnati and opened at Mozart Hall on April 26, 1869, where they stayed one week and then went to St. Louis. Johnny Allen left in May, 1869, and J. R. Kemble, C. S. Fredericks, Jules Seidel and Sig. Marks joined them. The party then became known as EMERSON & MANNING'S.

EMERSON'S (BILLY) MINSTRELS: were organized in Chicago, Ill., and gave their first performance February 11, 1870, at Ottawa, Ill., with the following in the company: Billy Emerson, John Pierce, H. Meismer, Lew Brimmer, Charles A. Boyd, Henry Schultz, William Butler, W. B. Rudolph (later known as Carl Rudolph, and whose right name was Wilber Barrill); A. W. Hall, A. Rider, Yates, F. King, A. Johnson; C. B. Griste, agent; Beaumont Duhring, treasurer. The Reynolds Bros. were shortly after added to the company. After a successful traveling season, a reorganization took place and they left Cincinnati for California on November 13, 1870, under the management of Thomas Maguire, at whose opera house, Washington Street in San Francisco, they opened on November 23. Billy Emerson, J. H. Budworth, George and Charles Reynolds, Charles Fostelle, M. Ainsley Scott, Con T. Murphy, Charles A. Boyd; and C. B. Griste, business manager, were all that went from Cincinnati. But after arriving there they were strengthened by the addition of Charley Rhodes, Johnny De Angelis, George T. Evans, H. Eytinge, Louis Broharm, T. Blamfin, J. Book, and an orchestra of ten pieces. They closed at Maguire's on Sunday, February 26, 1871, and opened at the Alhambra on Bush Street, February 27. During the season Bideaux, S. S. Purdy, James Collins, Martha Wren, A. M; Hernandez, Sheridan and Mack, Charles Vivian, J. H. Milburn, and Cool Burgess appeared. When the party first opened in San Francisco, C. B. Griste was the business manager; but when they appeared at the Alhambra he was the manager. On November 5. 1871, Emerson, with a portion of the band, closed and went on a traveling tour. The Reynolds Bros., Fostelle, Scott and others were in the party. On November 7, Kelly and Leon and S. S. Purdy, with a newly organized band, opened. Charles Howard, bones; Purdy, tambo; Arthur Stanley, Robinson, Bideaux, and Fanny Gibson were the additions. They closed in San Francisco, May 26, 1872, and went on a tour. They opened in New York September 2, 1872, at Lina Edwin's Theatre, under the management of Thomas Maguire, and Emerson and Carl Rudolph opened November 11, and the season closed November 16, owing to bad business.

Emerson and Maguire left for California. On the 12th of May, 1873, he organized a small party, consisting of M. Ainsley Scott, G. W. Rockefeller, Charles Boyd and W. Verner, and sailed for Australia under George Coppin's management. On their arrival in Melbourne they added to their party several performers then in that city and opened at St. George's Hall August 2, but did not at first meet with success owing to their having doubled the usual prices of admission. Holly, Buckley, and W. H. Campbell were the new faces added to the party. They afterwards played at the Prince of Wales' Theatre in Melbourne for nine weeks to the largest houses ever known in the colonies. On June 6, 1874, Emerson left the party and sailed from Sydney for California, and soon after his arrival in San Francisco he joined Maguire's party at the Alhambra.

EMMETT & BROWER'S MINSTRELS: had Dan Emmett and Frank Brower as the chief attractions and the party was one of the strongest on the road.

EMMETT & LUMBARD'S PARTY: were organized April 26, 1858, and opened at Irvine's Hall, St. Paul, Minn., for the summer. Dan Emmett, Frank Lumbard, Johnny Ritter and R. Moore were in the party.

EMPIRE BAND: was traveling in January, 1860, and were composed of Frank Applegate, L. H. Freeman, Harry Bull, J. Brown, H. Barnes, G. Barnes, Master H. Nobles, and C. Weir. They organized in Auburn, N.Y.

ETHIOPIAN SERENADERS: held forth a Vauxhall Garden, New York, late in 1844 and afterwards appeared at the Elysian Fields, Hoboken, N.J. Jerry Bryant, H. Mestayer, J. P. Carter, Raymond, and Jim Sanford were in the company. Sanford made a feature of the performance with his Congo drum.

ETHIOPIAN SERENADERS: See VIRGINIA SERENADERS.

EUREKA MINSTRELS: in January, 1864, were holding forth in San Francisco. Fred Wilson, who arrived from Shanghai, opened January 31, and on February 28 Backus and Bernard appeared. David Wambold, Sam Wells, and Master Lewis had appeared on February 22. Maguire opened the Metropolitan Theatre, Sacramento, on February 26, 1864, with Backus, Burbank, Bernard, Abecco, Barnwell, DeAngelis and Fred Wilson. In March they made a tour of the interior.

EUREKA MINSTRELS: See BACKUS' (CHARLEY) ORIGINAL MINSTRELS.

EXCELSIOR OPERA TROUPE: were traveling in Indiana in December, 1860, with Smith, Pierce & Manning, managers.

EXCELSIORS: See CAMPBELL'S MINSTRELS.

FARNSWORTH'S MINSTRELS: consisting of Ned Farnsworth, Lewis Wilson, George R. Penn, Frank Preston, W. E. Lorraine, Archy Ray, George Scott, Colin Mayne, E. Kendall, Charles Long, R. D. Gillette, and C. H. Brace, organized in December, 1863, and traveled East.

FARR & THOMPSON'S MINSTRELS: a re-organization from CHRISTY'S MINSTRELS, took place with J. T. Ainsworth, Matt Thompson, and George Gray joining, while Lewis Tracy, Silberberg, Laurence, Florence, and Chilcoat withdrew. In July, W. S. Farr became sole proprietor. They organized a brass band in conjunction with their troupe. They closed the season in Newark, August 2, 1661, but took to the road again in a few weeks. A reorganization took place in New York in June, 1863.

FARR & THOMPSON'S: See CHRISTY'S MINSTRELS.

FARRENBERG & BROWN'S (JOE) OHIO MINSTRELS: See OHIO MINSTRELS.

FERDINAND & SOLOMON'S MINSTRELS: were organized in December, 1863, and consisted of M. B. Leavitt, tambo; J. Ferdinand, bones; Frank Solomon, J. L. Sanford, Fred Ashley, Charles La Borde, E. J. Hirst, and C. Swain.

FISKE & HOLTON'S HARMONIANS: were organized in Worcester, Mass., in May, 1866, with Billy Taber, bones; Billy Dixon, tambo; Harry Richardson, Wally Parks, H. Stanley, Justin Joslyn, Bob Evans, Henry Hankley, and J. Hessions. They closed the season at Clinton, Mass., July 7, 1866. Leban Fiske sold out his interest to Holton and retired from the profession. The company was reorganized by Holton with Billy Dixon, Bob Evans, Billy Taber, Thomas McCone, Ned West, Harry Richardson, John B. Gates, W. Joslyn, Wally Jason, E. H. Howe, Harry Lincey, and Ed D. Horton. They opened in Providence.

FITZ GERMAN MINSTRELS: were composed of Hughey Hagert, Richard Gorman, Harry Brown, Howard Egbert, Harry Blanchard, W. H. Stanley, Bideaux, Fred Romher, G. A. Bernard and a silver band of eleven pieces. George Cole was proprietor and Val Rolewski, leader. They started early in March, 1873, and they had not been out many days when Cole deserted them, leaving salaries due to all.

FLORENCE'S ALABAMA MINSTRELS: was a new party that was organized in Boston, Mass., and opened May 2, 1863. Joseph Nugent, bones; Dan Wheeler, tambo; George W. Florence, John Ryder, R. A. Birchley, Ben Shepard, W. Cannon, Harry Jordan, J. H. Andrews, H. Schipp, A. Jigger, L. Brown, W. F. Asche, C. H. Greene, and Prof. Gilbert.

FORD, WEST & BLANCHARD'S CREOLE MINSTRELS: started in July, 1859, with Dad Edwards, bones; Harry Blanchard, banjo; Frank West, Prof. Brisco, violin; and J. Studley, basso.

FORREST'S MINSTRELS: were traveling in Kentucky in July, 1865. F. Ransom, Sile Weed, Early Miller, Jim Morris, J. M. Forrest, Lewis Walters, P. Marks, and J. C. Carroll.

FOSTER'S MINSTRELS: organized in New York in January, 1863, and traveled East and New York State with W. H. Brockway, Jules Stratton, W. Blythe, W. Waters, Carl Spentz, Johnny Booker, O. H. Carter, George Wrightman, W. Butler, E. Mills, J. Gaynor, and Charles Wood. In July, 1863, this party was called THE AMAZONS. Foster quit them in Albany soon after starting out. Johnny Booker also withdrew, as he stated at the time that there was no responsible head to the concern. There was a regular breaking-up, but H. S. Rumsey took charge and after reorganizing started out calling the party RUMSEY'S MINSTRELS.

FOX & SHARPLEY'S MINSTRELS: opened at Stuyvesant Institute, New York, October 7, 1861. George Gray, ballads; S. Sharpley and C. H. Fox had the ends. Dave Reed and Joe Childs were in the company. They closed there October 20.

Richard M. Hooley

FOX & WARDEN'S MINSTRELS: occupied St. James Hall, London, England, in October, 1859. They did a very good business. H. Drummond, C. Fox, and Mert Sexton were in the party. The proprietors dissolved partnership in May, 1860. Fox became sole proprietor and continued in the company. They appeared shortly after in Liverpool.

FOX'S OPERATIC TROUPE (not Charles H. Fox): organized in Maryland in November, 1859, and traveled. Fox, F. Buckingham, R. Turner Jr., D. Porter, H. Talbot, R. Sullivan, S. J. Stean, and Master Harry comprised the party.

FRONTIER MINSTRELS: were organized in Eastport, Me., where they first performed, January 11, 1866. George Patterson was interlocutor; Harry Harrington, bones; Samuel Patterson, tambo; W. Braddish, George Clark, Master Toney (clog), and Charles Scott.

GALESBURGH MINSTRELS: were organized in Galesburgh, in May, 1858, and opened at the Opera House under Pardy & Daniels' management with Gus Howard, T. B. Johnson, J. O. Noyes, S. V. Shelly, Frank Gray and S. S. Shepard. They were located there for the summer.

GAYLORD & DUPONT'S: during the season of 1854, this party opened in Philadelphia at the old Southwark Hall in Second Street. They occupied the premises nearly four years.

GAYLORD, FOWLER & HOGAN: opened in Kansas City, March 24, 1866, with a party. D. Camp was the manager and true to his name he "decamped" the second night with what funds there were.

GEMS OF CAMPBELLS: See ORIGINAL MATT PEEL'S MINSTRELS.

GEORGIA CHAMPIONS: was one of the many troupes that started out, emboldened to try their fortunes. They organized and opened in Providence, R. I., July, 1845. They had the original Jake Hunter (Mr. Ryder), banjoist; also the original Juba, then in his best trim; Tom Fluter, Juba, tambo; Pierce, bones; Russell, accordion.

GEORGIA MINSTRELS: a band organized by Sherry Corbin of colored performers in San Francisco for Australia. They opened in Newcastle, December 18; 1876, and appeared in Sydney, N. A. W., December 26, at the School of Arts. After playing there two weeks they proceeded to Melbourne, where they soon after burst up.

GEORGIA MINSTRELS: a party of gentlemen of color which was formed by C. H. Hicks, who opened with them at the Broadway Opera House, 600 Broadway, New York, July 20, 1867, with Lew Johnson, bones; C. Arlington, tambo; Smith, Benson, C. B. Hicks, ballads; Dick Little, banjo; A. L. Smith, essence. In April, 1868, they were in Aspinwall. They occupied the Empire Rink, Third Avenue and Sixty-third Street, New York, in June, 1869, with George Danforth, bones; Bob Height, Alf Smith and C. B. Hicks in the party. McMillan and Coats were managers. They sailed for Hamburg, Germany, January 25, 1870, arriving there early in February and opened February 10. They made a tour of the provinces and closed in April and several of them joined SAM HAGUE'S SLAVE TROUPE. C. B. Hicks started with this party September 9, 1871, for a tour through Pennsylvania. George Skillings, Bob

Height, Dick Weaver, Banks, Kersands and T. Drewette were added to the forces. On December 22 they appeared in New York at the Eighth Avenue Opera House. In March, 1872, Charles Callender bought the interest of Mr. Temple in this troupe and became sole proprietor. They opened at Lina Edwin's Theatre (formerly Kelly & Leon's Hall), New York, June 10, with Bob Height, Dick Little, Billy Wilson, James Grace, Pete Devonear, Kersands, Smith, L. Pierson, and C. B. Hicks. In March, 1873, the company was made up of the following people: Height, Little, Kersands, Devonear, Grace, Al Smith, L. Pierson, Jake Zabriskie and others. C. B. Hicks was agent. This party temporarily disbanded in December, 1874, and reorganized in January, 1875, with W. A. Mahara as manager and the following company: C. A. Crusoe, William Sanders, Locke Warinch, Mills, Master Burnham, C. Wright Harris, Samuel Butler, Alf White, Bob Turner, Benjamin Jackson, F. Burnell, D. A. Bowman, J. R. Matlock, A. Jackson, C. Morton and C. B. Hicks. D. B. Hodges, who started with the party in January, was relieved by John A. Warner in February.

GIBBS' (CLARK) MINSTRELS: consisting of Jim Wood, Clark Gibbs, John C. Murphy, J. W. Corcoran, Juan Costello, John Freeberthyser, George Wallace, Sig. Forresi, Harry Alberts, George Barker, and Master Francis. They opened November 12, 1866, in Indianapolis, Ind.

GIRARD'S MINSTRELS: organized in July, 1859, in St. Louis, Mo., and opened at Girard Hall under the management of A. McDonald with Frank Lynch, Frank Forester, Tommy Pell, Charles Correll, J. Wood, M. Lutz, J. Donniker, J. Smith and Pete Morris.

GLOBE MINSTRELS: opened at the Globe Theatre, Broadway, New York, November 27, 1871, with G. W. H; Griffin, James H. Budworth, bones; William Budworth, tambo; D. S. Vernon, Arthur McKoun, Stiles, Phelps and others.

GOOGIN'S (DAN) MINSTRELS: organized at Winona, Minn., where they opened June 20, 1872. They collapsed in six weeks at Lake City. Hi Price was in the company.

GRAVELEY'S (EDWARD) MINSTRELS: started from Baltimore, Md., October 8, 1878, with Harry T. Leonard, Barry, Gray, James Woodie, Charles Wattell, William Baker, William B. Harris, John Larmer, R. H. Tarrcent, Dave Graham, George Pritchard, George Browning, Master George Miller, Henry Silver, Ed Gerst, Ed Burton, and Ed Graveley.

GREAT ETHIOPIAN SERENADERS: was the title of a party so billed in 1845 to distinguish them from numberless "Serenaders." They performed at F. S. Myers' saloon, Eighth and Chestnut Streets, Philadelphia, as early as January 14. The prices of admission were: parquet, 25¢; recess, 12½¢. Young Sweeney, Purcell, Master Mitchell, Sam Sanford, "Ole Bull" Myers, B. Boyce, Frank Rosston, and Miss Shaw were in the party.

GREAT MINSTRELS OF THE UNITED STATES: was the title of an organization formed in Cincinnati, Ohio, and who gave their first show on December 1, 1873, in Troy, Ohio. They consisted of Charles Bartine and John Maur, end men; "Cincinnatus," St. Leon, Harry De Lave, Billy Harland, George M. Hill, Edwin

Logan, Alf De Witt, Frank Leon, W. E. Harlan, R. Crandall and orchestra. George A. Russell and Alf De Witt were managers. The company collapsed at Rock Island in December, 1874.

GREEN'S MOCKING BIRD MINSTRELS: Green & Hillsburgh, proprietors, consisted of Jules Stratton, C. Melville, Myers, Emmett, Mike Kannane, Lewis Mairs, Myron Lewis (wench), C. B. Reynolds, and Johnny Booker. They opened December 15, 1865, in Troy, N. Y. Green and Hillsburgh dissolved partnership January 2, 1866. At Columbus, Ohio, the company collapsed, February 20, 1866, owing to too much female management. It was reorganized and opened March 5, but burst up for the second time March 23, at Schenectady, N. Y. They reorganized, the company took to the road, opening at Meriden, Conn., March 12, 1868, with Pete Celeste, J. G. H. Shorey, Lon Chapin, Willis Armstrong, S. Benedict, H. Wray, and J. E. Green.

GRIFFIN & CHRISTY'S: See BUDWORTH'S MINSTRELS.

GRIFFIN & CHRISTY'S MINSTRELS: with Billy Sheppard and Johnny Collins, from California, opened January 21. Collins on the bone end and Christy, tambo. J. Stohr and T. Condron were proprietors. Otto Burbank also appeared in the olio. They closed June 27, 1867, and went traveling. They shortly after leased Union Hall, corner of Twenty-third Street and Broadway, which they opened July 29, 1867: George Christy, bones; Otto Burbank, tambo; W. Hodgkins, C. F. Shattuck; G. W. H. Griffin, interlocutor; George Leslie, Neil Rogers, Fred Abbott, Hogan, John Savori, Hughes, C. Percival, Joseph Prendergast, and James Morrison. They closed and went traveling September 23, 1867.

HAGUE'S (SAM) GEORGIA SLAVE TROUPE: were organized in Georgia by W. H. Lee in June, 1865. They traveled North and visited Utica, N. Y., in 1866. The party was then and there secured by Sam Hague and sailed for Europe June 16, 1866. They arrived in Liverpool and opened there at the Theatre Royal, July 9. Japanese Tommy, Sam Pride, Mallory, Slatter, Brooker, Neil Solomon, John Graves, Fernando, Johnson, and Jacobs, all colored, were in the party. Lee accompanied them as business manager. A minstrel performance with real Negroes proved a failure and Hague went on a traveling tour, which was anything but successful. After a trial of a few months, Hague advertised in the London papers for a partner; then, after eighteen months, he changed the troupe into a white one, secured St. James Hall, Liverpool, which he opened on October 31, 1870, with but three colored in the party. The company now consisted of E. D. Beverly, tenor, late of the Pyne and Harrison Troupe; J. E. Johnson, bones; Billy West, tambo; Thomas D. Fenner, interlocutor; Japanese Tommy, Beaumont Read, and J. Carpenter. In December, C. B. Hicks took the bone end. Wilson, Wherry, G. Campbell, Read, Beverly, and T. Medley were the sextette. There were also in the troupe A. Jacobs, Harry Webb, J. Carpenter, George Dolby, Billy Richardson, T. Lott, F. Smith, Aaron Banks, F. Peri, Sheppard, and Clamo. Harry Leslie opened on the bone end May 8, 1871, Hicks closing May 6. M. B. Leavitt opened with this party October 14, 1872, followed on October 21 by Rollin Howard. Eph Horn appeared January 13, 1873. In April two extra end men appeared, making six in all. Johnny Booker opened with them on February 21, 1876.

The company opened at the Duke's Theatre, London, April 10, 1876, for three weeks, then dedicated their new quarters at St. James' Hall, May 1, 1876, just one year after the fire. After a traveling tour of nine months, Hague's Minstrels re-opened at St. James' Hall, May 20, 1878. They shortly after took another tour, returning to Liverpool and opening for the winter season on December 2, 1878.

HALL'S (E. M.) MINSTRELS: started from Chicago, Ill., June 29, 1878, for a summer tour. Mark Hughes, E. M. Hall, the Rankin Bros. and others were in the company.

HALL'S (J. S.) NEW YORK MINSTRELS: consisted of J. S. Hall, Joseph Arthur, Andy McGee, Charles Sutton, Bernardo, the Clark Bros. (Ed. and Lew), the Landis Bros. (William and Charles), and John Philbin. They sailed for Glasgow, Scotland, on April 20, 1878, from New York. They opened in Greenock, Scotland, appeared in Glasgow May 15, and went thence to Dublin, where they disbanded in June.

HAMALL'S SERENADERS: were organized in Montreal, under the direction of Hugh Hamall, and opened in that city December 3, 1867. A. Lenox, J. S. Danvers, A. Hamall, Master Shea, Johnny Cole and Bob Simmons were in the company.

HAMALL'S (HUGH) TROUPE: started from Montreal, Canada, with a band consisting of Ned West, Hank Howard, Hugh Hamall, and the Leaux Bros. They opened in Quebec on August 19, 1873. On September 1, 1874, this company consolidated with La Rue's Minstrels.

HARMONEONS: after a lengthy traveling tour, appeared June 18, 1846, in the White House, Washington, D.C., before President Polk and family. J. Simmons Davis was manager; Marshall S. Pike, soprano; John Power, tenor; Frank Lynch, James Power, alto; and L. V. H. Crosby, basso. One of the songs sung by this company was Marshall Pike's "The Grave of Washington," the first verse of which was:

> Disturb not his slumbers, let Washington sleep
> 'Neath the boughs of the willows that over him weep;
> His arm is unnerved, but his deeds remain bright
> As the stars in the dark vaulted heaven at night.
> Another one was called "He Led Her To the Altar:"

> He led her to the altar, but the bride was not his chosen;
> He led her with a hand as cold as though its pulse had frozen.
> Flowers were crushed beneath his tread---a gilded dome was o'er him
> But his brow was damp and his lips were pale as the marble step before him.

This company was quite popular.

HARRINGTON & THOMPSON: opened in Memphis, Tenn., March 9, 1863, with a party, among whom were Nelson Kneass, Joe Childs and Ned Palmer.

HARRIS & CLIFTON: formed a party in New York and opened in New Brunswick, N. J., April 25, 1864, under the management of J. L. Harris and George Clifton. The party consisted of M. Bogan, tambo; Dick McGowan, banjo; G. W.

Charles, wench; J. Norcross, middle man; F. Campbell, S. Hosfield, Gus Edwards, bones; Dick Black, J. J. Gunn, George Hosfield, G. Clifton, and Eugene Gorman.

HARRIS' SERENADERS: William B. Harris, manager, opened December 5, 1876, at Annapolis, Md. The company consisted of James Wheeler, J. B. Hennings, John Atwell, James Wilson, Frank Hooley, J. W. Johnson, Frank Watson, Charles H. Stonley and Prof. John Spaun.

HARRISON'S MINSTRELS: opened June 3, 1869, at Newark, N. J., with: G. W. Jackson, J. H. Surridge, Johnny Brassell, and H. F. Dixey, who called themselves the "Associated Artists of Kelly & Leon's Minstrels"; W. H; Brockway, Johnny Hart, L. Myers, M. Gallagher, and J. Queech, in the party. Charles Melville was agent. Charles Harrison left the party the first week.

HART & SIMMONS' MINSTRELS: were organized in New York, and opened, February 2, 1863, in Paterson, N. J. Bob Hart and Lew Simmons were the managers; Col. T. Allston Brown, business manager; and William Nichols, treasurer. The party consisted of: Bob Hart and Lew Simmons, ends; Sam Cole, J. H. Surridge, J. H. Sadler, G. Droskin, George Smith, William Blakeney, D. Rist; William Blythe, F. Wells, J. Charles, J. R. Taylor (Kemble), G. Germain, William Walton, C. Smith and Harry Kenton. John R. Kemble made his debut in burnt cork with the party. While the party were playing in Warren, Bob Hart deserted them in March and the company was afterwards were called NICHOLS & SIMMON'S MINSTRELS.

HATCHER (M.) & E. MORROW: organized a band in July, 1875, and traveled in Indiana. E. Morrow and Jake M. Dinnison were in the company.

HAVERLY & MALLORY'S MINSTRELS: formerly COMBINATION MIN- STRELS, opened at Titusville, Pa., December 27, 1864. [See COMBINATION MIN- STRELS.]

HAVERLY & SANDS: started in April, 1866, with a band through Michigan. Dick Sands, J. H. Haverly, Charley Benedict, George Mankin, Harry Campbell, C. M. Torney, Prof. Eckart, F. D. Abbott, H. F. Bowers and others were along. They collapsed in Chicago, Ill., early in July.

HAVERLY'S MASTODON MINSTRELS: opened in Chicago, October 21, 1878. There were forty-two people seen in the first part, seated in four rows, one tier above another. The vocalists, interlocutor, and musicians were attired in black suits; the eight end men were dressed in blue and white plaid suits. Billy Rice, Barry Maxwell, Thomas Sadler and William Arnold occupied the tambo ends; Pete Mack, Sam Price, John Styles and Bob Hooley, the bone ends, accompanied by John Rapier, Henry Roe, John Styles, Thomas Dixon, J. W. Freeth, the four Arnold Bros., the three Gorman Bros., Thompson, Adams, Lee, and the California Quartette. One of the acts given was a song and dance and clog by twelve men. William Foote was manager; W. H. Strickland, agent; and Harry Mann, business manager.

HAVERLY'S MINSTRELS: was a party that J. H. Haverly started from Chicago, November 9, 1868. They gave their first show at Peoria, Ill., November 11, with Charles Reynolds, Sam Cole, William Barry, Rollin Howard, Brandisi, Gustave Bi- deaux, William Taylor, R. J. Tooke, H. W. Gifford, William H. Butler, Otis H.

Carter, E. G. Kneeland, J. H. Russey, M. Stanton, A. E. Voos, Charles Koehl, and George L. Bishop. Eph Horn joined them for awhile, leaving May 13, 1869, and S. S. Purdy opened. On March 26, 1873, Milt G. Barlow joined. A re-organization was made in November and they opened in the West. The party consisted of: Fayette Welch, Billy Courtwright, George Wilson, Charles James, Ned Goss, James Fox, W. H. Morton, Bernardo, Charley Howard, Bassett, Rapier, Rushby; Robert Eckhard, leader of orchestra; H. J. Clapham, business manager. Canfield and Booker opened on December 8, 1873. Kelly and Leon were added to the company August 10, 1874. George H. Primrose opened November 20. Billy Courtright joined this company in June, 1875. In August Milt G. Barlow, Wilson, Primrose, West, Frank Bell, Edwin French, Burton Stanley, Thomas B. Dixon and Henry Welling were in the party. Cool Burgess opened January 10, 1876. Barlow left March 25, 1877. Primrose withdrew June 14. Add Ryman was the next middle man. On August 20 Frank Moran and George Thatcher occupied the ends. On September 3, Bobby Newcomb took Thatcher's position. On March 11, 1878, J. R. Kemble, Ned Kent, Ernest Linden, and Billy Arlington joined them in Chicago. Harry Clapham severed his connection with this party on March 23. The season closed in Chicago March 30, and they started for California. They opened at the Bush Street Theatre, San Francisco, on April 22 with George Thatcher, Harry G. Richmond, Billy Carter, Frank Cushman, Billy Rice, J. R. Kemble, Charles Diamond, Welch and Rice, T. B. Dixon, H. W. Roe, John W. Freeth. and John L. Rapier. Haverly united his minstrel troupes into one under the title of HAVERLY'S MASTODON MINSTRELS.

HAWVER & FERGUSON MINSTRELS: opened October 13, 1873, at Battenville; N. Y., and the party consisted of G. Hall, A, Hawver, Brainard, Harkness, J. Allen, J. Ferguson, H. Russell, W. Harper, E. Brownell, Mart Gilmore and Lew Miller.

HAYES & SMITH'S BAND: was organized by Tim Hayes and J. R. Smith and gave their initial performance February 22, 1864, at Reading, Pa., with Tom Murray, Harry Talbott, Tim Hayes, Sam Hague, Miss May Walton, and Billy Fields.

HAYWORTH AND HORTON'S MINSTRELS: commenced a traveling season in 1852. George W. Moore, bones; A. M. Hernandez, Master Williams (the bushel measure dancer), Master Totting, and Jim Hunter were in the company. They traveled South and in six months the managers ran away and left them at Richmond, Va., to pay their own bills. The boys reorganized under the name of the PARROW MINSTRELS:

HEDDEN, ADAMS, & KNEELAND MINSTRELS: organized and traveled south in 1859. They consisted of W. Hedden, Johnny Adams, E. G. Kneeland, Nick Foster, J. Pfaffenschlager, J. Cassiday and S. S. Pretty.

HERNANDEZ & MORNINGSTAR'S MINSTRELS: were organized for a traveling trip through the South. The Seigel Children and A. M. Hernandez were the features.

HERNANDEZ & SMITH'S MINSTRELS: was one of the many minstrel parties that organized in Richmond, Va. They started under the management of A. M.

Hernandez and John P. Smith in 1853 and went to Norfolk, Va., just after the yellow fever. They returned to Odd Fellows Hall, Richmond; then made a tour of North and South Carolina, Georgia and Tennessee with Frank Weston, bones; R. Jean Buckley, J. K. Campbell, tambo; Joe Dewsbury, Lauer, Hernandez, John P. Smith, and Charles Harris. At Nashville, John P. Smith left them and they joined with another party (who had stranded there) and traveled as BILL PARROW'S MINSTRELS. At Louisville they disbanded.

HOLTON & GATES' HARMONIUMS: was a band that was organized for the purpose of joining with the Simon Pure American Circus in New York, October 1, 1866. The party consisted of C. Smith, E. H. Ross, O. P. Sweet, Frank Webb, Dick Thompson, Harry French, F. T. St. Clair, J. A. Herman, J. C. Morris, Ed W. Holton and Charles A. Gates.

HONTZ'S MINSTRELS: were organized in Dover, Pa., in September, 1860. W. Hontz, T. Bell, Jack Taylor, R. Sands, and Gill Tate were in the party.

HOOLEY & CAMPBELL'S MINSTRELS: R. M. Hooley having separated from George Christy in the management of Christy's Minstrels in New York, organized a party for the road and opened at the Melodeon, Boston, February 6, 1860. Hooloy, S. C. Campbell, and G. W. H. Griffin were announced as the proprietors. S. C. Campbell, Hooley, Griffin, J. A. Herman, A. J. Hobbs, J. K. Edwards, J. C. Reeves, J. H. Hilliard, Unsworth, Frank Brower, J. B. Donniker, F. Dickson, and T. Gaynor composed the company. Louis Zwiler was agent. When they first started they were called Christy's Minstrels, but soon after were known as Hooley & Campbells, considered one of the best minstrel parties ever organized for the road. Tim Hayes joined them soon after, also Charles H. Fox. They opened at the French Theatre, 585 Broadway, New York, June 25, 1860. After playing there one week they traveled East for a time. Returning to New York, they re-opened at 585 Broadway on August 13, with Unsworth, Eugene, S. C. Campbell, G. W. H. Griffin, R. M. Hooley, Donniker, J. C. Reeves, E. J. Melville, August Asche, and R. M. Howland. They opened at Niblo's Saloon, Broadway, August 27, with Billy Birch, Add Weaver, Master Barney, Hilliard, and Signora Oliveira. Wash Norton, who had left Bryant's, opened with this party in November. Then Cotton took Birch's place in November. Tim Hayes, clog dancer, who arrived in America in December, 1860, opened December 7. After an extended tour, they disbanded in Philadelphia in 1861. Unsworth and Eugene left in January, 1861, and Johnny Duley, Donniker and Rollin Howard opened. G. C. Charles (wench) opened in February. They closed in New York in consequence of increase of rent of Niblo's Saloon. They made a traveling tour, opening in Philadelphia at the Walnut Street Theatre, June 3, 1861. Birch and Brower joined them June 10 and they disbanded July 13.

HOOLEY & CHRISTY'S: [See GEORGE CHRISTY'S MINSTRELS] returned to New York and opened at 444 Broadway, May 23, 1859; but George Christy was enjoined by Henry Wood and not allowed to perform. It appears that when he withdrew from Henry Wood, George signed an agreement not to perform in New York for a year and a half, as George designed being away during that time. But his California trip not proving profitable, he returned just one year after leaving. The court granted the injunction and George did not appear but the company did. J. H. Budworth took the position vacated by George. Herman, Koppitz, Lothian, Eugene, George Coes (end), and E. Bowers were in the party. Coes retired in June and Gallagher took his place. The party went on a traveling tour in July, 1859. Cool White joined them August 15. Coes returned to San Francisco in July, 1859. The time of injunction having expired on November 1, they opened at Niblo's Saloon, New York, on that date. In October they were on the road again with Eugene, Cool White, J. A. Herman, Lothian, J. Reeves, S. C. Campbell, G. W. H. Griffin, J. K. Edwards, A. J. Hobbs, E. Byron Christy, J. Hilliard, and Master Gus Howard. The quartette of this company become justly celebrated and we doubt if it has ever been surpassed in artistic excellence. It included Herman, Coes, C. S. Campbell, and G. W. H. Griffin. Gustave Bideaux opened January 30, 1860. Owing to some misunderstanding between Christy and Hooley as to the proprietorship of the concern, they separated January 28, 1860. Hooley started a troupe on the road and Christy remained at Niblo's Saloon. W. White was interlocutor and M. C. Campbell, balladist. Billy Arlington appeared in March and W. White sailed for California March 5 to attend to some private business. The company closed at Niblo's Saloon July 28 and opened in Philadelphia at the National Theatre. They made a Southern tour with the following people: George Christy, manager; Frank Tryon, treasurer; John P. Smith, agent; E. Kelly, ballads; E. Hallam, flute; W. Arlington, tambo; Leon, wench; T. McNally, violin; O. P. Perry, cornet; W. Cross, basso; John Felk, second violin; Julian Clairville, piano; and Master Willie, jig. They were in Charleston, S.C., the night of the evacuation of Fort Moultrie by Major Anderson. On their return to New York they opened at Irving Hall, in May, 1861. George and C. Fox were on the ends. J. A. Herman, F. Carletta, G. W. Wrightman, J. Bayley, Haslam, Blanque, Master Bobby Lynnes, and Master Leon, wench. Cool White left June 10 and E. Byron Christy opened as middle man. Owing to very bad business, they closed there and opened at Stuyvesant Hall, where they closed late in September. Herman left them and Stratton took his place in August; also Charles Fox, whose position was filled by Arlington. After making a brief traveling tour, they collapsed at Buffalo, N. Y., May 27, 1862. The party consisted of Arlington, Haslam, Clairville, C. Abbott, R. M. Corwin, Japanese Tommy, and others. Frank Tryon was treasurer. During the summer of 1862, Christy occupied 585 Broadway, New York, and continued up to the end of November, when George and his partner, Briggs, dissolved partnership and vacated the place. Arlington, William Reeves, Cooper, Corwin, Moreland, Dick Sands, Eugene Florence, Jules Stratton, W. H. Lewis, Walter Birch, and Billy Allen were in the company. Once more he took a party on the road in December: Billy Quinn, N. W. Gould, J. S. Marland, Eugene Florence, Frank Spear, F. Boniface, T. Warren, L. Jacobs, R. Thompson, and A. Wood. In January, 1863, they visited Havana, Cuba, but their stay there was a very brief one, as they burst up. George, with a portion of the company, came North and traveled up the Hudson River, N. Y., in February; but they closed up in May. They then re-opened at 585 Broadway, October 5, 1863, with S. S. Purdy, T. B. Stevens, W. Randolph, B. Thompson, R. Lindley, J. Turner, D. L. Hargrave, F. Boniface, M. J. A. Keane, C. Hammond, J. C.

Kempe, E. Florence, P. Gillen, T. B. Prendergast, Henry Percy, E. Bowers and George Christy. They closed January 9, 1864. James Budworth joined just prior to closing. His next managerial venture was at the Fifth Avenue Opera House on the south side of Twenty-fourth Street, between Broadway and Sixth Avenue and adjoining the rear of the Fifth Avenue Hotel (afterwards Daly's Fifth Avenue Theatre), which he opened November 30, 1865, with W. S. Budworth, Walter Birch, J. Green, G. Hall, F. Abbott, J. Tannenbaum, C. Gardner, G. Wrightman, Hodgkin and George Christy in the party. On December 11, George Brant, Charles Duval and T. Donaldson appeared. On December 18, Charles Melville; January 15, 1866, Frank Leslie; April 23, J. H. Surridge; April 30, Lew Meyers; May 4, G. W. H. Griffin; June 25, S. S. Purdy. And they closed July 4, 1866. His next venture was opening Union Hall, corner of Broadway and Twenty-third Street, New York, on July 29, 1867, in conjunction with G. W. H. Griffin. Otto Burbank, Ford Abbott, Prendergast, George Leslie, E. Percival, Shattuck, W. W. Hodgkins, and James Morrison were in the party. They closed in September.

HOOLEY & HAWKHURST: (John Hooley and W. Hawkhurst) opened Hooley's Opera House, Brooklyn, September. 2, 1872, with the following party: James H. Budworth, Dick Ralph, Canfield, Baker, Andy Collom, McPhail, J. B. Carter, H. Williams, T. Waddee and Sig. Constantine. Fayette Welch appeared September 9; McKee & Rogers September 30; G. W. Griffin and Oberist appeared December 2, 1872, on which occasion Griffin assumed the management. De Angelis and Hughes were the end men. S. S. Purdy appeared December 16. The next managers were Griffin & Little, who commenced their campaign December 14, 1874, with Harry Talbot, Hawley, O'Rourky, Murphy, Shannon, and Thomas Hedges, Frank Gayton, Burton Stanley and others. They closed abruptly January 8, 1875.

HOOLEY & RICE'S MINSTRELS: [See HOOLEY'S MINSTRELS] opened in Brooklyn on February 5, 1877. A variety entertainment was added in which W. W. Newcomb, Little Mac, Baker, Doyle and others appeared. They closed on February 17, and traveled. During the matinee performance on February 17, W. W. Newcomb fell on the stage and broke his leg.

HOOLEY'S MINSTRELS: opened at Stuyvesant Institute, Broadway, opposite Bond Street, New York, on October 28, 1861. Hooley and G. W. H. Griffin were the proprietors. The party comprised the following performers: G. W. H. Griffin, R. M. Hooley, Charley Fox, Dave Reed, Joe Childs, T. McAnally, E. J. Melville, George Gray, and J. Malone. Billy Arlington joined shortly after. Early in the spring of 1862 the party made a traveling tour and returned to New York June 7 for a brief stay. They visited Philadelphia, where they opened June 16. In August they disbanded and returned to New York. In September, 1862, Hooley opened the Opera House, corner of Court and Remsen Streets, Brooklyn: R. L. Hooley, manager; T. B. Prendergast, stage manager; Gustave Percy (Geary), Prof. Straub, Charley Neil, George Rae, Master Eddy, J. P. Wernig, Archie Hughes, Tim Hayes, J. H. Hilton, George Wrightman, T. McAnally, J. Hemple, and V. Sambamani. J. Bryant and Johnny Booker appeared late in October; also E. N. Slocum. E. Bowers joined them in December. On June 1, 1863, George Christy joined and on June 29 Mert Sexton appeared. G. W. H.

Griffin joined October 5, 1863. Hooley's Opera House in Brooklyn was destroyed by fire May 12, 1865. The performers lost nearly, if not all, their entire wardrobe and instruments. The company then went on a traveling tour. They re-opened in Brooklyn at their new Opera house (which had been rebuilt), September 4, 1865, with the following company: George Christy, Tony Denier, G. W. H. Griffin, J. K. Campbell, Denny Gallagher, J. A. Herrman, George H. Charles, George H. Parkerson, L. Stanwood, J. W. Sandford, L. Collins, A. Goodwin, Tannenbaum, C. Gardner, Mons. Bauch, A. Ziln, T. R. Deverell, D. Willis, J. Williams, J. Bauchman, J. Conway, Peter Ally, and B. Northrop. Christy and Gallagher occupied the ends. E. Warden, after an absence of six years from America, returned May 9, 1866, and opened with Hooley's, May 14. Frank Girard opened the same date as interlocutor. John Mulligan joined the same season. Mr. Hooley commenced his next season on September 21, 1867, with the following company: Cool Burgess, Hank Mudge, R. Davis (first appearance in America), J. R. Ricci, Archie Hughes, Louis Nevers, Dave Reed, Dick Carroll, J. W. Glenn, E. Edwards, T. Deverell, H. Goodwin, W. Bell, E. Florence, T. Joseph, C. Thomas, A. Walters, C. Irving, Cool White, and H. Schwicardi. The season terminated June 6, 1868. Mr. Hooley then leased the Seventh Street Opera House on Seventh Street between Market and Arch Streets, Philadelphia, which he opened June 15, 1868, with his Brooklyn company. He closed in Philadelphia, July 18, and re-opened in Brooklyn, July 20. He re-opened the Seventh Street house, Philadelphia, September 7, 1868. Archie Hughes, S. S. Purdy, Charles Reynolds, Billy West, Sheridan and Mack, George Leslie, J. W. Hilton, Cool White and others were in the company. Mr. Hooley re-opened his house in Brooklyn on the same night---September 7, 1868, with George F. McDonald (interlocutor), Prof. Cornu, R. M. Carroll, C. L. Pierson, John Mulligan, Dave Reed, J. K. Campbell, J. W. Glenn, Percival, Louis Nevers, F. Shattuck, Fred Abbott, Steve Rogers and John Savori. Mr. Hooley closed his Philadelphia house on October 17, 1868, the speculation proving a bad one. His next venture was the old Odeon, Williamsburgh, L. I., which he leased; and after handsomely refitting the place, opened it as Hooley's Opera House, October 19, 1868, with Archie Hughes and Purdy on the end, Cool White in the middle, J. K. Emmett, Ricardo, Billy West, T. H. Jefferson, and others in the company. Dave Reed closed a year's engagement with this party, April 3, 1869, and was married (the second time) on the 4th and went on a pleasure trip. This party re-opened in Brooklyn, June 28, 1869, with Add Ryman, bones; John Collins, tambo; Cool White, middle man; Leslie, Templeton, Glenn, McPhail, Prof. Cornu, John and Joseph Trigg, Peter Ali, M. Risley, Andy McKee, Johnny Quinn, Myron Lewis, and others. Mr. Hooley re-opened in Brooklyn for his eighth season on September 4, 1869. Dick Ralph, Fayette Welch, tambo; Billy Rice, bones; and Cooper and Fields were in the company. The season closed June 11, 1870. Mr. Hooley leased Bryon Hall, 80 South Clark Street, Chicago, July, 1870, and at once commenced altering it into a first class minstrel hall. He also purchased a block of stores in Madison, Wis., known as Dayton Block (once the site of the post office), which he converted into an opera house. He commenced his ninth season in Brooklyn, September 5, 1870, with the following company: Charley White, G. W. H. Griffin, William Sheppard,

William Rice, Otto Burbank, J. K. Campbell, George Powers, J. Johnson, Fred Abbott, Frank Campbell, J. A. Basquin, W. Howard, Barron, Lester, Prof. Cornu, and others. He closed in Brooklyn on December 26, 1870. He opened his new opera house in Chicago January 1, 1874, with a first class party: Richard M. Hooley, proprietor; Charles T. White, business manager; A. L. Parkes, advertising manager; G. W. H. Griffin, stage manager; James Unsworth, John Mulligan, James Johnson, George Powers, William Rice, J. K. Campbell, J. Corwin, W. Butler, J. A. Basquin, J. Brandisi, William Freeth, C. Nichols, F.. Cardella, Beeler, Guilo, Hinchelie, Rick and Rick, and Heiser. The season closed May 20, 1871. They were burned out October, 1871. Mr. Hooley closed his Brooklyn house, June 1, 1872, and traveled for two weeks, producing the burlesques of "Divorced," "Black Crook," and "Article 48." He opened in Brooklyn for the summer on June 17. J. W. Clark, banjoist, was added to the company. Mr. Hooley leased the Globe Theatre, Chicago, July 22, 1872, with John Mulligan, Billy Rice, Cool White, Archie Hayes, F. B. Naylor, Charles Hunneman, Frank Bowles, W. P. Grier, D, S. Vernon, Hurley, and Marr. They closed in Chicago August 17, 1872, and went traveling. Then re-opened in Brooklyn, December 18, 1872, with Cool White, Unsworth, Eugene, Don Pedro Dorego, Stiles, Phelps, D. S. Vernon, J. H. Cook, J. Basquin, E. Cornu, F. Bader, Sig. Lapini, R. W. Harrington, J. Martin, W. P. Grier, A. McKown, Surridge, T. Deverell, J. Badger, and R. McNally. Mr. Hooley commenced his season of 1875-76 in Brooklyn, November 15, with Frank Moran, Archie Hughes, Billy Courtright, William Gray, Brockway, Add Weaver, E. M. Hall, W. H. Norton, Bernardo, James Lamont J. Kelly, C. Foster, G. Stanton, E. Cook, T. M. Palmer, T. Deverell and others. On November 22, Dave Reed took the bone end in place of Archie Hughes. On December 18, 1875, Cool White, J. A. Herrman and J. W. McAndrews appeared, and the season closed in February, 1876. Hooley then visited Chicago, opening the New Chicago Theatre, Clark Street near Randolph, May 1, 1876. In the company were E. M. Hall, Percy Ashton, Charles Benedict, Bobby Newcomb, Bernardo, Billy Rice, J. Lamont, John Hart, Murphy, Morton, Little Mac, Brockway, Garatagua, McAndrews, King and Drew. John Hart occupied one end for a few nights, when E. M. Hall assumed that department. On May 22, Pat Rooney and Bob Hart appeared. They closed there June 17 and the party went to Cincinnati. They re-opened in Chicago (at the same house) August 7 and the house was called "The Minstrel Palace." Billy Rice was business manager; Cool White, stage manager; and the following people were in the company: E. M. Kayne, J. W. Martin, George S. Knight, John Hart, Johnson, Bruno and others. They closed there November 23 and opened in Brooklyn November 27. Fayette Welch and Billy Rice on the ends; Cool White, interlocutor. They closed there January 6, 1877. After a brief traveling tour they re-opened in Brooklyn January 15 with Karl Steele, Bernardo, Charles Sutton, Baker, Doyle and others. Hooley next associated himself with Billy Rice and they opened the Third Avenue Theatre, New York, January 29, with a party called HOOLEY & RICE'S MINSTRELS.

HOPPER & BROS.' MINSTRELS: consisted of A. C. Miller, John Cole, C. Williams, James Canada, A. Hopper, C. Hopper, and Little Alice. The party traveled through Michigan in October, 1861, and in the summer traveled and performed under canvas. In September, 1862, a re-organization took place, when the party consisted of Abe T. Hopper, Jerry Hopper, Charles Meyatt, Ed Smith, Hank Wild, Charles Nicholls, Ed Tophoff, Mr. and Mrs. A. C. Miller, Carrie Walbey, La Petite Jennie, and Mons. Laurent.

HORN & BACKUS' MINSTRELS: composed of the principal members of the company that had been playing at the Lyceum Theatre, San Francisco, organized and started in March, 1859, for a tour of the interior.

HORN & COLLINS' MINSTRELS: organized in December, 1878, for a trip through New Jersey. They consisted of Eph Horn Jr., Harry Brown, Walter Wray, Add Collins, Al Mortimer, Charles Price and W. L. Hirst.

HORN AND NEWCOMB: organized a band and opened in Bridgeport, Conn., April 8, 1863, and made a tour East. The party consisted of Horn, Newcomb, Walter Birch, J. Hilton, J. F. Dunnie, W. H. Lewis (William Henry Rice), W. T. Emerson, L. H. West, Thomas Simpson, J. H. Kellogg, R. A. Perry, William St. Clair, W. Rice, and Little Bobby. Philo Clark was agent. They located at Smith & Ditson's Hall, Cincinnati, Ohio, in July, where Eph Horn left them, and the proprietorship devolved upon Newcomb alone. He started on a traveling tour with the party, and they were called NEWCOMB'S MINSTRELS.

HORN'S (EPH) TROUPE: who, after an absence of eighteen months on the Pacific Coast with the San Francisco Minstrels, Eph returned to Philadelphia in July, 1856, and, organizing a band, he opened July 7 at the Arch Street Theatre, that city. Sam Sharpley, Cluskey, Conrad, Paul Berger, Keisler, Penn Lehr, F. Solomon, Thompson, Simmons, and Read. In the spring of 1857, he organized a band and traveled with Sloat & Sheppard's Circus through Michigan during the summer months. He appeared with this circus as clown in May. This troupe closed in the fall of 1857.

HORN'S MINSTRELS: (not Eph Horn) organized in Boston in February, 1859: John Killeen, banjo; George W. Burton, bones; Malory, tambo; Knapp, jig; and John Green, tenor.

HOWARD & O'BRIEN'S MINSTRELS: gave their first performance on November 18, 1873, in Batavia, Ohio. C. P. Howard, Dan Kinkel Jr., Harry Nilson, Harry E. Pike, Harry Osborn, Joseph E. Manning, Dan Kinkel Sr., and Tony Backus were in the company.

HOWARD'S EUTERPEAN MINSTRELS: opened in Detroit, Mich., in July, 1858, under the management of Frank Howe. They then went traveling. T. Gilligan, Dick Berthelon, Frank Howard, William Allen, J. H. Horsie, Herr Lyle, Herr Odell, George Wilson, L. J. Donnelly, C. Sanford, Prof. Spiegle, William Allen, and T. Clifford. They afterwards made a tour and returned to Detroit.

HUNTLEY'S (J. T.) MINSTRELS: opened in Philadelphia in April, 1859, with David and J. Wambold, John Daley and Willie Roome in the party.

HUNTLEY'S MINSTRELS: was a party that was organized for the season of 1872-73 at Providence, R. I. They made a brief tour, closing at Birmingham, Conn., October 22, 1873.

HUSSEY & TAYLOR'S "ORIGINAL" CALIFORNIA MINSTRELS: was an organization under the management of Frank Hussey and Joe Taylor, and consisted of Hussey, Taylor, Pete Sterling, C. Shattuck, S. Purdy, Frank Leslie, Walter Fields, C. Delamore, Joe Childs, H. Isaacs, B. Isaacs, W. Sinclair, W. Hearn, Buckley, and Gibson. They opened Hope Chapel, which they called "The Academy of Minstrelsy," August 20, 1866. Adolph Nichols and M. J. Solomon closed soon after, but the house closed up a few days later.

HUSSEY (FRANK) MINSTRELS: was a party organized in New York, and sailed October 11, 1866, for China, Bombay, etc., by steamship. At Sandy Hook, a terrific gale was encountered the first night and which lasted three days, in consequence of which the ship sprung a leak and was obliged to return to New York, arriving October 16. The minstrel band had their baggage ruined by water. On October 21 they once more sailed, this time by way of Liverpool. In the party were John H Surridge, Frank Hussey, H. Sweeny, T. McNally, Pete Sterling, H. T. Mudge, Frank Myering, H. McDonald, W. Scott, and John Felten. After playing in the English provinces, they opened April 20, 1867, at the Paris Expedition in the Imperial International Theatre. Mudge and Hussey returned to America, arriving in New York in August, 1867.

HUSSEY'S (FRANK) TROUPE: was in Kingston, Jamaica, July 8, 1865, among whom were C. E. Collins (the "Cure"), J. Wallace and C. Clinton.

HUSSEY'S MALE AND FEMALE MINSTRELS: consisting of F. Hussey, Charles Backus, W. M. Barker, Sam Wells, C. Shattuck, Harvey Sterling and others, opened at the New National Theatre, San Francisco, Cal., August 20, 1861.

HUSSEY'S TROUPE: opened by Frank Hussey at Platt's Hall, San Francisco, February 5, 1866, with the following people: Joe Taylor, J. H. O'Neil, Johnny Collins, Clinton, Naublom, Hamilton, Wyant, and McDermott.

HYNSON'S CAMPBELLS: was organized by G. W. Hynson and traveled West in June, 1859, with C. Sanford, pianist; George Cushing, violin; Tom Chatfield, basso; J. W. Smith, wench; A. Howard, balladist; and Tim Woodruff an one of the ends. In July this party was under the management of Tim Woodruff and Charles Sanford. Sile Weed was added to the company.

JACKSON EMERSONIANS: was a party that organized and started from Dayton, Ohio in 1870 with George W. Jackson as manager. Milt G. Barlow first appeared in public with this party as end man and comedian. They collapsed in four weeks.

JEFFERSON'S MINSTRELS: traveled through the South in November, 1859, with Billy Jefferson, tambo; Charles Grape, Old Joe Kelly, banjoist and jig; J. T. Boyce, bones; Master William Boyce, and J. Rush.

JOHNSON'S MINSTRELS: organized and made a tour in New York State in November, 1858. Frank Pell, J. Van Husen, Johnny Pettit, Conklin, and Jeff Johnson were among the party.

JOHNSON'S (LEW) PLANTATION MINSTRELS: were performing at a hall, 232 South Clark Street, Chicago, Ill., in January, 1875. Charles Delaney, Dave

Brown, F. D. E. Haight, White, Allen, Buck, Gus Green and W. Muse were the principal "lights" of the company. They closed June 29, 1878.

JULLIENS' MINSTRELS: were on the road early in 1855 under the management of H. S. Carter, with M. Hernandez, Old Bill Parrow, J. N. Pierce, bones; J. K. Campbell, C. Harris, Frank Weston, tambos; Jules Benedict, T. Donaldson, George Cooper, R. Buckley and Mons. Lerommo. During the season Ben Cotton joined them and remained nine months.

KAYNE, HALL & WAMBOLD'S MINSTRELS: with E. M. Kayne and W. S. Warren as managers, opened on April 10, 1875, at the Grand Opera House, Chicago. The performers were Kayne, interlocutor; E. H. Hall and Ned Wambold, end men; Surridge, C. S. Fredericks, Wayne and Lovely. Cal Wagner appeared on April 19.

KELLY & LEON: leased Hope Chapel, Broadway, New York, in September, 1866, and having fitted up the second floor as a minstrel hall, opened it October 1 with Edwin Kelly, Francis Leon, Johnny Allen, Frank Moran, T. McNally, John Oberist, Ed P. Fairbanks, G. W. Jackson, Nelse Seymour, Sam Price, William Butler, Sig. Bretano and Garatagua in the party. Dick Sands, George and Willie Guy and George Christy opened October 8. In December, George Christy withdrew and Nelse Seymour appeared on the end. Johnny Allen left in March, 1867, and William Budworth took his place. Eph Horn opened April 15. The season closed June 22, 1867, and the party opened in Boston, June 24, at the Theatre Comique. They re-opened in New York July 29, 1867, with Add Ryman on one end. On August 12, Delehanty and Hengler commenced. The performances were brought to an abrupt termination on December 11, 1867, by the shooting of Tom Sharpe by Edwin Kelly, and were not resumed until the 17th, when G. W. H. Griffin appeared as interlocutor, Rollin Howard as prima donna, and George Percival as balladist, Mr. Kelly not being well enough to appear and Leon quitting the profession for awhile. On the 30th of December, S. S. Purdy appeared with this party, followed on January 6, 1868, by George Christy. And on January 13, Charles Heywood, female impersonator, made his first appearance on the stage. Leon made his re-entree February 3, 1868. Joe Murphy opened on the bone end April 20, 1868. J. Blamphin, who had arrived from Europe April 16, 1868, made his debut April 27, also F. J. Naylor, balladist. They commenced their next season August 31, 1868, with W. H. Brockway, S. S. Purdy, G. W. H. Griffin, J. H. Surridge, Leslie, Rayner, the Guy Brothers, R. M. Carroll, M. Schenet, Summer, Grey, Richard Davis, J. C. Campbell, Warren Kelps, and Myers. Mr. Kelly re-appeared June 8 and the season closed June 27. When they commenced this season they had twenty-nine people in the first part. There was one row of seventeen, consisting of two end men, thirteen voices in the chorus, interlocutor and balladist. The second line in the rear was composed of eleven musicians, besides the pianist in the orchestra. Having received tempting offers to visit Europe, they closed their season in New York, January 9, 1869, being their six hundred and twenty-fifth performance of this company at 720 Broadway. They then made a traveling tour of a short period, opening in Harlem, June 11. Mr. Kelly sailed for Europe in February, 1869. The traveling season closed April 10, on which date Leon sailed for London. Kelly and Leon opened in London, May 17, with

Montague's "Christy's," at St. George's Hall. They afterwards organized a party which they called KELLY & LEON "CHRISTY'S."

KELLY & LEON "CHRISTY'S": opened July 6, but bad business caused them to close and they returned to America, arriving in New York August 6. They shortly after organized a band in New York and started on a tour, opening in Hartford, Conn., on December 5. S. S. Purdy, Surridge, Brockway, Zulig, Kelly and Leon were in the party. Having regained possession of their old place, 720 Broadway, they opened February 7, 1870, with Leon, Kelly, Cool Burgess, bones; S. S. Purdy, tambo; Sam Price, James Clark, Mons. F. Fraulig, W. H. Brockway, Surridge, Sig. Brochelli, J. R. Clinton, Dick Quilter, Pete Goldrich, F. Meyering, T. G. Withers, J. B. Carter, L. W. Ball, G. Field, F. Lake and others. Early in May, 1870, a portion of the company went on a brief tour, opening in Washington, D. C., in March. Add Ryman and Johnny Hart appeared with the New York party, April 4. J. T. Gaynor, C. R. Clinton, James Clark, and Francis Violo appeared May 14. On June 6, Dan Donegon appeared. The traveling party re-appeared on June 27 and the season closed July 16. They opened their new hall (formerly Dodworth Hall) on Broadway, opposite Eleventh Street, New York, August 29, 1870, but closed December 3, 1870, and went traveling. In March, 1871, they (Kelly and Leon) appeared in a play called "St. Domingo" in white face at Hooley's Opera House, Brooklyn. They closed there April 1 and went on a brief traveling tour, appearing in white face. They then re-appeared at 720 Broadway, New York. In the party were Cool White, J. K. Campbell, Dave Wilson, Don Pedro Dorego, Billy Rice, H. T. Mudge, Devon Nelson, H. Nichols, T. Le Strange, Corrister, Zaulig, G. R. Fields, Charles Pratt (pianist), W. H. Wallace, J. H. Carter, G. Le Strange, A. Hoffman, S. Stiles, Ramponic, and James Collins. On September 18, S. S. Purdy opened, and the season closed September 30. Kelly and Leon then went to San Francisco, appearing there in November, 1871. They returned East, organized a party, and opened at Jersey City, N. J., November 19, 1872. They re-opened their old hall, 720 Broadway, November 25. In the party were Delehanty, Hengler, John C. Campbell, S. H. Holdsworth, W. H. Nichols, Charles H. Storms, George Guy, Corrister, Zaulig, Charles Lester, Agnes Nelson (vocalist), Emily Krauss (pianist), and Kelly and Leon. On the opening night in New York, Edwin Kelly appeared on the tambo end in consequence of the non-arrival of Dave Wilson. J. A. Palmer was interlocutor. The hall was totally destroyed by fire on the morning of November 28, 1872. Kelly and Leon took a benefit at the Olympic Theatre, New York, December 7, they having lost heavily by the fire. Many of the performers lost their instruments and wardrobe. They then went on a traveling tour, opening in Bridgeport, December 23, and closed January 4, 1873, as Kelly and Leon were engaged to open in New York at the Olympic Theatre, January 13, in the spectacle of "Alhambra," to do their specialties. After this they organized another party and opened the Lyceum, Washington Street, Brooklyn, March 31, but remained only one week. They went to Philadelphia for two weeks and then Kelly and Leon sailed for California, April 27. Early in February, 1874, another band was started by Kelly and Leon, with Dick Sands, Cooper, Fields, James Clark, Ramponie, Ned Wambold, Charles Foster and Kelly and Leon. They closed May 30. Kelly and

Leon then settled down in Chicago at the Grand Opera House, opening August 31, where they remained until April 8, 1875, when they suddenly closed. They re-opened in Chicago at the Grand Opera House, November 15, with Cool Burgess and Harry Talbot in the party. On January 1, 1876, they closed and went traveling. They opened in New York at the Twenty-third Street Opera House (formerly Dan Bryant's) May 11, 1876. In the organization were Charles Walters, John Morton, Edwin Lester, tambos; Dave Reed, bones; Huber, Glidden, Japanese Tommy, Surridge, C. R. Clinton, Kelly, Leon and others. C. H. Gordon (tenor), from Australia, opened May 8; Lew Benedict, May 15; Walters and Morton closed July 15, and dissolved partnership. Lew Benedict withdrew in September and John Allen appeared. C. H. Gordon withdrew September 30 to enter the operatic profession and is now known as C. H. Turner. Sam Price opened October 16. Lew Benedict and W. H. Norman were added to the company on January 1, 1877. The season closed in New York on March 10 and the party traveled. Lew Benedict was "given permission" to retire from the company April 21 and William Courtright occupied his chair. The season closed on June 2. They reorganized and opened in Brooklyn, August 6, 1877, with Edwin Kelly, Leon, Courtright, Japanese Tommy, Surridge, Edwin Lester, Tierny, Cronin, W. H. Norman, C. R. Clinton, William Ball, Frederick Willard, and Thomas Howard in the company. In January, 1878, Kelly and Leon, with a small company, sailed for Australia and opened at the Queen's Theatre, Melbourne, with Al Havman and Hiscocks as managers. The company consisted of Courtright, Lester, Surridge, Beaumont Read, Japanese Tommy, Ball and C. S. Fredericks. In April, 1878, they had possession of St. George's Hall, Melbourne, for two weeks, and in November were in Auckland, New Zealand, playing to crowded houses. Their success since they have been abroad has been unparalleled. During their first four weeks in Melbourne their receipts are said to have been £2,200 (about $11,000).

KELLY'S MINSTRELS: organized in Omaha, where they opened a new minstrel hall December 2, 1872, with Lew Reese, tambo; Billy Blair, bones; Thomas Sands, interlocutor; Prof. Glubb and Thomas Kelly managers.

KENTUCKY MELODISTS, PEE DEE MINSTRELS, and PEE DEE ETHIO-PIAN OPERA TROUPE: were the next troupes in the field. In the latter party were F. Stanford, G. De Duke, V. Price, and L. A. Wilson.

KENTUCKY MINSTRELS: were organized in Bridgeport, Conn., in August, 1860.

KENTUCKY MINSTRELS: were organized in Spottsville, Ky., May 22, 1875, and traveled under the management of William Woolley. The company consisted of James Murphy, the Radican Bros., Harry H. Wallace, James Day, Dave O. Lynch, W. H. King, Charles Steadman, Norman Malcolm, Childers and Barr.

KENTUCKY MINSTRELS: were playing at the Chatham Theatre, New York, in March, 1843. During the summer of the same year this troupe appeared at the Vauxhall Garden, New York. The party consisted of Billy Whitlock, bones; H. Mestayer; T. G. Booth; Charley White, accordion; Frank Lynch; Richardson; and Barney Williams, tambourine. In one of the programs of the day we find the following attractions announced: Overture, "Dandy Jim of Caroline," "Get Along,

John," "New York Gals," "Lucy Neal," "Old Aunt Sally," Cotton Plantation and Jig by Barney Williams and T. G. Booth. Shortly after this they appeared at Barnum's Museum, Ann Street and Broadway.

KENTUCKY RATTLERS: was an organization that lived but a short time with Charley Jenkins, Harry Mestayer, A. L. Thayer, John Diamond, S. Richardson, and T. G. Booth.

KENTUCKY SERENADERS: who had been on the road a brief time and laid off in Bridgeport, Conn., took to the road in September, 1859, with D. W. Thompson as manager and E. Cunkleman, Johnny Hanford, tambo; William Dwyer, J. Conley, W. Dowd, F. Hogue, W. Anderson, and J. Cook in the party.

KIMBERLY'S CAMPBELL MINSTRELS: were organized in 1848 by George A. Kimberly at New Haven, Conn., and soon after organizing were joined by S. C. Campbell. After traveling for a while they came to New York and opened at Vauxhall Garden, where Matt Peel joined them. In 1849 they located at the Society Library Rooms, Broadway and Leonard Street, New York. The company then included Bob White, interlocutor; Luke West, bones; Matt Peel, tambourine; J. A. Herrman, tenor; A. H. Barry, basso; Lewis Burdett, alto; Jacob Burdett, baritone; Charles Abbott, first violin; and L. V. N. Crosby, vocalist. This party soon became great favorites and they remained at this hall for a long time. Taking a traveling tour for a while, they returned to New York in 1851, when Mr. Kimberly retired from the management, having made considerable money.

KITCHEN MINSTRELS: were organized by Charley White in 1843 and they opened at Palmo's Concert Room, on the second floor, on the corner of Broadway and Chambers Street. They then went to Barnum's Museum, where they were for a while quite successful, after which a new band was organized and called the VIRGINIA SERENADERS.

KUNKEL'S NIGHTINGALE SERENADERS: put on the road by George Kunkel in 1853. R. M. Hooley was in the party. They were very successful for some time. During the season of 1855, he had in the party Master Adams, William Penn Lehr, J. K. Search, Harry Lehr, Levi Brown, T. L. Floyd, Joe Brown, Theo Ahrens, W. H. Morgan, Paul Berger and George Kunkel; John T. Ford, agent. In July, 1856, he appeared in Baltimore, Md., with Harry Lehr, Harry Johnson, Search, Levi Brown, E. T. Herman, Joe Whittaker, Thomas Floyd (wench) and John Germon. He closed up about this time.

KUNKEL'S NIGHTINGALES: reorganized in Baltimore, Md., in September, 1861, and opened at the Baltimore Museum. The party consisted of Harry Lehr, Thomas L. Floyd, Johnny Boyd, J. B. Donniker, G. W. Charles, Nelse Seymour, W. H. Lewis, R. S. Colton, W. Clinton and George Kunkle. Another re-organization was made in July, 1866, when the Nightingales opened at the Front Street Theatre, Baltimore, July 23. In the party were George Kunkel, John Purcell, T. St. John, J. Fredericks, Master J. Askew, J. Clary, William Gardner, J. Reynolds, T. Bayless, T. L. Moxley (wench), with Hughey Dougherty and Frank Pell on the ends. They shortly after went South. Tommy Winnett and Charles Holly (Keystone Boys) soon after joined them. They closed up in a few months.

LA RUE & BUNDY'S MINSTRELS: were organized in Madison, Ind., in March, 1861, with Johnny Bundy and C. LaRue as end men and Tim Parker, Joe Bates, Tom Wells, Jack Burnes, Billy Jones and George Allen in the company.

LA RUE'S CARNIVALS: See BURGESS, PRENDERGAST, HUGHES & DONNIKER'S MINSTRELS

LANDIN & SHARPLEY: a party with this title was visiting the towns in the vicinity of New York in May, 1854.

LANDIS' MINSTRELS: were traveling South and visited Washington, D.C., in January, 1858. Harvey Johnson and B. Mallory were in the party. They opened at the Athenaeum, Pittsburgh, Pa., September 29, 1860, with James Flake, J. W. Landis, J. Conrad, H. Conrad, H. Hamilton, J. Donnelly, J. Baldwin and John Bishop. On October 15 they closed in Pittsburgh and traveled.

LEAVITT & CURRAN'S MINSTRELS: opened December 1, 1866, in New Bedford, Mass., with the following in the company: M. B. and Johnny Leavitt, J. C. Curran, Frank Dayton, George M. Parker, William Crumbie, W. H. Briggs, N. Turner, J. C. Coffee, H. Frail, James Norton, Ed Fitzgerald, J. C. Leslie, J. J. Barry and Young America. They reorganized and opened May 13, 1867, at Marlborough, Mass. The party consisted of: M. B. and Johnny Leavitt, Harry K. Howard, J. F. Riley, Charles McCauley, William Crumbie, W. R. Sutherland, J. H. Gardner, William Brackett, H. E. McDevitt, Henri Muller and Young America. Leavitt was sole manager and occupied one of the ends, while Howard had the other. In November another reorganization was made and they gave their first show November 11, at Stoneham, Mass. L. B. and Johnny Leavitt, Edwin Holmes, Frank Dayton, E. Fitzgerald, J. A. Riley, Harry Jordan, W. H. Sutherland, Muller, and America continued in the party. C. T. Caldwell was agent.

LEAVITT'S TROUPE: under M. B. Leavitt, organized a party in Boston, February, 1866, and traveled through the East. The people consisted of M. B. Leavitt, Harry K. Howard, J. F. Riley, J. H. Carroll, Johnny Leavitt, J. A. Riley, Charles La Barde, William Henry, Stephen Lowery, Frank Dayton, C. M. Bassett, Henry Aulbman, George Barton and George W. Nixon. They collapsed July 23, 1866.

LEE & TREE'S MINSTRELS: opened in Washington, D. C., November 27, 1862. The company was Billy Hooper and Ritchie Mack, ends; Sim Morton, Pat HcGowan, Jake Cotter, Tom Painter, J. McGrath, J. J. Myers, Ed Burns, Ned Allen, Mike McLaughlin, J. D. McMahon, W. and J. Lee, A. Fleming, J. L. Caster, Master Fred and D. D. Poel.

LEE & WHITE'S MINSTRELS: organized in Salem, Mass., in April, 1861, with Pete Lee, Johnny White, Frank Carley, George Morton, Fred Ashley, J. A. Morrill, and J. Ambrose.

LEE'S (PETE) EMPIRE MINSTRELS: were a party traveling through the East in July, 1858.

George Christy

LEON'S SERENADERS: organized in Honesdale, Pa., and gave their first performance at South Canaan, Pa., in May, 1869. Manson and Davis were on the ends.
LEWIS AND MURPHY: started a band from St. Louis, July 24, 1869, consisting of Con T. Murphy, Johnny Smith, Frank Frayne, J. McNally, Eddie Haley, the Berger Bros., "Cincinnatus," and Johnny Murphy.
LEWIS' MINSTRELS: was organized in July, 1859, by Charles Lewis. Andy Morris, Robert A. Lindley, John Hinctcliffe, F. D. Frazee, James Holt, George Hertzog, Harvey Benedict, and George Chilcothe were in the company.
LLOYD'S MINSTRELS: was a first class organization that was made up in New York by Lloyd, of maps, etc., notoriety. The party consisted of Charles A. Fox, Billy Birch, Cool White, J. Andrews (McAndrews), Gustave Bideaux, Asche, David Wambold, A. Lehman, Albertine, N. Oehl, A. Breitkopf, C. Blass, J. Eastmead, and W. Bruns. They opened at Niblo's Saloon, New York, February 25, 1861. They shortly after went on a brief traveling tour and returned to New York, opening at Niblo's Saloon, April 1, with Herman, Fox, Bideaux, Wambold, Birch, Asche, H. Wilks, Eastmead, Lehman, Andrews, N. Oehl, Bruns, Breitkopf, C. Blass, Master Albertine, and Cool White. Wambold withdrew May 6 and sailed for Europe May 18. Fox joined George Christy's party; Herman also left. Bideaux withdrew and sailed for Europe May 30. Asche was also among the seceders. Business was very bad with the party in May, 1861, which was attributed to the fact of the manager being the proprietor of a Southern publication. Salaries were reduced in order to keep the troupe together but they disbanded June 6, 1861. LLOYD & BIDEAUX' MINSTRELS were organized in New York and opened on February 2, 1867, at Bridgeport, Conn. In the company were Charles Reynolds, bones; Cal Wagner, tambo; Johnny Booker, J. B. Murphy, interlocutor; M. Ainsley Scott, Delehanty, Hengler, Harry Stanwood, James Koehl, Billy Preston, Gustave Bideaux, Walter Neville, H. O. Arelli; Charles Wilkinson, agent; R. E. Ward, Edwin Seymour, and Carlos Fornesi. In April, 1867, Bideaux withdrew and the party was known afterwards as LLOYD'S MINSTRELS. While the company was in the West, trouble entered the wig-wam. A portion of the company was left at Adrian, Mich., in July, 1867, by Lloyd, who had run away leaving the majority of the company penniless and unable to get out of the town. Among those who belonged to the "can't-get-away club" were Charles Pettengill, Norrie, Joe Mack, Rockefeller, H. J. Jackson, William Ashcroft and Prof. Fred Zaulig. An appeal to the public was published for assistance to get them out of town. A "benefit" was given at the hall and the receipts amounted to $28. Some of the company were compelled to raise funds on their trunks to get out of town.
LONE ROCK MINSTRELS: opened in Lone Rock, Wis., March 4, 1870. R. Richardson, bones; J. Richardson, tambo; E. Castle, middle man; Williams, Danforth, Hays and Benoit were in the company.
LONG & DINMORE'S SABLE HARMONISTS: formerly the PHILADELPHIA SABLE HARMONISTS, were made up of Mr. Jenkins, banjo; William La Conta, bones; Adams, violin; Rudolph, tambo; Henry, second banjo; and Cripp, triangle. In June, 1848, they reappeared at the Chestnut Street Theatre. While there, they

produced a burlesque in which George Holman, Mr. Deaves, Mr. Kavanaugh, J. Weaver, D. Kelly, F. Solomon, Mrs. Harriet Phillips (afterwards Mrs. George Holman), Mrs. McCormick, and Mme. Burette appeared. In 1849, Dan Bryant joined this party and traveled South with them.

LONG'S (CHARLEY) MINSTRELS: commenced operations October 2, 1866, in Warren, Mass. The company consisted of Charley Long, Harry Buckley, Dick Carlton, J. W. Martin, D. Chase, C. P. Edwards, A. C. Moore, Master Billy, J. Ryan, F. Paige, and T. H. De Witt.

LOSEE'S MINSTRELS: were traveling in 1848 and it was with them that Dan Bryant first appeared in burnt cork.

LOZARDO'S COMPANY: who had a minstrel party traveling through the Southwest by boat, enlarged the boat while in Columbus, Ky., adding fifty more seats, making the total seating capacity four hundred. In his party were Billy Wellington (colored) and his father, Duke Wellington. On December 18, 1875, they opened in Tiptonville, Tenn.

LYCEUM MINSTRELS: was the name of a party that opened at the Lyceum Theatre, San Francisco, Cal., in 1858, the same night that George Christy's Minstrels opened in that city. S. A. Wells, Charles Henry, Charles Backus, C. D. Abbott, Frank Hussey, Frank Medina, Max Zorer, T. Raleigh, W. M. Barker, Tom Romaime, M. D. Edmonds, Master Lewis, and Mike Mitchell were in the troupe. After playing there seventy-five nights, they made a tour of the mountain towns. Eph Horn joined them January 3, 1859.

MACKIN, WILSON, SUTTON & BERNARDO'S MINSTRELS: left Philadelphia May 21, 1877, with Sam S. Sanford as business agent, for a Western trip with Mackin, Wilson, Charles Sutton, Bernardo, J. H. Stout, the Levino Bros., and Prof. Froside.

MAGUIRE'S EMPIRE MINSTRELS: consisted of Charles Petrie, John Marks, Tom Allen, Alex Ross, W. H. Brownell, and Ida Brown. Clark and Fletcher were managers. They started in August, 1861, and performed through the South under canvas.

MAGUIRE'S MINSTRELS: were organized in the fall of 1855 by Thomas Maguire, the principal members of whom were of the San Francisco Minstrels, including R. M. Hooley, S. A. Wells, Billy Birch, Max Zorer, Charles Henry, John W. Smith and E. Deaves. Maguire took from San Francisco in July, 1865, a band to Virginia City, Nev., and played them in his theatre there with Walter Bray Stephenson, Lew Rattler, De Angelis and others. He organized and opened at the Academy of Music, San Francisco, February 22, 1866, with Charles E. Collins, Jake Wallace, C. R. Clinton, George Edmunds, Frank Medina, Senor Pinto, Dan Delaney, A. J. Talbot, Frank Hussey, Joe Mabbott, E. Naublom, Harry Williams, J. Heating, Prof. Freeman, and Joe Taylor. They closed March 26 and went to Sacramento, but reappeared at the Academy, April 3.

MAHARA'S GEORGIA'S: opened in March, 1876, with Billy Wilson, Taylor, Brown, Charles Crusoe, Charles Benson, Keenan, and Morton. They were sent to

California in March by J. Haverly. In February, 1877, Haverly and Maguire had no further control of this party and they sailed on March 29 for Australia under the management of C. B. Hicks. This party was in Melbourne in November, 1877. They then made a lengthy tour through Queensland and New South Wales, returning to Melbourne in May, 1878. In June, 1878, Haverly became sole proprietor, with Callender as manager. They opened the season of 1878-79 at St. Louis, August 26. On January 6, 1879, they opened in San Francisco. Also see CALLENDER'S GEORGIA'S.

MAINSTER'S MINSTRELS: started from Albany, N. Y., and opened at Kinderhook N. Y., July 19, 1875, with the following company: John Henshaw, the Haley Bros., George Hunter, Walter Gale, Alf Lawton, Ed Kane and others.

MANNING'S MINSTRELS: formerly EMERSON & MANNING'S, closed their season in Chicago, May 28, and traveled. For several weeks after this party had opened in Chicago, the theatre was inadequate to accommodate the crowds, the receipts ranging from $1,000 to $1,200 nightly. Billy Emerson could not stand success and the consequence was a dissolution of co-partnership. Ben Cotton happened to arrive in Chicago from California just at that time and he took Emerson's place and became a great favorite. The company closed in Chicago, June 3, 1871, but reopened the season in that city August 21 with Kemble, Cotton, J. H. Budworth, Schoolcraft, Coes, Harry Talbot, Peasley, Fitzgerald, Stevie Rogers, C. S. Fredericks, James Lamont, C. Markham, Long, Frank Kent and Charles Hunneman. The house was burned down during the great fire of October 1871 and the party traveled. They located in St. Louis, in October, but closed there on December 21. See EMERSON & MANNING'S MINSTRELS.

MARDO & HERNANDEZ CAMPBELLS: was a party made up in New York from the company that closed at 444 Broadway. They went on the road in April, 1859, under the management of Mardo and A. M. Hernandez, and consisted of T. Simpson, musical director; J. K. Campbell, Dick Berthelon, L. R. Crandall, D. Gallagher, T. Campbell, Add Weaver, and Master Barney.

MARINE MINSTRELS: started from Cincinnati, O., October 12, 1874. They had a boat on which they gave their entertainments, visiting all the principal towns along the Ohio River below Cincinnati. Abe Lee, S. A. Howard, Ned Belmont, J. K. Larrimore, John Barlowe, Prof. Louis Graeber, L. Brand, Charles Felix Echenez, Sam Newton, and P. W. West. They closed September 1, 1875, in Evansville, Ind.

MARSH'S MINSTRELS: organized and started for a tour through Pennsylvania in November, 1869. On November 16, S. S. Purdy joined them and they were called S. S. PURDY'S MINSTRELS with Purdy and Gardner on the ends.

MARTIN'S MINSTRELS: were organized by M. W. Martin in 1855 for a tour. Their last performance took place May 9, 1857, at Levering's Hall, Philadelphia, Sixth Street and Germantown Road with J. M. Harvey, Billy Martin, C. Stokes, J. M. Briggs, H. F. Pell, C. B. Myers, B. F. Wiley, John Darragh, A. S. Reeves. Wiley, Stokes, Harvey, Pell and Briggs are dead.

MAY'S CAMPBELLS: traveled in the West in September, 1858, and consisted of Jimmy Martin, Frank May, William H. Silver, J. H. Bryant, J. C. Abbott, J. C. Davitt, R. J. St. Clair, C. Brightmore, E. and R. Ray.

MAZEPPA MINSTRELS: were organized in Newark, N. J., in August, 1864., with Billy Hart, bones; Frank Howard, tambo; Matt Ward, George W. Howard, Dick Burt, Master Johnny, Mark Sanderson, Henry White, Charles W. Porter, C. Parkhurst, W. W. Jones, S. W. Pierson, Henry Price, George Thompson, M. Savage, and Master Moore.

MCALLISTER & POLEY: started from Whitehall, N. Y., August, 1873, with a company for a tour through New York State, but their trip was a short one as they collapsed at Whitehall, N. Y., in November.

MCALLISTER'S MINSTRELS: were organized in Troy, N. Y., and consisted of Billy McAllister, proprietor and manager; Flynn, Enson, Ripley, Reede, Charles M. Bassett, R. H. Salter, Thomas Desney, John Sharp, D. W. Clark, John Ryan, Edward Martin, William Straub and Charles Morton. They opened in Cohoes, N. Y., September 23, 1878.

MCCHESNEY & BRIGGS: opened Apollo Hall, Columbus, Ohio, in August, 1861, with a band consisting of Charles Sanford, Ned Foster, Harry Thompson; W. E. Manning, bones; J. W. Smith, J. Stout; W. H. Griffin, jig; Gus Clark, H. Herman, and Wallace. The company was later called WILSON'S MINSTRELS.

MCDONNALL & DEWEE'S HARMONIANS: were organized in Philadelphia in September, 1859, with Ned McDonnall, Mrs. E. McDonnall, Tilly Ludwig, Carl Eckman, J. B. Jennings, A. Williams, C. Augusta, J. Dewee, Billy Brown, and Ralph Rees.

MCFARLAND'S MINSTRELS: was organized in Detroit, Mich., in 1867. George H. Primrose was in the company, he making his debut as "Master Georgie, the Infant Clog Dancer."

MCGINLEY'S MINSTRELS: consisted of C. Chatwick, Mike Quinn, Emma Perkins Tony Ward, John Cook, Sarah McGinley, J. Wilson, Master Bobby, T. Vaughan, and Tony Ward. They gave their initial performance October 27, 1886, in Salt Lake City.

MCGOWAN'S (DICK) MINSTRELS: with Johnny Boyd, Hugh Clark, Dick and Johnny McGowan, Jerry Learey, Joe Reynolds, Frank Stephens, H. W. Long, Charles Sanford, and Prof. Latine as the party, were in Kentucky in July, 1865. They intended making a trip to Mexico but collapsed at Hickman, Ky., July 4.

MEAD'S TROUPE OF ETHIOPIANS: consisting of S. B. Mead, proprietor; J. M. Warriner, manager and stage director; H. M. Wood, treasurer; and C. N. Beeker, agent; and the following performers: Bideaux, Harvey Paul, bones; R. I. Turner, guitar; G. C. Rich, violincellist; G. C. Stanley, contra basso; J. M. Warriner, middle man; Joseph Breckly, cornet; William C. Wertner, basso; William Walsh, second violin; Charley Mead, William H. Lewis, T. J. Huntley, banjo and jig; Andrew Keller, piccolo; Master Thomas Paul, wench; Little Bobby Mead, snare drum; Dan Evans, tambo; Joe Morris, S. B. Mead, Joseph Emmett, and J. Henry Murphy traveled through the East in 1862. In June several changes were made in the party. W. C. Buckley, C. Maurettie, Master M. Snow, and Master Tom Donnelly were added and the party was called HOOLEY'S MINSTRELS.

MELODEON MINSTRELS: consisted of Max Irwin, H. W. Eagan, Fenno Burton, Johnny Williams, Joseph Whittaker, Bob Hall, Johnny Winans, J. Vincent, and T. Johnson. John P. Smith was business agent. They opened at the Melodeon, Baltimore, September, 1860.

MELVILLE'S (CHARLES) MINSTRELS: was organized in New Jersey and gave their initial performance, December 15, 1860, at Jersey City. The company consisted of Charles Melville, C. Lewis, D. M. Holt, Frank Wells, D. P. English, A. Morris, William Blythe, L. H. Rink, George Chilcothe, William Wilson, Charles Arthur, G. S. Williams, J. G. Van Duyn, George Akerman, and James Gordon. Melville and Akerman were proprietors.

MERRILL'S MINSTRELS: organized and opened in Milwaukee, Wis., on April 30, 1875, with F. N. Merrill as proprietor and the following performers: W. L. Forsyth, Will Sutherland, George Duncan, Gus Edgar, Harry Robins, Frank Dean, Nick Webber, Joe Dickey, D. J. White, C. A. Campbell, W. A. Hathaway, August Giest, J. M. Nathans, J. P. Henderson, Fred Marsh, and Henry Eicks.

METROPOLITAN MINSTRELS: commenced in December, 1858, with C. H. Mortimer, C. G. Foster, J. H. Rice, G. W. Melville, George Douglass, G. Dunbar, H. Thompkins, Add Weaver, and Master Barney. They traveled through Ohio.

MILLIMAN'S (ZEKE) MINSTRELS: opened in Barrington, Mass., on September 28, 1869, with Billy Frear and Zeke Milliman on the ends and G. Green, Master Zeke, Gus Newhouse, H. D. Maston, M. W. Clifton, B. Fredericks, M. Isaacs and C. Muller in the company.

MILLWARD, MC CAULEY & OTES: organized a party and opened at Norfolk, Va., March 14, 1864, with G. W. Herman, F. Welch, W. Blythe, F. Harrison, A. Manahan, F. Newhold, Master Stewart, E. May, W. Anderson, T. A. Smith, J. Gastel, and W. Sanderson.

MINOR'S ETHIOPIAN: consisted of Johnny Minor, W. Bassie, Joe Bryant, Frank Wilson, John Richards, Robert Beale, John Collins, Robert Hughes, Edward Ripley, Dick Shelly, and John Mulligan. They organized in the South in May, 1860.

MITCHELL'S MINSTRELS AND JESTERS: was a company organized and opened April 30, 1855, at Melodeon Hall, Cincinnati, Ohio, with Mike Mitchell, Johnny Booker, Paul Berger, E. G. Kneeland, Maestro Ronero, Edwin Deaves, N. G. Foster, Woodruff, A. Hanley, Master Ralph and George Cadedo.

MOCKING BIRD MINSTRELS: was composed of a party of darkies belonging to Philadelphia who organized and played in barrooms for pennies during 1855-56. They were afterwards engaged by three white man who organized the Alabama Slaves and played Philadelphia and vicinity.

MONITOR MINSTRELS: opened in Vicksburg, Miss., July 21, 1863, under Frank Berger's direction. The company consisted of Tom Clannon, bones; Frank Berger,

Ed Palmer, Master Harry, John Freeberthyser, Frank Small, Cecile Berger, and Kate Sauffey.

MONSTER MINSTREL ORGANIZATION: was a band formed in New York, made up from the company that Hooley had had in Williamsburg and Brooklyn. They opened in Newark, N. J., March 22, 1869, and consisted of G. W. Jackson, Billy Rice, J. K. Campbell, Joe Mack, M. B. Leavitt, Masters George and Tommy, Joseph Cook, Kaufman, Thomas Whiting, G. P. and Robert Barnard, Lenzberg, John White, G. F. Hemmings, and John P. Smith, agent.

MOORE, CROCKER & RITTER PARTY: who, in November, 1864, withdrew in Liverpool from the Montague-Wilson's Christy's and organized a band of "Christy's." The band consisted of G. W. Moore, J. P. Crocker, J. Ritter, H. Hamilton, F. St. Clair, L. Rainford, J. C. Norman, J. Lumbard, D. Crosby, F. Medex, J. Williams, and L. Williams. They gave their first performance at Chester, England, November 20, and afterwards went on a tour. Unsworth and Eugene joined them soon after they commenced traveling.

MOORE & BURGESS CHRISTY'S: Nelse Seymour appeared on the tambo end in July, 1869. Wambold and Bernard also appeared for three nights during July, Backus taking the opposite end to Seymour, and Bernard in the middle. After they closed, S. S. Purdy appeared. Moore's Christy's increased their first part in June, 1870, to forty-one performers. Hughey Dougherty opened with Moore & Burgess' Christy's party May 20, 1872. McKee and Rogers and Billy Emmett opened with Moore & Burgess Nov. 3, 1873. Hughey Dougherty arrived in London from the Cape of Good Hope on November 25, 1874, and opened with Moore & Burgess' party on December 7. Quilter and Goldrich opened with Moore & Burgess' party in April, 1875. Canfield and Booker opened with the Moore & Burgess party July 3, 1875.

MOORE & DEARY'S VIRGINIA SERENADERS: started from Pennsylvania in July, 1859, and went on a traveling tour through the East.

MORAN'S (FRANK) MINSTRELS: formerly DIXEY'S & MORAN'S, before C. F. Dixey retired to private life. James H. Budworth opened September 30. On October 28, Billy Manning took Moran's place on the end. E. M. Hall appeared the same date. Eugene and Unsworth opened November 25. J. J. Kelly left January 21, 1873, and his place was filled by S. Holdsworth. The season closed April 5, 1873, and the party traveled under the title MORAN & MANNING'S MINSTRELS until June 24. See also DIXEY & MORAN'S MINSTRELS.

MORAN'S MINSTRELS: was organized and opened at Concert Hall, Chestnut Street, near Twelfth, Philadelphia, September 5, 1864. They called it the Chestnut Street Opera House and featured Frank Moran, E.. Bowers, M. Bryan, J. Purcell, W. Norton, S. C. Campbell, T. Gettings, and T. R. Deverell. In October, Allison and Hincken were announced as managers. They suspended performances for a while late in November, but re-opened December 12, 1864, to close altogether shortly after.

MORGAN & LUMBARD'S ALPINE MINSTRELS: was organized in Glovers-ville, N. Y., in February, 1860, and traveled with Ruff Williams, J. C. Morgan, W. Nathan, H. Lum, M. Marcy, Mark Deross, and J. H. Foller.

MORNINGSTAR'S MINSTRELS: under the management of Charles A. Morningstar, started from Memphis, Tenn., May 30, 1865. Hugh Hamall, Ned Stanley, Harry Causland, O. P. Sweet, John Rushton, and Ned Raymond made up the party, which was of short duration.

MORRILL, WAYNE & GLEASON'S PARTY: organized in Eastham, Mass., in February, 1861, and started on the 4th for a tour with William Wayne, Charles Gleason, George Hartford and John Morrill.

MORRIS & WILSON'S MINSTRELS: formerly MORRIS, BROCKWAY & JOHN E. TAYLOR'S MINSTRELS, after an extended tour through the country, located at their new opera house, Fifth and Pine Streets, St. Louis, Mo., opening April 10, 1865, with the following company: C. A. Morris, Fred Wilson, H. G. Thomoson, O. H. Carter, Johnny Pierce, Billy Manning, Mike Kannane, L. Cook, Frank Wells, Mike Miller, Jules Seidel, C. Kommefsky, James Barney, Oscar Kress, and Harry Pelt. In January, 1866, Fred Wilson and J. K. Emmett occupied the ends. In February, 1867, Charles A. Morris retired from the management and Fred Wilson became sole manager and proprietor.

MORRIS, BROCKWAY & JOHN E. TAYLOR'S MINSTRELS: organized in Boston in July and gave their first public performance July 28, 1861, at Gloucester, Mass. They made an extended tour. In April, 1862, a re-organization took place, with the following people in the company: Dick Sands, W. E. Brockway, A. Jones, C. A. Morris, W. P. Spalding, E. Miles, A. H. Carter, Master Henry, D. Webster Collins, W. Blythe, De Witt Goodwin, George French, and Stratten. In February, 1864, Lew Simmons and Cal Wagner were on the ends. The company closed for the summer in June, 1864. They reorganized for the fall and winter season of 1864-5, with Jules Stratton, C. A. Morris, Charles Fox, Cal. Wagner, Blakeney, Ned West, T. Russell, and Japanese Tommy. Fred Wilson soon after became a partner with Morris and the company was known as MORRIS & WILSON'S MINSTRELS.

MORRIS, DEMONT & GARDNER'S MINSTRELS: opened on March 5, 1870, at Rockford, Ill., with Ed White, Fred Alexander, Prof. Horgan, Carl Knowles, William Tucker, John Manning, Ned Freeman, McFisher, John Steger, Pete Baker, C. J. Williams, Mons. Boening, S. Andrews, Harry Wright, and Sam Cole.

MORRIS BROS, PELL & HUNTLEY: having withdrawn from the Ordway Aeolians, organized a band December 14, and opened at the Howard Athenaeum, Boston, December 20, 1857. After a brief stay there, they opened at Horticultural Hall, January 4, 1858, and in a few weeks opened at the School Street Opera House, adjoining Parker House, same city. Dick Sliter appeared February 15. Shortly after, this party went on a tour, opening in Philadelphia, May, 1858, at S. S. Sanford's Minstrel Hall. They returned to Boston and re-opened at the School Street house October 18. On January 9, 1859, they appeared at the Boston Theatre for the benefit of E. L. Davenport. A benefit was given to the troupe March 19 at the Boston Museum. They were called MORRIS BROS., PELL & TROBRIDGE'S MINSTRELS.

MORRIS BROS., PELL & TROWBRIDGE'S MINSTRELS: [See MORRIS BROS., PELL & HUNTLEY] on May 14 gave the last performance of the season at the Boston Museum. They started May 16 for a tour, with Frank Brower, Fred Wilson, Dick Sliter, Ambrose A. Thayer, Lon Morris, Billy Morris, Johnny Pell, J. C. Trowbridge, W. H. Brockway, Carl Troutman, E. W. Prescott, J. C. Gilbert, Masters Rentz and Tommy. They, having leased Ordway Hall, opened it on August 29, after giving up the School Street house. Dick Carroll was added to the party. David Wambold, who had closed at Wood's in New York, opened December 19; and early in January, 1860, Eph Horn and Add Weaver opened, followed on the 23rd by Little Barney. Fred Wilson left for England February 22. In May 21, 1860, they started on their third tour, with Gilbert, Troutman, Wilson, E. Bowers, Wambold, Thayer, A. Werner, R. Carroll, Herr Endres, Herr Hess, Barney, C. A. Morris, E. Sutton, Master Kent (Welch), Lon Morris, Billy Morris, Pell, Trowbridge, Brockway and Prescott. They re-appeared in Boston, August 11, at the Museum and opened their hall August 20. In November several changes were made. Wilson and Brockway re-appeared. Edwin Kelly joined them May 10. And on May 18 the party closed their season in Boston and commenced a tour on May 20. In November, 1861, F. Wilmarth, tenor, joined. After another season in Boston they closed May 24, 1862. During the last week of the season Napier Lothian, A. B. Chase, D. B. Boardman, and Johnny Queen joined the party. After a tour they re-opened in Boston, August 4, and among the newcomers was R. Fredericks, baritone. They closed the season May 16, 1863, and made a summer tour. They commenced their next season August 3, 1863, and it proved a most brilliant one. The next season opened with about the same company. Eph Horn appeared August 3, 1864, and remained until October 25, when the hall was destroyed by fire. The Morris Brothers lost the scenes and properties of the pantomime of "Magic Horn," valued at $1,000. All the instruments of the company were saved. This hall was previously known as the Old Province House, afterwards Ordway Hall, and the Morris Bros. had occupied it some four years. The company then went to the Tremont Theatre, Boston, where they remained during the rebuilding of their opera house, which they opened December 21, 1864. At the close of the season they made their regular summer trip; and returning to Boston, re-opened August 7, 1865, with the following company: Lon and Billy Morris, Johnny Pell, Trowbridge, George F. Ketchum, M. Koerber, N. Lothian, J. L. Gilbert, D. W. Boardman, J. P. Endress, G. W. Jackson, E. W. Prescott, R. M. Carroll, Johnny Queen, Charles Pettengill, Aug Schnieder, D. J. Maginnis, M. Van Stane, and E. C. Clements. Trowbridge withdrew from the co-partnership in April, 1867, and Lon and Billy Morris continued to manage the show, while Trowbridge remained in the company on salary. On the 19th of August, 1867, they commenced another season in Boston with the following company: Johnny Mack, Hughey Dougherty, Lon Harris, J. L. Blodgett, D. W. Boardman, Ball, Heep, Sawin, Coleman, White, Moore, Gilbert, Prescott, Jackson, Barney, Kelly, Master Barney, Sheridan and Mack, and Miss Frank Christy. This company of managers sold out their interest in their hall in Boston and went on the road, traveling in October, 1869. The party then consisted of Lon, Charles, and Billy Morris, Master Lon Morris, Billy

Sweatnam, M. Ainsley Scott, Henry Young, C. A. Jones, E. W. Prescott, E. Holmes, G. W. Jackson, Charles Knowlton, William Henry, E. Kirwin, F. Adams, Fred Emerson, J. Humphreys, and Bernardo, with Charles A. Jones, agent. Having secured Wilson & Harris' Opera House, they did not remain long; as they soon took to the road, with Lon Morris as manager and the following company: Charles Sutton, Bernardo, W. A. Barlow, F. Adams, E. W. Prescott, C. Lavalee, E. Holmes, Walter Bates, Charles A. Jones, Billy Emmett, Japanese Tommy, J. F. Barlow, George F. Clarendon, Frank Campbell, W. Henri, C. W. Knowlton, J. McPhail, M. Keogh and others. They were traveling through the East in June, 1870, with Lon and Billy Morris as proprietors. Billy Morris and Sweatnam occupied the ends and M. Ainsley Scott, interlocutor. The party was on the road for the season of 1872-73. They opened in New Bedford, Mass., December 3, 1877, under the management of Charles Morris, with Flem Adams as agent; Billy Morris, J. Garland, Charles Sutton, Frank Campbell, Bernardo, D. Holbrook, the Barlow Bros., E. Kirwin, and R. Melville.

MORRIS' ETHIOPIAN OPERA TROUPE: was a party of colored individuals who gave a performance at Rochester, N. Y., April 26, 1858. Johnny Codey, jig dancer, was in the party. After visiting a few places, they closed.

MORRIS' NEW ORLEANS MINSTRELS: reorganized in Chattanooga, Tenn., December 1, 1875, with Charles Duprez as manager and with the following people: Prof. William A. Tobin, James Lilley, J. B. Jackson, George Morton, James Henessy, Charles Foster, M. Jones, and William Lewis.

MORRIS' (C. A.) PARTY: organized in Pittsburgh, Pa., in November, 1868, and opened at Buffalo, November 2. Add Ryman, Billy Sweatnam, Jimmy Quinn, Rosenthal were in the party. Johnny Hart soon after joined and took one of the ends. Joe Rainer appeared January 13, 1869.

MUDGE & GAYNOR'S MINSTRELS: organized in Pittsburgh, Pa., and left there on November 29, 1876, to travel through the oil regions. Hank Mudge, James Gaynor, Johnny Bowman and others went along.

MUDGE & PARMELEE'S MINSTRELS: gave their first show May 28, 1868, at Hartford, Conn.

MUNROE'S MINSTRELS: started from Reading, Pa., under the management of John N. Shearer, December 13, 1875, with H. J. Munroe, Harry Morgan, Billy West, Weidner, Shaich, Clorne and a full brass band. They reorganized in October, 1876.

MURPHY & BRAY'S MINSTRELS: opened the American Theatre, San Francisco, Cal., June 1, 1864. In the party were the Worrell Sisters, W. H. Smith, Sterling, Corrister, Stadfelt and Edmunds. In November, this party having returned to San Francisco from a tour in the interior, appeared at the American Theatre, San Francisco.

MURPHY & SESSIONS' SABLE AEOLIANS: started in February, 1860, for a trip down the Mississippi River with S. Purdy, Harry Pell, A. G. Cooper, Fitzgerald, West, Stay, E. W.. Straight, and Sprung. In April they located at the St. Louis Museum.

MURPHY AND MACK: opened in Salt Lake City August 18, 1869, with a party consisting of Joe Murphy, Ben Cotton, Johnny Mack, Theodore Jackson, Armest Beaumont and others.

MYERS & LANDIS' VIRGINIA SERENADERS: was organized in 1855 with J. R. Myers, H. Conrad, R. Moore, Paul Berger, R. F. Myers, J. Williams, B. S. Bowen, J. Cluskey, J. Conrad, and J. M. Landis. In 1857 they performed at the Melodeon, Chestnut Street above Sixth, Philadelphia. In consequence of the hall being destroyed by fire in June, 1857, they went traveling and continued on the road for several seasons. In July, 1860, Ford and Smith were in the party.

MYERS' (DICK) MINSTRELS: were organized in Philadelphia in January, 1858, with J. R. (Dick) Myers, J. Unsworth, Paul Berger, J. and H. Conrad.

NATIONAL MINSTRELS: was a party formed in San Francisco, Cal., in May, 1863, for a tour of the mountain towns with Walter Bray, J. H. O'Neil, Ned Hamilton, T. F. Barnwell, George Edmunds, J. C. Brown, and Max Zorer.

NEW HAVEN SERENADERS: were made up July 4, 1860, in New Haven, Conn., with G. A. Ford, bones; G. M. Boardman, A. C. Stone, Barnes, W. E. Harvey, H. H. Stephens, J. C. Osborne, R. Robinson, E. Burney, E. T. Hendricks; and R. D. Gillette, tambo.

NEW ORLEANS AND METROPOLITAN BURLESQUE TROUPE: was organized in 1857 under the management of J. G. H. Shorey, W. Carle and C. H. Duprez. They continued traveling for some time, meeting with success. In August, 1858, they visited the Eastern country with Shorey, Scott, Harrison, Carle, Green, Johnson, Mlle. Estelle, Celestine, and Madame Howard. In May, 1859, E. Bowers took Shorey's position for a few weeks. In consequence of sickness in July, this party chartered a steamboat and visited the principal points in Rhode Island frequented by pleasure seekers. In November, the title of the company was changed to SHOREY, CARLE, DUPREZ & GREEN'S MINSTRELS.

NEW ORLEANS BURLESQUE TROUPE: started from Jersey, in March, 1859. They consisted of Charles Melville, C. Bovee, W. Jacobs, M. A. Scott, W. Herman, J. Welply, E. Harrison, Master Warren, H. Hill, and E. Perrine. They disbanded at Harrisburg, Pa., September 18, 1859.

NEW ORLEANS MINSTRELS: [See NEW ORLEANS SERENADERS] Nelson Kneass, S. S. Sanford, J. H. Collins, J. C. Rainer, G. Swaine Buckley, Max Zorer, Master Lewis, Master Ole Bull, and J. Burke comprised the company. In September they visited Philadelphia and appeared at Sansom Street Hall, then to Masonic Hall, same city, where they remained during the holidays of 1849-50. At the breaking out of the California fever they became desirous of visiting that golden El Dorado and, after giving concerts in various cities and towns in Mexico, they landed at San Francisco, Cal., in 1852. During their sojourn in California they gave concerts in the principal towns and visited the mines where they were compelled to perform in tents, which were overcrowded, notwithstanding the price of admission was three dollars a ticket. They made money rapidly but experienced great suffering and some startling risks of their lives. When the rainy season had submerged the country, they were obliged to swim their mules through the most dangerous torrents to return to San Francisco, where they performed for fifty consecutive nights to crowded houses. During their traveling, George was the advance agent and principal performer. They visited all the mining regions, climbing and fording their way on mules over mountains, rivers, and through flood. They returned to New York in June, 1853, where they determined to locate permanently. Accordingly, they leased the building then known as the Chinese Rooms, which they converted at considerable expense into an opera house, where they produced, with all the concomitants of scenery, costumes and properties, a succession of burlesque operas to crowded and fashionable audiences. "Cinderella" had a consecutive run of six months. They remained there three years. They were the first to give burlesque operatic performances. Their operas were magnificently mounted and elegantly costumed. Eph Horn and Tom Briggs joined them at 539 Broadway in March, 1854. In the early part of 1856 they resolved upon erecting a more commodious building where they could have greater scope for the scenic and dramatic effect of their operas. They secured a lease of the premises, No. 585 Broadway, directly opposite the Metropolitan Hotel, which they converted into a beautiful bijou theatre. It was first opened to the public on the evening of August 25, 1856, with a minstrel entertainment, which concluded with a burlesque upon the opera of "Il Trovatore." Encouraged by the success they had met with in the performance of their burlesque operas, they attempted to give the same in white faces. The novelty attracted for a few weeks but it was found that without the Negro dialect and make-up their performances lacked spirit and the attendance fell off. Eph Horn left them in the spring of 1857. They closed in New York, June 22, 1857. On August 22 they started for a tour of the Western country, playing in white face. They appeared at Jayne's Hall, Philadelphia, in December. They returned to New York and opened at 585 Broadway in December and, after giving the burlesque operas for a while, returned to the old style minstrel performances. On January 9, 1858, owing to bad business, they closed; and on January 11 appeared at 444 Broadway, previously occupied by Christy & Wood's Minstrels. Dick Sliter was then in the party. Their stay there was a brief one, for they soon took to the road (February 27). They opened at Ordway Hall, Boston, 1858, while the Ordway's Aeolians went traveling. They remained there only two weeks, as business was bad. They opened at Allston Hall, Boston, as BUCKLEY'S SERENADERS.

NEW ORLEANS OPERA TROUPE: organized for a tour through the East, in July, 1859, with Harry Sprague, manager; A. C. Smith, S. A. Jordan, L. B. Patterson, T. F. Craig, J. H. Curran, Pete Lee, and Bob Pratt.

NEW ORLEANS OPERA TROUPE: was under the management of Mr. Sanford. They started in Philadelphia in 1849. April 19, 1852, they appeared in the Astor Place Opera House, New York, with Lynch, Kavanagh, Sanford, Rainer, Collins, McKenna, Leibenstine, Master Sanford, "Ole Bull" (A. Wyatt), and George Linguard. On August 12, 1853, Sanford opened the first minstrel opera house ever built expressly for that business. It was located at the corner of Thirteenth and Chestnut Streets, Philadelphia. In the company were J. H. Kavanagh, George Holman, Nather, Lynch, Collins, Rainer, S. S. Sanford, R. H. Sliter, A. Wyatt, Master Schmitz, Von

Bonhorst, and Nelson Kneass. The house was destroyed by fire December 9, 1853. Sanford at once started out on a traveling tour with Collins, Rainer, Lynch, Wyatt, Holden, Cool White, Amici, King, Kavanagh, Sliter, and Master Sanford. In August and September, 1854, Sanford had a party in New York (at the Stuyvesant). Cool White joined Sanford in Philadelphia in September, 1856, Charley White having opened there two months previous. In May, 1857, the company went traveling. They re-opened in Philadelphia, January, 1858. J. L. Carncross, ballads; B. S. Lowen, banjo; and Young America, jig. During this month he distributed five thousand pounds of bread to the poor of Philadelphia. Harry Huntington, banjoist, appeared in March. In May he went on his annual tour. Cool White withdrew in October but returned in January, 1859. E. F. Dixey, bones, and J. T. Huntley opened here October, 1858. The company went on a tour in March, 1859, with the following people: Cool White, Von Bonhorst, Dixey, Kavanagh, Holden, Carncross, Paul, Finnie, Rainer, Perry, Strum, Hughes, Lindsay, James, Julia, Pauline, S. S. and Master Sanford. In consequence of sickness, Cool White withdrew soon after starting but recovered his heath after an illness of three months. In August, 1859, Bideaux, Dick Sliter, Archy Hughes, C. Brittinghoffer, C. Parrine, Dan Gardner, W. C. Dickinson, R. S. Lindsay and Prof. Kreistzer were in the company. Bob Simpson, "cloggist," joined this party in October. In December, 1859, while traveling South, quite an incident took place during the visit of the company to Milledgeville, Ga. While Mr. Hughes, the dancer, was performing an act, considerable excitement was created by the sudden appearance of a six-footer, making his way down the aisle towards the stage; and as he reached the dancer he exclaimed, holding out a gold watch: "Here, stranger, by -----! Take my watch. You beat hell!" At the conclusion of the dance, Mr. Hughes offered to return the watch; but the senator, for it was the Hon. Mr. Tatum, said: "No Sir-ee! I mean it. And you can go to the penitentiary and have your name engraved on it, for the only engraver we have in the state is in prison." In May, 1860, Sanford started from Philadelphia on his eleventh summer tour with the following people: Robert White, J. M. Landis, Sam Sharpley, Dixey, J. R. Myers, O. Perry, Holden, T. A. Beckett, James Glenn, Finnie, Morris Edmunds, Von Bonhorst, Master Frances, Julia Sanford, Dick Sliter, J. Paul, C. Campbell, Abecco, Carncross and Williams. A walk-around called "Go, Bear the News, My Lady," written by Artemus Ward expressly for Sanford, was produced in Philadelphia in August, 1860. In November, 1861, the company consisted of Carncross, Dixey, Cool White, Holden, J. L. Palmer, J. T. Cocks, W. Shackleton, Hughey Dougherty, G. L. Hall, Frank Moran, T. A. Beckett, James Arnold, Wagstaff, M. C. Campbell, S. Hilsee, Archie Hughes, J. Paul, P. Buch, Joseph Glenn, C. Pearce, Ira Paine, R. Lindsay, J. Ward, Julia, Master and S. S. Sanford. This was a double company, as Sanford had leased the opera house in Harrisburg, Pa., and alternated his company between Harrisburg and Philadelphia for several weeks. In May, 1862, he closed and went traveling. He fitted up the small lower concert hall, 1219 Chestnut Street, Philadelphia (formerly used as a carriage repository), which he soon after closed up and went traveling. In June, 1862, the party closed very abruptly out West. In August he re-opened in Harrisburg, with J. Flake, J. Sanford, Haven, J. Williams, J. Woodsides, J.

R. Myers, W. Batchelor, and J. Arnold. He re-opened the lower concert hall, Philadelphia, October 20 and closed November 15, taking to the road again, closing the Harrisburg place at the same time; which he re-opened December 1 and again closed March 3, 1863. After a traveling tour he opened at Barnum's Museum, New York, July 6, with S. S. Sanford, J. Williams, E. T. Turner, F. Myers, J. L. Hall, and Haven.

NEW ORLEANS SERENADERS: in 1846 visited England; and after a tour of England, Ireland and Scotland of sixteen months, they returned to America and opened at the Society Library Rooms, New York, in November. This was their one hundred and sixty-eighth night there and they were then known as the NEW ORLEANS MINSTRELS.

NEW ORLEANS SERENADERS: organized in Poughkeepsie, N.Y., in September, 1860. Mike Runnell, Charles Tilvernsell, D. Atherton, Master Freerer, Mat Greyton, J. C. Smith, A. Wheeler, and R. Sweet were in the party.

NEW YORK MINSTRELS: started from New York under the management of Charles G. Clarke on November 30, 1865. Taylor, Delmae & Beasly were the proprietors. L. M. Reese, J. D. Roome, Dave Worden, Will Pierce, Goff Bishop, and Master Tommy.

NEW YORK MINSTRELS: was a new party formed in San Francisco, Cal., September 9, 1865, by Frank Hussey, C. Clinton, C. E. Collins (the "Cure"), and Jake Wallace. They opened September 13 at the Academy of Music, that city. They collapsed early in October.

MORRIS (C. A.) PARTY: organized in Pittsburgh, Pa., in November, 1868, and opened at Buffalo, November 2. Add Ryman, Billy Sweatnam, Jimmy Quinn, Rosenthal were in the party. Johnny Hart soon after joined and took one of the ends. Joe Rainer appeared January 13, 1869.

NEW YORK SERENADERS: were organized in 1849, and played in all the small towns through New Jersey (being the pioneer minstrel band in that state) and up to Philadelphia. George Winship was on the bone end.

NEW YORK SERENADERS: played in Honolulu for five months, then returned to San Francisco and embarked for Van Dieman's Land with the same company. Owing to a mutiny on the ship, the troupe left the vessel at Otaheite, one of the Society Island group, where the vessel touched to leave the mutineers. They gave six concerts there and then visited the Palace, having received a demand from Queen Pomares to amuse her. From there they took passage on a ship bound to Tasmania and arrived in Launceston in 1850. There they met John Mitchell, McManus and other expatriated Irishmen, who received the Serenaders with paternal cordiality. At that time (1850) they were the only Americans there. They played five months between Launceston and Hobart Town; thence to Sydney and were the first to introduce minstrelsy in Australia. They often had the patronage of Sir Arthur Fitzroy and Lady Keith Stewart. They then visited Melbourne, and back to Sydney; thence far off to India's burning sands and were in Calcutta in 1851. They were the pioneers of minstrelsy in India. They were honored by the patronage of the Marquis of Dalhousie and Lady Dalhousie, the Duke of Wellington's sister. They played before many of the rajahs and celebrities of Hindustan and went thence to Madras, thence to Ceylon, playing in that country for five months, performing at Point De Galle, Columbo, Kandy and thence to Bombay, still the pioneers. They returned over the same ground, playing the second time in Calcutta, traveling in India in the Peninsula and Oriental Steam Navigation's steamer. There were six persons in the party and they paid 20,000 rupees to the steamer for six days' traveling on that line. They soon after closed and returned to California. See also CALIFORNIA MINSTRELS and PRENDERGAST'S MINSTRELS.

NEWCOMB'S MINSTRELS: were formerly HORN & NEWCOMB. Billy Arlington became associated with Newcomb on November 6, 1865, and appeared on one of the ends, and the company was called NEWCOMB & ARLINGTON'S MINSTRELS. Arlington retired in March, 1867. It was while he was running this traveling troupe in his own name that he made his protracted stand at Wood's Theatre, Cincinnati, and that he made olio features of acrobats, gymnasts, wire walkers, Dutch comedians like J. K. Emmett, and Chinese Giants. He opened at Wood's Theatre July 8, 1867, remained open (except for two weeks courteously conceded to other parties) until June 13, 1868, then re-opened on the following July 3, and remained until November 7, when he resumed traveling. During his last three weeks at Wood's his receipts were $26,000, larger than ever before taken in at a minstrel entertainment in the same time. This was due in a great measure to his having revived the gift-enterprise scheme so familiar from 1850 to 1854. At first he gave away $200 every night, and $100 at the matinees. This was increased during the third week to $350 every night, and $200 at the matinees. The wheel-of-fortune was on the stage and the drawings took place in the presence of the purchasers of tickets. The Bamford and Norman shooting affair took place an the afternoon of July 26, 1867. [See Brown's Burnt Cork History, Firsts and Oddities.] The occasion of Messrs. Bamford and Norman's reappearance was also that of Johnny Thompson's debut. In the olio were Bob Hart, Billy Emerson, Frank Pell and Johnny Thompson. Joseph Rainer retired for a brief rest and Bob Hart took his place in the middle. Newcomb closed in Cincinnati, June 13, 1868. The hall was renovated and repaired and they re-opened at Wood's Theatre, Cincinnati, July 3, 1868, with the same company, with the addition of Cool Burgess, A. J. Talbott and Joe Brown. "Cincinnatus," a song and dance boy, who had been a newsboy in Cincinnati and had learned to imitate almost exactly Billy Emerson in his songs and dances, made his debut with this party October 12, 1868. The company closed in Cincinnati November 7 and went traveling. A change was made in the management early in October, 1868, C. A. Morris withdrawing and W. W. Newcomb becoming sole manager and proprietor. J. T. Gulick took the place of Mr. Morris. Several changes were made in April, 1869. L. H. West took R. Willis' place as second violinist; Dick Parker left, and J. K. Campbell, banjoist, appeared; Ned West, clog dancer, left, and Justin Robinson, wench dancer, joined; Fayette Welch was replaced by Billy Rice as tambo; James T. Gulick left May 15, and the company closed for the season on August 21, 1869, at Columbus, Ohio. They reorganized in Indianapolis and opened there September 27, with J. Gulick, basso; Charles Hudson, tenor; T. McNally, leader; John Fielding, tambo; and Dave Wilson, bones. Joe K. Emmett appeared for a few weeks. They closed their season at Bridgeport, Conn., May 6, 1870. On March 1, 1871, Newcomb & Arlington secured the lease of the lower Apollo Hall, on Twenty-eighth Street (north side), a few doors west of Broadway, which they fitted up for a minstrel hall. They opened on April 17, 1871, with the following people: Newcomb, tambo; Arlington, bones; C. Reynolds, Charles Walters, Harry Stanwood, Willie and Tommy, Percy, Walz, Daly Bros., W. H. Rice, Charles Henry, J. J. H. Murphy, H. Schwicardi, J. B. Carter, Surridge, H. Percy, Donniker, F. Meyering, Charles Barton, Joseph and John Trigg, D. S. Lippe, J. Hammond, A. M. Brooks, J. G. Withers and F. Maly. Walter Bray opened May 8. "Cincinnatus" appeared May 15, Sam Price May 29, and the season closed June 10, and they made a traveling tour. They re-opened in New York September 4, 1871, with about the same company. Andy McKee, D. S. Vernon and Jesse Williams were the new people. Business was bad and the season closed September 30, 1871.

NICHOLS & NORRIS' MINSTRELS: traveled west in December, 1859. They had several of the tender sex in the troupe.

NICHOLS & SIMMONS' MINSTRELS: formerly HART & SIMMONS' MINSTRELS, Sam Cole took the end lately occupied by Hart. Col. T. Allston Brown shortly after withdrew from them, as salaries were not forthcoming and the party broke up in Ohio soon after.

NIGHTINGALES, THE: consisted of F. L. Fitch, H. B. Clark, Billy Roach, Master Eddy, E. H. Dudley, E. D. Groding, and Mad. Eloise. After a short stay in Chicago they went traveling.

NISH'S CHRISTY'S: were at Auckland, New Zealand, in October, 1865, and left October 6 to go further South. Wash Norton was with the troupe. On their farewell appearance there they appeared in white face, the occasion being for the benefit of Nish and Melvyn. Joe Brown left the Christy party March 15, 1866, for England, and opened at the St. James Hall, London, June 11.

NORRIS AND DUNCAN: started a party through the West in November, 1868. They lasted only one week. Bowman and Harris occupied the bone and tambo ends. Oscar Kress was the manager.

NORTHERN SERENADERS: were organized in 1844. Jackson, Freeman, Hanover and Robinson comprised the company.

NORTON'S (WASH) CHRISTY'S: arrived in Cape Town with a party on September 2, 1868, and played in Georgetown, Cape of Good Hope, October 23, 1868, and went thence to Mosel Bay, opening at the Theatre Royal, Port Elizabeth, November 2. They traveled through South Africa by their own wagons, making from sixty to seventy miles each day, performing the same night, which was done by no other company before. On February 10, 1869, they reached Murraysburg, South Africa, and reached St. Helena, May 22. On May 27 they sailed for Rio de Janeiro, where they arrived June 19, and Buenos Aires July 5, and opened there July 13. In the company were C. Steele, musical director; Cole and Wash Norton. Mr. Norton returned to London, arriving there October 2, from Rio de Janeiro. After visiting Paris he returned to London and opened with Christy's at St. James' Hall, March 19, 1870.

NORTON'S (WASH) MERRYMAKERS: was the name of a minstrel party that was organized in San Francisco for a tour around the world. They consisted of the following: Wash Norton and wife; Karl Steele, violinist and pianist; and Kirk and Drew, song and dance. They sailed from San Francisco December 4, 1877, and arrived in Yokohama, Japan, December 27, where they played to a fair business only. They left there January 9, 1878, and opened in Shanghai, China, January 16, and remained there two weeks. They appeared in Hong Kong on February 7 and left there February 14 for Singapore, where they did not perform in consequence of Dave Carson having possession of the principal hall. Next, they visited Penang and Calcutta, thence overland to Bombay, stopping at several places on the road. They opened in Calcutta April 6 for one month. Thence they went to Ceylon, Singapore, Java and Australia. At Calcutta, Kirk and Drew dissolved partnership.

O'NEIL (DICK) MINSTRELS: were organized in February, 1864. Add Weaver and Lew Brimmer were on the ends and Bob Hart in the middle.

OAKS' MINSTRELS: had their origin when D. H. Oaks organized this party in May, 1854, for a traveling tour, but their existence was a brief one. R. M. Hooley was musical director; Johnny Booker, bones; Joe Brown, dancer; G. H. Gardner, tenor; and Young Dan Emmett, banjoist.

OHIO MINSTRELS: was the name of a party performing in the Adelaide Rooms, London, England, in December, 1858. They shortly after traveled through Ireland and Scotland and settled down in Liverpool in June, 1859, where they opened a new hall and were called FARRENBERG & BROWN'S (JOE) OHIO MINSTRELS. The party then consisted of J. Farrenberg, A. Humboldt, J. Stuckley, Ben Brandon, James J. Buckley, W. Jeff, J. Wallace, S. Brown, and Joe Brown.

OLD DOMINION MINSTRELS: were organized in Richmond, Va., in 1850, where they played for three weeks in Odd Fellows Hall. Then they went on a traveling tour, stopping at Norfolk, Portsmouth and Suffolk, at which place they disbanded and returned to Richmond. In the party were John P. Smith (then known as John P. Weston) and J. H. Irwin (afterwards of the City Jail in Baltimore and a prominent politician) as tambo. The quartette consisted of J. Albert Allen (who afterward married the sister to James H. Taylor, the well known actor), Miles Phillips (now merchant in Richmond), Lawrence Kearns and John P. Weston (Smith). William Bailey and Tim Hays were also in the party.

OLD DOMINIAN SERENADERS: were organized in Richmond, Va., in 1844 with Old Bill Parrow, Joe Sweeney, John Sherman, Dick Swims, and Master Smith.

OLYMPIC MINSTRELS: opened in Detroit, Mich., on July 14, 1868, under the management of O. W. Blake. The party consisted of J. W. McAndrews, Pete Lee, J. S. Stout, Master Harry, J. H. Carle, J. S. Edwards, T. H. Williams, B. K. Hodges, F. McAvoy, O. W. Blake, and N. Tenette.

OLYMPIC MINSTRELS: opened in Norfolk, Va., April 25, 1864. Ole Bull Myers, H. Walters, Henry Talbott, C. C. Lewis, Billy Fields, and John P. Smith (manager). They traveled East under the management of S. J. Carroll in October, but during that month collapsed, Carroll taking leave of the party in a hurry, leaving all the boys without paying the hall rent or hotel bill. They again started from New York and open on October 18, 1864, with Joseph Wadsworth, T. H., Jackson, M. B. Leavitt, Billy Blair, E. J. Kelly, George Germain, Fred Williams, J. L. Davenport, Masters Goodwin and Collins, J. H. Ackerson, H. Schultz, August Spech, and J. Driscoll. J. H. O'Neil and S. J. Carroll were proprietors.

OPERATIC BROTHERS AND SISTERS: were started early in 1845 and consisted of Dan Gardner, Sam Johnson, J. Myers, S. Cole, Charley White, Jerry Bryant (bones) and Barney Williams (tambourine). Barney also did a single act called "Dandy Jim of Caroline." They played at Palmo's Opera House, Vauxhall Garden and the Elysian Fields. It was with this party that Dan Gardner danced the first double polka in character.

ORDWAY'S AEOLIANS: were organized in Boston the latter part of 1849 by John P. Ordway and they opened at Harmony Hall, corner of Washington and Sumner Streets, December 16, 1849. G. Warren White, Howe, Reddington, Fabens, Gilmore (later known as P. S. Gilmore), King, Colburn, Edgar, and Donaldson. The following season J. R. Hector, Jerry and C. A. (Neil) Bryant, Abijah Thayer, S. B. Balls, E. Colburn, Master Wells and Gilmore were in the company. In January, 1852, their lease of Harmony Hall expiring, they went traveling through the East. E. H. Winchell, S. C. Howard, and H. M. Williams were engaged. Mr. Ordway then leased the old Province House, rear of 165 and 171 Washington Street, Boston, and nearly opposite the old South Church. They opened early in 1852. It was called Ordway Hall. John Diamond and young Dan Emmett joined them. They continued to occupy this hall for several years. In April, 1855, J. C. Trowbridge took a benefit, when Earl H. Pierce, John P. Ordway, Johnny Peel, E. W. Prescott, Tom Christian, J. C. Trowbridge, M. S. Pierce, Lewis Mairs (M. Lewis), Lon Morris, J. B. Donniker, and J. C. Howard appeared. In May, 1856, Johnny Peel, Billy and Dan Morris opened. In December, 1857, a rupture took place, when the Morris Bros., Peel and Huntley withdrew and opened at the Howard Athenaeum, Boston. E. Bowers and J. H. Budworth joined the Ordway's in January, 1858. J. B. Donniker opened in February, Budworth and Bowers left in May, and in June the company went traveling. They re-opened in Boston August 30, 1858, with G. W. White, E. Kelly, Johnny Pierce, Tim Norton, Albert Jones, W. Norton, Ed Taylor, D. P. Kincaide, John Norton, and Master Edward. Mr. Ordway, while managing this party, had a music store in partnership with his brother at 339 Washington Street. He retired from the profession in September, 1859, to devote his time and attention to the study and practice of medicine and surgery in Boston. The Mr. Gilmore mentioned is P. S. Gilmore, who originated the "Peace Jubilee" in Boston. Edward Colburn retired and engaged in business in Boston as a locksmith. John P. Ordway died April 27, 1880.

ORGAN MINSTRELS, THE: opened at Thomeuf's Opera House, Philadelphia, in March, 1858.

ORIGINAL AND ONLY NEW ORLEANS OPERA TROUPE: was a party so called that opened at the School Street Opera House, Boston, Mass., November 21, 1859, with S. A. Jordan, L. B. Patterson, Harry Blanchard, C. G. Mortimer, M. Leon, L. Buckminster, George Thomas Cram, and A. S. Williams. Harry C. Sprague was business manager.

ORIGINAL BOSTON SERENADERS: were organized in Boston, Mass., in 1843. They came to New York and performed with success at the Chatham Theatre. The party consisted of George Harrington, banjo; Gilbert Ward Pell, bones; Moody Stanwood, accordion; Frank Germon, tambourine; Tony Winnemore and Quinn. Gil Pell never played under the name of Pelham except when he was a pupil of his brother, Richard, and then he went under the name of Master Pelham. Early in 1844 this party gave a special performance at the White House, Washington, to the President (Tyler) of the United States, his family and friends. The following is a copy of the program:

FOR THE ESPECIAL AMUSEMENT
of
THE PRESIDENT OF THE UNITED STATES, HIS FAMILY AND FRIENDS,
will be sung the following songs, by the original
AMERICAN ETHIOPIAN SERENADERS:

> Mr. F. Germon .... Tambourine
> Mr. F. Stanwood .... Accordion
> Mr. Warren .... First Banjo
> Mr. Harrington .... Second Banjo
> Mr. Pelham .... Bones

PART I: "Dan Tucker," "Come, Darkies, Sing," "Old Colored Gem'men," "Bress That Lovely Yaller Gal," "Ginney Maid," Solo on accordion, "Good-Bye, Dine."
PART II: Quick step, "Lucy Long," "Virginia State," "Old Jaw Bone," "Dis Nigger's Journey to York."
PART III: Railroad Overture, "It Will Nebber Do To Gib It Up So," Lecture on Phrenology, Duet---Accordion and Bones, "Wild Goose Nation."

They were men of strong individuality and force of character and of immense ability in their roles. The members of the original troupe were men of education and refinement and their performances were most fascinating and instructive. Harrington was the basso and had a remarkable organ of great power and sweetness. Stanwood played the accordion and every evening performed a solo on this little-known instrument that brought down the house with an encore. There was no violin and these five constituted the entire troupe. They played dandy niggers exclusively, did not change their dress during the whole performance, and there was no dancing. Stanwood wore spectacles and played the accordion with much skill. They took a traveling tour as far south as New Orleans, returning to New York in the spring of 1845, and shortly after sailed for Europe with Dumbolton. They opened in 1846 at the St. James Theatre, London, and so great was the rush to see them that they had to give morning concerts. W. White was also in the party, and Dumbolton was agent. By the above program it will be seen that it consisted mostly of songs, duets and glees; none of the present olio style of Ethiopian performances being introduced, but little progress in that direction having been made up to that time. They were patronized by the Queen, Prince Albert, and the nobility, having played before the Queen and royal family, the Duke of Wellington, and others of the nobility at Arundel Castle by command of the Queen. It was here the conundrum was given out so often spoken of. Bones says to Tambo:

"Why am I like the Duke of Wellington?"

"You look more like a stove-pipe!."

"I'll tell you why I am like the Duke of Wellington. 'Cos I beat the bony part."

This was received with great laughter and applause, the duke being fairly convulsed with laughter. The Iron Duke being a little deaf, considerable loud talking had to be indulged in. They soon after returned to America to reorganize and took a brief traveling tour. They appeared at the Chestnut Street Theatre, Philadelphia, in July, 1847, and opened in New York, August 14 at the old Minerva Rooms, Broadway. Eph Horn played the bones; J. R. (Ole Bull) Myers, violin; A. F. (Tony) Winnemore, banjo; Kelly, Chinese chimes; F. Solomon, accordion; and James Sandford, tambo. When this party went to England the second time they were then known as DUMBOLTON'S SERENADERS.

ORIGINAL CAMPBELL MINSTRELS: were organized in June, 1847, by John Campbell and consisted of W. B. Donaldson, Jerry Bryant, John Rae, James Carter, H. Mestayer and David Raymond. They played at the American Museum, New York. Jerry played bones and did the act "Lucy Long." Soon after they organized Rae withdrew and joined Christy's and Luke West joined and took Donaldson's place.

ORIGINAL CAMPBELLS: was a so-called party organized in August, 1860. Ross, Leslie, Rainer, Lascelles, Eph Horn, Daley, and others were in the party.

ORIGINAL CAMPBELLS: was a party so-called that opened in Washington, D. C., in August, 1861. Charles Dupont, Lou Gaylord and Tom Frazier were in the company.

ORIGINAL CHRISTY MINSTRELS: were organized by A. P. Christy in Buffalo, N.Y., in 1843, and gave their first public show in that city in Water Street. In the company were A. P. Christy, George N. Christy, Lansing Durand, and T. Vaughn. They were then called the VIRGINIA MINSTRELS. They traveled principally in the Western and Southern country. Soon after their organization they called themselves CHRISTY'S MINSTRELS. Enam Dickerson and Zeke Backus joined them. They first appeared in New York April 27, 1846, at Palmo's Opera House, afterwards Burton's Chamber Street Theatre. On their second engagement in New York they appeared at the Alhambra, in Broadway near Prince Street, and from thence went to the Society Library, afterwards Appleton's Building, and thence to Mechanics' Hall, 472 Broadway, afterwards occupied by the Bryants. They located here March 22, 1847, and gave concerts every night up to July 13, 1854. Their entertainments there became the rage. The hall was nightly filled to overflowing with the most fashionable audiences and an early attendance was necessary to secure seats. E. P. Christy was the ballad singer. He was not a great vocalist, yet a pleasing one. His ballads became very popular and were hummed and whistled in the streets. As soon as one became familiar to the public, Mr. Christy was ever ready with a fresh one. Many of the ballads sung by him were written by Stephen C. Foster, one of the most popular of American song writers. George Christy, who became an immense favorite with the public, played the bones; Earl H. Pierce, tambourine; and E. P. Christy, balladist. When this party commenced at Mechanics' Hall, the company consisted of E. P. Christy, George N. Christy (bones), R. Hooley (violin), T. Vaughn, Earl Pierce (tambourine and banjo), and Sam A. Wells. In the latter part of October, 1853, a dispute occurred between George Christy and E. P. Christy and George left. He then became a partner with Henry Wood, with whose minstrels he commenced October 31, at what was then known as 444 Broadway. During the last two years and eight months that George was with Mr. Christy, he received the sum of $19,680 as his salary. He left the company and he and his benefactor became partially estranged and from that time George never prospered. Although not related to E. P. Christy, his real name being Harrington, that gentleman entertained a strong affection for him and treated him as if he were his own son. During the season George retired from the company, the title of the hall used by the Christy's was changed to Christy's American Opera House.

ORIGINAL MATT PEEL'S MINSTRELS: was a party so announced, under the management of Frank Converse, who appeared in Albany, N. Y., January 2, 1860. They traveled West and were soon after called the GEMS OF CAMPBELLS. They shortly after were called FRANK CONVERSE'S CAMPBELLS. They returned to New York in March, 1860, and started on the 17th for a tour west.

ORIGINAL METROPOLITAN BURLESQUE OPERA TROUPE: formed in 1852, with Frank West, bones; Joe Ford, tambo; Harry Blanchard, banjo and middle man; Billy Moore, violin and tenor; J. E. Farrenberg, alto; and A. S. Harris, bass.

ORIGINAL VIRGINIA SERENADERS: composed of Cool White, James Sandford, J. R. Myers and Robert Edwards, was organized in 1843. They played at the Chatham Theatre, New York; then made a tour of the country. A split took place in the party, some joining the Ethiopian Serenaders and Cool White organized a party called The Three Dark Unapproachables.

ORMSBY & STONOKER'S MINSTRELS: consisting of Dan Howard, H. M. Williams, C. King, Joe Miller and Jenny Williams, were traveling through Pennsylvania, in July, 1865.

OTTO COTTAGE MINSTRELS: was a band of minstrels that performed in the summer of 1844 at the Otto Cottage, Hoboken, N. J. This party was organized by Louis Schwartz in opposition to McCarty, who had a band performing at Elysian Fields, Hoboken. The Otto Cottage party had Sam Johnson and Master Ben Mallory as the principal attractions. Sam Johnson played the triangle.

PAGE & CREE'S MINSTRELS: were a party of performers traveling in Vermont in December, 1862. They existed only a month. Cree enlisted in the Thirteenth Vermont Regiment.

PAGE BROS.' MINSTRELS: organized in Plainfield, Vt. James Batcheller, N. Lumbard, M. S. Page, J. O. Page, Julian Lease, A. Lane, and Master Lon Page were in the party. They started in January, 1863.

PAGE'S MINSTRELS: organized and traveled in New Jersey in April, 1860.

PALMETTOS, THE: was a band organized in Savannah, Ga., in January, 1861, with J. Murphy, bones; B. L. Jackson, W. Darrall, W. Hill, F. Leslie, Johnny Lewis, and old Alex Kreuse, tambo.

PARROW'S MINSTRELS: were organized in Richmond, Va., in 1851 with old Bill Parrow, tambo; John P. Smith, bones; John Lacey, Tim Hays, John P. Smith, and Parrow, the quartette. They opened in Lynchburg, where they played a week and then disbanded. William Parrow was stabbed at Lebanon, Tenn., November 21, 1870, by an Indian, a student at the Cumberland University in that town, and Parrow died the day following. See HAYWORTH AND HORTON'S MINSTRELS and HERNANDEZ & SMITH'S MINSTRELS.

PAUL & SLOCUM'S PARTY: made a traveling tour through the East in April, 1859, with Frank Rivers, Maldin, Wright, A. K. Miller, Billy Sortet, and Master Thomas.

PEEL'S (MATT) MINSTRELS: was organized in May, 1857, and made a brief tour in the West. The party soon after took the name of Peel & Huntley. Master Arnold, Young "Ole Bull," Charles Palmer, H. Arnold, and J. Lyon were added. Farrenberg left for Europe in June. The company returned to New York for a while but closed in July and went on the road. On the 11th of October they reorganized in New York for a tour through the East and opened in New Haven, Conn., with Adams, ballads; T. J. Peel, jig; Mert Sexton and others. In a few days A. M. Hernandez, who had left Sniffin's Minstrels, joined; but left equally as abruptly and returned to Sniffin. In a few weeks R. Abecco, Max Irwin, Paul Berger, E. C. Huntley, W. Low and R. Perry were added. In December they visited the Eastern towns with Matt Peel, G. W. Moore, Mert Sexton, T. J. Peel, G. G. Minor, A. M. Hernandez, J. B. Donniker, F. B. Converse, L. Condis, J. Brown, J. Farrenberg, J. Adams, R. Abecco, E. H. Winchell, and E. Page. In February, 1858, they made a tour of the South and were called MATT PEEL'S CAMPBELLS. When Matt Peel died, Mert Sexton took his place and the party closed up May 9 and returned to New York.

PEEL'S (MRS. MATT) CAMPBELLS: organized in New York in September, 1859, and made a traveling tour through the East, opening in New London, Conn., September 27. J. T. Huntley was the manager. The party then went South and, in November, J. Pearce, E. N. Slocum, Add Weaver, Little Barney, August Sontz, and Frank Converse were in the party. On January 23, 1860, the party consisted of L. Reese, J. Neil, Dave Reed, J. M. Byer and E. Coles. They opened at the Chatham (late National) Theatre, New York, having taken a brief rest in New York previous to opening. Charley Whit appeared there with the company. Business was not good and they closed late in January. In February the company left for a tour through the South. In May, S. Price and Frank Peel occupied the ends. In June, Charles Melville was the tenor. In July, 1861, a re-organization was made, excepting Price and Walsh, and they opened in Chicago, May 17. Ben Cotten joined them in August and the party then consisted of J. T. Huntley, George Winship, J. W. Andrews, A. J. Talbot, J. V. Chadduck, Joe Gibbs, Frank Beeler, Walsh, Price, and Brekport. George Massett and J. L. Stout left them in July in Chicago. The party located in Chicago in October for the winter and G. Bishop, G. Bideaux, James Wambold, J. Winship, Theodore Duvergne, Walter Saunders, Theodore Merkes, Fred Graham, Eugene Albertine, Matt Thompson, Barry Coyne, Frank Massett, and August Watson comprised the company. In February, 1862, several changes were made in the company. Add Weaver, Master Barney and others joined.

PELHAM'S (GIL W.) MINSTRELS: consisted of Barney Williams, Little Bobby Williams, "Jawbone" Daniels, Robert Hoffman, and Dick Sliter. They commenced a traveling tour in 1846.

PELHAM'S (PHIL) MINSTRELS: organized in Portsmouth, N. H., where they opened on March 12, 1863. Phil Pelham, tambo; E. L. Dunbar, bones; J. H. Long, banjo; L. M. Devereaux, Ned Kelton, Frank Morse, A. M. King, R. P. Danforth, M. J. Blake and E. H. Bond constituted the organization.

PELHAM'S TROUPE: opened in Boston at the Melodeon, July 21, 1856.

PENNINGTON'S SERENADERS: occupied Concert Hall, Albany, N. Y., in January, 1861, with T. Hutchinson, D. M. Holt, J. P. English, T. Pennington, C. Lewis, and J. Campbell.

PERHAM'S OPERA TROUPE: was organized by Perham (not Josiah) early in 1858 and traveled East.

PERHAMS TROUPE: organized by Josiah Perham (of lottery renown) in 1850, this party visited the principal Eastern towns. John Mulligan was with them one year.

PETTENGILL, BONTER & MUDGE: organized a band and started on a tour August 27, 1868, with Charles Pettengill, Charles Dobson, David Hawley, P. Bremmer, C. H. Platt, G. C. Bonter, J. W. Hilton, Thomas Deverill, Frank Schmidt, J. H. Hilliard, H. T. Mudge, Frank Campbell, J. Vogel, F. B. Naylor, Harry Wilson, E. W. Webber, and James Deverill. Charles Melville was agent for the first week, after which C. B. Griste took the position.

PETTENGILL'S (CHARLEY) MINSTRELS: was a party organized in New York in September, 1866, and consisted of Pettengill, Glendy Burke, Paul Underner, Frank Weston, Carl Hemmell, Joe Mac, Ed Merley, Young America, H. J. Hentz, H. Blanchard, H. Byron Newcomb, J. Moncrief Ford, H. Freyberthuyser, J. H. Rice, Frank Ellenger, W. C. Mortimer, and Sig. Francisco. Pettengill's company opened April 6, 1868, at Brooklyn, N. Y., with A. J. Talbot, Charles Pettengill, M. Ainsley Scott, Harry Robinson, E. A. Marston, Rockefeller, Carl Ebbcock, Frank Campbell, Walter Neville, Justin Robinson, J. J. Hilliard, S. S. Simmons, Joseph Wadsworth,

James Watters, Julius Thiele, James Grantz, Edward Morton, Billy Reed, Charles Forrest (wench); George Warren, Jacob Bayer, Hinchcliff, and Master Charlie. In two weeks they took to the road, but closed at New Haven, Conn., in June, 1868, for the purpose of re-organizing. They opened in Albany, N. Y., in July with Hank Mudge, Charles Vivian, Frank Campbell, Harry Robinson, Vogel, C. Pettengill and others. C. B. Griste was agent. They closed in Saratoga in about one month.

PHILADELPHIA SABLE HARMONISTS: were organized in Philadelphia, in 1847. William Horn, brother of Eph Horn, was the agent. The company consisted of Charley Jenkins, aeolian banjoist and musical director; Mr. Adams, Congo, tambourine; Johnson, violinist; La Conta, bones; and Rudolph, guitar-banjoist. Looking over their program, we note the following announced: "Mary Blane," "Stratling Our Long-tail Blue," "Dearest May," "Stop Dat Knocking," "Come Back, Darkies, to You I Call," "Come, Sit Thee Down, My Pretty Yaller Gal," "Floating Scow of Old Virginny," "Walk in de Parlor," "Picayune Butler," and banjo solo of "Cuddy Inko Dinko Bim." For voices and harmony this company was excellent. They appeared at the Chestnut Street Theatre and afterwards at the National Theatre (Circus), that city. They were afterwards called LONG & DINMORE'S SABLE HARMONISTS.

PICKERING'S MINSTRELS: were organized in New York and sailed December 23, 1865, for the West Indies, arriving at Barbados, where they performed several nights. They opened in Demerara, South America, February 12, 1866, and went thence to Brazil and back through the West Indies. Joseph F. Pickering was manager. He had in the company Harry Mestayer, Joe Childs, W. Sinclair, J. Miller, W. Clarke, H. L. Parker, Mrs. Marie Mazzocchi, Prof. Gardner, J. Carroll, and Miss McFarlane.

PIERCE & HUNTER'S MINSTRELS: made a tour of the country in the summer of 1854. William Pierce, J. H. Hunter, G. H. Burr, Sheldon, and G. Buckley were in the company.

PIERCE'S "ORIGINAL" CAMPBELLS & FRANK PHELPS' GREAT TROUPE: was organized in December, 1860, and traveled through New York State with the following people: Frank Phelps, Johnny Pierce, Frank Pell, D. W. Collins, A. J. Tabor, W. H. Howard, E. Lamb, Prof. Gaynor, and W. H. Davis.

PIERCE'S (EARL H.) MINSTRELS: were organized in opposition to E. P. Christy's party. They opened at the old Olympic Theatre, 442 Broadway, New York, April 8, 1850. J. B. Fellows was musical director. Eph Horn and Jerry Bryant were in the party. Shortly after, Pierce associated himself in management with Fellows and opened at the Society Library Room on Broadway and the party was called PIERCE & FELLOWS' MINSTRELS.

PIERCE & FELLOWS' MINSTRELS: They afterwards appeared at Mitchell's Olympic for seventeen nights. Eph Horn was one of the end men. Owing to a quarrel between Dick Myers, Jim Sanford and the manager, there was a change in the company.

PIERCE'S (EARL HORTON) MINSTRELS: opened at Academy Hall, 663 Broadway, opposite Bond Street, on December 10, 1855, with E. H. Pierce, J. W.

Raynor, N. W. Gould, Louis Main, J. B. Donniker, L. Condit, B. Mallory, T. Christian, J. Murphy, E. Huntington, and W. P. Collins. They remained there but a few nights. On July 11, 1857, Earl H. Pierce and J. W. Raynor sailed with the company for England on the *North Star*. Nish, Raynor, Pierce, Wambold, Burton, Christian, Collins, Brown, and Donnelly were in the party. They gave a private rehearsal at the St. James Theatre, London, on July 28 and their first public performance took place August 3 there. They were then called CHRISTY'S MINSTRELS. After meeting with great success, they appeared at the Surrey Theatre and in January, 1858, opened at Polygraphic Hall, in King William Street, London. They afterwards made a tour of the provinces. George W. Moore, who sailed from New York, June 11, 1859, opened with his company, taking Pierce's position, who had died. J. W. Rayner took the company for a long tour through Great Britain and Ireland. On July 11, 1869, Mr. Rayner retired from the business with a fortune (so stated at the time) and returned to America, arriving in New York August 15. Before he left the party he secured the services of G. J. Wilson. During the season of 1860-61 the party consisted of W. J. Collins, A. and G. Nish, managers; Harris, basso; C. Murray, baritone; W. Meeker, J. Spiller, Mert Sexton, J. Howard, Tom Christian and G. W. Moore. Joe Brown left and W. H. Howard was substituted. The party opened in London, at Her Majesty's Concert Rooms,

PIONEER MINSTRELS: consisted of Harry Conley, Lee, Walter Allen, Harvey La Pert, Billy McClellan, and Billy Hart. They started from Dallas, Tex., April 17, 1874, under the management of Lew Ginger. They were of short duration. They reorganized under the management of Fudge & Whaley and traveled through Texas by wagons.

POSTLETHWAITE'S MINSTRELS: See BELER, POSTLETHWAITE & CO.'S CAMPBELLS.

PRENDERGAST'S MINSTRELS: gave their first show at the Olympic Theatre, New York, October 26, 1857, and in the party were Tim Norton, T. B. Prendergast, J. H. Budworth, Charley White, J. Carroll, H. Stephens, W. W. Snow, R. Montgomery, H. Wilson, J. Waddee, L. Donnelly, J. Barker, H. Troutman, H. Carlton, and M. Gallagher. Business proving bad, they closed November 14, 1857, and, reorganizing, went out again as WHITE'S SERENADERS. Returning East after a brief tour, they started out again through the East as the NEW YORK SERENADERS, several changes being made.

PRICE'S (SAM) MINSTRELS: formerly HAPPY CAL WAGNER'S MINSTRELS, closed June 12, 1875. Cal Wagner reorganized and started on his annual tour August 30, 1875, with F. N. Merritt, George C. Roberts, John Clark, Thomas O'Brien, Greenville, F. K. Ainsworth, F. G. Fisher, W. K. Lavalle, Cal Wagner and others in the party. They reorganized August 14, 1876. Sam Price, J. K. Campbell, Emerson, Clark, Hoey, Fields, Leon H. Wiley, Joe Garatagua, Fred W. Otis and others.

PRICE'S (SAM) MINSTRELS: See WAGNER'S MINSTRELS.

PURDY & WHITE'S MINSTRELS: gave their first show on May 19, 1873, at the Thirty-fourth Street Theatre, New York. S. S. Purdy, tambo; J. Niles, bones; Cool White, interlocutor; Abecco, J. Manning, H. Wells, Evans, J. W. Clark, H. T. Mudge, and B. Carroll.

PURDY, SCOTT & FOSTELLE: formed a band consisting of S. S. Purdy, M. Ainsley Scott, Fostelle, Frank Jones, A. Stanwood, T. Baker, L. Zimmerman, S. Schubert, P. Boam, S. Jackson, R. Williams, and W. Sidell. They started from San Francisco in February, 1872, for a Winter campaign.

PUTNAM, WRIGHT & MASTERS: organized a company December 17, 1859, and traveled through the East with Joe Emerson, Carl Lambler, T. R. Wright, J. M. Sullivan, Johnny Masters, and J. S. Farrenberg.

RATTLERS (LEW) MINSTRELS: consisting of Rattler, Sheppard, Tommy Peel and Taylor were traveling through Idaho Territory in May, 1865. In November the company left San Francisco for a tour. Rattler, Joe Taylor, C. E. Collins, Clinton, Johnny O'Neill, Hamilton, and Williams.

RAYMOND & WARING'S: the circus managers, organized a band to travel with their circus in 1847. Tony Pastor, Bob Hall, Turner, and G. W. Hoyt made up the party.

RAYMOND'S MINSTRELS: organized in New York and started for Stamford, Conn., where they rehearsed eleven days. They opened in that city in 1846, under the management of Raymond (whose right name was Dr. Burr). In the party were Billy Birch, Hi Rumsey, Goodsell, Raymond, and others. They existed only four weeks.

RAYNOR (LESLIE) & SMITH: having secured a lease of Congress Hall on Bush Street, San Francisco, in October, 1867, and having altered it and made a temple of minstrelsy, opened October 25, with Harry Leslie, Harry Raynor, Henry Herbert, Nordblom, Kemp, Storms, Loomis, Harry Williams, G. F. Smith, H. Thomas, Frank Medina, J. Mundweller, and George T. Evans in the party. The house was called the "Temple of Music." Frank Hussey joined February 24, 1868, and Fred Sprung opened March 2. Leslie and Raynor shortly after disposed of their interest to William H. Smith & Co.

RAYNOR-CHRISTY MINSTRELS: started on a traveling tour in June, 1864, with John P. Smith as agent and with J. W. Raynor, George Christy, A. Buckam, H. Talbott, George Germain, Dick McGowan, William Fields, J. Cooper and J. Bailey. They opened at the Bowery Theatre, New York, July 10, 1865, and closed there August 11. George Christy left them August 5 and his place was filled by Master Bobby (Bobby Newcomb). After being idle for a week, a re-organization took place and they re-opened August 21, 1865, at Trenton, N. J. Master Bobby, Japanese Tommy, and John Rushton were in the party.

REED & BARROW'S MINSTRELS: opened in Cincinnati, Ohio, April 28, 1866, and the party consisted of: Ned Reed, C. H. Barrows, Tom Murphy, Tom Wilson, George Scott, George King, J. Thompson, George Wallace, Domingo Donego, Otto Hubert, W. B. Adams, and Billy Stewart.

REESE'S MINSTRELS: started from New York in February, 1867, for a trip up the Hudson River, with the intention of performing in Yonkers on Monday and Saturday evenings of each week with Billy Coles, Frank Dumont, George Durand, W. H. Elstob, J. Madigan, A. S. Clark, M. J. Kavanagh, Billy Morris, Master Buck, and Jerry Dashington, manager.

REMINGTON & KIRBY: took a party on the road, opening December 30, 1867, in Jackson, Mich. In the company were: Billy Remington, A. R. Kirby, Prof. Heller, H. Woodland, B. Kaltan, J. Decker, C. Gillott, J. Neillan, R. Gibbons, F. Wobell, J. Williams, and G. Decker.

REMINGTON & MILLER'S MINSTRELS: traveled through Illinois in November, 1865. A. S. Remington, Jerry Leary, F. Ransom, Early Miller, and Susie Star made up the company.

REMINGTON'S MINSTRELS: when "Bones" Remington organized a party in New Bedford, Mass., in November, 1862, and opened in Hartford. The party consisted of "Bones" Remington, bones; L. Dunn, S. Hutchinson, J. W. Florence, M. B. Levi, Master George Ross, C. A. Hamilton, and J. B. Edwards.

REYNOLDS' MINSTRELS: were traveling through New England in 1855. J. Edwin Green was one of the managers. While in Newfoundland, under the management of W. Warren, of Lowell, Mass., the same year, and being the first that had visited St. John, the citizens pronounced them a set of impostors, being only white men blacked up instead of the "real stuff."

REYNOLDS, NEWCOMB & BURGESS' MINSTRELS: consisting of Cool Burgess, Reynolds, Wally Thomas and others, started and opened September 24, 1862, in Canada. In November, Sam Sharpley bought out this show, and, re-organizing, called his party **SHARPLEY'S MINSTRELS.**

REYNOLDS' OPERA TROUPE: was organized November 25, 1858, for a tour through the East with E. S. Gray and Wally Thomas in the party. In November, 1859, they were still traveling in the East, but shortly after closed.

REYNOLDS, SHOREY & THOMAS' NEW ORLEANS METROPOLITAN TROUPE: was a band organized in New Hampshire in April, 1861, by J. G. H. Shorey, Reynolds and Thomas. The party consisted of A. H. French, L. A. Boyd, N. Burton, James Clark, John Norton, J. F. Sullivan, L. H. Books, E. St. Johns, William Butler, O. Underwood, and Master Kent. They gave their first performance April 10 at Nashua, and disbanded June, 1861.

RICE'S (WILLIAM HENRY) MINSTRELS: consisting of Billy Manning, Walter Bray, Fayette Welch, W. H. Rice, Charles Fostelle, Gustave Bideaux, R. T. Tyrrell, W. W. Newcomb, Sam Gardner, George Hill and the orchestra, formerly with Newcomb's company just closed. They opened September 2, 1872, at Melodeon Hall, Cincinnati, Ohio. Walter Bray, W. W. Newcomb, E. M. Hall and Cool White joined the party. They inaugurated Music Hall, Cincinnati, Ohio, October 14, 1872, with Charles Bartine, Joe Mairs, Horace Rushly, James Semple and W. Pope in the company. They collapsed October 28, 1872, but reorganized for a traveling tour, opening November 7, at Cynthiana, Ky.

RICE'S MINSTRELS: was a new troupe that opened at the New Chicago Theatre in April, 1877, under the management of George Miller. In the Company were Pat Rooney, Fayette Welch, Baker and Doyle.

RICHARDSON, GRAY & LYONS' METROPOLITANS: were organized in Rochester, N. Y., and took to the road December 15, 1875; opening in Bath with Sage Richardson, Joe Lyons, Sam Unsworth, Lynch, Churchill, W. F. Gray, S. Grant Green, Alfred Clark and Thomas McDorrand.

RIVERS, WHITE & LEWIS' MINSTRELS: were organized in Boston, Mass., in August, 1860, and performed there in Gothic Hall.

ROBERTS & WILSON'S PARTY: started in July, 1864, for a tour with Billy Emerson, George Warren, M. B. Leavitt, Johnny Leavitt, James A. Barney, J. H. Barton, Charles M. Cawley, Frank Wilson, J. H. Reiley, Joseph Davenport, J. Roberts, F. A. Burgess, R. Howard, R. A. Farren, and J. W. Gilmore.

ROBINSONS (HARRY) MINSTRELS: as "The Men with the Silver Horns," were organized in August, 1872, and consisted of Billy McAllister, Dick Gorman, Frank Carlton, Milt Barlow, John Henshaw, D. Clark, H. Clark, Seymour, David Schiff, W. Sheridan, John Crawford, J. C. Wallace, H. P. Linder, James Dalton, Alonzo De Forrest, John H. Polley, G. W. Morgan, Charles Dearborn, and John Ricaby, advance agent. They rehearsed and started from Troy, N. Y. J. H. Polley and Harry Robinson were proprietors. In eight weeks Polley sold out his interest to Robinson and withdrew from the company. In February, 1872, six end men and a lady doorkeeper were announced. They closed the season May 31, 1873, at Niagara Falls. They commenced the next season with the following people: Bernardo, Quilter, Goldrich, John McVeigh, James A. Gulick, Oscar Blakeley, W. H. Workman, Henry Bray, Charles Webster, George Morgan, D. Clark, Henry Grant, C. A. Simpson, Thomas Latimer, B. Templeton, A. Withers, and T. Watts. On September 27, 1873, Billy Gray joined the party. They reorganized and started from Syracuse, N. Y., January 15, 1874, but closed the season at Bloomsburg, Pa., February 18, 1874, the business having been bad. They reorganized and started August 24, 1874, with James Roche, Harry Armstrong, Kline Bros., C. M. Basset, Frank S. Morton, C. Simpson, Frank Welch, Charles Gisling, Justin Robinson, Delos Clark, Thomas and Heeney. They closed the season at Sydney, Ohio, June 26, 1875, and started out on another tour in September, 1875, with Green, Sadler, Oscar Willis, Charles Armstrong, Billy McAllister, Mike Foley, George Robinson, Hi Henry, Delos Clark, John Stout, Hank Walters, J. W. Sells, T. Seymour and John Grick. W. S. Belknap severed his connection with the company early in 1877. George Robinson changed his name to Eustache in February, 1878. Harry Robinson opened with his company in Chicago, July 29, 1878, and was joined by Arlington, Cotton and Kemble. Robinson left his company in Omaha in October, 1878. Several members of the company also withdrew to join other bands. The company as then organized consisted of Welby, Pearl, Irving H. Bush, Harry Shirley, George Franklin, W. S. Belknapt J. G. Ruben, George Hastings, Charles Riggs, John Oberist, Horace Rushby, George Sala, and O. F. Seymour.

RODEMYRE & TUCKER'S CAMPBELLS: was the title of a band that organized in Alton, Ill., in February, 1860.

ROSS, SPRUNG, SMITH & CHADDUCK'S MINSTRELS: who had been confining themselves to the West, closed their season in June, 1863, in St. Louis, Mo., and in July started for a tour to perform under canvas. Alex Ross, Fred Sprung, Shaddock, J. W. Smith, W. F. Bush, E. D. Strong, Charlie and Ned Straight, and Alice Gibson. In December, 1863, as BOSTLEWAITE & SHADDOCK'S MINSTRELS, they occupied Wyman's Hall, St. Louis. They burst up in a few weeks.

RUMSEY & NEWCOMB'S CAMPBELLS: consisted of W. W. Newcomb, Harry Lehr, Charles M. Currier, John Ritter, Charles Sprouse, Alfred Herman, Richard Carroll, Frank Beler, Little Bobby, A. Neitsall, C. W. Gaul, E. C. Hunley, L. Minirie, Frank Leslie, Little Arthur, Billy Hedden, J. Morrison Jr., and W. McAndrews. One of their features was a brass band. H. S. Rumsey was the first man to appear before a Cuban audience in a banjo solo. In April, 1861, they reorganized in New York and opened in Connecticut April 8 with Rumsey, Newcomb, Leslie, B. Braham, Bobby, M. Lewis, W. T. Emerson, Richard Willis, J. Burgess, William Blakeney, Charles Rumsey, S. Manning, Rudolph Hall, W. Reeves and C. Osborn. They sailed from Halifax June 13 for England and opened at Clayton Hall, Liverpool, July 1, 1861. Brookhouse Bowler, tenor, went with them. Unsworth joined them there August 5; also Master Eugene. After giving one hundred and twenty-four consecutive performances in Liverpool, they started on a provincial tour. They opened in London February 17, 1862, at Astley's. They then went into Saxony and Prussia. In Germany they had trouble. The Germans expected to see real Negroes and would not tolerate the imitation article. Returning to London, they appeared at the Oxford Music Hall April 21, and afterwards the Canterbury Music Hall, where they disbanded in June, 1862. Little Bobby (afterwards known as Bobby Newcomb) was in the party. After playing for a while at the Oxford, Rumsey returned to America and started Rumsey's Minstrels on his own hook.

RUMSEY & NEWCOMB'S MINSTRELS: consisted of W. W. Newcomb, J. Farrenberg, S. Gardner, J. W. Adams, Matt Peel, H. S. Rumsey, Tommy Peel, C. Keene, Dickinson, Currier and Donniker; Dr. Jones, agent; and Richard Ennis, secretary. During the season of 1857, they traveled South. In 1858 the name of "Campbell" was abandoned. They reorganized and made a tour of the South, and in 1860 went to Havana. Hernandez, Bideaux, Master Bobby, Harry Lehr, Owens, Stanley, French, B. Yates and others were in the troupe. At Havana they cleared $30,000 in forty performances. They arrived in New York from Havana, January 12, 1861, and disbanded. Master Eddy's (who had been with the troupe) right name was Edward Hughes. It was while traveling in the West, in February, 1858, that they were called RUMSEY & NEWCOMB'S CAMPBELLS.

RUMSEY'S MINSTRELS: consisting of Brockway, Butler, W. Herman, Wrightman, Gaynor, Carter, Thomas Deverill, Ned West, Stratton, Perry, Butler, Master Henry, William Price and Harry Hapgood, agent. In March, 1864, the party consisted of Johnny Pierce, Fred Sprung, W. Manning, W. S. Mullaly, D. W. Collins, F.

Rheinholt, John Woolsey, J. H. Stout, C. E. Rumsey, Ned West, F. Schwitzer, H. Perkins, J. H. Clifford, J. H. Carleton, S. Lemain, and D. Tongue.

RUMSEY & NEWCOMB'S MINSTRELS: See CAMPBELL'S MINSTRELS.

RUMSEY'S MINSTRELS: See FOSTER'S MINSTRELS.

SABINE MINSTRELS: were a party organized in 1858 and made up of the crew of the U. S Frigate, *Sabine*. In June, 1860, they gave a performance at City Hotel, Aspinwall, New Granada. In July, they made a trip through the country with William Wallace, tambo; John Jeffers, bones; Charles Clifton, T. H. Goodwin, William Candelin, Ed Olmsdale, Aug Wagner, J. W. Martin, Ed Knause, A. S. Kennedy, J. W. Turner, and William Whitford.

SABLE BROTHERS, THE: This party consisted of Turpin, Cleaveland, and a few others. They appeared in New York at Convention Hall, Wooster Street, and thence went to Burnum's Museum.

SABLE HARMONISTS: consisting of J. W. Smith, J. B. Murphy, Martin Freeberthyser, E. D. Gooding, J. H. Stout, John and Henry Freeberthyser, John Cole, Charles Sandford, George Northrop, La Belle Louise, and Mlle. Thudom, were traveling through Arkansas in February, 1863.

SABLE HARMONISTS: were organized early in 1846 and consisted of Plumer, Archer, J. Farrell, W. Roark, Nelson Kneass, J. Murphy, T. F. Briggs, R. M. Hooley, and Tichenor. In November, 1847, they played in New York at the Minerva Rooms. They went to England in 1847 under the management of R. M. Hooley and visited London, Paris, Boulogne, Brussels, and the smaller cities of the British Isles. In London they occupied the Hanover Square Rooms, so celebrated as the locale of H. M. Ancient Concerts.

SABLE HARMONISTS: was a party organized in November, 1858, and consisted of T. L. Newcomb, W. S. Stevens, P. Dalton, J. E. Stevens, R. Stewart, W. Seymour, and W. E. Mellish. They made a tour of the British provinces.

SABLE HARMONISTS: started on a tour in April, 1859, with O. L. Elliott, A. J. Bailey, C. Folsom, and Mary Dancy.

SABLE MELODISTS: were organized by Cool White in 1845 at Lynchburg, Va., and they traveled South and West. Cool White, William Perron, Mead Harris, Franklin, Alexander, and Dick Swims were in the company. They lasted only two months, as they closed in Gallipolis, Ohio.

SABLE SISTERS AND ETHIOPIAN MINSTRELS: commenced in November, 1844, with Barney Williams, Charley White, J. Hallett, R. White, Charley Howard, and three females known as Annette, Angeline and Pauline. They went on a traveling tour, appearing at Washington Hall, Newark, N. J.; then returned to New York and appeared at the Northern Hall in Bleecker Street; thence to Apollo Hall on Broadway. They were very popular then. In January, 1845, they appeared at Franklin Hall (Franklin Theatre), Chatham Square; after which they went on a traveling tour through the East under the management of William Magee. The popularity of the company became very great; and, hurrying on to Boston, they prepared themselves for a hearty reception. Before their arrival, however, William B. English announced Lucille and Helen Western as the original Sable Minstrels. The result was the minstrel party disbanded and returned to New York.

SALVO MINSTRELS: was an amateur party organized in Philadelphia, August, 1859, with Charles Salvo, bones; James Salvo, tambo; John Petit, guitar; William F. Brown, banjo; T. Rhoads, violin; Ben Van Lew, violin; J. Greenwood Watson, Master Stuart, and Ben F. Lewis. James K. Early was manager.

SANDS & HERBERT: with a company, opened in Paterson, N. J., September 10, 1866, consisting of Charles Pettengill, R. W. Smith, W. Emmett, J. R. Surridge, T. Waddee, C. Church, F. Voss, M. Solomon, Fred Herbert, T. Mortimer, Sig. Hess, N. Terry, W. Scott, Mons. Valarde, C. Wilson, J. Shaus, Dick Sands, and Tim Hayes. Pettengill withdrew the second week.

SANDS' PARTY: Dick Sands, with a party consisting of William Ashcroft, Dick Melville, James Fish, Mike Foley, Harry Williamson, Master Christopher Fish, and P. W. Richards started in September, 1867, but closed up November 30, in consequence of the illness of Ashcroft.

SANDERSON'S MINSTRELS: were organized in Baltimore, Md., where they opened in July, 1864, with George Gray, Lew Brimmer, Frank Campbell, George Edwards, J. Norrie, M. Wiliiams, Leon Berger, Spigel Blum, and J. Tannenbaum. On September 12, Low Gaylord joined. They collapsed at Cumberland, Md., December 24, after a long and severe season of bad management.

SAN FRANCISCO MINSTRELS: appeared at Maquire's New Opera House, San Francisco, in June, 1864. Birch, Wambold, Backus, and Abecco opened Eureka Hall, San Francisco, September 15, 1864, under the management of Maguire. This party was transferred to the Academy of Music, where they appeared January 21, 1865. Bernard was then in the party. In March, 1865, the quartette of managers sailed for New York, and the balance of the company returned to the Eureka on March 6. On March 30, Clara Day appeared, followed by Fred Sprung, J. E. Taylor (tambo), George Winship, and A. J. Talbot (bones). Birch, Wambold, Bernard and Backus, managers and proprietors, organized in New York and gave their first performance May 4, 1865, at Newark, N. J. They opened in New York on May 3 at 585 Broadway. he company consisted of Birch, Wambold Bernard, Backus, Cooper, Fields, W. S. Mullaly, Dick Sands, E. Haslam, Hays, Ira Paine, Shattuck, W. H. Rice, J. B. Donniker, M. Ainsley Scott, and Templeton. The season extended up to July 7, 1866, and was the most successful one (financially) ever known in New York, being an uninterrupted season of sixty-one weeks. The receipts for the first two months amounted to $14,970, a greater sum than ever before received by a minstrel band in that length of time. On July 9, 1866, they started on a traveling tour. They commenced their next season in New York September 3, 1866, with Donniker, M. Ainsley Scott, Briebkoff, A. Schmidt, Joe Bailey, C. Templeton, Cooper, Fields, and William Henry Rice. On November 19, M. Ainsley Scott suddenly withdrew from the company, leaving his name in the bills. He secretly got his clothes away from his dressing room and left the city without giving the least notice to his managers. W. P. Grier, basso, opened December 3, followed on June 3, 1867, by Master Barney, and June 10 by J. H. Williams, cornetist. The season closed June 29 and they opened in

Washington, D. C., July 1. They re-opened August 12, 1867. Bobby Newcomb commenced October 14. The receipts of this company for the year 1867, commencing January 1 and ending December, were $92,279. This is probably a greater sum received in the same length of time than by any other minstrel band. They had never given a matinee up to this time. In March, 1868, there were ten performers in the first part: Billy Birch, bones; Backus, tambo; W. H. Bernard, interlocutor; Clarendon, clarinet; J. H. Williams, cornet; J. B. Donniker, first violin and musical director; W. H. Bernard, second violin; and Fowler, violincello; David Wambold, Grier, Templeton and Fowler, quartet; Bobby Newcomb, song and dance; Cooper and Fields, cloggists; and William Henry Rice, wench. The eight hundred and fifth performance of this party in their hall, 585 Broadway, took place March 9, 1868. They gave three hundred and sixty-five uninterrupted performances. Joe Brown opened June 15, 1868, and the season closed June 27. On June 29 they opened in Boston at Selwyn's Theatre. They re-opened in New York on August 31, 1868. Harry Raynor, having returned to New York after an extended tour over Australia, Africa, etc., opened here October 5, 1868. Tim Hayes commenced November 2, followed, December 7, by Billy Emerson. On December 14, Daddy Rice's Ethiopian Opera of "Bone Squash" was presented. Master Jerry, jig dancer, opened January 8, 1869. Ira Paine appeared April 12, 1869. The season closed June 12. They re-opened August 30, 1869, with John Mulligan, Frank Kent, Johnny Queen, W. Blakeney, W. Richards, E. J. Hartigan, J. Jack, G. Clarendon Corrister, M. Ainsley Scott, Billy West, Ira Paine, J. Oberist, Billy Emmett, Bobby Newcomb, Birch, Wambold, Bernard, and Backus. Backus, Wambold and Bernard had arrived from Europe, August 24. Leggett and Allen arrived from Europe September 21 and made their American debut September 23. Harry Norman took Wambold's place February 21, 1870, and, Mr. Wambold went to the Hot Springs of Arkansas, where he remained over two months. He re-appeared May 9 and the season closed May 14. Leggett and Allen were the originals in this country of the act known as the pedestal dancing. They commenced their next season August 29, 1870, which closed April 1, 1871, and they went traveling. They re-opened August 28, with Oberist, William Dwyer, Bobby Newcomb, Charles Gibbons, J. Cheevers, Ed Kennedy, Billy West, and Signor Salcedo added to the company. Pedro Sterling, impersonator of monkey characters, who returned from England in October, opened October 30, in a monkey sketch. They closed the season and their performances at 585 Broadway, April 27, 1872, and they made a short tour. They inaugurated the next season at the St. James Theatre, Twenty-eighth Street, near Broadway, New York, on August 26, 1872. William H. Bernard withdrew from the company and retired from the profession at the close of the previous season. Beaumont Read, balladist from London; C. Fredericks; Joe Norrie, interlocutor; Johnson and Powers, and Mullally were in the company. Ricardo opened November 11. Frank Converse appeared in January, 1873, and the season closed March 1 and they traveled. They opened at Hooley's Opera House, Brooklyn, September 8, and closed there November 1 when they again traveled. They opened their new hall on the westerly side of Broadway, in the block between Twenty-eighth and Twenty-ninth Streets, September 3, 1874, with Add Ryman, interlocutor; Birch,

Wambold, Backus, Carl Rudolph, Eugene, Tremaine, A. H. Pelham, D. Barron, Ricardo, Mackin, Wilson, W. Mullally, Bent and others in the organization. They closed the season June 5, 1875, and re-opened August 30 with J. A. Barney, Mullally, Carl Rudolph, Ricardo, Ryman, Johnson, Powers, Billy Carter, C. Warde, A. Bent, Blakeney, and J. Ross. On January 17, 1876, they made a change in the arranging of the first part. Instead of the performers sitting in a row as was the custom, in the center of the stage was a large easy chair for the interlocutor and in front of it a small table upon which was seen an elegant silver vase, containing a bouquet of flowers. On either side of the interlocutor were a single chair, a sofa capable of seating three persons, and two chairs. The general appearance of the stage was that of a handsome parlor. This innovation was claimed as having been original with them, but this was disputed by E. N. Slocum, who claimed to have originated it two years previous, but who did not carry out the idea until the opening of the sixth season (1876) of Simmons & Slocum's Minstrels in Philadelphia. But Sam Hague claims to have introduced it in England long before either party. The season closed June 3 and they traveled. They re-opened in New York August 28, 1876. Add Ryman, interlocutor; Carl Rudolph, Charles Stevens, W. H. Hamilton and H. W. Frillman were in the company. Charley Backus visited Philadelphia October 17 to be married to Lizzie Mason, and during his absence (16 and 17) E. M. Hall occupied the tambo end. The season closed April 21, 1877. They re-opened August 27 with Edwin French, Bob Hart, W. H. Hamilton, Frillman, Carl Rudolph, Ricardo, Johnson, Powers and Charles Gibbons and others. Thomas Wilmot, tenor, opened September 3. George Thatcher appeared December 10, also Bobby Newcomb. Thatcher closed March 25, 1878, and the season closed April 27 and they went traveling. Backus was unable to start with them, but joined them May 8. His place was occupied by E. French. They re-opened in New York City September 2, 1878. Add Ryman, interlocutor; H. W. Frillman, basso; W. Raymond, tenor; J. G. Russell, baritone; Johnson, Powers, Ricardo, Thatcher, Birch, Wambold, and Backus were in the company. That the San Francisco Minstrels were one of the institutions of New York, and deservedly so, no one will dispute.

SAN FRANCISCO MINSTRELS: in 1854 Jerry Bryant, Eph Horn and Sher Campbell organized this band made up principally from performers who had remained there from the E. P. Christy party. S. C. Campbell, Jerry Bryant, W. M. Barker, Eph Horn, W. D. Corrister, C. D. Abbott, Stadtfeld, and A. Morgan were in the party. In 1856 a party was formed for a trip through Australia, New South Wales, Victoria, Queensland, Van Diemon's Land and New Zealand. Among the party were Tom Brown, Otto Burbank, W. A. Parker, G. W. Demerest, D. F. Boley, J. O. Pierce, David Garson and others. They also called themselves the San Francisco Minstrels. Backus took the end, which he filled with so much credit, while Carson kept the bone end. It was Charley's second trip to that country and, not liking it as well as he did the first, he left for California, via London and New York, in about 1860. Early in 1861 the company was under the management of Samuel Colville, when a snug sum was realized by all in the concern. Finally, in July, 1861, the company dissolved partnership, Burbank going to London and joining the "Christys." The original San

Francisco Minstrels went to Sacramento in 1857, where they shortly after had a split, one-half returning to San Francisco and the rest going through the interior. Billy Birch, Sam Wells, George Coes, S. C. Campbell, W. Barker, George Demerest (wench), and Hooley were in the party. They landed first at San Andrase, where they played to $2 a ticket, the house being crowded with miners. There was no stage or scenery of any description, which necessitated some change in their program. It was a flat floor they played on, with eight candles for footlights. On the program was an act announced that required scenery, but the boys did a walk-around instead. This was supposed to finish the show but the audience would not have it; and seeing them waiting Micawber-like, Birch stepped forward and with one of his characteristic speeches attempted to soothe their aching hearts. When he retired, loud calls were made for "some more," whereupon Wells attempted to lay the flattering unction to their souls but they shouted, "Kill him!" etc. Birch once more came to the front but the audience indulged in much loud talk as to what they would do. The following day, soon after reaching a ranch, they were waited on by Judge Dudley (a distant relative of Birch), who showed him a letter from San Andrase pronouncing the members of the company frauds and indulging in a few other very indelicate epithets. The judge endorsed the minstrel boys as being all right and they had a good house that night. Birch visited San Andrase several times afterwards but he never approached the town without a flag of truce. A party consisting of Billy Birch, George Coes, Sam Wells, W. M. Barker, C. D. Abbott, F. Medina, W. D. Corrister and E. Deaves, opened at the Opera House, San Francisco, in September, 1859, under Maguire's management.

SAN FRANCISCO MINSTRELS: was a band organized November 10, 1865, and opened at Eureka Theatre, San Francisco. Joe Taylor, Frank Medina, Johnny De Angelis, Jake Wallace, Lew Rattler, Charles Talbot, Clinton Murphy, Williams and Abbott were in the party.

SAN FRANCISCO MINSTRELS: was the title of a party that opened a new hall over Badger's Auction Store, Montgomery Street, San Francisco, June 2, 1866. In the party were A. J. Talbot, Jake Wallace, Mons. Charles, Lewis Morton, Medina, Lorclain, Moss, and James Murphy. They closed up in June of the same year.

SAN FRANCISCO MINSTRELS: was the title given a band that opened October 3, 1866, at the Academy of Music, San Francisco, Cal., and consisted of A. J. Talbot, Billy Sheppard, Jake Wallace, Frank Medina, H. Nordbloom, J. R. Taylor, L. Mundweller, Prof. Fiedler, T. F. Barnwell, Prof. Freeman, Sig. Pinto, and J. Mundweller.

SANFORD & SMITH'S TROUPE: was located in a hall in Louisville, Ky., in September, 1859. After making a brief traveling tour they returned to Louisville. The party consisted of J. W. Smith, Sile Weed, Charles Kendall, John Cantine, Charles Sanford and Mlle. Margueritta.

SANFORD'S (S. S.) MINSTRELS: was a party organized and opened in 1843 at the old Southwark Hall, Philadelphia, and went thence to Temperance Hall, same city, where Sanford introduced Eve (Eph) Horn. After a brief stay there, the party went traveling in Pennsylvania; and at Pottsville, Pa., Eph Horn made his first appearance (accidentally) as Bones. John Diamond, who occupied the bone end with the company, got into an altercation with and stabbed a night watchman. Diamond was arrested and lodged in Harrisburg jail. This was during the inauguration of Gov. Shunk. The next day Horn took the bones, being his first appearance on the end, as previous to that he played the triangle. Dan Rice was one of the features of this show. The company returned to Philadelphia in the summer of 1844; and early in November they visited Baltimore, Md., opening at the Museum, November 2. John Diamond rejoined them there. The following is a copy of their program loaned us (some years before his death) by Frank Brower:

PROGRAMME
PART I: Northern Dandies

Overture... Full Band
Sing, Darkies, Sing... Tonton and Chorus
Cynthia Sue.. S. Sanford and Band
Lucy Neal... S. Sanford
Juliane Johnson..Percell and Chorus
Ole Bull and Dan Tucker...................................Sanford and Band
Yellow Gals... Tonton and Chorus
De Ole Gray Goose.. Sanford and Band

PART II: Slaves of the South

Railroad Overture... Full Band
Song and Dance "Whar Did You Come From?"..........S. S. Sanford
Going Over the Mountains...................................... Percell
Boatman's Glee.....................Sanford, Diamond, Horn and Tonton
Baltimore Ladies, Come Out To-night............................ Full Band

The whole to conclude with a trial dance by Master Diamond and S. S. Sanford. As danced by them in New York and Philadelphia, to thousands of the elite. The afternoon Concert at 3 o'clock. Admission, 25 cents. Children, half price.

SANFORD'S MINSTRELS: were at the new Seventh Street Opera House, Seventh Street, near Arch, Philadelphia, formerly a church, which was fitted up for a minstrel hall by L. V. Tunison and H. Parsons, who opened it September 18, 1867, with S. S. Sanford's Minstrels. Eph Horn, Frank Moran, Frank Girard, W. L. Hobbs, J. Morrison, F. Williams, C. Church, C. F. Shattuck, W. Allen, Devin Bros., W. Budworth, and J. Edwards. were in the party. On January 6, 1868, M. Ainsley Scott, G. Rockefeller, Master George, and Miss Maggie opened. The managers gave a good show but failed to meet with much encouragement and they closed February 22, 1868. After making a brief tour they returned to Philadelphia, re-opened at their old hall, March 9, but disbanded March 28, 1868.

SANFORD'S (S. S.) TROUPES: leased McDonough's Olympic Theatre, Race Street, above Second Street, Philadelphia, In November, 1864, which Sanford opened November 14 with the following band: Frank Schaffer, Prof. Hasfelt, J. Orr, J. Williams, F. Basquin, J. Mortimer, J. Buckley, Larry Tooley, J. J. B. Whitman, J. Rainer, Master Willie, Young America, Julia and S. S. Sanford. They closed there in

January, 1865. Mr. Sanford next became associated in management with Sam Sharpley and was with him during the season of 1865-66. On July 6, 1866, Mr. Sanford opened at Tony Pastor's Opera House in the Bowery, New York, with a band. Mr. Sanford shortly after took a company to Pleasantville, PA., and then traveled through the state, closing up in April, 1869. In September, 1869, Mr. Sanford organized a small party which he called the PICKED NINE and traveled through Pennsylvania and New Jersey. During the summer of 1870, Mr. Sanford traveled with Gardner's Circus as writer. In October, 1870, he organized a party to travel through New Jersey, consisting of Billy Chambers, bones; S. S. Sanford, tambo; Paul Berger, John Edwards, Holmes, Mortimer, Smith, Solomon, Brown, Creed, Stout, and Julian Reed. His next venture was the leasing of the old church, 928 North Second Street, above Poplar Street, Philadelphia, which he opened as a minstrel hall December 17, 1870. In the company were: John Forbes and W. Howard, end men; Master Julian Reed, Fulton Myers, W. L. Hirst, C. Wilson, Berger and others. After a successful season, he closed and went traveling; re-opening in the Second Street hall August 26, 1871, Eph Horn appearing as bones, Sanford as tambo, Paul Berger, "Ole Bull" Myers, J. E. Dougherty, Joseph Barth, J. Paul, Joe Saunders, J. Sterling, A. Holmes, A. Davis, Casha, J. Mitchell, Miss Rosalinda, La Petite, Master Freddie, and James W. Sanford. The house burned down October 17, 1871. Sanford leased Sanderson Opera House, Baltimore, Md., which he opened April 8, 1872. George Kunkel, W. Porter, Dan Conner, Fulton Myers, F. A.. Howe, Sanford and others were in the company. They closed May 9. He next organized a party for the Eleventh Street Opera House, Philadelphia, which he opened May 18, 1874, and closed June 6, when he went on a tour. Dan Gardner, Billy Porter, "Ole Bull" Myers, George W. Horn, Paul Berger, Frank Devere, W. Howard, J. Lynch, A. Harmer, C. Chase and others comprised the company in Philadelphia. Mr. Sanford organized a party in September, 1878, consisting of Frank Campbell, Fred Herting, W. Bell, C. Wilber, P. Cassel, G. Rudolph, C. Gardner, P. Holly, Paul Berger, B. Acherd, S. S. Sharkey, and F. Hall. Sanford leased Friendship Hall, corner of Norris and Sepviva Streets, Philadelphia, which he opened September 30, 1878, but it was of short duration. Once more Sanford took to the road but collapsed at Newark, N. J., on January 11, 1879.

SCHOOLCRAFT & COES: organized a party in Portland, Me., to take a traveling tour. They opened April 2, 1877, at Lawrence, Mass., with Ben Gilfoil, Luke Schoolcraft, James Fox, Bernardo, Schaffer, Slavin, D. Barron, Arthur Cook, George Coes and others.

SEARCH & MOXLEY'S NEW ORLEANS MINSTRELS: organized and opened in Baltimore, Md., at Maryland Institute, July 22, 1857, with Jake Search as the manager. They made a tour through the West.

SEAVER & COES': opened the old Odeon, Brooklyn, N. Y., March 5, 1866, with the following talent: Charles Pettengill, J. K. Campbell, Johnny Allen, George Coes, W. P. Spaulding, M. Warren, G. W. Jackson, Walter Fields, G. H. Frugior, B. Isaacs, M. Riley, C. White, J. J. Hilliard, H. Isaacs, C. Curry, F. Bowen, G. Belden, and the Thompson Bros. They closed July 28 and went traveling.

118

SHARPLEY & ALLEN'S MINSTRELS: opened in Boston in July, 1869, for a few weeks. While playing there, they combined with Delehanty and Hengler's party.

SHARPLEY & COTTON'S MINSTRELS: Sharpley, Cotton, M. T. Skiff, Master Bennie (Cotton), J. E. Green, William H. Chambers, Harry Bloodgood, Little Willie, George Schubert, Prof. Tannenbaum, Ira A. Paine, Edward Holden, Alfred Moe, George Monk, W. C. Schurb, Mons. Schultzhold, G. W. Pike, J. H. Cooper, and Master Charlie comprised the party. They closed August 24, 1867, Sharpley having secured a lease of the Theatre Comique, Broadway and Spring Street, New York, in conjunction with Charley White, and the company opened there August 26, giving a minstrel first part followed by a variety show. They closed there January 4, 1868, and disbanded. Reorganized, they opened at Newark, N. J., February 10, 1868. Dick Ralph, Masters Willie, Bennie and Ben Cotton were in the party. After a short tour they closed, but reorganized for the fall and winter season and opened November 12, 1868, at Arlington Hall, Chicago, with Sharpley, Cotton, Charles Church, George Gray, Alfred Moe, Harry Stanwood, Masters Willie and Charlie, Frank Kritta, J. Tannenbaum, Joseph Norrie, W. H. Chambers, and J. Reilley. Ben Cotton withdrew in January, 1869, and Sharpley took possession of Wood's Museum, Chicago, on January 19. Charley Benedict took Cotton's position on the end. Shortly after this the party was known as SHARPLEY'S MINSTRELS.

SHARPLEY'S MINSTRELS: on September 6, 1869, started out from Boston for a fall and winter tour, with Sharpley and Harry Stanwood on the ends, Joe Norrie in the middle, and Charles Atkinson, Frank Campbell, E. M. Hall and J. Henry Reynolds in the party. In May, 1870, his show was called "Sharpley's Silver Show," and Prof. Logrinia, with his birds and cat, as a portion of the entertainment. Sharpley reorganized a party in New York and opened at the San Francisco Minstrel Hall, 585 Broadway, May 13, 1872, with Sam Sharpley, tambo; Nelse Seymour, bones; James W. Lamont, interlocutor; Frank Campbell, Monroe Dempster, Charles Henry, Gen. Grant Jr., Harry Macarthy, and Charley White. Mackin and Wilson appeared June 17, and on June 29, the company closed and traveled until July 20, 1872, when they closed. They made a tour of the West, returning East in April, 1869, with Harry Stanwood on one of the ends. J. G. Withers, Jesse Kane, Church, and E. M. Hall were in the company. In June, 1869, he formed a co-partnership with Johnny Allen, and the party was then called SHARPLEY & ALLEN'S MINSTRELS.

SHARPLEY'S MINSTRELS: was the title of a company traveling in Kansas in October, 1857.

SHARPLEY'S MINSTRELS: organized in New York and opened in Middletown, Conn., August 20, 1861, with Abecco, T. McAnally, Dave Reed, James Lamont, James Granger, H. T. Mudge, C. King, and R. Edwards. They closed their traveling tour, came to New York and appeared at the Canterbury, under Fox & Curran's management.

SHARPLEY'S MINSTRELS: were known as the "Iron Clads," also the "Monitors." The company was made up of the following: Sam Sharpley, C. A. Boyd, J. F. Sullivan, Frank Kent, J. D. Newcomb, J. Danford, John Williams, Richard Escott,

Cool Burgess, Frank Bowles, Wally Thomas, G. W. Bailey, O. D. Underwood, Fred King, Herr Koenig, William Frazee. In the spring of 1863 Sharpley returned to New York, and, after a short rest, reorganized his company and started on another prosperous tour, which lasted, without interruption, until June, 1865. In April, 1865, S. S. Sanford became an equal partner with Sharpley, and the party traveled South. Sharpley opened at Bowery Minstrel Hall (afterwards Tony Pastor's Opera House), 199 and 201 Bowery, opposite Spring Street, New York, June 12, 1865. The company consisted of S. S. Sanford, Cal Wagner, Hughey Dougherty, A. C. Stone, Little Archie, Jules Stratton, Dick Escott, Frank Bowles, E. T. Blackmar, Thomas Sears, Edwin French, William Chambers, Gil Pond, John Williams, J. Ambrose, John Masterson and J. F. Sullivan. Sharpley was tambo, and Wagner, bones. The season closed July 29, 1865. The company then went on a traveling tour through the East, starting in August, with Sanford, Wagner, Dougherty, F.. Myers, Archie Sharpley, Young Hengler, Isaac Perry, Walter Birch, E. T. Blackmar, Pond, Masterson, Escott, Chambers, W. T. Emerson, Williams, and H. Walsh. Wagner and Dougherty on the ends. Sharpley did not go with the party, but re-opened the house as Tony Pastor's Opera House on July 31, and continued in partnership with Tony Pastor for some two years. In March, 1866, Tony Pastor's Combination and Sharpley's Minstrels united. After traveling for a while, Sharpley formed a co-partnership with Ben Cotton and opened the Fifth Avenue Theatre, on Twenty-fourth Street, near Broadway, New York, on August 5, 1867, with a company which was called SHARPLEY & COTTON'S MINSTRELS.

SHARPLEY'S MINSTRELS AND SHERIDAN & MACK'S COMBINATION: started from New York for a traveling tour in August, 1873. They closed at Lynn, Mass., October 3, 1874.

SHARPLEY'S SERENADERS: See REYNOLDS, NEWCOMB & BURGESS' MINSTRELS.

SHELBY'S (DAN) MINSTRELS: started for a tour in December, 1863, through New York State. Billy McCracken, F. B. West, C. Willis, G. Dunbar, R. Lane, N. C; McElroy, and Mrs. Dan Shelby were in the party. They disbanded February 13, 1864. The company was later reorganized in Chicago in November, 1868, consisting of P. O. Hudson, W. Hindmonston, Bob Lindly, Dan Shelby, Master Willie, A. B. Kennedy, E. M. Hall, Devere, Frank Fisher, and Prendergast, and opened at Kankakee, Ill., November 9. They started from St. Louis August 3, 1869, for a summer tour with a party consisting of George Powers, Billy Pash, Frank Curtis, P. O. Hudson.

SHIMER & BARNEY'S MINSTRELS: were organized in Buffalo, N. Y., in January, 1867, and were advertised to open at Attica, N. Y., January 3; but the musicians not putting in an appearance, those who did go to Attica returned to Buffalo, "leaving footprints in the snow."

SHOREY & MOWRY'S NEW ORLEANS METROPOLITAN MINSTRELS: were organized in Providence, R. I., and opened in Milford, Mass., April 9, 1866. The party consisted of Shorey, H. G. Mowry, Charles Gleason, M. Clark Clement, H.

Drew Clement, L. Ball, Billy Weston, Flem Adams, Frank Bean, Billy Hammond, Harry Wilson, J. A. Reid, Charles Ball, W. W. Mayn, Ned Clark, and A. Young.

SHOREY, CARLE, DUPREZ & GREEN'S MINSTRELS: [See NEW ORLEANS AND METROPOLITAN BURLESQUE TROUPE.] continued traveling, Duprez being the business manager; Master Tommy, clods; W. Carle, E. Green, C. Bovee, M. T. Skiff, G. W. Bailey, J. P. Griffin, W. Herman, F. Bowles, Mons. C. Lavallee; Masters Tommy, Hope, and Shorey; Misses Estelle, Celestine, Duprez and G. Bates comprised the party. Owing to trouble among the managers, they disbanded at Baton Rouge, December 26, 1860, and reorganized on the 28th at New Orleans under the management of Duprez & Green, Shorey drawing out. A newspaper war was indulged in by Shorey and Duprez, each one calling the other some pretty hard names and each one making anything but complimentary state-ments about the other. As reorganized, the party consisted of Green, Lavallee, L. J. Donnelly, Nelse Seymour, W. D. Frazee, C. Bovee, J. F. Bowles, John Pratt; Master Charley, jig; W. B. La Point, G. P. Wright, E. N. Slocum, J. H. Carlton, M. Ainsley Scott, Peter Duprez, P. J. Pratt, George H. Surgeons, and C. H. Duprez. In March, 1861, they made many changes. E. N. Slocum and Charles Gardner joined. They closed their season July 4, 1861. They reorganized in October, 1861, and the John Denier & Warren pantomime troupe was added to the party. The party as now organized consisted of John Denier, E. Green, F. Bowles, C. Boyd, D. C. Rice, L. Havacki, M. Boynton, Duprez, C. Reynolds, George Bailey, E. Denier, A. Hathaway, Miss J. Lovell, F. Taineniu, William Warren, W. Thomas, T. Thorpe, P. Wilkins, S. Davis and S. Vienaire. They started from Boston by steamer for Newfoundland. The Denier pantomime company left there in January, 1862. On April 7 they started for a Western tour. In June, M. Ainsley Scott was middleman. F. S. Sprung joined them; also Cool Burgess, who, with C. Reynolds, had the ends. On June 18, they opened at the Boston Museum for two weeks. J. D. Newcomb was the advance agent. Closing in Boston July 2, they soon after took a steamer for New Orleans, under engagement to Spalding & Bidwell. They opened at the Academy of Music in November. Scott, C. Lavallee, J. H. Kellogg, A. S. Prentiss, L. L. Fabbrisco, W. J. Eagan, F. Adams Jr., William D. Benoit, George Duban, A. Connair, Master Florence, E. Holmes, J. Keth, H. Slate, Duprez, and Green were in the party. They closed in New Orleans, January 24, and sailed on the 25th for Havana, where their stay was very short. They returned to New York, February 6, 1863, and went West. J. Campbell left them in February. The season of 1863-64 closed in July, 1864. In November, 1865, Green withdrew from the company after twelve years' connection with them, Duprez buying out his interest. Lew Benedict was engaged and opened November 22. J. B. Murphy, balladist and inlerlocutor; Tom Baker, bones; and Mons. Navoni joined the same time. The company then became known as DUPREZ & BENEDICT'S MINSTRELS.

SHOREY, MELVILLE & GREEN'S MINSTRELS: showed in Providence, R. I., August 19, 1869.

SHOREY'S SOUTHERN MINSTRELS: made a tour in February, 1854, with the following company: J. G. Wentworth, Durand, Lamos, F. A. Shorey, Cardelow, Wanton, and J. Austin.

SIMMONS & SLOCUM'S MINSTRELS: organized a band and opened their new opera house on Arch Street, above Tenth Street, Philadelphia, on August 29, 1870, with Lew Simmons, John S. Cox, E. N, Slocum, William Blakeney, Johnny Hart, Andy McKee, W. P. Sweatnam, Eddie Fox, Robert Fraser, William Eiseman, Charles Folly, William Ewers, William Sester, Charles Brown, Charles Heywood, George Clairidon, Joseph Norcross, William Clark, William A. Brisco, George Harris, John Crosher, William Blaber, J. S. Stout, Ed G. Stone, W. H. Chambers, and Charles Dettro. The season closed May 20, 1871, and they went on a traveling tour. They re-opened August 28, 1871. John Crosher closed late in January, 1872, intending to quit the business. Their hall burnt down March 20, 1872. They opened in New York, April 15, 1872, at Niblo's Garden in the burlesque of "Poll and Partner Joe." They opened in San Francisco, Cal., at the Alhambra Theatre, May 27. On July 8, David Wambold appeared, followed on the 15th by Cool Burgess, Charles Sutton and M. Ainsley Scott; July 29, Delehanty and Hengler, and they closed August 4. They re-appeared in Philadelphia, August 25, 1872, and in the company were Matt Wheeler, Luke Schoolcraft, W. L. Hobbs, Slocum, Simmons, Eddie Fox, J. J. Reiley, Fred Walz, Charles Stevens, Hurley, Marr, William Henry Rice, William Hamilton, Justin Robinson, Barlow Bros., John Crosher, C. F. Shattuck, Jasper R. Ross, J. H. Stout, and J. H. Beck. Joseph Allsop, basso, opened December 9; and Richard Magee, tenor, on December 23, made his first appearance on the stage. William Newcomb appeared September 29, 1873, followed on October 25 by Kelly and Leon. Billy Manning appeared as end man on March 23, 1874, and on the same date Primrose and West appeared. The season closed May 16, and the company traveled for the summer. On August 31, 1874, the season opened with Charles Reed, Harrington, McGlone, Pete Mack, Fostelle, J. L. Woolsey, Sweatnam, Simmons, Slocum, George Thatchert Welch, Johnny Rice, Shattuck, Hamilton, Charles Stevens, J. H. Stout, Eddie Fox and orchestra. Abecco opened January 11, and the season closed May 29, 1875. They then started on a tour, but closed late in June. In August, Billy Sweatnam became one of the partners and the company opened in Philadelphia, September 6, 1875, as SIMMONS, SLOCUM & SWEATNAM'S MINSTRELS. Abecco, George W. Harley, Sweatnam, Simmons, Slocum, Charles Reynolds, George Thatcher, Billy and Johnny Rice, and Gus Mills were in the company. In April 24, 1876, they made a new departure from the ruts of minstrelsy, appearing in their first part in continental costumes and they were called the CENTENNIAL MINSTRELS. The season closed July 15, 1876. They commenced their next season August 28, 1876. On October 31, Simmons and Slocum severed their connection with this troupe, owing to trouble with the proprietor of the opera house. They organized a party for a traveling tour, which they called SIMMONS & SLOCUM'S MINSTRELS. They opened at Easton, Pa., November 21, 1876. The party consisted of Welch, John Rice, George Thatcher, W. Henry Rice, George W. Harley, T. B. Dixon, Charles Stevens, Vincent Barone, Simmons and Slocum. A re-organization was made by Sweatnam and the party was called SWEATNAM'S MINSTRELS. They had J. J. Kelly, tenor, and C. F. Shattuck, interlocutor. They re-opened December 6, 1876. On Christmas Day the company was called SWEATNAM &

FRAZER'S MINSTRELS. J. G. Russell, baritone appeared January 29, 1877. Milt G. Barlow opened March 24, appearing on the end and in the olio. He closed May 19. Simmons & Slocum's party did not last long. The Arch Street Opera House opened for the next season on August 27, 1877, with SIMMONS, SLOCUM & SWEATNAM'S MINSTRELS, and consisted of Simmons and Frank Cushman, on the ends; Slocum, interlocutor; Charles Reynolds, Welch, Johnny Rice, Fred Walz, C. F. Shattuck, Eddie Fox, J. J. Kelly, Charles Stevens, Sandford and Wilson. Sweatnam did not arrive from California to appear until October 15. The season closed on February 16, 1878. They re-opened April 15 and the season closed in May. They re-opened September 16, 1878, with Billy Sweatnam as sole manager, as Simmons sailed for Europe June 12. In the company were Charles Reynolds, Charles Banks, Billy Carter, Burt Sheppard, Johnson, Bruno, J. R. Kemble, W. F. Holmes, C. P. Shattuck, Carl Rudolph, Fred Walz, John S. Cox, and J. H. Cox. The set for the first part represented an arbor with a garden at the back, set without any wings or entrances. The performers in the first part did not sit in the usual semi-circle but were scattered in various parts of the arbor.

SKIFF & GAYLORD'S MINSTRELS: were organized in Philadelphia in November, 1864, and they went to Trenton, N. J., to rehearse. They opened November 17 in New Brunswick, N. J., and not, as has been erroneously published, in 1859. Delehanty and Ward, Harry Stanwood, John Purcell, John Howard, J. J. Kutz, Samuel Hosfield, D. Sufflebine, Jacob Steeg, Ed Sullivan, P. Masterson, William Schaffer, J. P. Skinner, Thomas Prestwich, Low Gaylord (bones), M. T. Skiff, and C. Forrest (wench) made up the party, and C. E. Richardson, as agent. This company was organized and put on the road with the money of "Coal Oil Johnny," as he was familiarly known---the sole condition being that portraits of himself as "financial agent" should adorn the posters and programs.

SKIFF'S MINSTRELS: were organized by M. T. Skiff, who commenced September 26; 1863, at Liberty Hall, Alexandria, Va., with G. W. Charles, Low Gaylord, John Purcell, J. H. Collins, Harry Bloodgood, Paul Andria, M. T. Skiff, and J. H. Reynolds. They remained there a very short time and went traveling, calling themselves SKIFF'S ARMOR PLATED ETHIOPIAN GUNBOATS. J. Tannenbaum and M. Ainsley Scott were in the party. M. T. Skiff retired from the stage for a while and was, in July, 1864, proprietor of the Beach House, Nantucket, Mass.

SKIFF, WHEELER, HORN & BRAY'S MINSTRELS: started from Boston and opened November 8, 1869, at Lynn, Mass. M. T. Skiff, Eph Horn Sr., Eph Horn Jr., Walter Bray, Cooper, Fields, Charles Church, William Chambers and others comprised the company, with C. B. Griste as agent.

SLITER & WOOD'S MINSTRELS: were playing through the states of Michigan and the far West in 1857 and in May appeared in Detroit. Dick Sliter and Mickey Warren were in the company.

SLITER'S (DICK) EMPIRE MINSTRELS: were traveling in 1850 and consisted of G. G. Snyder, G. B. Brown, E. D. Palmer, J. Gardiner, H. L. Sloan, G. W. Sherwood, H. L. Powers, Cool White, and R. H. Sliter. G. B. Brown, announced as the champion bone player of the world, performed a bone solo with imitations of birds, drums, horses, races, etc.

SMITH & SLAVEN'S ABOLIANS: made a tour of the Eastern states in February, 1867, under the management of Jerry Dashington.

SMITH AND TAYLOR: organized a party in New York, consisting of John Taylor, Archie Hughes, J. Brown, Fred Abbott, Billy Sheppard, J. H. Hilton, A. Campbell, W. Neil, Masters George and Willie Guy, and G. Percival, and sailed for Europe June 21, 1869. They played in Liverpool two weeks, after which they made a tour of the provinces. John E. Taylor left London for Australia November 15, 1875. He arrived at Melbourne January 1, 1876, and became partner in the management of the United States Minstrels in Sydney in June, 1876.

SMITH'S (BILL) MINSTRELS: were organized in New York in January, 1859, and appeared at the theatre in Albany but closed up in a few weeks.

SMITH'S (W. N.) ETHIOPIANS: organized in August, 1860, to travel South with Van Amburgh's Menagerie. W. N. Smith, bones; A. Pierce, tambo; Master Smith, banjo; Otto Horn, violin; M. Corrigan, triangle; L. C. Bremmer, banjo; and Bobby Williams, clog.

SNIFFEN'S CAMPBELLS: was a first class band organized late in 1858 and opened at 444 Broadway, New York. They consisted of Matt Peel's company, B. Golden, clog; Master Charles, wench; A. M. Hernandez, R. Abecco, J. A. Herman, ballads; B. A. Cotton; G. W. Moore, tambo; J. B. Donniker, J. T. Boyce, J. Unsworth, C. Howard, T. J. Peel, J. W. Adams, E. H. Winchell, N. W. Gould, Asche, and L. Condit. They opened August 30. Matt Peel withdraw in October, when a reorganization was made. A. Montgomery, H. Hempe, J. Warren, R. Carroll, Cotton, and Gould remained. Cool White opened November 15, as middle man, and Howard left to join Matt Peel's Minstrels. B. A. Cotton returned in December, taking Unsworth's place as bones. In January, 1859, another re-organization was made with Billy Birch, bones; E. Bowers, interlocutor; G. W. Moore, tambo; J. B.. Donniker, violin; B. Golden, clog; J. B. Herman, ballads; R. Abecco, harp; A. M. Hernandez, B. A. Cotton; R. M. Carroll, jig; and Master Charles, wench. Cool White left soon after. They disbanded in February, 1859, owing to bad business.

SOUTHERN MINSTRELS: organized in the month of February, 1859, and made a lengthy tour with Dan Wilson, bones and jig; J. Williams, tambo; Young Master Walter, ballads; J. Brown, basso and guitar; E. Bowen, banjo; Charles Heep, violin; and .W. C. Shearn, manager.

SPRAGUE'S MINSTRELS: organized and opened in Nashville, Tenn., in March, 1863. They consisted of Fred Reinbolt, Charles Vogt, Gus Shaw, Von Humel-bacher, Billy Sweatnam, Tim Woodruff, and La Belle Louise.

STAR BAND OF METROPOLITANS: were organized in the South in March, 1859, by a Mr. Wright. In the party were Murphy, Foster, Purdy, Kendall, Holt, etc.

STEAMER *BANJO* MINSTRELS: was a party under the management of Frank Cardella that started December, 1859, on the steamer for a trip on the Mississippi River with Sam Long, B. A. Cotton, N. G. Foster, J. T. Wambold, Joe Mais, Sam

124

Gardner, John W. Adams, George M. Hill, J. V. Chadduck, C. Keene, C. Young, and Tom Allen. In the spring of 1860, M. Herman, T. Chatfield, Joe Kinslow, and J. Pfaffenschlager joined.

STEWART BROS.: organized a party and traveled through Indiana and Ohio, commencing in Fort Wayne, in December, 1869.

STRONG & BURGESS MINSTRELS: organized a band in New York early in 1860 and started for California.

SWEATNAM'S (BILLY) MINSTRELS: organized in September, 1866, for a tour through Ohio. Billy Sweatnam, C. Howard, Prof. Spirls, G. Wallace, G. Barker, Tommy Manning, W. J. Jacobs, Dan Sweatnam, and J. Thorne were in the company.

TAYLOR'S MINSTRELS: J. H. Taylor, proprietor, opened in Newark, N. J., January 14, 1865, with A. C. Morrison, J. L. Marchant, J. H. Richie, A. Force, J. H. Hilton, Reeves, W. N. Smith, Joe English, Mons. Gibbonoise, Anna Lee, and Emma Birch. A re-organization occurred at Bristol, R. I., where they opened on July 30, 1868. G. H. Coes, T. L. Merchant, Tom Yates, Walter Birch, Frank Dumont, H. Lockwood, E. Harrison, James Johnson, F. Blakeley, and George Warren were in the company. J. H. Taylor and Frank Dumont occupied the ends.

THAYER AND NEWCOMB'S BAND: organized in 1849 by A. L. Thayer and William W. Newcomb. This party continued together for four years. In 1849 the party was located at the hall at the corner of Court and Hanover Streets, Boston.

THAYER'S MINSTRELS: were organized in the fall of 1848, with A. L. Thayer as manager. The company consisted of Edward B. Gray, called the "Boston Rattler and King of Dancers"; Charles Howard, left hand violinist; A. L. Thayer, banjoist; John G. Brown, tambourine; Charley Huntley, bones; W. Newcomb; and Fred Wilson, clog dancer and walk-arounds. Gray gave imitations of all the principal dancers in the country, including Dick Pelham, John Smith, Frank Brower, Master Juba, John and Frank Diamond, and George Christy. They played at the Park House, Boylston Garden, Boston.

THOMAS' (JERRY) TROUPE: organized a minstrel party and opened the Brighton Theatre, located on the west side of Broadway, above Thirtieth Street, on December 30, 1878, with the following minstrel band: A. H. Pelham, Billy Bryant, Harry Percy, Lew and Charles Dockstader, Charles Storms, Bob Hart, Emil Ames, Charley White, Gibbons, Davenport, George W. Woods, John H. Mack and an orchestra.

THOMPSON'S LONE STAR MINSTRELS: consisted of John A. Thompson (better known in the dramatic profession as representative of old men), interlocutor; T. R. Murphy, tambo; William McCellan, bones; Master Johnny, Charles Duffy, Harry De Vere and Charles Frazer. They started in August, 1874, for a tour through Texas. They closed September 15, 1874.

THORNTON & FISH: made a tour of the Canadas with a party in September, 1867, and then traveled East with T. Fish, F. L. Thornton, C. Austin, M. Foley, C. Fish, J. Fish, A. Nix, M. Dempster, G. R. Winship, H. Fish, F. G. Butler, R. B. Taylor, F. Hendricks and Master J. Sweeney.

THORPE & OVERIN'S MINSTRELS OF ALL NATIONS: opened November 27, 1665, at Masonic Hall, northeast corner of Grand and Crosby Streets, New York, with the following people: George Guy, Joseph Braham, Masters George and Willie Guy, Willie Martini, T. Donaldson, Oliver White, Bolus, H. Clifford, Dick Healey, Field, Gonzalez, and Clark Bros. They collapsed December 13 but reopened December 23 with George Guy, Warren White, Walter Field, Frank Dey, Dick Healey, Jessie Robinson, Grace Duvernay, and Mlle. Gertiani. They closed Christ-mas night.

THREE DARK UNAPPROACHABLES, THE: This was the title given to John Diamond, Chestnut and Hoyt when they appeared at the Park Theatre, New York, succeeding the Virginias in 1842.

TOLEDO OPERA HOUSE MINSTRELS: consisted of O. M. Blake, James A. Hayes, Prof. Luckner, Lew Benedict, J. F. Oberist, J. G. Tomaze, John H. Carle and daughters, Estella and Celestine; Charley Rivers, and Miss Victoria. This party occupied the Opera House, Toledo, Ohio, in May, 1862.

TOPLIFF'S MINSTRELS: composed of Harry Haviland, G. W. Herman, Tim McIntyre, Fulton Knight, Harry Wells, C. M. Reese, Louis Gumphert, Howard, and Cobburn made a tour of the oil regions in December and January, 1867-68;

TROY'S VIRGINIANS: were traveling in Kentucky in 1861. They opened in Louisville in February. Old Matt Bork, banjoist, was with them. In November this party took the name of TROY'S UNION MINSTRELS, J. Nelson, banjoist; Johnny Troy, bones; Tom Cannon, tambo.

TURNER & MACK'S PARTY: consisting of Ned Turner, J. H. Thayer, J. N. Davis, G. M. Smith, Herr Clinger, Master Charles, A. M. Palmer, Sid Thayer, Billy Matthewson, J. H. Quirch, Master Tinsley, J. A. Johnson, Frank Master, Billy Harwood, George Florence, and Sig. Garriga, made a tour of the Canadas in September, 1863.

TWILIGHT SERENADERS: organized in Pennsylvania in 1860, and opened in Erie, Pa., on the 25th with J. F. Oberist, C. A. Swartz, F. McWhaster, E. F. Clark, J. C. Burns, and D. J. Lockwood.

UNION MINSTRELS: organized in January, 1861, for a tour of Indiana and the South with Nick Ryan, Mike Phelan, Dan Trotter, W. W. Patterson, Sam Messenger, Dan Cleveland, C. W. Campbell, Jim Gray, and H. Peel.

UNION STAR MINSTRELS: were made up in New Bedford, Mass., in April, 1863, and consisted of A. S. Remington, bones; M. B. Leavitt, tambo; S. W. Hutchinson, Dan Ashley, banjo and interlocutor; Nat Luce, Paul Leon, wench; Lew Hart, J. H. Lawrence, E. M. Leslie, and B. T. Whitemore. They made a tour through Massachusetts.

UNITED STATES MINSTRELS: was a party organized in Melbourne, Australia, after Billy Emerson had closed his engagement there in June 1874. G. W. Rockefeller, Charles Holly, Buckley, Tommy Hudson, Campbell and West appeared at Apollo Hall, Melbourne, and played to very good business. In July they formed a coalition with Louis Braham, T. Rainford, and Nick Fullade and opened at the Opera House in that city. In July, 1875, they occupied the School of Arts in that city, after which they made a tour of the interior. Returning to Apollo Hall, they attracted crowded houses. They then moved to St. George's Hall in that city and opened April 9, 1877, with William Horace Bent and Richard W. Kohler added to the company. They again appeared at the School of Arts, where they closed in August, 1877, and visited Brisbane. They afterwards went on a tour, appearing in Castlemaine in April, 1878. In November, 1878, they occupied St. George's Hall, Melbourne. E. Amery, basso; Browning, baritone; Walter Hawkins, male soprano; Charles Holly, jig; Brown and Newlands, end men; Owen Conduit, Johnny Thompson, G. W. Rockefeller, Tommy Hudson, Louis Braham, and R. W. (Dick) Kohler comprised the company. Washington Norton left the company a short time previous. The business of this company has been very large in Australia.

UNSWORTH'S MINSTRELS: organized and opened at Bridgeport, Conn., February 25, 1861. Unsworth, Eugene, and Donniker were proprietors. R. Abecco, Julius Stratton, T. Hayes, C. O'Neil, Signor Maro, J. Frost, H. Trigg, J. M. Loomis, B. O. Jones, and Johnson were in the party. They returned to New York and closed in May, 1861.

VIRGINIA MINSTRELS: were traveling in Pennsylvania in September, 1858, and shortly after went South. John W. Landis, J. R. Myers, J. A. Williams, Paul Berger, and Ben Yeager were in the company.

VIRGINIA MINSTRELS: under the management of O. F. Drew started from Richmond, Va., December 1, 1875, on a tour. In the organization were Prof. Mereo, Charles Norris, bones; Torie Zerlini, Hamilton, tambo; W. Wagner, Morris Bros., Willie Hart and Joe Wilson.

VIRGINIA MINSTRELS AND PEARL BELLRINGERS: organized in New York and gave performances in a small hall on the corner of Center and Pearl Streets. This is the same place where Matthew T. Brennan afterwards kept a public house. Frank Brower and Johnny Reynoldson were the features of the show.

VIRGINIA SERENADERS: in which Eph Horn, David P. Bowers, and J. Moran were the leading features. They traveled with Raymond and Waring's Menagerie, performing under canvas. In December, 1844, the Virginia Serenaders consolidated with the ETHIOPIAN SERENADERS. The party consisted of Cool White, J. R. Myers (Dick Myers), Tony Winnemore, Eph Horn, James Sandford, Edwin Deaves, Master Diamond, and Robert Edwards. Some of the great attractions with this party were Horn and Sandford in the "Dutch Farce." The arrival of the New Orleans Serenaders with their intention to locate in Philadelphia, caused the disbandment of the old Virginia Seranaders, except upon special occasions.

VIRGINIA SERENADERS: with Mr. Deaves as one of the principal cards. This party appeared in Philadelphia at the Masonic Hall, Chinese Museum, Temperance Hall (Northern Liberties), Arch and Chestnut Street Theatres at stated intervals. Charley White remained but a brief time with the party. From Philadelphia they went on a traveling tour, visiting Boston, where they did the act for the first time called "The Black Shakers." This was in May, 1849, at the Howard Athenaeum.

VIRGINIA SERENADERS: was the title of a band that was organized at Kittery,

Me., and gave their initial performance in that town March 21, 1867. J. Burns, Al Withim, Oscar Marr, Frank Pearl, and Master Dixie were in the party.

VIRGINIA STAR TROUPE: was organized in Newark, N. J., in July, 1859, and opened on the 4th with H. Sexton, W. F. Nutter, William B. Hunter, R. Carter, J. Lorckey, Bobby Hunter, Billy Griffin, Hen Sexton (brother to Mert Sexton); Andy Campbell, bones; and Billy Lester, tambo.

WAGNER & COTTON'S MINSTRELS: started out early in August, 1878, for a season's campaign with Johnny Brooks, Harry Stanwood, Girard Bros., Cal Wagner, Ben Cotton, W. W. Rankin, George Eustache, and Jacob Riley. The partnership was dissolved November 23, 1878, and Cotton left the party.

WAGNER (CAL) & CO.'S MINSTRELS: opened in Orange, N. J., November 7, 1865, and consisted of Jimmy Wright, Henry Ide, J. C. Carter, G. W. Rockefeller, E. H. De Coo, D. H. Smith, George Watt, Neil Rogers, Dion De Marbelle, George W. Clark, Masters Rogers and O'Brien, Henry Stewart, E. F. Baggage, W. C. Hadley, Asa La France, George S. Norris, Joseph B. Otis, George Peckham, Charles Smith, and C. A. Jones. This party was shortly after called THE PONTOONS. They closed up in the summer of 1866.

WAGNER & HALL: organized a company in Wheeling, West Va., and took to the road May 1, 1875, with Johnny Hall, Leon Bruce, Billy Wagner, C. A. Conners, Charles Dumont, Fred Kent, George Gans, Billy Boyd, Harry S. Campbell, Joe Kramer, Max Feinler, Theodore Roller, Charles Turner, and Harry Diamond.

WAGNER (CAL) & SAM HAGUE'S MINSTRELS: started on a tour West in February, 1866, with Cal Wagner, Sam Hague, T. D. Fenner, J. T. Carter, G. W. Rockefeller, D. H. Smith, Harry Wagner, Little Stevie (Stevie Rogers), W. C. Hadley, James M. Otis, J. H. Raymond, George E. Peckham, George S. Norris, George W. Clark, Henri Stewart, George Roberts, Neil Rogers, and E. F. Baggage ("Phat Boy"), agent.

WAGNER & SIMMONDS: organized a band in Newark, N. J., and opened in Bloomfield, N. J., January 1, 1866, with Charles Wagner, H. Simmonds, Frank Howard, T. L. Johnston, T. M. Curtis, William Dayton, T. L. Brennan, J. E. Thomas, T. H. Howe, and S. Rankin.

WAGNER'S (HAPPY CAL) MINSTRELS: opened in Baldwinsville, N. Y., October 18, 1869. In the party were Cal Wagner, Ben Hayes, J. H. Roberts, George Barbour, Bob Edwards, James Weston, Gus Clarke, Mike Stanton, John McDonald, Master Steve Peel, and George McDonald, agent. They commenced their next season on August 15, 1870, at Syracuse, N. Y. Lew Hallet, P. O. Myers, George Wilson, W. W. Barbour, G. A. Barbour, George Bagley, Teal Seymour, Archy White, Harry Wayne, Ed Morris, and Ed Tinkham were in the party. In November, 1870, J. Haverly took Cal Wagner with a minstrel party on the road. May 22, 1871, Johnny Booker joined, and in August, 1872, Billy Arlington was a member of the company. The partnership between Haverly and Wagner was dissolved November 8, 1873. A re-organization took place with the following people in the company: Johnny Booker, Sam Price, Edwin Harley, Earl Bruce, John H. Murphy, J. G. Gross, James

Green, Thomas Sadler, and others. The season closed June 20, 1874. The next season he traveled with several changes in the company and had a prosperous tour, which closed at Evansville, Ind., March 20, 1875. This company soon after started out for a summer's tour and was called SAM PRICE'S MINSTRELS.

WAMBOLD & BACKUS' MINSTRELS: See BACKUS' (CHARLEY) ORIGINAL MINSTRELS.

WAMBOLD'S MINSTRELS (not D. S.): was an organization traveling South. They disbanded at the St. Charles Theatre, New Orleans, April 15, 1860, in consequence of bad business.

WAMBOLD'S MINSTRELS: consisting of G. H. Harris, Harry Wilson, Charles Hamilton, Louis R. Lindley, Frank Parent, James Russell, George Boyd, Hamilton Shelly, Harry Johnson, and Howard Marvello, opened October 13, 1865, in New Albany, Ind. They were in existence but one or two weeks.

WARD & WEBB'S MINSTRELS: opened March 4, 1878, in Philadelphia. The party consisted of Charles Sutton, Dave Holbrook, Frank Campbell, Frank Bonner, John Sheldon, Walter Wallace, Charles Busby, Phillip Freeman, Cummings, Hines, Bernardo, John A. Armstrong and others. After a season of two weeks' bad business, they disbanded.

WARDEN'S BURLESQUE TROUPE: appeared in Baltimore, Md., in March, 1858. Frank Weston was in the company.

WARDEN'S TROUPE: consisted of Charles Melville, Billy Boyd, Warden, F. Lynch, Nish, Paudert and Sutton. They traveled in 1855.

WAVERLY MINSTRELS: confined themselves to the small towns in the immediate vicinity of New York. B. Garno, a gentleman afterwards well known in the theatrical and billiard world, was one of the principal performers.

WAYNE, HARRISON & WIGGINS' BAND: was organized in Manchester, N. H., and opened in Concord, N. H., May 1, 1865. In the party were J. Morton, F. Rivers, B. Hoytt, E. B. Hamblin, C. E. Danforth, C. Stearns, J. L. Lefavour, A. Riddelle, and Master J. Lang.

WEAVER & LAWTON'S MINSTRELS: opened December 27, 1876, at Reading, Pa. Add Weaver, Alf Lawton, Henderson, White, Campbell, Green, and the Barlow Brothers were in the company. They disbanded on December 30 after three days' existence.

WELCH, HART & CLARKE'S MINSTRELS: gave their initial entertainment on December 23, 1872, at Springfield, Ill. The company consisted of Fayette Welch, James W. Clarke, Thomas, Reed, J. Rapier, Frank Harrison, Ned West, George Pierce, H. Rushby, Henry Milton and a brass band. On January 31, 1873, W. W. Newcomb joined and the company was thereafter called WELCH & NEWCOMB'S. On March 31, 1873, Newcomb severed his connection with them and they soon after disbanded.

WELCH & HUGHES' MINSTRELS: consisting of Welch, Hughes, Harry White, Albert Welling; Dick Willis, Dave Wilson, A. C. Proctor, C. A. Mathews, George Franchew and others opened in Newark, N. J., November 8, 1877.

WELCH & NEWCOMB'S: See WELCH, HART & CLARK'S MINSTRELS.

WELLINGTON & CHATWICK'S MINSTRELS: made a tour of Utah and Arizona Territories in December, 1866. After crossing some four hundred miles of mountain and sandy desert while on their way to California, the first town they reached was Lanburnolio, where they played in June, 1867, to crowded audiences. In the party were Budd Wellington, Charles Chatwick, Thomas Arlington, Ned Sweet, C. L. Merrill, T. Owen Prentiss, Mat Cannon, J. T. Maxadow, C. E. Hall, Ben Wood, J. Carlton, J. F. Moore, and Master Clarence.

WELLS & HUSSEY'S MINSTRELS: organized in San Francisco and went on a traveling tour through the mountain towns and returned to San Francisco in July, 1859, opening at the Lyceum Theatre, where they remained only two weeks and then disbanded.

WELLS AND KANE: started from St. Louis, Mo., in May, 1869, to travel. George Cushing, J. Clark Wells, manager; Kane and Carroll were in the party.

WESTERN MINSTRELS: opened in Nebraska City in April, 1860, and then traveled with J. A. Grubb, S. F. Baldwin, H. S. Whitten, Thomas Lorten, A. J. Harding, and W. H. Wilson.

WESTON AND HUSSEY: took a minstrel band, consisting of H. Ackland, Harry Kelly, Frank Hussey, N. La Fenillade, J. Stewart, T. Campbell, Max Maretzie, D. Warren, G. Fitch, W. Harrison, Frank Weston, Charles Holly, T. J. Peel, T. Rainford, J. Herman, N. Reeves, Cullimore, T. Buckley, H. Reynolds, and J. Hart, and opened at St. George's Hall, Melbourne, Australia, in June, 1869.

WESTON & PRENDERGAST'S MINSTRELS: consisting of: Frank Weston, J. Prendergast, D. A. Crow, W. T. Anderson, Edward West, B. S. Warren, and L. Miners, organized in February, 1865, and traveled in the far West.

WHITE'S (CHARLEY) MELODEON: in 1850, Charley White had a minstrel company at the Melodeon, 59 Bowery, New York, consisting of R. White, C. White, F. Stanton, W. Smith, H. Neil, Master Juba and Dan Bryant. Dan remained one year on the end. In September, 1853, Mr. White associated with him in the management, Dan Emmett. The admission fee was 12½ and 6¼ cents. The Melodeon closed on April 22, 1854. Charley was very successful here, having introduced to the public E. Bowers, R. M. Carroll (made his debut here as Master Marks), Dan Emmett, Frank Stanton, Lilly Coleman, John Murray, Pic Butler, M. Turner, W. Roark, J. Huntley, John Donnelly, M.. Lewis (Lewis Mairs), G. White, Billy Smith, Master Juba, Boston Rattler, W. Donaldson, W. Quinn, J. Carroll, Tim Norton, Tom Briggs, H. Rumsey, James Budworth, Dan Gardner, William Budworth, Joe Brown, T. D. Rice, Mike Mitchell, John Mulligan, Luke West, Sam Wells, Johnny Pell, Billy Newcomb, Charles Fox, P. B. Isaacs, D. S. Wambold, John Savori, Rayner, E. Deaves, Pierce and Warren. Charley White then opened at the St. Nicholas Rooms, 495 Broadway, three doors above Broome Street, with White's Serenaders.

WHITE'S (COOL) BROADWAY MINSTRELS: started from New York, May 21, 1866, and opened in New Brunswick, N. J. The party consisted of Cool White, T. McNally, J. E. Green, Dick Ralph, J. Wilson, Z. Mortimer, T. Schapcott, Sig.

130

Navoni, J. P. Maguire, S. Coley, H. Stewart, Walter Fields, W. Schwab, J. Celona, J. Wilkinson and Thomas Warhurst, agent. The company collapsed early in June, 1866.

WHITE'S SERENADERS: formerly PRENDERGAST'S MINSTRELS, with Dan Emmett as banjoist. Dan Bowers made a success of "Old Bob Ridley." He opened his new house, 49 Bowery, opposite the Bowery Theatre, New York, in August, 1854. Pell was in the company. John Diamond opened in May, 1855. In July, 1857, the party appeared at Barnum's Museum. The Opera House closed in October, 1857. The party was known as White's Ethiopian Opera Troupe while at 49 Bowery. Charley White is the originator of afterpieces in minstrel bands, having introduced them at the Melodeon. In August, 1856, Charley White located his minstrels at the Chinese Assembly Rooms, 539 Broadway, New York. Eph Horn was in the party. In May, 1860, he opened 598 Broadway in conjunction with A. Adams. It was a few doors above the Metropolitan Hotel.

WHITE'S SERENADERS: were organized by Charley White in 1846 and consisted of R. White, Charley White, F. Stanton, W. Smith, H. Neil, and Master Juba. They appeared at the Melodeon, 53 Bowery, New York.

WHITING'S MINSTRELS: opened in Schuylkill Haven, Pa., July 14, 1865. Eugene F. Gorman, J. H. Whiting, George Hill and others were in the party.

WHITMORE & CLARK'S MINSTRELS: reorganized in May, 1866, with the following performers: George M. Clark, A. White, Andy Weaver, Boyle Bros., C. A. Whitman, E. P. Hardy, Jimmy Porter, Thomas Mayo, Andy Wyatt, E. C. Clements, Thomas Maynard, F. Packard, Johnny Armstrong, J. K. Strong, F. Perkins, and W. Thorbahn. They traveled East. They reorganized the next season with George M. Clark, Hank White, Johnny Morrisey, Eddie Lincoln, Otto Newbert, Johnny Dunbar, Fred Britton, L. A. Reed, J. G. Bishop, S. W. West, J. Holt, G. E. Kinsley, J. T. Maynard, E. P. Hardy, O. S. Holden, and M. Chiniski. In December, 1869, this party was playing through Massachusetts with C. H. Colborn, cornet; Johnny Morrisey, bones; Hank White, trombone; George M. Clark, middle. Whitmore & Clark reorganized at White River Junction, Vt., on January 5, 1874, with Clark and Hardy as proprietors. In the party were Frank Morton, Hank White, George M. Clarke, Thomas Maynard, Master Freddy Conway, Mack, Carl Rudolph, Andy M. Wyatt, and L. C. Read. This company closed at Windsor, Vt., November 22, 1875.

WILD, BARNEY & MAC'S MINSTRELS: gave their first show at Providence, R. I., October 25, 1869. In the company were Sam Devere, Frank Meyring, Byron George, R. T. Tyrrell, B. Tyrrell, G. W. Barnard, H. J. Milliken, J. Hayden, C. T. Smith, and Charles Wilson.

WILLIAMS' EMPIRE MINSTRELS: was the title of a party on the road early in 1847. William Morris was among them.

WILLIS & THOMPSON'S MINSTRELS: opened in Mobile, Ala., May 27, 1865, with Oscar Willis, Willis Armstrong, E. K. Collins, James Snyder, C. G. Spinola, Master Bobby, J. W. Thompson, James Livingston, John Stuart, James Weaver, Ed Magruder, J. T. Murphy, Frank and Emilie Siegel.

WILSON & MORRIS' MINSTRELS: were started from Boston, Mass., in December, 1860, for a traveling tour. The party consisted of Fred Wilson, clog; Charles A. Morris and W. H. Brockway, managers; George W. Shepard, C. Reynolds, M. T. Skiff, Add Weaver, Little Barney, S. P. Emery, A. Jones, C. A. Boyd, W. Field, W. Blair, F. Fordukes, and J. D. Burton. C. Backus joined them in January, 1861. They closed a two weeks' stay at Austin Hall, Boston, March 16, 1861. After a short travel, they disbanded in April.

WILSON & WILSON'S NEW YORK MINSTRELS: was a band that consisted of John and R. D. Wilson, W. Merrill, W. Carlton, Charles Florence, John Freeman, John Godley, Francis De Moore, Master Clarence, H. H. Gardner, A. J. Talbot, Jake Wallace, William Vincent, Frank Medina, and Tommy Bree. They opened at Platt's Hall, San Francisco, Cal., February 8, 1867, and lasted just four days, as the party was too big (seventeen in the first part) to make the "ghost walk," and the manager closed up.

WILSON'S CIRCUS MINSTRELS: consisting of Fred Sprung, Frank Wilson and George Winship, was a party that accompanied Wilson's Circus over the mountain towns in California during August, 1865.

WILSON'S (FRED) MINSTRELS: gave their first show at Jacksonville, Ill., March 2, 1873. Fred D. Goslee was the tenor. In May, Fred Fox, George Wilson, John Rapier, Will Morton, and R. M. Tileston were in the party. The season closed June 16, 1873, at Lafayette, Ind.

WILSON'S MINSTRELS: [See MC CHESNEY & BRIGGS] consisting of Billy Norwood, Ned Turner, F. Lapham, N. B. Shimer, Dr. D. Wilson, Master Tommy, and Frank Mintford started late in November, 1864, for a tour through New York State.

WILSON'S MINSTRELS: On June 27, 1868, they closed their season in St. Louis and went traveling. In the party were J. R. Kemble, Cal Wagner, Harry Talbot, C. S. Fredericks, J. J. Kelly, Rollin Dano, J. G. Withers, Prof. Blakeney, Frank Cardilla, F. Wilson, Tommy Queen, Ed Montgomery, Jules Seidel, Charles Kommefsky, Lucas Cooke, and William Collins. They re-opened in St. Louis September 7, 1868.

WINNEMORE'S SERENADERS: consisted of A. F. Winnemore, manager and proprietor; F. Solomon, leader; G. Harrington, musical director; J. Rudolph, W. D. Laconta, D. W. Lull, J. Thompson, Tom Brower, J. Donnelly, Paine, and Mitchell. They appeared in Philadelphia in November, 1849.

WINSHIP'S OPERA TROUPE: was organized in 1853 by George Winship. They traveled from New York to New Orleans, meeting with fair success. They disbanded in 1854 but reorganized in 1856 and traveled the Northern States and Canada, disbanding in Montreal.

WINTHROP SERENADERS: organized and traveled through Massachusetts in July, 1858, with J. B. Dunton, E. Cutter, J. Crowell, N. J. Hall, Billy Whitney, Harry Blanchard, Frank West, and J. Woodworth.

WOOD & NIXON'S MINSTRELS: appeared at Apollo Hall, New Orleans, in November, 1859. In December they started traveling with Dan Wood, Hank

Wakeley, Jimmy Carroll, Charles Rand, Joe Nixon, and Master Reede. They afterwards went through the West.

WOOD'S EMPIRE MINSTRELS: commenced a western tour in December, 1859, with Charles Sanford, J. Smith, Sile Weed, and J. C. Willis.

WOOD'S ETHIOPIAN TROUPE: was a party that organized in September, 1860, for a traveling tour, but were soon after known as BELROY'S ETHIOPIANS.

WOOD'S METROPOLITAN MINSTRELS AND JULIAN'S OPERA TROUPE: organized in Providence, R. I., by Samuel Corry as manager in April, 1863. They consisted of F. J. Wood, Charles Slocum, Harry Bloodgood, Dan Pell, S. W. Lagee Jr., George D. Horance, W. Harrington, B. J. Donniker, H. H. Massey, C. Hill, Daniel Lang, H. Walsh, J. Cane, and Charles Karavell. Fanny Wood appeared in the first part in white face as interrogator.

WOOD'S MINSTRELS: under the management of James H. Budworth, consisted of W. S. Budworth, R. Howard, J. K. Campbell, H. Wheeler, M. G. Solomon, Master F. Budworth, and J. H. Budworth. They opened at Barnum's Museum, New York, in July, 1860, where they closed August 18 for a traveling tour, under the title of BUDWORTH'S MINSTRELS. J. Slater, Mons. Delvidie, Mr. Ketter, A. H. Wood, Rollin Howard, Mons. Strakosch, Thomas Hall, W. S. Stratton, Master Tommy, and W. S. Budworth were in the party.

WOOD'S MINSTRELS: started December 24, 1869, and opened in Lawrenceburg, Ind., with Marsh Adams, interlocutor; Tim Woodruff and Harry Nickerson, end men; Harry Parker and others. Harry Wood was manager.

WOOD'S MINSTRELS: under the management of Cool White, started from New York and opened January 4, 1866, in Morrisania, N. Y., with S. S. Purdy, J. H. Budworth, H. T. Mudge, J. Clark, T. McNally, Walter Fields, J. Wilson, T. Simpson, Z. Mortimer, Sig. Vayo, J. Bergness, N. C. Dumaille, J. Bishop, J. Chitry, and Chit Moore, agent.

WOOD'S MINSTRELS: was another party organized by Sylvester Bleecker in June, 1862, and started for a traveling tour on the 7th. Theodore Jacobs (brother to Mrs. George Holman), J. H. Carleton, Billy Allen, S. Myers, W. Herman, J. Eastmead, J. Kelk, M. Brooks, R. Thompson, J. Owens, and J. Francis. Sylvester Bleecker was manager for Tom Thumb for a long time.

WOOD'S MINSTRELS: was the title of an organization started in December, 1862, by Palmer and company. The performers consisted of Prof. Rhinehart, Frank Berger, Billy Sweatnam, Gus Shaw, Tim Woodruff, C. W. Morgan, Frank Wilson, Moses Rumney, and Master Willie.

WOOD'S MINSTRELS: were organized in New York in January, 1860; immediately after, Henry Wood closed. They started West with the following people: L. Meyer, R. Thompson, F. Edwards, J. H. Budworth, Ned Davis, C. Crosby, R. Abecco, H. W. Ellis, Sylvester Bleecker (the manager and middle man), and H. Guyon. Budworth left early in March and Dave Reed took his place. J. W. Beyer, L. M. Reese, and F. Wyant also joined. In June, E. Harrison, violinist, was engaged.

They returned to New York October 25 for a few weeks' rest, after which they traveled again, but finally returned to New York April 24, 1861, and disbanded.

WOOD'S NEW YORK MINSTRELS: was the name of a party performing at Yazoo City, in January, 1859. They were on the steamer, *Banjo*, at the time; and consisted of S. Gardner, George W. Hills, T. L. Chatfield, M. B. Fox, J. H. Cassiday, J. Mairs, T. H. Jefferson, and Young Master Tommy. They visited New Orleans in March, and in April they left the *Banjo* and opened at the Amphitheatre, that city. C. Young, M. B. Jefferson, and G. H. Cushing added to the party.

WOODRUFF & FOSTER'S MINSTRELS: In 1858, Tim Woodruff and N. Footer had a band on the road in Cincinnati. They opened at the New Museum (late Western Museum) in October with Barber, Woodruff, Sutton, West, Shelton, Richardson, and Howe. They soon after were known as TIM WOODRUFF'S MINSTRELS.

WORLD RENOWNED AND FAR FAMED NEW ORLEANS MINSTRELS: was the title of a party playing at Otto Cottage Garden Theatre, Hoboken, N. J., in July, 1860, and consisted of W. C. McCall, T. McAnally and others.

WRIGHT'S (BILLY) MINSTRELS: were organized for the summer season of 1876. Eph Horn Jr., Al Hulmes, Ad Collins, Billy Brown and others were in the party. They opened in June at Rihl's Hall at the extreme southern section of the city of Philadelphia.

WYATT'S MINSTRELS: was organized in Boston, Mass., by George W. Wyatt, the well known actor and manager, in March, 1843. The party, after traveling through Massachusetts for a brief time, closed up owing to a quarrel between Jenkins and Diamond (No. 2). The party consisted of A. L. Thayer (banjo), John Diamond (bones), Harry Mestayer (violin), and Charles Jenkins (tambourine). George W. Wyatt, on the night of January 18, 1860, played Phineas Fletcher in "Uncle Tom's Cabin" at Waterbury, Mass. Soon after the play he complained of faintness and in fifteen minutes was a corpse.

YANKEE HILL'S MINSTRELS: with Yankee Hill as proprietor; Dr. William Valentine, business manager; George Gray, Frank Mumford, George Whiting, and others traveled West in December, 1863.

YANKEE HLLL'S MINSTRELS: were organized in Boston, Mass., in 1854 and visited the principal towns in the East with George Long, Frank Spencer, D. W. Norton, G. W. Buckley, G. Bones Rose, and John Norton.

YOUNG AMERICANS: were organized in Chicago, Ill., July, 1860. H. Henneman, bones; W. Hollister, J. Clark, Albert Henderson; J. H. Bishop, interlocutor; Charles Walker, tenor; Johnny Dunlap, Tony Waters, and Billy Murphy, tambo. They played at Simons' saloon, Chicago, for four nights, and then went traveling.

YOUNG CAMPBELLS, THE: started in December, 1862, for a trip through the East. They consisted of Johnny Duley, Billy Train, F. Brundage, J. D. Lyman, G. Campbell, R. Dana, F. L. Bennett, Harry Stanley, H. Beach, George Havens, H. Kammering, and Master Edwards.

Frank Brower

BROWN'S BURNT CORK BIOGRAPHY

ABBOTT, D. C.: died in La Salle, Ill., May 20, 1864.

ADAMS, JOHN A.: of Moore & Burgess' party, died in London, England, January 24, 1873. He visited Europe with Rumsey & Newcomb's party.

ALLEN, JOHNNY: was born in Newark, N. J., April 20, 1844. He first appeared before the public in 1861 in burnt cork. He first appeared in New York at Hitchcock's place in Canal Street. He was at the French Theatre, 585 Broadway, in January, 1863, when a miscellaneous entertainment was given. He made his debut on the dramatic stage March 24, 1871, at Brooklyn, N.Y., in "Schneider." He first appeared on the dramatic stage in New York, April 24, 1871, at the Bowery Theatre. There was an ease and grace in the personations of Mr. Allen which were particularly noticeable and distinguished him from the great mass of performers who attempted the acts which he executed so successfully.

ARLINGTON, WILLIAM: right name Burnell, was born in New York City. He was considered a good end man.

ARMSTRONG, WILLIS: died in a hospital in New York on April 18, 1877, of consumption.

BACKUS, CHARLES: had the remarkable good fortune to have been born in the year 1831, in the city of Rochester, N. Y.; in which city and Cleveland, Ohio, his boyhood's days were passed. In 1832 he emigrated to California. At San Francisco he organized a band of minstrels known as the Backus Minstrels and gave performances in that city and throughout the state during four years with a degree of success unparalleled in the history of the profession. In conjunction with S. C. Campbell and Jerry Bryant, Mr. Backus next proceeded to Australia, stopping on their voyage at the Sandwich Islands, where they had the honor of appearing before his highness the King at his palace by special request of his majesty. Arriving at Sidney, Backus and troupe gave a series of performances and met with such encouragement as to induce him to repeat them in the principle cities and towns of the colony, extending then to Van Dieman's Land. Returning to Sidney, he next went to California, the scene of his first professional successes. There he remained about two years, when, relinquishing for a while the minstrel business, he attached himself as Negro clown to Buston's Circus and in this capacity accompanied the circus all through the interior of Australia for some six or eight months. Finding the circus business not congenial to his taste, he formed a small company of performers and proceeded to England by the overland route, stopping at Ceylon, Asten in Nubia, Bombay, up the Red Sea, through the land of Egypt, giving performances at all these places, including Cairo. Sailing down the Mediterranean, he paused time enough to perform at Gibraltar and the historic isle of Malta. He played as clown at Astley's Amphitheatre and Canterbury Hall in London, England; and then returned to his native place. He played star engagements in Philadelphia, Baltimore, and Washington. In 1861, he returned to California and played there two years; then organized a band of minstrels and went to China, playing at Shanghai, Hong Kong, Canton and Moccos. Remaining in China four months, he again returned to San Francisco, where he was engaged by Thomas Maguire in conjunction with Billy Birch, D. S. Wambold and W. Bernard. These three, with Mr. Backus, formed the San Francisco Minstrels and came to New York a short time since. And on the 8th of May, 1865, they opened at Heller's Hall, 585 Broadway, where, night after night admiring crowds attested their claims to superiority and excellence. Mr. Backus' specialty was mimicry, imitations and delineations of popular actors.

BAKER, TOM: died in the City Hospital, at Memphis, Tenn., in October, 1870, of congestion of the brain, aged 32 years.

BAMFORD, H.: died in the hospital, in San Francisco, on April, 1871.

BARKER, WILLIAM H.: died in San Francisco, Cal., December 11, 1863, aged 38 years.

BARLOW, MILT G.: was born in Lexington, Ky., June 29, 1843, and entered the minstrel profession in 1870 as an end man.

BASQUIN, J. A.: one of the best Ethiopian minstrel performers ever before the public, died at Brooklyn, N. Y., on January 27, 1872, at the age of 42 years. He was supposed to have been a native of France. For a long time he was connected with Hooley's Serenaders, and was also with Unsworth and Eugene in England, and had been prominently before the American public for a number of years as a member at various times of many prominent minstrel bands. As a performer he was very popular, not only with the public but with his professional brethren. He had been ailing for some time past in Philadelphia, Pa., and was recently engaged by R. M. Hooley for his opera house in Brooklyn. Some two weeks prior to his decease, he was placed in the Long Island Hospital, the expenses of his illness and burial being defrayed by R. M. Hooley and the members of his company. His remains were interred at the cemetery of the Holy Cross.

BENEDICT, LEWIS: was born in Buffalo, N. Y., December 7, 1839 and studied law for some time; but finding that profession not in accordance with his tastes, he went to Buffalo, N.Y., where he determined to adopt the minstrel profession. And in the year 1858 he opened the stage of the Metropolitan Theatre in that city. He made his debut in a black face and dance, an "Essence," then very popular, and met with a hearty reception. At St. Louis, Mo., his style being so much different from the host of comedians in the field, he secured a place in a troupe then organizing, called Johnson's Empire Minstrels. In the company at that time were the veterans Frank Lynch, Mart Flavin, Dick Moore and several others. The company went as far as St. Joseph, Mo., and met with great success in the West. Lew then became the favorite in Chicago, Detroit, Milwaukee, Cleveland, Toledo and fifty other places of interest. Lew was always the lion, making hosts of friends both on and off the stage. In 1863 he became a partner with Mr. Duprez in the company now known as Duprez &

& Benedict's Minstrels. In deportment, Lew is the ideal of a gentleman, the members of the company being strongly attached to him. He has a joke and smile for everyone and some very amusing incidents could be related of this prince of comedians.

BERGER, PAUL: retired from the business in June, 1864, having received an appointment as transcribing clerk in the Philadelphia Post Office but he shortly after went back to his "old love."

BERNARD, WILLIAM H.: was born in New York in 1833. The first we heard of him in the minstrel business was in 1849 when he sailed for California by the ship *Brooklyn*. He was two hundred and twelve days getting there. He organized the first minstrel party in California in August, 1849, and played in the Parker House at five dollars per ticket. He then hired Alfred Green's Hall, over the Aguilla d'Oro. During the winter of 1849 he went to the Sandwich Islands with the company known as the New York Serenaders and played in Honolulu for five months, the Island being full of Californians avoiding the hardships of California incidental to the hard times of 1849. He returned to San Francisco and embarked for Van Dieman's Land with the same company. Owing to a mutiny on the ship, the troupe left the vessel at Otabeite, one of the Society Island group, where the vessel touched to leave the mutineers. They gave six concerts there and then visited the palaces, having received a demand from Queen Pomares to amuse her. From there they took passage on a ship bound to Tasmania, and arrived in Launceston in 1850. There they met John Mitchell, McManus and other expatriated Irishmen, who received the New York Serenaders with fraternal cordiality. They also met many of the Chartists—Jones in particular. At that time (1850) they were the only Americans in Van Dieman's Land and the troupe did an immense business. They played five months between Launceston and Hobart Town. From the latter city they went to Sydney and were the first to introduce minstrelsy in Australia. They often had the patronage of Sir Arthur Fitzroy and Lady Keith Stewart. They then visited Melbourne, and back to Sydney; thence far off to India's burning sands and were in Calcutta in 1851. They were the pioneers of minstrelsy in India and were a great success. They were honored by the patronage of the Marquis of Delhousie and Lady Delhousie, the Duke of Wellington's sister. They played before many of the rajahs and celebrities of that section of Hindustan; and went thence to Madras, where success attended their efforts. From Madras they went to Ceylon, that beautiful land of edifices and temples. For five months the troupe played in that country, performing at Point De Galle, Columbo, Kandy, and thence to Bombay, still the pioneers. The company then returned over the same ground, playing the second time in Calcutta, traveling in India on the Peninsula and Oriental Steam Navigation's steamers. The company consisted of six persons, who paid the agents of that company 20,000 rupees for sixteen days' traveling on that line. Mr. Bernard then sailed around the Cape of Good Hope and landed all right in New York. He returned to California and associated himself with Charley Backus and Billy Birch. David Wambold soon after visited California and was a great success, filling the Eureka and Academy for months. From the quality of material then professionally associated, the Birch, Wambold, Bernard and Backus' San Francisco Minstrels, knowing that if it were possible to secure a hall in New York, success would attend their efforts. They left San Francisco, the city of their great success, guided solely by their own judgment and business qualifications. They secured the hall known as Heller's, previously a sepulcher for all who had the audacity to try it, having proved an ulcer to the profession in general and swamped the Buckley's and hosts of others. But the master hands went to work with a determination to succeed and the receipts of the company exceeded those of any other minstrel band in the United States for the same length of time. They are one of the institutions of New York, and deservedly so from their originality. Mr. Bernard fills the very responsible position of interrogator, and as such has no superior, if an equal, in the business. He is very original in everything he does and is possessed of a deliciously comic laugh. It is not the dry cackle or the senseless chuckle sometimes given out as the laugh Ethiopian. It is rich, unctuous, the expressive juice of careless mirth and jollity. It strikes the heart with a positive shock of fun. He mingles his humor with occasional bursts of serious intensity, which give the speeches designed for the purpose their fullest significance. Mr. Bernard is also a most excellent musician, playing the violin very well.

BIDEAUX, GUSTAVE: was born in France in 1830. He came to America in 1858.

BIRCH, WILLIAM: was born in Utica, N.Y., February 26, 1831. His first attempt at minstrelsy was in 1844 in a small town called New Hartford, N.Y., under the management of Ned Underhill's father, occupying the bone end. He shortly after joined Raymond's Minstrels. He joined the Virginia Serenaders in Philadelphia. He appeared in New York in 1850, at 444 Broadway, with Fellows' Minstrels, where he remained one year. Then he traveled with the Eph Horn, Wells & Briggs' party. He returned to New York and engaged with Wood's Minstrels at 444 Broadway. After a trip West, he re-appeared in New York with Wood & Christy's Minstrels. He went into partnership with Dick Sliter and Sam Wells, sailed for San Francisco, and opened at Maguire's Opera House in 1851. He remained in California six years. He was married on August 19, 1857, and the following day the twain took passage on the steamship *Central America*, for New York. On the passage the steamship was wrecked off Charleston, S.C., on September 12. Just before being sent into one of the lifeboats, Mrs. Birch took a pet canary bird from its cage in her state-room which she nestled in her bosom. During the excitement, Billy became separated from his wife. Mr. Birch was picked up by the Norwegian bark *Ellen* and taken into Norfolk, Va., more dead than alive. After playing in Baltimore one week (doing Negro acts between the pieces at the Holliday Street Theatre), he opened with the Bryants in New York. He was with Hooley & Campbell's at Niblo's Saloon; with Sharpley in Philadelphia, Lloyd's Minstrels, Hooley & Campbell's, back to California for three years, and then returned to New York and established the San Francisco Minstrels. As an end man and general comedian, he was one of the best in the business. For originality and the ability to play on words, he was excelled by few, if any. His manipulations of the bones were also good. His elaborate exordiums to nothing in particular, his unctuous representations of meaningless phrases, his apparently unconscious transition from pathos to bathos, and from the logical to the ludicrous, kept the audience in roars of laughter. Birch was quite as funny in the "Virginia

Mammy" as ever Daddy Rice was. Billy Birch died April 20, 1897, in New York City.

BLOODGOOD, HARRY: right name Carlo Moran, was born in Providence, R. I., in 1845. He first appeared in public at the age of fifteen with Hoffman, the pianist. He first put on burnt cork with Wood's Minstrels and remained with them nine months. After that he was connected with some of the best variety theatres and minstrel bands in the country. He was the originator of the present style of song and dance, which he first introduced in "Anna Maria Jane," written by himself and brought out at Hooley's, Brooklyn. He was also author of "The Yellow Girl That Winked at Me," and other popular songs and dances. Mr. Bloodgood died June 12, 1886.

BOLEY, DAN F.: was one of the original Backus Minstrels. He was a fine banjoist, and his deep, sonorous, bass voice will be recollected with mingled feelings of regret and pleasure. In 1855, he, in company with Backus, Burbank, and others re-organized the Backus Minstrels and made a trip to Australia. After a time all except Boley returned. He married a wealthy widow and remained there.

BOOTH, T. G.: made his first appearance on the stage (as a low comedian) at the Metropolitan Theatre, Buffalo, N.Y., in 1853. He died in Toronto, Canada, August 18, 1855, and his remains were brought to New York.

BOWERS, EDWARD: made his debut on the minstrel stage at Charley White's Melodeon, No. 49 Bowery, New York, some time between 1850 and 1854; and he played there for several months. In January, 1856, he joined Ordway's Aeolians in Boston, Mass., and left them in May. When Henry Wood and George Christy opened a new marble building on the westerly side of Broadway, near Prince Street, as a minstrel hall, October 31, 1857, Mr. Bowers was a member of the company. George Christy withdrew from the firm in May, 1858, and the company was thenceforth known as Wood's Minstrels. In the summer, Mr. Bowers left the company to become co-manager of Birch, Bowers & Fox's Minstrels, who opened in the Museum, St. Louis, Mo., September 6, 1858. They disbanded December 25, that year. Returning to New York, he joined Sniffen's Campbell Minstrels, 444 Broadway, January 3, 1859, and that company disbanded the following February. In May of that year he filled for a few weeks the place of J. G. H. Shorey in the New Orleans and Metropolitan Burlesque Troupe, under the management of J. G. H. Shorey, W. Carle & C. H. Duprez. In August, 1859, he joined Wood's Minstrels in New York; but remained only a few months, as on December 12 he opened with Anderson's Minstrels in the Melodeon, Boston, Mass. After a season of five weeks and four nights, this company disbanded. He then joined the Morris Brothers, Pell & Trowbridge's Troupe, remaining with them until the fall of 1862. In the latter part of that year he joined Holley's Minstrels in Brooklyn, N.Y., and continued there until about November, 1863. In company with T. B. Prendergast, he organized a company which opened in Newark, N. J., January 3, 1864. In June of that year the company was reorganized, and its title changed to that of the Aeolians. After this troupe disbanded, he played for a time with Moran's Minstrels in Philadelphia, Pa., and subsequently fulfilled engagements in variety theatres. He made his last appearance on any stage in the Varieties, in the Bowery, New York, February 11, 1865, while fulfilling a star engagement with John Mulligan. He was then taken ill and died on the 27th at the age of 38 years. He was an excellent interlocutor, a good business manager, and one of the best writers or adapters of Negro farces and sketches of his time. He also wrote many songs which became popular. Being of a genial disposition, he made many friends and acquaintances.

BOYCE, CHARLES: died in Providence, R. I., July 1, 1862, aged 24 years, of consumption.

BOYCE, JOHN: died in Brooklyn, N.Y., June 11, 1867, aged 38 years and three months. His remains were interred in Evergreen Cemetery. He was born in Covington, Ky., in 1829. The first band he played with was Birch, Bowers and Fox, in 1857. His last appearance was in New York with Griffin & Christy's Minstrels on June 4, 1867. As an end man he was a most excellent performer. His great specialty was singing Irish songs. He possessed a good brogue and also sang his songs with much humor. He also did a good stump speech.

BRIGGS, T. F.: was, we believe, a native of New York City and early in life was employed in a butcher shop in East Broadway. When he first went on the minstrel stage (Billy Birch informs us), he played under the name of Tom Fluter; but shortly thereafter, owing to his success, he resumed his own name. In 1846, when the Sable Harmonists were organized, he was of the company, which also included Plumer Archer, J. Farrell, W. Roark, Nelson Kneass, J. Murphy, R. M. Hooley, and Mr. Tichenor. In November, 1847 they played for a brief time in the Minerva Rooms in New York and subsequently went to Europe under the management of R. M. Hooley; and we presume Mr. Briggs accompanied them. They performed in London, Paris, Boulogne, Brussels and the smaller cities in the British Isles. In 1851 he was a co-manager of Horn, Wells & Briggs' Minstrels, who in July of that year played in the Boston (Mass.) Museum, the troupe then including J. K. Campbell, S. A. Wells, Eph Horn, Tom Christian, Calsianno, Billy Birch, J. W. Farrell, and T. F. Briggs. In the same year he joined Wood's Minstrels, 444 Broadway; and we find that in 1853 he was still a member of the company. In March, 1854, he joined the Buckley's, then playing at 539 Broadway. And on September 20 of that year, in company with E. P. Christy, Earl Pierce, J. B. Donniker, Tom Christian, Lewis Mairs, Tom Vaughn, S. C. Campbell, Eph Horn and others, he sailed in Vanderbilt's steamship *North Star* for California. While crossing the Isthmus he caught the Panama fever and from its effects he died after his arrival in San Francisco, Cal., without having performed there. He was an excellent banjoist, and some time before his death he played in sketches in partnership with Eph Horn, they proving a very strong attraction. At the time of his demise he was about 30 years of age. He was a good banjo player. There have been few as good but none better in his peculiar line. Horn was very much attached to Briggs and was deeply affected by his death. He declared he would quit the business as soon as his engagement was up, as he could never get another acting partner to fill Briggs' place.

BROWER, FRANK: was born in Baltimore, Md., in 1820. His first appearance in public was in 1837 as Master Brower. He then became the confidante of Weldon, the magician. He next traveled with the Cincinnati Circus Company, under the management of Charles J. Rogers. It was while Richard Myers, Frank Brower, and others were practicing in Philadelphia that Mr. Rogers happened to hear the party playing; and of what he thought and did on that occasion, we excerpt the following from a private letter of Mr. Rogers:

> I soon made up my mind that Frank Brower possessed all the talent there was in the party; so I engaged him, and we left the depot, corner Eleventh and Market Streets, at 12 o'clock the same night. We opened in Cincinnati soon after our arrival, and spent the season traveling in Ohio, Indiana, Virginia and Kentucky.

During the season the manager found a banjo player named Ferguson, who played the banjo and worked on the canvas for ten dollars a week. Brower and Ferguson soon became the greatest cards of the day. About this time Henry Clay and Tom Marshall of Kentucky were engaged on opposite sides in a very important lawsuit in Versailles, where the circus played during the trial. Marshall gained the suit and was so much elated at beating his old political opponent that he indulged a little too freely; and, being much pleased with Frank Brower---who was very temperate at that time---induced him to join him in a "drinking bout." At daybreak Frank and the great "Kentucky orator" were snoozing in the barroom of the hotel, one on the counter and the other on the floor. Ferguson went South and died of cholera. Brower returned to Philadelphia and the company laid up. In the spring of 1841, Brower again joined Rogers' Circus and Emmett played the banjo in the ring to Brower's dancing. We have already spoken of him as one of the original band. In 1851, he again visited England as clown to Gen. Rufus Welch's Circus. As a performer, he stood at the head of his profession. He was very versatile. As Gumbo Cuff in "Oh, Hush!" he was immense. His dry wit was well understood by the audience and its freedom from vulgarity commended it to the lovers of genuine fun. His "Happy Uncle Tom" was as perfect a piece of acting as has ever been witnessed upon any stage. In 1867, he retired from the profession and opened a saloon on Ninth Street below Market, Philadelphia. He died in Philadelphia, June 4, 1874, and his remains were interred in Woodlands Cemetery, that city.

BROWER, THOMAS P.: died in Philadelphia, March 15, 1867, aged 39 years.

BROWN, JOE: Ethiopian comedian and jig dancer, was born in Buffalo, N.Y., January 2, 1830. He first entered the business in 1844 in Albany. He had a match dance with Earl Pierce the same year and won it. He first appeared in New York at the Melodeon, opposite the Old Bowery Theatre, in the fall of 1852. He went to England July 11, 1857, and, after an absence of eleven years, returned to New York, June 2, 1868. He danced a match game with Dick Sliter in Chicago, Ill., in 1856 and received the champion belt (silver), which he lost when shipwrecked. He left New York for England in 1857. In August, 1866, he paid a flying visit to New York but returned to Europe in a week. He was the first man to do "Old Bob Ridley" in a regular minstrel band.

BROWN, JOHN G.: died in New Bedford, Mass., October 8, 1853.

BRYANT, JERRY: was born in Chesterfield, Essex County, N.Y, on June 11, 1828. He commenced to learn the printing business but left it at thirteen years of age to make his appearance as a ballad singer. Having met with some success, he obtained an engagement at Vauxhall Garden, New York, in 1844, enlisting with him in the same company the talent of his brother, Dan. About this period negro minstrelsy came in vogue and the humor of the thing hitting Jerry's fancy, he united himself with the first troupe which was known under the name of Campbell's Minstrels; and it was on July 14, 1845, for Pete De Laru's benefit that Jerry danced "his match for $1,000 with Master Tommy Teaser from Troy; the audience to be the judges!" In October, 1848, he sailed for London, England, and performed with Dumbolton's Serenaders at the St. James Theatre, then made a tour of Scotland. He returned to New York in 1849 and traveled through the States. He then appeared at Mitchell's Olympic Theatre, New York, with Earl H. Pierce in a minstrel organization. Then he went to Boston and appeared with Ordway's Aeolians. He returned to New York and joined E. P. Christy's Minstrels in 1853. In the latter part of 1854, Jerry yielded to the common fever of all American "professionals" and went to California, where he soon became as great a favorite as here and divided popularity with the first comic stars then figuring in that country. The writer well recollects him in the trial dance with Horn; and well does he recollect, too, that not even Tom Briggs, whose talents and whose gentle nature made him the pet of every circle, was more highly esteemed for correct conduct and amiable qualities than Jerry Bryant. From California, after a year's stay, Jerry made a trip to the Sandwich Islands and Australia, returning by the same route in 1856; and, after a short stay in the principal Pacific cities, reached New York again in the winter of the latter year. Jerry now made no more wanderings abroad but, gathering his two brothers around him, he on the 23d of the following February (1857) fixed himself and them permanently at 472 Broadway; and there laid the foundation of a business name and fame in the title of the Bryants' Minstrels. He was "a fellow of infinite jest." In him was confined the true spirit of drollery and all the elements of fun without vulgarity. He was at once the perfection of dry, telling fun and extreme physical whimsicality; and those who were forced to roar at his impassive countenance or were transfixed by his astonishing grimaces, would, if they met him the next morning, be hardly able to recognize in his handsome and somewhat serious features, the comic actor of the night before. There was a peculiarity in his style that seemed to preclude all idea of successful imitation. He was himself alone, a host of talent, a delineator of eccentric Negro character never surpassed and but rarely equaled. In private life he was a social companion, gay, lively and generous. Jerry made his last appearance in public April 2, 1861. He died on April 8 of congestion of the brain. His remains were interred in Calvary Cemetery.

BRYANT, NEIL: died in St. Mary's Hospital, Brooklyn, March 6, 1902, aged 72 years. His right name was Cornelius O'Brien. He retired from the profession in August, 1883, and secured a position in the Bureau of Engraving and Printing at Washington, where he remained until taken to the hospital.

BRYANT, DANIEL WEBSTER: was born in Troy, N.Y., on May 9, 1833. He made his first appearance on the stage in 1845 at Vauxhall Gardens, situated on the west side of the Bowery, just below Cooper Institute, on the occasion of his brother Jerry's benefit. Shortly after this he determined to enter the profession as a regular performer and he was engaged with a number of companies until 1848, when he joined Losee's Minstrels. In 1849 he joined the Sable Harmonists and traveled through the South and West. On returning to this city in 1850, he became a member of Charley White's Minstrels, then located at the Melodeon in the Bowery. After performing there for one year, he joined Wood & Fellows' Minstrels on Broadway and remained with them one season. He then joined the original Campbell's Minstrels, occupying the place on the end formerly filled by Luke West. They traveled South and West until 1856, disbanding in July. Mr. Bryant then managed a company styled Bryant's Campbell Minstrels. During that season he made an immense hit in his "Essence of Old Virginny"---a characteristic dance which has since been attempted by many men in the business; but, up to the day of his demise, Dan never met with a successful rival. The following September he visited Philadelphia, where he met with great success. In February, 1857, his brothers Jerry and Neil arrived in New York from an extended tour of California and Australia and with them he formed a co-partnership; and, getting together a company, they opened Mechanics' Hall, 472 Broadway. Dan Bryant made his debut on the dramatic stage for the benefit of his intimate friend, William R. Floyd, at the Winter Garden, July 2, 1863, when he acted Handy Andy in Mr. Floyd's comic drama of that name. On July 26, 1864, he began a summer season at Wallack's Theatre, acting in "The Irish Emigrant" and "Handy Andy," and subsequently in "The Colleen Bawn." He played a few weeks only. In May, 1865, he sailed for Europe and acted upon the dramatic stage with success in both Dublin, Ireland, and Liverpool, England. And on July 17, 1865, he began another brief season at Wallack's Theatre, which closed August 26. On June 11, 1866, he began a third summer season at this theatre, producing on July 30 "Shamus O'Brien." He closed September 1 and then went on a starring tour, visiting the principal cities of the country. On June 10, he commenced his fourth annual engagement at Wallack's, which closed July 27. On August. 10, he sailed for California under engagement to Thomas Maguire. In 1868, Mr. Bryant abandoned the dramatic stage and returned to minstrelsy, opening a new hall in the Tammany Building. On August 2, 1869, he began an engagement at Niblo's Garden, acting Shawn in "Arrah-na-Pogue," which ran until September 5, when he terminated his performances. His last performances on the dramatic stage were at Wallack's Theatre in the fall of 1874, when he kindly helped the management out of a dilemma by consenting to perform for a brief season during the illness of J. L. Toole. His last appearance in public was at his own opera house on the evening of April 3, 1875. The announcement of Mr. Bryant's death carried poignant grief to the hearts of a large circle of friends and acquaintances, not only throughout the United States but to many residing in the principal cities of Great Britain. Both privately and publicly he was extremely popular and we do not believe he had an enemy. He was thoroughly unselfish, generous to a fault, and ever ready to assist those in distress. Although he had accumulated a fortune by his professional labors, the qualities above referred to caused him speedily to scatter it with a prodigal hand; and, at the time of his demise, we regret to say, his pecuniary affairs were so involved that he left his family without any provision for the future. As a performer, both on the minstrel and dramatic stage, Mr. Bryant occupied high rank and was greatly respected by all with whom he came in contact. The sudden death of Nelse Seymour gave a severe shock to Mr. Bryant's system; and the demise of James Unsworth, following so closely thereupon, added to his mental depression. These matters were kept constantly before his mind while arranging the weekly programs for his Opera House. After the performances of April 3, he complained of being ill; and, upon a physician being summoned, he pronounced the disease pneumonia. On April 6 a consultation of physicians was held and it was thought that he could not live through that night. But he rallied and the symptoms became more favorable; and, until Saturday, a few hours before his death, it was thought that he would recover. He was delirious much of the time; and, during such intervals, he would hold conversations with Nelse Seymour, James Unsworth and his late brother, Jerry, all of whom seemed to him to be present. Mr. Bryant suffered greatly from lack of sleep and his physicians found it impossible to induce a state of somnolence, even subcutaneous injections of morphine failing to produce the desired effect. For some three or four hours preceding his death, he was in a state of delirium. He left a widow (formerly Nelly Fitzgibbon of St. Louis). He died on April 10, 1875.

BRYANT, WILLIAM T.: died in New York, September 23, 1865.

BUCKLEY, FRED: violinist and interlocutor, was born in Bolton, England in 1833 and died from consumption in Boston, Mass., September 16, 1864, aged 31 years, eleven months and four days. He came to this country with his father and brothers in 1839. On January 29, 1857, he was married to Fanny Brown (afterward Mrs. Carlo), but in a short time after a separation took place. His talents were fine, and to aid them nature richly endowed him with a handsome, genteel and attractive person. There was a charm in his society---a peculiar influence that left a fond desire for a further and lasting intimacy. He was an excellent violinist, his solo performances being great features of the entertainments. He was, moreover, a composer of no mean order. The last time he ever appeared upon any stage was at the Temple, Portsmouth, N. H., June 22, with his brothers; and his last solo was "The Dream." By his death the company sustained a serious loss.

BUCKLEY, R. BISHOP: the eldest of the Buckley brothers, died in Quincy, Mass., June 6, 1867. His remains were interred in Mount Hope. A few months previous to his death, while traveling with his company, he received a stroke of paralysis, which resulted in his death. He was born in Bolton, England, in 1826. He was a quiet, close and philosophical observer of Negro character and, being gifted with great imitative powers and facial elasticity, his delineations were irresistibly effective. In characters of rustic simplicity and marked stolidity there was no sign of effort in his acting, but an ease and truth that were unobtrusively convulsing. In dramatic scenes his most heroic characters were extremely ludicrous. Easy, good natured, musical, and jolly was he. Some things that he did no other man could do as well. Many of his songs were "jolly" in the extreme and we shall always remember him with feelings of pleasure and esteem. He filled a place which very few men in the profession will ever reach. His musical abilities were of a high order of merit. His performance on the Chinese fiddle rendered that instrument entirely his own, outside of the "flowery land"; while as a vocalist, possessing a round and mellow voice of high tenor caliber, he gave the most difficult operatic music with artistic skill and finish.

BUCKLEY, JAMES: father of the Buckley brothers, died at Quincy, Mass., on April 27, 1872, of disease of the heart, aged 68 years. On September 3, 1872, George Swaine Buckley and Sam Sharpley started out with a show, which closed in March, 1873.

BUCKLEY, GEORGE SWAINE: was born in Bolton, England, in 1831 and came to this country with his father and brothers. He made his first appearance in public as the "Infant Prodigy" at Harrington's Museum, Boston, in 1840. It was at this time that he first commenced the study of the banjo under the celebrated Joe Sweeney; and in a short time acquired such remarkable proficiency that Joe adopted him as his protégé and starred him throughout the States for several seasons under the appellation of "Young Sweeney." In 1843 he joined with his brothers in the formation of what afterwards became the celebrated Buckley's Minstrels. He was the principal tenor singer and comedian. In making their tour through the mountain towns of California, in all their difficult movements of toil and peril, George was the *avant courier* and principal performer in the band; frequently riding fifty miles a day to engage halls, advertise, and return in time to keep his end up with the boys at the evening performances. That he was always considered the "bright particular star" of this troupe there is no doubt. He was a capital delineator of the Negro character. Everyone must acknowledge his "Sally, Come Up" to be as near perfection as anyone could wish. "Susan's Sunday Out" was another one of his finest exhibitions and "Music on the Brain" a combination of qualities which made it a marvel.

BUDWORTH, JAMES H.: was born in Philadelphia, December 24, 1831. In early life he evinced a decided taste for music and theatricals. He possessed a powerful voice and a wonderful gift of imitation and, when quite a young boy, amused and astonished those who heard him with his correct imitation of persons whom he had heard speak or sing. He made his first appearance at the Park Theatre, New York, in 1848, and was performing there at the time the building was destroyed by fire. He then engaged himself at the Broadway Theatre, appearing in several characters with success. Minstrelsy being at that time in the ascendancy, he changed his complexion and joined an Ethiopian company under the management of the celebrated Luke West. He traveled with this company through the South for a while and then left to join Charley White's party, who were then performing at White's Opera House in the Bowery, N.Y. While with this company he improved very fast. Being versatile in his performances, he became a very useful member of the profession. His services were shortly after secured by Mr. Henry Wood for George Christy & Wood's Minstrels, then performing to crowded houses at the old Hall, 444 Broadway. There he became quite a favorite with the New York public. Since then he has traveled through the United States and Canadas, everywhere giving entire satisfaction. On the 26th of

May, 1865, he appeared at the Park Theatre, Brooklyn, in the farce of "The Perse-cuted Dutchman." The piece in which he appeared is a mere sketch designed for a display of broad humor. It gives the actor an opportunity to air his aptitude for imitating the "sweet German accent" and Teutonic stolidity of habit. Few actors have ever attempted this line of business and only one or two "stage Dutchmen" have ever achieved even passing success. Whether it is that the character is difficult to imper-sonate or lacks the necessary humorous element to make it popular, we do not know. Mr. Budworth succeeded in keeping the house in a roar of laughter from the time he stepped on the stage till the curtain went down. His make-up was capital, his natural figure being much in his favor. His imitation of the Germanized English was exceed-ingly good. Mr. Budworth has a natural vein of humor, without which no actor can become a successful comedian---humor in action, gesture, or expression, which sets the audience laughing before he opens his mouth. He is at present engaged with Budworth's Minstrels at the Fifth Avenue Opera House. For the past four or five years he has been studying hard to perfect himself in several comic characters, espe-cially Dutch, as he intends shortly to bid adieu to his dark brothers and appear again upon the legitimate stage. With this natural qualification and the aptitude he has displayed, Mr. Budworth may, if he sees fit, make his mark on the stage, if he chooses to abandon minstrelsy and take to the regular walks of the profession. The latter is more laborious and uncertain than the business he is now engaged in, but the reward of success is much greater. It is for Mr. Budworth to elect whether the in-ducements are sufficient to change his professional complexion. Budworth died very suddenly of strangulation, after a sickness of but a few days, on March 11, 1875, in New York, aged 44 years.

BULL, TOMMY: right name William Howe, a jig dancer, joined the Twenty-fifth Regiment of Missouri Volunteers on March 1, 1862, and served as drummer. He died in New York January 31, 1868.

BUTLER, JOHN: died in New York, November 18, 1864, of heart trouble.

CAMPBELL, J. K.: banjoist, was found dead in bed at the Boston House, Pitts-burgh, Pa., on the morning of February 6, 1878. He had retired in his usual health and was found dead early in the morning. Members of the profession in Pittsburgh had his body embalmed, placed in a casket, and expressed to Philadelphia, where his wife and children resided. He was born in this city in 1835 and his right name was John Kelly, under which name, along with J. C. (Fatty) Stewart, he made his first appearance at Dan Wright's Music Hall on Water Street, this city, about 1846. In 1850 or 1851, when playing with George Lea at the Franklin Museum, Kelly was given by Lea the name of J. K. Cameron, taking the name from that of the well-known theatrical printer. By a typographical error the name appeared on the first night in the playbills as J. K. Campbell; by which he was ever afterwards known, with the exception of a short time while he was with Hooley & Campbell's Minstrels. At the request of Sher Campbell, he appeared as J. K. Edwards. He is said to have been the original "Ham-fat Man;" and in dancing "The Essence of Old Virginny" he was considered at one time as a great card. He also at one time ranked as one of the best banjo players in the profession. His remains were interred in Philadelphia.

CAMPBELL, JOHN C.: right name J. St. John, died in Brooklyn, N. Y., on January 26, 1875, of consumption, aged 31 years. His remains were interred in Cypress Hills Cemetery by the B. P. O. Elks.

CAMPBELL SHER C.: right name Sherman Cohen, was born in New Haven, Conn., May 16, 1829, and during his early life he learned the trade of carriage trimming, which he followed for some years. He was very fond of music and, possessing a fine alto voice, he soon gained a local reputation. He first put on burnt cork with Kimberly's Campbell's Minstrels in 1849. In 1854 he visited California with E. P. Christy's party. In the following year he engaged with the Backus Minstrels and visited Australia. While performing there his phenomenal baritone voice attracted the attention of Catherine Hayes, who invited him to sing at one of her concerts, which invitation he accepted. His rendering of "Dermot Asthore" on that occasion not only proved a great hit with the public but led Miss Hayes to personally compliment him and urge him to at once commence a course of study for the operatic stage. In 1856 he returned to San Francisco, where he remained three years, following his profession and increasing his reputation. In 1862 he joined Bryant's Minstrels, then located at Mechanics' Hall, 472 Broadway, and continued with them for some years. Shortly after this time, he determined to try his fortune upon the operatic stage and a company was organized under the management of Lafayette Harrison who gave performances at Niblo's Saloon. Shortly after this he joined William Castle, formerly a minstrel, in the management of an operatic troupe with the late Fanny Stockton as prima donna and made a tour of the country. Then he was engaged with Caroline Richings' Opera Co., with which he continued some years. From 1869 until 1872, he was a prominent member of the Parepa Rosa English Opera Co. In the fall of the latter year he accompanied Mme. Rosa to Europe; and while she fulfilled an engagement at Alexandria, Egypt, he went to Milan, Italy, where he pursued his studies. At the conclusion of Mme. Rosa's engagement, Mr. Campbell re-joined her in London, England, and became the chief baritone of an English opera troupe under the management of her husband, Carl Rosa. Bryant's Minstrels was the last burnt cork party he played with. He died at Chicago, Ill., November 26, 1874. His remains were interred in Graceland cemetery.

CARLTON, PAUL: cornet player, died at Cairo, Ill., January 9, 1873, of smallpox.

CARROLL, JAMES: died at Cheyenne, W. T., on May 19, 1874.

CARSON, DAVE: was born in March, 1837. He has visited, professionally almost every part of the globe. He left New York in 1853 when only 16 years of age for Melbourne, Australia, where he arrived after a voyage of one hundred and five days. After visiting the principal gold mines, and performing with success at each, in 1856 he joined a party consisting of Tom Brower (Frank's brother, since dead), Otto Burbank (now with George Christy), W. A. Porter, G. W. Demerest, D. F. Boley, J. O. Pierce and a number of others. The company was styled the San Francisco Minstrels, under which appellation they performed throughout New South Wales, Victoria, South Australia, Queensland, Van Dieman's Land and New Zealand. In 1859 the company was materially strengthened by Charley Backus, who took the end, which he filled with so much credit, while Carson kept the bone end. It was Charley's second trip to that country, and not liking it as well as he did the first, he left for California via London and New York in about 1860. Early in 1861 the company were under the able management of Samuel Colville (late of the Broadway Theatre), when a snug sum was realized by all in the concern. Finally, in July, 1861, the company dissolved Christy's while Boley and Demerest organized a company for Mauritius, where they performed with success. But, alas, little good did it do them; for after leaving Mauritius and on their way to the island of Bourbon, the ship went down and all hands, with the single exception of one of the company (a cloggist), perished. Carson and Brower organized a company for India, which left Australia in August, 1861. They arrived in due time at Calcutta, where they astonished the Hindus and Mohamedans not a little with their representations of the sports and pastimes of the Ethiopian race in the United States of America. After performing a season at Calcutta with satisfaction to themselves and the public, they left the "City of Palaces" for a tour through Hindustan. The boys gave their entertainments all through the country, including Benares, the Holy City of the Hindus, Allahabad, Lucknow (where they performed in one of the palaces), Cawnpore (where the terrible massacre occurred in 1857), Agra (formerly the residence of one of the greatest of the "Great Moguls"), Meerut (where the mutiny of '57, which came near costing England her magnificent Eastern Empire, first made its appearance), Delhi (in the absence of whose king, who was enjoying for the benefit of his health the balmy breezes of Rangoon, Carson did himself the honor of seating himself upon the celebrated "Peacock Throne"). From Delhi to Umballa, Loodianna, Anarkullee and Lahore, all in the Punjab, thence to Cashmere, where Dave was presented by the Rajah with a beautiful Cashmere shawl. From Cashmere our traveler took his company to Simla in the Himalaya Mountains, a beautiful sanitarium, situated at about a height of 8,000 feet above the level of the sea. From Simla the company went back to Calcutta, showing on their return at nearly all the places they had visited before. After a second successful season at Calcutta, our hero went to Madras and from thence through to the Malabar country, touching at "Goa," an ancient Portuguese settlement; so on to Bombay, the emporium of Western India, where their audiences, consisting of Parsees, Europeans, Hindus, Musselmen and a host of natives from all parts of Asia, greeted them at each performance with delight and hard silver, there being no greenbacks in that country. The company remained in India over five years, all the time as the San Francisco Minstrels; and there is not the slightest doubt that, owing to the facility with which Carson attained Hindustanese, the language of the country, and the manner in which he mimicked and caricatured a certain class of the native people, the great success with which the company met with was obtained. In May, 1866, the boys dissolved partnership, owing to the desire to see their native land once more. Brower died on the 15th of March, eight months after arriving home. Carson attended to him up to the last and was one of the chief mourners at the funeral. Brower had been away sixteen years, Pierce about seventeen, and Carson nearly fourteen. Previous to their leaving India, Carson and Pierce entered into an agreement with Tom McCollum, the great two horse rider, who had been coining money at Bombay with his circus, to bring out a circus, minstrel and ballet troupe. We clip the following from the *Times of India*, May 3, 1866:

> We are glad to be able to inform our readers that arrangements are in progress for providing Bombay with entertainments of a superior nature during the approaching cold season. The names of Messrs. McCollum, Carson and Pierce---the promoters of the scheme---will be a sufficient guarantee that it is no mere bubble. These gentlemen have determined upon proceeding at once to Europe for the purpose of organizing an equestrian troupe, for which no one is more qualified than Mr. McCollum, a ballet troupe and a band of minstrels, to be presided over, as usual, by the facetious "Dave." This latter gentleman wishes it to be particularly understood that he has no intention of laying aside the characters and impersonations which have made him so well known in India, but that he is merely proceeding to Europe by the overland route to pick up a renewed stock of health, fresh ideas and the latest novelties. To supply the want of a suitable theatre, it is proposed to erect on the Esplanade a large marquee, which would at once serve for a circus tent and for music pavilion, a portable stage being erected for the ballet, the minstrels, etc.

The arrangement fell through, owing to Pierce backing out at the last moment. Carson left India for Europe on the 6th of May, 1866; and on the voyage he visited Aden, on the Red Sea, a portion of Arabia, Grand Cairo and Alexandria in Egypt; also Malta and Gibraltar on the Mediterranean; thence through England, Ireland and Scotland, returning in July, 1866, after an absence of fourteen years to New York where his family reside. Mr. Carson proposes leaving for Europe early in June to organize another entertainment for India, in which country he is known as a favorite and established caterer for public amusements. Mr. Carson wears some magnificent diamonds, presented to him by Mr. Cowasjee Manockjee Limjee, a wealthy Parsee merchant of Bombay.

CARTER, JACOB: baritone singer with Courtney & Sanford's Minstrels, died at Rio de Janeiro on August 27, 1873, of yellow fever. His right name was Jacob Werwertz.

CASTOR, W. H.: committed suicide at Sydney, N.S.W., in March, 1865, by swallowing poison. He was connected with Joe Brown's party.

CEDA, WILLIAM: real name William Price, one of the Sable Harmonists, died in Liverpool, England, March 9, 1873. His remains were interred in Hofield Cemetery.

CHASE, HORACE A.: died in Bath, N. Y., on September 24, 1870, aged 36 years.

CHRISTIAN, TOM: whose right name was S. B. Siddings, was born in 1810. He became quite blind in June, 1863. He went to the war as corporal in the Second Connecticut Battery and contracted a series of colds, which resulted in the losing of his sight. He died in London, January 29, 1867. His remains were deposited in Brompton Cemetery. He was one of the oldest of the Christy Minstrels. He originally associated himself with that gentleman (E. P. Christy) in 1847 and continued with him until he withdrew from management in 1851. He then went to Europe with the Rayner-Pierce party and remained in England up to his death. He was unable to perform for many months prior to his death, but Messrs. Moore & Crocker paid him his full salary all the time, in addition to defraying all the expenses consequent of his death. He was taken to the hospital in London October 12, 1866, very sick. He had a cancerated throat, one cancer located under the tongue (to cut which, he had to bleed to death) and two more in the throat.

CHRISTY, E. P.: originator of Christy's Minstrels, organized in Buffalo, N.Y., in 1842. He married Harriet Harrington in Buffalo. After performing in Water Street, that city, he removed to Seneca Street, where the oddity and genius of the exhibition brought him full and respectable houses. At the solicitation of numerous citizens, he was given the use of the dining saloon of the American Hotel. From this moment he laid the foundation of a fortune. The company which Mr. Christy had succeeded in bringing together did not contain any really artistic gentlemen in the musical line; but their rendering of plaintive melodies, which are always calculated to touch the tender chord of sympathy, enlisted the patronage of persons who delighted in the simple style of the singers, unadorned by musical decorations and embellishments so common with all "great" singers and which are seldom understood by those who listen merely because it is fashionable. For a number of years Mr. Christy had the Ethiopian field to himself and well did he profit by it. About the middle of July, 1854, he abandoned the business and retired to private life to enjoy his gains, which were afterwards largely added to by other speculations and enterprises. He left a fortune of about $200,000. On May 9, 1862, in a fit of temporary insanity, he jumped out of the second story window of a house in which he resided in New York. He died on May 21 and his remains were interred in Greenwood Cemetery. On the plate on the lid of the coffin were inscribed the words: "Edwin P. Christy died May 21, 1862, aged 47 years 6 months and 23 days." Of the causes which led to the act of self-destruction, various stories were current. Some attributed it to insanity, some to family troubles, some to one thing, some to another. The immediate cause was the mental disturbance produced by one or two suits at law, which, with ordinary men, would scarcely have been sufficient to ruffle their equanimity of temper. He had succeeded in defeating the same parties in two similar suits but their pertinacity in maintaining a third irritated him to an extent beyond endurance; and a week before he committed the rash act which terminated so fatally, he declared to some friends that he knew he should yet become insane and do himself some serious injury. Mr. Christy was a man of violent temper and not a pleasant man to deal with. He was entirely too self-willed and had too little regard for the feelings of others. He had none of the self-abnegating qualities, none of the personal dignity, none of the *suavite in modo*, which constitute a gentleman. And yet, though illiterate, he affected to use grandiloquent words and often employed them on the most inopportune occasions.

CHRISTY, E. BYRON: son of E. P. Christy, died in New York, April 6, 1866, aged 28 years.

CHRISTY, GEORGE N.: died in New York May 12, 1868, from inflammation of the bowels. His right name was George Harrington and he was born in Palmyra, N. Y., in 1827. His first public appearance was made at the old Eagle Street Theatre,

Buffalo, N.Y., in 1839. He had been engaged by E. P. Christy, who had brought him out as a jig dancer. He left Buffalo with E. P. Christy and traveled with his legerdemain show. George Weldon was the "faker" and George was his confederate. Our hero had a dog that he used to perform a number of tricks with. George was with this "faking" show until 1842, when E. P. Christy organized the original Christy Minstrels and George Christy took the bone end, with Lansing Durand as tambo. George was the first to do the wench business. He was the original Lucy Long and Cachuca. Our hero accompanied the troupe all over the country until 1846, when they opened for a brief season at Palmo's Opera House in Chambers Street, this city. He was then considered the best performer that put on burnt cork; and to this day there is no performer in black face who is a greater favorite with the public than was George Christy at that time. His name was a tower of strength to the original Christys. He was considered one of the funniest of the funny in everything that he did. George was well cared for while he was with E. P. Christy, and during the last two years and eight months of his engagement he received the sum of $19,680.

CHRISTY, WILLIAM A.: died in New York, December 8, 1862, in his 23rd year. He was the youngest son of E. P. Christy, a brother to E. Byron Christy and half-brother to George. He was never considered more than a mediocre performer. He was somewhat effeminate in appearance and made up as a female very naturally.

CLARK, S. E.: basso and banjoist, died in New Haven, Conn., February, 1860.

CLIFFORD, J. C.: also known as J. C. Cross, an American baritone, died in Liverpool, February 16, 1877.

CLUSKEY, JOHN: died in Albany, N. Y., September 17, 1864, from consumption. He was a good jig dancer of the John Diamond school. In New York he played with Charley White's Minstrels.

COLEMAN, BILLY: died in New York June 4, 1867. He was a clever banjoist as well as a good general performer. At Charley White's Melodeon he was a favorite. He retired from the stage about five years prior to his death and engaged in other pursuits. He was 38 years of age.

COLLINS, ADD: right name A. K. Harding, entered the profession in 1852, being seventeen years old. He was born in Fosterville; Bucks Co., Pa.

COLLINS, DAN W.: right name Daniel Carpenter, died in Brooklyn, May 20, 1869, of consumption, aged 33 years. He was buried at Cypress Hills Cemetery.

COLLINS, JOHN: died in Havana from yellow fever, in December, 1860.

CONVERSE, FRANK: the celebrated teacher of and performer on the banjo, was born in Westfield, Mass., June 17, 1837, but his family shortly after removed to Elmira, N.Y. The Converse family were all excellent musicians, therefore the subject of our sketch may be said to have been born with music on the brain. As early as six years of age he commenced to study music, and before he had reached his twelfth birthday was an excellent player on the piano. At fourteen he first took hold of the banjo and devoted all his spare time to the study of that instrument, applying to it theoretical musical principles, arranging a complete system of study founded on correct musical rules acquired from his piano studies. So infatuated did he become with the old Cremona that he neglected the piano and devoted all his energies to the development of his favorite instrument. During all this time he was strenuously opposed by his parents, who tried to dissuade him from his course, they thinking the banjo an instrument of but trifling consideration, not susceptible of any improvement, and upon which labor and time would be foolishly thrown away; but in spite of all opposition he continued on and in two years he appeared for the first time in public at several amateur concerts. Shortly after this he accepted an engagement with McFarland, then managing the Detroit theatre. He took the position made vacant by the withdrawal of Hi Rumsey, who appeared between the pieces and played solos. His next engagement was with a minstrel company managed by Backus & Co., then performing at Metropolitan Hall, Chicago. This was in 1855. He remained with this troupe until it disbanded. We next find him permanently located at St. Louis, where he for some time gave lessons on the banjo. In 1856 he joined Matt Peel's Campbell Minstrels at St. Louis and traveled with them until the spring of 1858, visiting all the principal towns and cities in the United States and closed with the party at what is now known as 444 Broadway, New York. He then bent his steps Southwest and stopped at Memphis, where he organized a large school and taught the banjo. After a successful season there he returned North and betook himself to Coke and Blackstone, but he was not long in finding out that he was never carved out for a limb of the law; and after toiling over the books for six months, he returned to his old business and joined Campbell's Minstrels, then under the management of John T. Huntley, and they took a trip down through the New England States. His next engagement was to him the most important one of his whole career. He met Mrs. Hattie A. Clarke, widow of George B. Clarke, and one of the proprietresses of Congress Spring Hotel, Saratoga. This meeting sprang into friendship, then love, followed by an elopement and marriage. He then organized a company of corkers himself and, after a successful tour, for awhile retired from the stage. But he was doomed not to remain in retirement long; for he had tasted of the sweets of traveling and the hearty plaudits of the admiring audiences. He accordingly visited Denver City, Colorado Territory, and organized a company called Converse and Petrie's. The next place we locate him is at San Francisco, California, where he was playing and teaching. When he returned to New York he played a short engagement with Wood's Minstrels, at 514 Broadway, shortly after the place opened. Mr. Converse's principle motive has been to elevate the position of his favorite instrument and its music. He has taken advantage of every opportunity to further that end, introducing it when and wherever a proper occasion offered itself, more particularly to the notice of those musicians who, through ignorance of the capabilities of the instrument, have spoken against it. On the 29th of last December these self same musicians, through appreciation of his successful efforts, tendered him a very flattering testimonial concert at Niblo's Saloon, signed by the names of all the principal music dealers and minstrel managers. The affair was a great success. He has worked hard and done much to elevate and fully develop the banjo. He has written a complete work on the banjo for beginners (which will shortly be published by Messrs. Dick and Fitzgerald). Mr. Converse has established himself in New York as a teacher, and is really over-run with pupils, keeping all his time busily occupied; so much so that he has been compelled to obtain the assistance of Mr. Savori, the excellent banjoist. Mr. C. is also engaged at Wood's Minstrels, where he appears every night in one of his popular solos. He is one of the best performers on the instrument that we have ever heard. He died September 5, 1903.

COPELAND, ALFRED: for many years harpist with various companies of Christy's Minstrels, died in London, England, on March 22, 1872.

COTTON, BENJAMIN A.: was born at Pawtucket, R. I., July 27, 1829. In 1845 he joined VanAmburgh's Menagerie and in the side show played the bones and afterwards learned the banjo. He next learned cigar making, at which business he remained until 1855 when he joined the Julian Operatic Troupe. He then joined Matt. Peel's Campbell Minstrels with whom he remained fifteen months, after which he took to hotel keeping, but to his cost he soon found out that he "could not keep a hotel." He returned to the profession, joining Sniffen's Company at 444 Broadway, New York. Then he traveled with Billy Birch and afterwards was one of the Banjo Minstrels, playing on the Mississippi River. During this engagement he had the opportunity of seeing the customs, manners and habits of the Southern Negro. He visited the plantations, the cotton fields, and attended their evening festivals, played while they danced, and carefully watched all their amusements to make himself the better acquainted with their customs and actions. After a sojourn of about eighteen months among the Southern plantations, he returned to New York and engaged with the Hooley Campbell Minstrels. It was while with them he introduced that celebrated plantation scene of "Old Uncle Snow"; also "Abraham's Daughter" and "The Union, Right or Wrong," introduced for the first time. He next visited California, where he remained two years. In 1865 he returned East and with Joe Murphy organized the Cotton & Murphy Minstrels and up to about 1905 had been a great favorite with the public. Ben was a natural actor, chaste in everything he undertook, adhering closely to the character he represented, neither coarse in act nor language, never using vulgarity for an incentive to mirth. These, with his great desire to please, made him a great favorite. His "Bob Ridley" years ago was considered a wonderful bit of fidelity to Negro characteristics, while his "Uncle Snow" was considered as one of the very best representations of the aged darkie ever seen upon a stage.

CRAIG, TOM: returned to New York in January, 1863, after an eighteen months' campaign. He was orderly sergeant in Company E, Twenty-second Regiment, Massachusetts Volunteers.

CROCKER, J. P.: died in London, England, December 17, 1869, aged 35 years. He had been suffering for nearly two years with consumption. Although unable to take any active part in the performances of the stage for nearly one year, yet he assisted in the business department up to December 15. He was an American by birth.

DALEY, JOHN H.: died in London, England, May 31, 1864, in his 29th year. He was born in Philadelphia in 1835. He was well known as one of the wittiest comedians in the business.

DANFORTH, GEORGE: colored, died in New York August 17, 1870, aged 33. He was a bone player.

DANIELS, R.: formerly of Kelly & Leon's, died at Elmira, N.Y., July 21, 1873, of consumption, aged 40 years.

DARLING, ISAAC: died of consumption June 10, 1871, aged 54 years. He had been with this troupe since its first organization.

DAVIS, EDMUND: died in New York on June 29, 1872, age 48 years.

DAVIS, HENRY: was born in Richmond, Va., and died in Wilmington, Del., January 9, 1865.

DE LAVE, MONS.: in the Fall of 1861 walked the tight rope at Volk's Garden, then opposite the Bowery Theatre. Leslie, being of an ambitious nature, sought permission to try the rope at a day rehearsal, which was granted by Mons. Da Lave with a smile. Leslie mounted the rope and with pole in hand started on his first trip; and to the surprise of all, accomplished the feat. This encouraging him, the next day he was the owner of a rope and commenced business in earnest. He then went to Frank Rivers' Melodeon on Broadway, then to 444 Broadway, and the summer of 1862 was at the Old Bowery Theatre when Sam Stickney was manager.

DEAVES, EDWIN: was born in Philadelphia in 1817. He was one of the originators of the Virginia Serenaders. He was a very clever performer in burnt cork. He originated the act called "The Black Shakers," produced for the first time in May, 1849, for Deaves' benefit. He appeared at Charley White's Melodeon in New York after he closed with the Virginias, where he remained for nearly two years. In 1855 he went to California with a minstrel party, among whom were Sam Wells and Billy Birch under R. M. Hooley's management.

DELEHANTY, WILLIAM H.: was born in Albany, N. Y., of Irish parents in 1846, where he made his first appearance on the stage in 1860. He joined Skiff & Gaylord's Minstrels in 1862 and remained with that party for four years. He formed a co-partnership with T. M. Hengler at Chicago in 1866.

DENLIN, PAUL: comedian and dancer, died of rapid consumption in London on August 13, 1878, aged 37 years. His remains were buried in Brompton Cemetery.

DIAMOND, JOHN: renowned jig dancer, was born in New York in 1823, and at an early age gave evidences of his abilities as a dancer. A contract was entered into between Barnum and Diamond and he performed in all the principal cities with great success. He visited England under the management of Barnum and performed to crowded houses.

DIXON, GEORGE WASHINGTON: made his first appearance on any stage at the old Amphitheatre, North Pearl Street, Albany, N.Y., under the management of Parsons in 1827. When Sloman commenced singing buffo songs some years ago, his success struck a spark in the bosom of Dixon and he commenced singing buffo at the Albany Theatre in 1830. He shortly afterwards left for Philadelphia and made his first appearance June 19, 1834, at the Arch Street and sang his prize extravaganza of "Zip Coon" for the benefit of Andrew J. Allen. In 1839, we find him in New York.

DONALDSON, WILLIAM B.: made his debut in 1836 at Poughkeepsie, N.Y. as the "Young Jim Crow," singing and dancing after the style of T. D. Rice. He died at Poughkeepsie, N. Y., April 16, 1873. In February, 1858, he was a Negro clown at the Broadway Circus, New York. In May, 1871, he leased Lockwood House, Poughkeepsie, N. Y., which he opened. Donaldson astonished people by his remarkable left-hand playing on the banjo, not simply picking and fingering with the left hand, but entirely reversing the position in which the instrument is ordinarily held.

DONNELLY, LEWIS J.: died in New York October 26, 1869.

DOUGHERTY, HUGHEY: was born in New York. He first appeared on the stage in New York at the Melodeon under Frank Rivers' management. He was then known as "Young America." He was a good minstrel performer and the best stump speech maker on the stage.

DUNNIE, J. F.: left the profession in August, 1872, and became passenger agent for the Baltimore Railroad. In January, 1875, he was connected with the Erie Railroad. He is said to have died in Cincinnati several years ago.

EAGAN, H. W.: was killed at the battle of Bull Run, July 21, 1861.

EDMONDS, D.: was born October 9, 1830, and commenced his public career in 1838 as violinist. He first blacked his face in 1839 and played for Stoddard in Jim Crow business. He commenced as a regular minstrel in 1846. He could play any instrument in the band, do middle business, and go on for fops or old men in afterpieces.

EDMUNDS, GEORGE: violinist, died at Walla Walla, Wash., on January 22, 1870. He was a native of Dublin, Ireland, and at his death was about 40 years of age.

EDWARDS, BOB: right name Robert O. Dean, was found dead on the morning of July 25, 1872, in his saloon in Buffalo, N.Y. He was born in Philadelphia in 1829. In 1842 he was known as Master Edwards and was one of the earliest of bone end boys and, as a jig dancer, was with the Virginia Serenaders. From 1864 to 1866, he was manager of a minstrel party. His wife was the widow of Bob Shadduck.

EMERSON, BILLY: was born in Belfast, Ireland, July 4, 1846. He came to this country in 1847. He joined Joe Sweeney's Minstrels in 1857 as balladist and jig dancer. In St. Louis, Mo., in 1868 he received a solid gold medal, valued at $175, for being the champion song and dance performer. He was married at Covington, Ky., June 25, 1869, to Maggie Homer.

EMMETT, DAN DECATUR: was one of the earliest devotees of burnt corkdom. In 1840 he was traveling with the Cincinnati Circus, playing in the orchestra. He was born in Mt. Vernon, Ohio, in 1815. He began life as a printer but soon abandoned his trade for a circus company. He was not long in discovering that he could compose songs of the kind in use by clowns. One of the finest of these was "Old Dan Tucker." Its success was so great that he followed it with many others. They were all Negro melodies. Finally he took to Negro inpersonation, singing his own songs in the ring while he accompanied himself on the banjo. In 1843 he was one of the original four that appeared in minstrelsy. When the party went to England, Emmett remained abroad for several years. He returned and joined Bryant's Minstrels at 472 Broadway. He was engaged to write songs and walk 'rounds and to take part in the nightly performance. He made his home at Mt. Vernon, Ohio. It was he who first discovered Ferguson, the banjo player and after much persuasion induced the manager C. Rolers to engage him. It was while traveling with this party that Dan learned to pick the banjo. The following season, 1841, he re-joined the circus and Frank Brower and Emmett became very popular. He was known in the East much earlier than Joe Sweeny. He was not only a fine banjo player but an excellent musician and to his genius the minstrel stage owes many of its most popular "walk-'rounds" and other comicalities. The piece by which he will be longest remembered is one of his inspirations of later years, which arose to the dignity of a sectional war song.

EMMETT, JOSEPH K.: Dutch comedian, was born in St. Louis, Mo., March 13, 1841. He made his first appearance as a song and dance performer at Jake Esher's Bowery, St. Louis, in 1866. He opened in New York with Bryant's in 1868 in Dutch songs and dances. He made his debut on the dramatic stage in his play of "Fritz," November 22, 1869, at the Academy of Music, Buffalo, N.Y. He opened in New York at Wallack's Theatre, July 11, 1870, as Fritz. He made his debut in England, November 30, 1872, at the Adelphi Theatre, London, in his play, rewritten and called "The Adventures of Fritz." He died June 15, 1891.

EUGENE: right name Eugene D'Ameli, was born at New York, June 4, 1836, his father being an Italian refugee engaged in the confectionery trade. At an early age Eugene was apprenticed to John P. Beauville, a hardware merchant; but displaying a predilection for the stage, he was soon afterwards allowed to join a minstrel company and was permitted to make his first appearance in public at the age of thirteen years. His initial steps were taken with the Christy & Wood troupe at No. 444 Broadway on May 16, 1853, as an impersonator of female characters. His success was assured at the outset. He was connected with prominent minstrel organizations at all times. He visited California twice, acting at San Francisco in 1858 in the drama of "Uncle Tom's Cabin" and taking the part of Topsy with success. He was a familiar and welcome caller at every city of note in the States and Canada and accompanied by Unsworth he made a Continental tour in 1861, appearing at the leading English, Scotch, Irish, French and German theatres. While in Berlin, it is stated that some of the officers of the Prussian army became so convinced of the impossibility of any man personating female characters so completely, that they came upon the stage behind the scenes and insisted upon being introduced to the charming "Fraulein Eugene." Returning to London, a four years' engagement was conducted in that city, after which they remained for nearly the same length of time at Liverpool, sailing for America again in 1868 and appearing for some time at Dan Bryant's Opera House in Fourteenth Street. He was found, when off the stage, to be a neatly dressed and very good looking gentleman, somewhat under the medium size, but of as fine a general figure in the manly attire of everyday life as he was in the gorgeous wardrobe of the sable prima donna at night. He was one of the most thoroughly artistic personators of burlesque female actors ever seen.

FARRON, WILLIAM: died in Lebanon, Tenn., November 29, 1870.

FORD, JOHN T.: was born in Baltimore, Md., in 1829. Before he had reached the age of 23 he was acting as business manager for George Kunkel's Nightingale Minstrels and traveled all over the country with that party. He then, in company with Mr. Knuckel and Thomas Moxley, leased the old Richmond, Va., Theatre, and the Holliday Street Theatre, Baltimore. Mr. Kunkel managed the Richmond establishment and Mr. Ford took charge in Baltimore. For twelve consecutive years Mr. Ford has managed the Holliday and is still in possession. Where is there another who can say as much? At the close of the season of 1857, he withdrew from the Richmond Theatre and Mr. Kunkel carried it on by himself. The next year he was elected President of the City Council of Baltimore and by force of circumstances was acting Mayor of the city for two years and filled the office with marked ability. He was also elected City Director for one term of the Baltimore and Ohio Railroad; also a Commissioner of the McDonough Fund on the part of the city. He was manager of the Washington Theatre where President Lincoln was assassinated. Shortly after the assassination, Mr. Ford was arrested on suspicion of complicity in the affair; and after undergoing imprisonment for forty days in Carrol Prison, he was released by the government, there not being the slightest proof against his loyalty.

FOX, CHARLES E.: died in New York December 26, 1864. He was born in Brooklyn, N.Y., November 14, 1828. He first appeared in burnt cork in 1848 as a banjoist. He was afterwards attached to the best minstrel organizations in America. He returned from England December 15, 1860, and opened a sample room at 512 Broadway in November, 1862. His last appearance on the stage was December 22, 1864, only three days before his death, at 444 Broadway, New York. His remains were interred in Greenwood.

GALLAGHER, DENNY: died in Philadelphia on November 23, 1868, and his remains were interred in Cathedral cemetery. Denny was born in this city in 1830 and made his first public appearance at eighteen years of age in white face in Irish songs and dances. He next appeared at the Old Franklin Museum in Chatham Square under the management of George Lea, appearing during the evening in white and black impersonations. He was not able to perform for several months prior to his death, as he was failing rapidly with consumption. Denny was one of the best general performers in the business. He could do almost anything in a minstrel band, although his forte was on the tambourine end.

GAUL: the instrumentalist, died in Havana, Cuba, in December, 1860.

GAYLORD, LOWRENZO: died in poverty and from consumption in Philadelphia, April 7. 1878. He was born in Westfield, Mass., on January 19, 1836. At the early age of twelve years he turned his back upon his home and launched himself into the show business, singing ballads with John Green's Circus. With that concern he traveled for several years, and then he joined Spalding & Rogers' Circus, with which he journeyed for a time as clown. Doffing the motley, he settled down in Philadelphia, where he began his career as a negro minstrel by leasing old Southwark Hall in Second Street below Green, which he opened as Gaylord & Dupont's Opera House. In 1877 he was taken sick and was confined to his bed until he died. Joe Gaylord, in whose arms he died, was attentive at his bedside. He was buried from St. Michael's

R. C. Church on April 11, the interment being in the new Cathedral Cemetery, Philadelphia. All that Low Gaylord possessed at his death---the title and fame of his troupe, with his wood cuts---is disposed of in the following directions, virtually constituting his last will and testament:

> Philadelphia, Pa., April 5, 1878.
> This certifies that I have this day assigned and transferred to Joseph Teals, better known as Joseph Gaylord, all my right and title to the name of Skiff & Gaylord's Minstrels, also all wood cuts belonging to the above firm; the said Joseph Teal, or Gaylord, to act as my successor, and to look to the interests of my children. (Signed) LOW GAYLORD. Witnesses: Mary A. Teal, Laura Gaylord, Mary Gaylord, Elizabeth Gaylord.

GEARY, GUSTAVUS: died of heart disease in Harlem, N. Y., April 25, 1877.

GETTINGS, THOMAS: died in New York November 23, 1866, of consumption, aged 22 years. His remains were interred in Calvary Cemetery.

GLENN, JAMES W.: died in New York February 26, 1870. His right name was McDonald. He was born in Philadelphia of Irish parents in 1839. He was first introduced to the profession by Cool White with S. S. Sanford's Minstrels while traveling in the season of 1858-59.

GOULD, JULIA: was born in London, England, in 1827, and joined Buckley's Minstrels in New York in September, 1850, as an impersonator of female characters in their Ethiopian burlesques. In 1864 she went to California. She was afterwards known as Mrs. Julia Collins.

GRANGER, W. H.: a musician with the BUCKLEY SERENADERS, died in Toronto, Canada, in April, 1867.

GREEN, J. EDWIN: was born April 9, 1834, and made his first appearance before the public at Nashua, N. H., as balladist with a company of white vocalists styled the American Bards, of which Mr. Green was one of the proprietors. He made his first appearance in burnt cork at Lowell, Mass., in 1855 with Reynold's Minstrels, of which the subject of our sketch was one of the managers. In the year 1857, Mr. Green entered into partnership with Messrs. Shorey & Duprez and with them he traveled extensively through the East and West and throughout every part of the Southern country and West Indies. During this time he appeared on both ends, acted as middle man, and took an active part in everything pertaining to negro minstrelsy. He was known all over the country as "The Great Mocking Bird Imitator." Mr. Green's first appearance in New York was at the New Bowery Theatre, July 24, 1863, for the benefit of M. C. Campbell.

GRIFFIN, G. W. H.: was born in Gloucester, Mass. His parents moved to Boston when he was six months old. At 15 he was placed in a lawyer's office, where he remained for two years. He was then apprenticed to the engineering business. But he evinced a passion for music and poetry; and when not engaged in the active duties incumbent on his position, his time was wholly occupied in the study of music. While an apprentice he became a member of the Boston Glee Club. In 1850, Mr.

Griffin assumed the position of manager of a minstrel company called the Boston Harmonists and made his first appearance in that capacity at Palmyra, New York. Soon after this he joined Gray's Warblers; and then, after traveling through the country with several troupes, he attached himself to Bryant's Minstrels. In July, 1853, he joined Wood's Minstrels at No. 444 Broadway, New York; and in 1858 became a member of the company organized by R. M. Hooley for the purpose of a tour to the El Dorado of the Western world. On his return to New York, he associated himself as a partner with Messrs. Hooley and S. C. Campbell at Niblo's Saloon. He was afterward with Bryant and also with George Christy, then with Hooley in Brooklyn. In September, 1878, he became business manager for the Theatre Comique, New York. Griffin won considerable reputation as an author. Among his most popular musical compositions are "Lonely No More," "My Greenwood Home," "Louie Lee," "Bird of the Wreck," "Not a Star from Our Flag," "Sister, Thou art Dear to Me," "Pleasant Dreams of Long Ago," "Tell Me, Little Twinkling Star," "I am Lonely Tonight," "Happy Days," and "Cherish Love While You May." He also composed sacred pieces for churches and authored comic acts.

HAGUE, SAM: was born Sheffield, England, in 1828. He commenced his career in the show business as a clog dancer. In 1850 he visited America and in company with his brothers, Tom and William Hague, traveled East and West as the Brothers Hague Concert Party. During this tour he introduced English clog dancing into America. Subsequently at different times, he was partner with Dick Sands and Tim Hayes. He traveled with Skiff & Gaylord's and other minstrel parties. He was partner with Cal Wagner, leaving whom until the latter retired from the show business and settled down in Utica, N. Y., as proprietor of the "Champion Shades" saloon. He then left for Europe with the Georgia Slave Troupe, where he remained until his death at Liverpool, January 7, 1901.

HAMALL, HUGH: singer, died in Montreal, Canada, October 10, 1875, of disease of the kidneys.

HAMILTON, JAKE: banjoist, died in San Francisco, November 4, 1877, of consumption, aged 57 years.

HARRINGTON, GEORGE N.: died in Frankford, Pa., in January, 1859, in obscurity and distress. He was the original "Mary Blane" and "Lucy Neal."

HARRIS, CHARLES: the banjoist, retired from the stage in Richmond, Va., in 1857, and for some time gave instructions on the banjo and guitar in Chicago.

HART, BOB: right name James M. Sutherland, was born, February 9, 1834. At twelve years of age he was train boy on the Erie railroad. At eighteen he became a regular engineer on the road. He was, soon after, a Methodist preacher. He removed to New York City, where, for a time he was engaged in the produce business. The possessor at that time of a fine baritone voice, he answered an advertisement for a ballad singer and was soon regularly engaged in a leading minstrel house, making his first appearance in this line of business in the fall of 1859. He afterwards visited New Orleans, where he became a manager in 1866 conducting the Olympic Theatre until the building was destroyed by fire on December 28, 1868. After this, he remained unconnected with any amusement enterprise for some little time, but was finally induced to make his bow to a Chicago audience in August, 1869. He was one of the best speech makers in the profession. Its very force lay in the fact that it was just such an oration as a pompous darkie, better stocked with words than judgment, might shoot off at an assemblage of terrified hearers. It was a purely original effort, differing in toto from the average burlesque address of the minstrel stage. He died April 6, 1888, in New York.

HAYES, TIM: was born in Dublin, Ireland, September 22, 1841. He came to America in December, 1860; and made his debut at the Melodeon Music Hall, Broadway, New York, where he remained one week and then joined Hooley & Campbell's. He died at the Asylum for the Poor in Washington D. C., May 12, 1877, of consumption. He reached Washington from Philadelphia a few days prior to his death in a pitiable condition and shortly after went to the hospital connected with the almshouse. His remains were interred in a lot in Mount Olivet Cemetery, that city. He has been credited with introducing the clog dance as a marked feature in minstrelsy; but this is not so, as there was clog dancing in America before Tim Hayes was born. James O'Connell, best remembered as "The Tattooed Man," but a versatile performer, used to dance in wooden shoes at the Bowery Amphitheatre, New York, in 1839. The Wood Children, sons of William Wood, the dancer and pantomimist, did a double clog dance during the season of 1843-44. Ben Yates also used to make clog dancing a specialty as early as 1848. There was also Johnny Goulding, who did clog dancing at the small concert saloons down Broadway, New York. Billy O'Neil, Irish comedian, was a clog dancer long before Hayes' time. Fred Wilson was one of the first to make clog dancing a specialty in the minstrel business.

HEDDEN, WILLIAM: died at the residence of the mother of Charley White in New York, January 3, 1861, and was buried in Calvary Cemetery. His style of jig dancing was very much admired. Five months prior to his death he was disabled by consumption.

HENGLER, T. M.: was born in Albany, N.Y., in 1845, of Irish parents. He made his *debut* at Albany in 1860, then joined Newcomb's Minstrels, remaining with them three years. He became connected with Sam Sharpley's Troupe in 1865 and with Delehanty in 1866. Their first engagement together was with Dingess & Green's Minstrels.

HERMAN, J. A.: right name Simonson, was born in Brooklyn, N.Y., January 1, 1823. He first appeared in public with a concert company in white face in 1840 at Croton Hall, located at the junction of the Bowery and Division Street, New York. He first appeared in black face with a small minstrel band, consisting of Duke Morgan, Alfred Delapere, William Charrington, and Raymond, who traveled with Mabie's Circus, appearing in the side show. In 1848, he appeared with Kimberly's Campbell Minstrels at Society Library Rooms, New York. He took his leave of the stage at Hooley's Opera House, Brooklyn, about 1871; then reappeared at Hooley's Opera House, Brooklyn, in 1874, but remained about two weeks, after which he retired from the profession. In November, 1874, he was proprietor of a hotel on the site of the old Union Racetrack, Long Island. He died January 23, 1901.

HERMAN, W.: violinist, died in New York, June, 1863, and was buried June 12.

HERNANDEZ, A. M.: died in Pontevideo, Uruguay, on October 25, 1874.

HILGER, JOHN: died in Indianapolis, Ind., on April 21, 1875, of pneumonia, aged 23 years. He played the tuba horn.

HILTON, JOHN W.: died in Liverpool, England, of consumption, January 2, 1871, aged 35 years. Everything that could be done for his comfort during his illness was attended to by Sam Hague.

HOBBS, ALFRED: died in New York, February 17, 1861, after a long and painful illness. He was 28 years of age.

HOBBS, WILLIAM L.: died in Philadelphia on July 15, 1874, aged 45 years. He was an instrumental performer and musical director. He had been connected with minstrelsy almost from the time of its origin.

HOOLEY, RICHARD M.: was born in Ireland in 1828 and was intended for the medical profession. He came to America in 1840 and, after residing in New York about ten months, he went to Buffalo and joined Christy's Minstrels in August, 1845. He was with them as leader for two years. Since that time he has been one of the principal performers and managers of negro minstrelsy. He visited California eight times within three years. In 1868 he visited Europe, returning home August 29, 1868. Mr. Hooley had worked himself up from the ranks, having for many years traveled through the country as violinist. From the opening night of his new house in Brooklyn, success crowned his efforts and he made a great deal of money. But the Fire Fiend came and in one night swept away his place. In a short time he had it rebuilt and his success continued very great. Mr. Hooley was rather below the medium height, compactly framed and the possessor of a pleasant, friendly face, adorned by a remarkably luxurious growth of beard, just softening into dove color in the highlights, flowing down across his breast; and his dark hazel eyes beamed with all the benevolence of a heart as big as a bullock's. Mr. Hooley was an affable gentleman, an experienced manager, a most excellent violinist, and a man of taste, judgment, and a fine musical education. He had the personal respect of all who knew him, for he had in his manner and disposition those hearty and kindly qualities which exercise a madnetic influence upon all who come within the sphere of their attraction.

HORN, EPH: whose right name was Evan Evans Hern, died in St. Vincent's Hospital, New York, Wednesday afternoon, January 8, 1877. His last appearance on the stage was at Taylor's Opera House, Trenton, N. J., Christmas Day, December 25, 1876. During this trip (it was a variety company), Mr. Horn took cold, from which pneumonia resulted. His funeral took place from "The Little Church Around the Corner" on January 6 and the remains were placed in a receiving vault in Evergreen Cemetery, where they remained until May 16, 1877, when they were committed to their final resting place in that cemetery. All the funeral expenses were borne by his old and dearly tried friend, Tony Pastor. Mr. Horn was born in Philadelphia in 1823 and first entered the minstrel profession in 1843 at Carlisle, Pa., as end man with S. S. Sanford's Troupe. He next traveled with a small band with VanAmburgh's

Menagerie. It was while the troupe of Virginia Serenaders were in Philadelphia at the lecture room of the Chinese Museum, corner of Ninth and Sansom Streets, now occupied by a part of the Continental Hotel, that attention was called to Eph Horn as one of the rarest of humorists. Eph Horn's first appearance in New York was in 1847 with The Original Virginia Serenaders. Horn continued with this troupe, whose time was mainly spent in traveling, until Earl H. Pierce organized his band as a rival to E. P. Christy's. Horn withdrew from Fellows' in March, 1851, and on April 2, in conjunction with Charley White, sought to establish a rival establishment six doors above, in the old Coliseum Building. It was opened under the name and style of Ethiopian Opera House. Without being exactly the meat, it occupied the meat's position in a sandwich whose outside layers were E. P. Christy's on the next block above and Fellows' house below, all three being on the same side of the street. It was a failure and therein silence was absolute after the performances of April 23. The band went traveling but even the road proved unprofitable. Horn then enrolled himself under the responsible banner of S. A. Wells. Reaching Gotham once more, Horn resumed with Fellows' on January 12, 1852. Horn's re-appearance in New York was on December 1, 1852 at Barmun's Museum for the benefit of C. W. Clarke. Shortly after this, Horn was engaged at the old hall, later occupied by Wood's Minstrels; and after several months spent there, he joined Campbell's Minstrels in the summer, withdrawing therefrom to associate himself with Buckley's. Eph Horn stood at the very head of the minstrel profession. Placed in almost any position in a company, he was able to fill the part. As an end man he was one of the best and as a delineator of the old Nergo he displayed remarkable talent. If Booth or Kean ever succeeded in "holding the mirror up to nature" in the true Shakespearean sense, then Eph Horn did so far as negro minstrelsy is concerned. Falling back upon burnt cork, in the summer of 1858 Horn was with Ordway's Aeolians, Boston, and there, on behalf of admirers in that city, he was presented by Dr. John P. Ordway with a valuable watch and chain. Thence he came to New York and was added to the forces at Wood's New Marble Hall. He retired from that establishment in November and on the 22d and 23d of that month was clown at the National Circus, Philadelphia, going thence to the Holliday Street Theatre, Baltimore, as clown for Tom King's Circus, which began there on November 24. Leaving Tom King in a hurry, he again set sail for California and on January 3, 1859, opened at the Lyceum, San Francisco. In the Spring, Horn & Backus took this strong party among the California hills and on April 30, in anticipation of his leaving the Pacific Coast, "Uncle Ephraim" had a grand testimonial benefit at the American Theatre, San Francisco. He got back here in June and after a brief visit to his family in Philadelphia, took Max Irwin's place at Wood's Marble Hall. His next notable engagement was probably his first of all with Bryant's Minstrels at 472 Broadway, March 2, 1860, and continued until the season closed, July 14. Among the extravaganzas he here made his own were "The Deserted Miner," the Stranger in the burlesque of that name, the Doorkeeper in "The Masquerade Ball," "The Breakneck Act" (with Jim Carrol), "The Locomotive Darkie," the pathetic ballad of "Lord Love! and his Lady Nan-cy-see-see," "The Burlesque Convention."

HOWARD, BILLY: right name William Donoghue, went to Europe with the Buckleys, remained there, and died at Nottingham, England, January 9, 1872, of consumption, aged 30 years. He was a native of Utica, N. Y.

HOWARD, GUS: formerly of Hooley & Christy's party, died at Alexandria, Va., on March 29, 1874.

HOWARD, SETH C.: at one time interlocutor with Bryant's, died in Hornellsville, N. Y., February 11, 1860, of consumption.

HUGHES, RUDY: right name James Quigg, was a partner with Hogan in song and dance, died in New York, November 10, 1871, of consumption, aged 24 years.

HUNTLEY, CHARLES L.: died in Mobile, Ala., May 12, 1860.

HUNTLEY, JOHN T.: retired from the profession several years ago and afterwards kept a hotel at Catskill, N. Y. He died August 4, 1895, aged 69 years.

IRVING, PHIL: former manager of the California Minstrels, died in New York City, February 17, 1906.

IRWIN, MAX: was born in Cincinnati, Ohio. He first appeared in New York with Wood's Minstrels. He was married to Augusta Lameraux, *danseuse*, in Philadelphia, August 19, 1859. He went to Australia in 1862, where he died on August 9, 1864, in Adelaide. He had assumed the name of Paul Maxey. He was a brother of Selden Irwin, the actor.

ISAACS, P. B.: died in a small town near San Francisco, Cal., September 6, 1865, while traveling with Maguire's Minstrels. His remains were interred in the town where he died. He was born in London, England, in 1831.

JACKSON, JOSEPH: professionally known as J. Arnold and formerly of Moore & Burgess' Minstrels, died at sea on board the steamer *Canada*, between Rangoon and Akyab, October 28, 1878. At the time of his death he was with Dave Carson's company.

JACKSON, THEO: basso and middle man for the Buckleys, retired from the profession in June, 1866, and entered into business with his father in Providence. Shortly after, he returned to the stage and in April, 1869, appeared in San Francisco, Cal., at Maguire's Opera House. On July 20 he was married to Susie S. Davis of Providence, Mass. He was born in Southport, Conn., May 27, 1838. He first appeared in the minstrel profession in June, 1862, with the Buckleys.

JOHNSON, SAM: whose right name was Isaac Ray, took the name of Johnson as it was a prominent character in T. D. Rice's sketch of "Oh, Hush!"---the dandy darkie in "Virginia Cupid." His career in the minstrel profession was a brief one. During the season of 1844-45 he joined the party known as the Operatic Brothers and Sisters. He shortly after retired from the profession and purchased an interest in a steamboat running on the Ohio River. He also became interested in real estate at one time and also associated himself in the circus business with Dan Rice. He died at River View, Ky., October, 1876. Although in his 62nd year, yet he was so well preserved that those who saw him just before his demise agree that he had the appearance of a man who was not more than forty-five or fifty. His reputation for neighborliness was good and as a business man he stood high, being both active and punctual.

KAVANAUGH, JOE: joined Sanford January 16, 1850, and remained in his employ until the day of his death, which occurred in Philadelphia, February 11, 1861, aged 50 years. His remains were interred in Mount Moriah Cemetery, that city. He was a printer by trade. During the visit of the Woods to this country, he sang in all their operas. He also sang with the Seguin Opera Troupe and played Dandini, Count Pompoline and other characters with that troupe.

KEARNEY, MICHAEL: died in Boston, October 26, 1877. He first appeared in public at 11 years of age, traveling with the Original Christy's. He joined Morris Bros. in 1868. In 1870, he was partner with James Moran, known as the "Irish Team." In the fall of 1876, he was stricken with paralysis.

KELLY, EDWIN: was born in Dublin, Ireland, in 1835 and educated in London for a surgeon. He was a life pupil of St. George's Hospital. He came to America and made his first appearance on the minstrel stage with Ordway's Aeolians in Boston. He appeared as tenor vocalist and interlocutor. After his engagement at Ordway's expired, he made several tours with various minstrel companies and became a very popular performer. At length he became partner and manager of the Academy of Music in Chicago, which was built under his supervision and where he collected a fine company. By his judgment and energy, as well as his efforts to elevate the tone of minstrelsy, his company was a popular one in Chicago and the great West. After five years of continued success, Mr. Kelly with his partner, Leon, transferred their attention to Cincinnati, where another and prettier minstrel hall was speedily erected and opened. But this gratifying result was of short duration, as a fire in a few hours swept away the beautiful hall, wardrobe and everything pertaining to the company, among which were some valuable operettas, ballads and minstrel acts, written by Mr. Kelly. After this, Kelly resolved to try the great metropolis, opening Kelly & Leon's Minstrel Hall October 1, 1866. As a manager, Mr. Kelly proved himself to be every way competent to conduct a first class troupe. As an interlocutor he was well up in the business, being posted in all its details. He was a sweet-ballad singer and possessed a clear tenor voice. He was a tall, powerfully-built man, with a large head and broad shoulders. His muscular system was well developed. He had light hair and heavy, drooping moustachios and was exceedingly gentlemanly in his manners.

KEMBLE, JOHN R.: was born in Kent, England, in 1838. He came to America in 1857. His first experience in minstrelsy was with the Hart and Simmons party. He soon after joined Morris' Minstrels and was with them for five years as interlocutor and stage manager. In 1868 he was attached to the dramatic company of De Bar's Opera House, St. Louis, Mo., but was prevailed to return to minstrelsy by Billy Emerson, who was with Manning at the time in management. He was a fine solo or quartette singer, a good interlocutor, and a most useful member of the profession. He died in London, England, June 11, 1908.

KNEASS, NELSON: was born in Philadelphia, in which city he made his debut April 22, 1828, at the Chestnut Street Theatre as Richard III. In 1845 he first commenced in the burnt cork business. Mr. Kneass continued in the business a great favorite with the public, having composed a great many songs that afterwards became very popular. In March, 1858, he was manager of the Hiawatha Concert Saloon, Chicago; and on Christmas night, 1859, he opened a minstrel hall there. He was leader of the orchestra. He died in Chillicothe, Ohio, September 10, 1869.

KNEELAND, C. G.: formerly musical director of Johnny Booker's Minstrels, left the business in June, 1861, and settled down in Shellsburgh, Wis., (having got married) and took to farming.

LA CONTA, WILLIAM: an old banjoist and bone soloist, died from consumption at the Presbyterian Hospital, Philadelphia, on April 27, 1878, in the 51st year of his age. In 1848, he appeared with the Sable Harmonists in song and dance ("Lucy Long") and the double-faced soldier and sailor specialty, which he was one of the first to dance in this country. His remains were interred in Odd Fellows' Cemetery, Philadelphia.

LA RUE, D. C.: died of pneumonia at Charleston, S. C., on March 15, 1875.

LAFFERTY, CHARLES: violinist, died in Pittsburgh, Pa., September 3, 1859.

LANDIS, JOHN: was employed in the Philadelphia Navy Yard in August, 1861, as a son of Vulcan, and in July, 1863, was proprietor of an oyster saloon in Reading, Pa. He died in Philadelphia, September 19, 1863. He had been ill for two or three months. His death was no doubt hastened by the death of his child the day previous. He had rare comic ability, his performances always eliciting well deserved applause.

LANE, PETE: the once famous champion jig dancer, was born in Philadelphia and made his debut as a jig dancer in 1852. He died in the arms of his friend, Mr. Sinclair, in his native city, June 13, 1858.

LANG, JOHN: tenor, died of consumption in Chicago, on December 5, 1874, at the hospital, corner of Fourteenth Street and Indiana Avenue.

LEE, W. H.: business manager, died of consumption in Liverpool, England, December 16, 1874, aged 33 years.

LEON, DAN: died in New York April 27, 1863. He was born March 1, 1826, and entered the profession in 1845. He was a clever interlocutor and did Shakespearean burlesque business. He was connected with E. P. Christy's, Murphy, West and Peel's and Campbell's minstrels at different times.

LEON, FRANCIS: right name Patrick Glassey, was born in New York. When only 8 years of age he sang in the choir of St. Stephen's Church in this city. He sang with great success the first soprano in Mozart's Twelfth Mass. He first made his debut in the minstrel business at Wood's Marble Hall of Minstrelsy on Broadway in operatic burlesque. He made a successful first appearance and remained quite a favorite with the habitués for a long time. He subsequently appeared with various first class troupes as prima donna and *danseuse*, until we find him in partnership with Mr. Kelly in the West, as manager of the Academy of Music, Chicago, and afterwards in Cincinnati. He then came to this city and, in partnership with Mr. Kelly, opened at 720 Broadway. Mr. Leon possessed a full soprano voice and could sing up to D in the ledger lines. As a dancer he was one of the best in the minstrel business. His terpsichorean movements were executed with wonderful rapidity and he did many steps that we have not seen attempted by any other performer in the same line of business. In his prima donna business he copied no one. His imitations of the principal operatic lady singers were very good. In addition to being well up in this business, he was also a clever impersonator of female characters, in light sketches written by himself, and in which he was ably assisted by his partner, Mr. Kelly.

LESLIE, HARRY: was born in East Troy, N. Y., January 30, 1837. His first appearance in public was as a "tambourinist" with a traveling company in the New England States. In the year 1857, he joined the celebrated Bryant's Minstrels, then at 472 Broadway, and remained with them one season as versatile performer. In 1860, he again joined the Bryant's Minstrels and played a successful engagement of one year. In January, 1861, he was at the Canterbury, this city, as a pantomimist, comic dancer, ballet master, etc. In Philadelphia he walked a rope stretched across the Schuylkill River, a distance of 1,400 feet and 100 feet in height, for nine weeks in succession. That was nothing comparatively, but it rather staggers the nerves to imagine oneself jumping three times a week from that height, as he did, into the not over placid waters below. In January, 1863, he was stage manager at Trimble's Varieties, Pittsburgh. He walked a rope across the Niagara River on June 15, 1865. He made a great many similar feats over rivers throughout the country. In the winter of 1869, he traveled with Tony Denier as pantomimist. He died in the insane asylum.

LINGARD, GEORGE ALEXANDER: brother of James W. Lingard, died suddenly in the Bowery Hotel, New York, October 28, 1876, of enlargement of the heart. His remains were conveyed to Cypress Hills Cemetery. He was born in England in 1827. As early as April, 1850, he appeared at the Astor Place Opera House, this city, as a balladist with Sanford's Minstrels. In the spring of 1853, he sang at the Chatham Theatre between the pieces. He afterwards became an actor.

LLOYD, COL. ALVIN: was first brought to the notice of the show world by being connected with the Sable Harmonists in 1847. He is said to have run away from this company while in the West, leaving them without paying any salaries, and also their board bills unpaid. Several of them, having no money, were arrested and locked up, where they were compelled to work out their indebtedness. For committing some crime, he was shortly after arrested and served out nearly his time in the penitentiary in Kentucky, when he escaped, but was pursued by the jailer and overtaken, having his chains on at the time. He was severely beaten by his captor and once more safely caged; but his health becoming so bad that, fearing he would die, he was set at liberty. Reaching Cincinnati, he published a questionable paper, and in consequence of publishing a slanderous article on Mr. Potter, a gentleman much respected as the proprietor of the Cincinnati Commercial, he was obliged to leave in a hurry. His next venture was the minstrel party bearing his name. He was very much disliked by every member of that company for his overbearing, insolent manner to everyone. And it is stated that he was fond of exhibiting a revolver, but he was cowed down once by David Wambold, who threatened to kick his head off. After failing with this company, he went South and entered the Confederate Army as a "tent colonel"; but deserted the cause, came North and entered the Federal army. Wending his way South, he was recognized by a rebel officer, who shot him in the leg five times. This was the cause of his lameness. While in Cincinnti with his minstrel troupe, he was served with so many warrants of arrests for many of his former acts of villainy that he could scarcely find time to return from any court before he was served to appear at another. In one day he was arrested over forty times. His company that burst up in July, 1867, in Jackson, Mich., he ran away from in the night to Chicago. He next appeared in St. Louis, engaged in soliciting subscribers to a railroad snap publication. After obtaining about $15,000, he is said to have run away and was extensively published throughout the West. He once more came to New York and became interested in the management of the New York Theatre (afterwards Globe), Broadway above Fourth Street, in partnership with D. H. Harkins. Going up Broadway one day he met Dan Bryant, Nelse Seymour, and William Newcomb, when an altercation took place, resulting in Dan giving Lloyd a good horsewhipping. What became of Lloyd we do not know.

LULL, DAVE: was well known as "Dad" Lull or "Hump-backed Dad." He was a hump-backed man and used to play for his own dancing with exceedingly grotesque effect. His enormous hump was not only of service to him as a means of amusing the public but was also useful as a weapon of offense, his favorite mode of attack in personal combat being to bore his antagonist therewith. He was celebrated as a banjo player, having played at the Old Eagle Street Theatre, Buffalo, in 1842. He was with the old Virginia Serenaders when Billy Birch was in the company.

MACK, JOHNNY A.: died at San Rafael, Cal., July 23, 1870, aged 34 years. He was born in Pittsburgh, Pa. He first appeared in burnt cork in Boston. He had been for some months too unwell to pursue his avocation and his final decline was very rapid. He died of consumption.

MANNING, WILLIAM E.: died in Chicago, Ill., May 15, 1876, in the 42nd year of his age, and his remains were interred in Piqua, Ohio, in the Forest Hill Cemetery. The bottom of the grave was covered with Brussels carpet and two flag-stones were placed upon the top of the coffin and cemented. He was born in Piqua, Ohio, and commenced the minstrel profession at 17 years of age. He was first with the Dixey Company in 1859; afterward, with the Campbell, Morris, Rumsey, Wilson and Newcomb troupes, and with the VanAmburgh, and Haight & Chambers circuses. In 1867 he became an assistant manager in the Emerson, Allen & Manning Troupe, afterward the Emerson & Manning, and the Manning Minstrels. Upon the stage in the first part, he was a model of an end man. Mystified at the rhetoric of the middle man, and disputations upon all points advanced by the opposite end man, he kept his auditors in merriment from the opening to the close of the scene. In the olio, whether in his horrible "pathetic ballads," or his unrivaled "magical" entertainments, he never failed to please. A clear, honest eye, face an over-healthy crimson, and general bearing unassuming, he was always self-possessed, and was considered one of the best representatives of the old river darkie extant. It was a curious but perfectly natural compound of simplicity, cunning, affection, dishonesty, earnestness, laziness and cowardice; all his bad qualities so manifestly the product of hard experience and sad necessity that one could not help a feeling of sympathy and liking for the worn-out, shuffling-gaited, whining-voiced old rascal. Although in deep consumption at the time of his death, his decease was hastened through the villainous actions of a supposed friend well known in the minstrel profession.

MASON, HARRY: real name Henry Davis, died in Wilmington, Del., January 9, 1865, of pulmonary consumption.

MASON, HENRY: died in New York, suddenly on February 22, 1873, of hemorrhage of the lungs, aged 33 years. He had been suffering from consumption for some time. He was a clever performer and attentive to business.

MCANALLY, THOMAS: violinist, died in Brooklyn, N.Y., of consumption, May 25, 1872, aged 35 years. He was buried in Evergreen Cemetery.

MEEKER, G. W.: violoncellist, better known as "Old Governor," died in Dublin, Ireland, March 12, 1861, of heart disease. He was one of the original old Campbell party with Murphy, West and Peel.

MELVILLE, CHARLEY: was born in Brooklyn, N.Y., and made his first appearance on the stage as a ballad singer at Plunkett's Olympic Theatre, New Haven, Conn., in 1852 for the benefit of Julia Turnbull. His first professional engagement was with the Original Campbell Minstrels as leading tenor vocalist. After their season closed, he joined the Original Christy Minstrels and continued with them until their departure for Europe. After a term with West & Peel's Campbells Minstrels, he retired from the stage and became an agent. He died in Newark, N. J., July 10, 1901, and his remains were interred in Woodlawn Cemetery, Newark.

MILLICENT, JOHN: a professional dancer for 39 years, died in London, January 10, 1865. He was an American.

MITCHELL, MIKE: jig dancer, died in San Francisco, January 13, 1862, aged 32 years. He was buried in San Francisco. A marble slab was arranged over his grave with the following:

> Here lies one who has taken steps
> That won the applause of man,
> But grim Death came and took a step
> Which he could not withstand.

MOORE, GEORGE W.: familiarly known as "Pony Moore," was born in New York, February 22, 1820. When reaching the age of 12, being so diminutive in appearance, he was looked upon as a second edition of Tom Thumb and was called "the little pony." And to his last day he was known throughout the profession as "Pony Moore." As soon as he had reached the age of 16, he ran away from home and joined a circus company, first leaving one company and then joining another. In 1844, he made his entree in the burnt cork business at the Halfway House, Broadway, New York, where the City Assembly Rooms Building afterwards stood. He joined here the old Virginia Serenaders. In 1852 he made his first appearance on the end as Brother Bones with Hayworth and Horton's company. He afterwards traveled with the Kentucky Minstrels, Ring & Parker's Troupe, the Congo Minstrels (afterwards known as Buckley's), and the Dumbolton's band. He opened at Mechanics' Hall in 1856. Their last performance there was February 21, 1857. When he left this party he went through the South with Tony Hernandez and a variety show. Pony used to stand as a target for Hernandez to throw knives at. He next traveled with Matt Peel's Campbell's Minstrels and remained with them until Peel's death, when he became manager and played through New York State, closing in Brooklyn. In the latter city he played at Burtis' Variety Show, working both places each night. On June 11, 1859, Pony sailed for England to join the "Christys," who were then in London. He met the party and took Earl H. Pierce's "posish." The chair that had been occupied by Pierce was covered with crepe and remained unoccupied until Moore took it. Moore played the tambourine, while in America he manipulated the bones. His salary was $15 a week, including board. He opened at Polygraphic Hall, London, England, then went on tour, re-opening in London in 1860. He left the company in Dublin, Ireland, and with Ritter, Crocker and Hamilton, started a Christy show of their own, opening in Chester, England, November 14, 1864. On September 18, 1865, he opened at St. James' Hall, London. Later Moore brought out Ritter and subsequently, through the death of Crocker, became the manager of the company. Moore took Burgess as partner. Pony died in London, England, October 1, 1909. He was the oldest minstrel living at the time of his death. In the callow days of minstrelsy, he was poet and composer and is credited with being the author of two songs, "Work, Niggers, Work," and "Dis Child's Tambourine." In the first he used to sing:

When the ebening shades am going down
An' sink in the West
Oh, den de nigger's work am done,
An' den he takes him rest.
CHORUS
Work, niggers, work, work, work, niggers, work,
What care we fo' de morrow?
Set ob sun, de day's work's done,
Den we'll banish sorrow.

In his second song Pony sang, in language forcible but not elegant, the fierce hand-to-hand combat of two colored ladies and varied the scene of the strife by the somewhat inappropriate chorus of:

De niggers dance upon the green,
To de music ob de tambourine;
Dan lightly touch de banjo string,
And den shake dis chile's tambourine.

It is a well known fact among the "old timers" that Pony claimed the authorship of all American songs and had effrontery of putting his name on the title page as author. When spoken to about it, he exclaimed, "Well, there is no international copyright."

MORRIS, WILLIAM E.: died in Boston, Mass., October 11, 1878, after an illness of several weeks. William E.. Morris was born at or inside of Fort Niagara, near Buffalo, N.Y., May 11, 1832, and was therefore in his 47th year. When 15 years of age he entered the minstrel profession, joining Williams' Empire Minstrels in Buffalo, N.Y. After appearing for a time in small parts, he gained popularity and made rapid progress. In 1852, he went to Boston, Mass., and joined Ordway's Aeolians. He, with his brother Lon, Johnny Pell and J. C. Trowbridge, seceded from the company and organized the Morris Bros. & Trowbridge Minstrels. Early in 1870 he was connected with his brother Lon in the management of the Mystic Trotting Park, Boston, and similar enterprises. He made his last appearance in Boston, at Beethoven Hall during the early spring of 1878, when he created a sensation by his whistling "The Mocking Bird," which was almost inseparably connected with his professional career. He was at one time one of the greatest favorites with lovers of minstrelsy that ever put on burnt cork. His cunning Negro look, his voice, his "feats," his whimsicalities, all conduced to make him one of the best end men in the business.

MULLEN, J. J.: died in New York August 17, 1869, and his remains were interred in Calvary Cemetery.

MULLIGAN, JOHN: died suddenly in New York on July 22, 1873, in the 47th year of his age. He was born in New York in March, 1827. His first professional engagement was with Raymond & Waring's Menagerie. He subsequently traveled two seasons with Robinson & Eldred, dancing in the ring, while Al Romaine performed upon the banjo. He then joined Perham's Minstrel Troupe, remaining one year and becoming a great favorite with the audiences. In 1854 he joined Mabie's Circus in Missouri, with which he traveled to New Orleans, La., and back, and at the conclusion of that season he was engaged by G. F. Bailey, with whom he remained three seasons. He then went to Philadelphia, where he fulfilled a profitable engagement at Thomas' Opera House, and the following winter he joined VanAmburgh's Circus and Menagerie at Macon, Ga., and continued with that show one season. He had by that time become a very attractive performer and managers sought his services. On his return from the South, he was engaged by Frank Rivers for his Melodeon in Philadelphia, and so great a favorite did he become that he remained two years. About this time he attracted the attention of George Lea, a well known manager, and in 1862 entered into a contract with the latter for a long period. He performed under Mr. Lea's direction in Baltimore, Washington, Philadelphia, New York, New Orleans and nearly all the principal cities of the Union. He was afterwards connected with the San Francisco Minstrels, Hooley's and others of note. Mr. Mulligan had been suffering from some disease of the heart for some time, but had been confined to his room but a brief period. On the day of his death he expressed a desire to look out of the window, and his wife had arranged a pillow on the sill for him to rest his head upon. And as he sat there with one arm around his wife's waist and gazing upon the passing pedestrians, his spirit winged its flight so quietly that his wife was not aware of his death until she saw his head droop upon the pillow. In attempting to raise it she discovered her loss. Mr. Mulligan, as an Ethiopian comedian, had few equals in his peculiar line, and in his special acts was without a rival. His appearance on the stage was ever a signal for hearty laughter. Being over six feet high, and his wardrobe of the most ludicrous description, it was not strange that he should evoke great enthusiasm.

MYERS, RICHARD: known as "Ole Bull" Myers, was born in Baltimore, Md., May 5, 1809. He was connected with minstrel companies for a great many years. In 1835 he played the violin accompaniment to S. S. Sanford's singing. He was considered one of the best violinists in the profession. His last performance in public was at the Cape May (N. J.) Court House, August 5, 1874. On the morning of the 6th he said, speaking to his violin, "I have played you for the last time. You go under my bed when I get home, and lie there." He died in Philadelphia on September 10, 1874.

NELLE, WILLIAM CYNES: tenor, of Moore & Burgess' Christy's, died October 22, 1874, aged 25 years.

NEWCOMB, WILLIAM W.: died in New York at the City Hotel, corner Broadway and Eighth Street, on May 1, 1877. With cords attached to the door latch, gas jet and bell pull, and with a rope so rigged that he might take at least a little exercise while lying in bed, he had lain in that room almost helpless for ten weeks, or ever since he broke a leg while performing in a pantomimic sketch at Hooley's Opera House, Brooklyn. Heart disease terminated a life that poverty long before rendered undesirable. He met his end unexpectedly and alone. He was found kneeling in death at his bedside with his hands supporting his face. It is surmised that a rheumatic affection, which not even his physicians deemed serious, suddenly went to his heart. His funeral was very poorly attended, there being only twelve persons present, among whom were Frank Leslie, the old time minstrel performer, one other professional, a few boarders in the hotel (non-professionals) and the writer of this. The service of the Episcopal Church was read by Frank Leslie and a hymn was sung by Mr. Leslie and his lady friend and myself. It was a sad sight. There, lying in his coffin, was the once great Newcomb, who in his day was a great favorite and a man of influence. Having been reduced to poverty, living his latter days on the charity of others, he was forgotten by all his old associates, more particularly those he had often befriended (pecuniarily), who, even when death had wrapped his mantle around him, failed to forget his little failings. Just as the mortal remains of poor Newcomb were about being conveyed from the hotel parlors to the hearse, the Rev. Dr. Houghton put in an appearance; and, after a short prayer, the once popular minstrel performer was taken to his last resting place. Mr. Newcomb was born in Utica, N. Y., August 4, 1823. At about five years of age he became an orphan and he was taken in charge by the gentleman who had been the chosen physician of his parents. It was his guardian's purpose to make a physician of him; but the boy as he grew up developed a taste for banjo songs and straight jigs and ultimately he placed himself under the wing of Fitzallan, one of the many solitary song-and-dance performers of that day. He traveled with him for three years at the tail end of circuses and then had an offer from S. B. Howes, whose circus he joined and with whom he remained as a jig dancer for three years. Then he and Abijah L. Thayer of Boston organized a minstrel band, from which the latter was forced by ill health to withdraw after a four years' partnership. Newcomb's first appearance in New York was in an olio at Tripler Hall on December 4, 1851. It was he who invented and danced for the first time before the public "The Essence of Old Virginia" with Fellow's Minstrels at 444 Broadway, Mert Sexton being the second one to do the act. He was also the first minstrel who produced burlesque stump speeches, his first being "Woman's Rights."

NISH, ANTHONY: musical director of Moore & Burgess' Christy's, died in London, England, October 3, 1873, of erysipelas, caused by the extraction of a sound tooth in place of one decayed. He was born at Newcastle-on-Tyne, England, in February, 1831. In 1850 he visited the United States. His remains were interred in Brompton Cemetery.

NORTON, TIM: died in New York on January 25, 1862, after an illness of three months of consumption. He was buried in Greenwood. He was a versatile performer and could make himself useful in almost any line of business. He was quite young, not being more than 23 years of age at the time of his death.

NORTON, WASHINGTON: was born in New Orleans, February 2, 1839, and first appeared before the public in Roxbury, Mass., when but 9 years of age. He joined Ordway's Aeolians in Boston in 1851. He opened with Bryant's in New York in 1859. He sailed for Europe March 2, 1861, and joined Nish's party, but left for the Cape of Good Hope, July 5, 1862. He re-appeared in New York in 1867, but returned to Europe in 1868, organized a band, and went to South Africa. On July 23, 1870, he had a match jig dance with Joe Brown at the Canterbury, London, and won the match. He returned to New York on July 5, 1872, and opened at the Bowery Theatre on August 5 in a play called "From Abroad." He died November 16, 1899.

O'BRIEN, MIKE: banjoist and balladist, died of consumption in Algiers, opposite New Orleans, April 28, 1869.

O'NEIL, CHARLIE: formerly with Hooley's party, committed suicide in St. Louis by drowning on July 2, 1863.

OYSTERMAN, PAUL: clarinet player, died in St. Louis, March 22, 1867, of consumption.

PEARCE, W. W.: died in Herkimer, N. Y., January 2, 1864, of consumption, aged 26 years. His wife was the former Marion Crapeau.

PEEL, MATT: was born in New York, January 15, 1830, of Irish parents. When he was about 2 years old his parents removed to Brooklyn, N.Y., where his father died in 1846. At an early age he evinced a talent for mimicry and a propensity for dancing. In 1840 he danced in public at a number of benefits at the Military Garden. In 1843 he organized a party to give Ethiopian concerts and traveled through Rhode Island. In 1846 he was engaged by June & Titus to travel with their circus. He was one of the best eccentric performers on the Ethiopian stage and was never at a loss for a point upon which to "bring down the house." He was extremely jealous of his reputation and would never permit another to eclipse him in fun and happy hits. He was the first one that brought forward that popular saying, "He was a good man; as good a man an over lived---but he can't keep a hotel." Matt Peel made his last appearance on the stage at Buffalo, N. Y., on May 2, 1859, and on the morning of the 4th, about 5 o'clock, while sitting up in bed, conversing with his wife, he instantly expired as he was exclaiming, "Oh, May, I am dying." His wife subsequently became the wife of J. T. Huntley.

PEEL, TOMMY: whose right name was Thomas Jefferson Reily, died in Melbourne, Australia, July 31, 1869, and his remains were deposited in the same grave with Billy O'Neil, the Irish comedian, which was Tommy's request. The pall bearers were Frank Hussey, Frank Weston, Frank Drew, John Smith, Harry Kelly, Charles Woodruff, T. Rainford and Henry Petchman. Weston & Hussey's brass band, assisted by other brother professionals, played the "Dead March" from "Saul." He was buried under the Roman Catholic faith. Tommy Peel was born in Albany, N. Y., in September, 1841. At a very early age he had a local reputation as a jig dancer; and while he was engaged at Rose's Tenpin Saloon, in Washington Street, Albany, near Congress Hall, he was often sought for by the getters-up of impromptu negro minstrel companies and to dance at various benefits. At 9 years of age, Master Tommy made his debut with a regular company, joining the Sable Harmonists in his native city, the company having halted there to give two or three performances; and it was at this time that he first had the pleasure of appearing in public in proper uniform, viz. pink shirt, blue plaid breeches, and brass-heeled shoes. The applause he received was tremendous and Tommy's appearance added largely to the receipts of said company, Dan Bryant being in the company. In 1852 he attracted the attention of Matt Peel, who took him under his fostering care and Tommy was soon well known to the minstrel profession and the public as Master Tommy Peel. The following account of the closing days of the earthly career of this once popular jig dancer is by Frank Russey. The sketch is correct in every particular, and there will be many an eye dimmed while reading of the jig dancer's desire to return home again, to rejoin his companions of old, then "ten thousand miles away."

On my arrival in Sydney, Australia, the first person I heard from was Tommy Peel, who, from Melbourne, some five hundred miles away, had sent me a letter asking all sorts of questions about home, his old professional friends, etc. After my engagement in Sydney was over I started for Melbourne, and the first person to greet me when the steamer reached the latter place was Tommy Peel. But not the Tommy Peel I had last seen in California. He was pale and sickly looking, and his eye, once so bright and cheery, was sunk in his head. Nevertheless, it was a joyful meeting. Tommy had many a question to ask me about 'the old boys,' as he called them. How was Dan Bryant, and Eph Horn, and Brower, and Backus, and a hundred others? I answered, in brief, that they were all well when I left home. 'But, Tommy,' said I, 'you are not looking well.' 'No.' he rejoined, 'I caught a heavy cold over in New Zealand, but am much better now.' I was not long in finding something to do in Melbourne, for, three days after my arrival, I leased, in company with Weston, Kelly and Holly, St. George's Hall, and began to refit it as a Minstrel Opera House. A company was organized to go up country until the Opera House was completed, and Tommy Peel was of the company. The first performance was given at Castlemaine, and Tommy, when he was about ready for his jig, saluted me with: 'Frank, how does Master Barney dance?' 'Well, Tommy, he is a great dancer.' 'Yes,' said he, 'but I hold the belt.' 'So you do, Tommy, and I hope you will always hold it.' 'Well, Frank,' he said, 'I shall try to. But you have not seen me dance for years. Now, I'm going to dance for you to-night.' And he did dance. Such another jig as was danced by Tommy Peel that night I have never seen. Poor Tommy! Next day at the hotel he said: 'Frank, when you go home, will you take me with you?' Little did I think that it would be his last home I should take him to, and I promised him I would take him with me to the states. 'For,' he explained, 'I want to meet Barney, and dance him.' And thenceforward his thoughts seemed to be entirely of home and Barney. Our opera house was finished at last, and we returned to Melbourne and opened. Tommy was on the bills every night in his 'Champion Jig,' but the steps were telling on him, and he was failing day by day. I advised him to 'lay up' for a week or two. But no! 'I shall be all right soon,' he said. On the last night that he appeared, he came to me at the wings and asked: 'Frank, can't you take my jig off the bills until I get a little stronger?' 'Certainly, Tommy; and you had better keep off the stage until you're all well.' 'All right, Frank,' said he, 'I'll be better soon.' I advised him not to dance that night. 'But my name is on the bills,' was his argument, 'and I must dance.' He tried to but he couldn't. Nature could not longer stand the strain. I called to him from the wings to 'cut it short.' He looked at me as much as to say, 'I don't like to do it, but I must.' When he came off the stage, he reproached himself with, 'What will the people say of a jig like that!' I told him not to mind what the people would say, but to go home and take good care of himself. From that time he began to sink rapidly; and on the morning of Saturday, July 31, 1869, the life passed from him. His last request was that we bury him by the side of Billy O'Neil, the Irish comedian. He was so buried; and now I never see a dancer on the minstrel stage without thinking of poor Tommy Peel and his Last Champion Jig. FRANK HUSSEY

PELHAM, RICHARD WARD: better known as Dick Pelham, was born in New York, February 13, 1815, and made his first appearance on the stage in 1835 at the Bowery Theatre, New York, with T. D. Rice in "Oh, Hush!" He afterwards traveled with Turner's Circus executing a song and dance. He afterwards traveled with his brother, Gilbert. After appearing at various theatres in New York, he became one of the original band and went to England. He never returned to America after leaving it with the "original four" in 1843. His last engagement was in August, 1856. He died in Liverpool, England, October 8, 1856, of cancer of the stomach and was buried in Anfield Cemetery. Several years prior to his death he was indebted to Samuel Hague, proprietor of the well known minstrels in Liverpool, for many kindnesses. He also conducted a column in Mr. Hague's monthly publication, headed "Ethiopian Anecdotes." He was the author of many Negro melodies. For many years he managed Pell's Serenaders in England and it was with them at the Surrey Theatre, London, in the spring of 1849 that Juba achieved the success which shortened his life. Gil Pell, who had been a prominent feature of the Dumbolton Troupe, which, by special invitation, had performed at the residences of many of the English nobility, was also with Pell's Serenaders along with Juba.

PELL, GILBERT WARD: the retired bone player, died on December 21, 1872, and was buried in the Cemetery St. Helens, Lancashire, England, aged 47 years.

PELL, HARRY: died on Blackwell's Island, New York, about May 1, 1866.

PELL, JOHNNY: whose right name was John A. Davin, died in Boston, January 24, 1866, aged 33 years. His last engagement in New York was with Charley White in the Bowery in 1854. He was a partner of the Morris Brothers from 1857 up to his death. Two days before his death he was married to Miss Moonie of Boston. His remains were brought to New York and interred in Calvary Cemetery. As an end man he was complete in everything pertaining to that position. His ornaments, his handkerchief, his vest, his wig, his movements, all his attitudes, stamped him a master spirit.

PETTENGILL, CHARLES: died in Albany, N. Y., on October 10, 1870, of consumption, aged 27 years.

PIERCE, EARL H.: died in London suddenly, June 5, 1859, and the house was closed until June 9. He had been indisposed and away from his duties one week prior to his death. On Sunday he said to his nurse he could not remain in bed and asked to be taken to a place of worship. He was taken to Highgate. He went through all his devotions with the utmost fervor and, on getting outside the building, he clasped his hands and fell down dead. He was born in New York in 1823. He was one of the greatest comic banjo soloists of his day and achieved fame by his song of "Hoop-de-dooden-do." His first appearance before the public was in Philadelphia with Ogden & Raymond's Circus. In 1842, he joined a minstrel party composed of Dan Emmett, Frank Brower, Jimmy O'Connell, Frank Diamond, Mestayer, and Master Pierce. At this time they were performing at the Franklin Theatre, N.Y.C. Leaving the minstrels for a while, he joined Turner's Circus. He later joined E. P. Christy's Minstrels. He went to England in 1856.

PIERSON, LEWIS: balladist and interlocutor, died at Washington, D. C., on April 24, 1874 of consumption.

PIKE, MARSHALL S.: was born in Westboro, Mass. He was one of the first impersonators of female characters on the minstrel stage, having performed in Boston in 1836. He became quite noted as a song writer. He traveled with minstrel bands for some years. He was taken prisoner of war early in 1861, but was paroled the same year. He died at Upton, Mass., February 13, 1901.

PRENDERGAST, THOMAS B.: left New York for the South with the 71st Regiment, April 22, 1861, and he was one of the first to set foot on Alexandria, Va., ground when that city was captured by the U. S. Forces. In June, 1861, he made a flying visit to New York on business and appeared with the Bryants (for that night only), June 13 and sang "Vive la America." He was presented with a beautiful gold medal by Dan on behalf of the company. He dropped dead an Sunday, March 6, 1869, in the arms of Charles Covelli, in Utica, N.Y. He was a first class ballad singer. He retired from the profession one year prior to his death and kept a saloon in Utica with Covelli. The funeral procession was one of the most imposing seen in that town for a long time. The fire department, citizen soldiery and many others attended. The cortege moved in the following order: Fire police, band (all the fire department band), citizens, the corpse, delegation from Fountain Hose No. 4, Binghamton, in carriages, and mourners and friends. The procession proceeded to St. Patrick's Church, where solemn high mass was celebrated. The delivery of the sermon occupied one hour. The remains were interred in St. John's cemetery. Mr. P. was a member of the fire department and, upon the organization of the fire police, he was chosen captain. He participated in the battle of Aquia Creek and received special mention for bravery from his officer. He was engaged in the Bull Run fight with the Seventy-first Regiment.

PRICE, HI: was born in Chatfield, Filmore County, Minn., September 30, 1857. His first appearance in public was with Googin's Minstrels. Since then he has been connected with various circuses in the concerts.

PRIDE, SAM: banjoist, died in Ireland on November 11, 1871, of bronchitis.

PRIMROSE, GEORGE H.: was born in London, Ontario, November 12, 1852, and first blacked up in 1867 as "Master Georgie, the Infant Clog Dancer."

PURDY, S. S.: fell dead in the street in front of the Barnes House, Chicago, Ill., on February 29, 1876, aged 40 years. He was buried in Chicago. He was born in Troy, N.Y., in February, 1836. He visited England in June, 1869, and appeared with Moore & Crocker's Christy's.

QUINN, BILLY: died in New York November 29, 1863, of consumption, aged 26 years. His remains were interred in Calvary Cemetery. Jig dancing was his line of business.

RAWLINSON, JOHN: a once popular vocalist, died in London, England, April 11, 1875, and was buried in Brompton Cemetery. He was 37 years of age.

RAY, JOHN: better known as "Fox" Ray, died at Walsall, Staffordshire, England in April, 1873, age 42 years.

RAYNOR, GEORGE: right name George James Rea, basso, died in Brooklyn, April 7, 1874, aged 44 years. He was brother to John Raynor. He was at Burton's, Chambers Street Museum, New York, in 1852.

REESE, A. H.: formerly of Happy Cal Wagner's Minstrels, died in Milwaukee, Wis., on November 28, 1877, of consumption.

REEVE, WILLIAM M.: died at Williamsburg, N.Y., August 11, 1872, age 37 years. He was interred in Greenwood Cemetery.

REIMER, A.: was taken ill with hemorrhage of the lungs, and died in Montreal on September 28, 1868.

REMINGTON, BILLY: died of heart disease at Grand Rapids, Mich., April 16, 1870.

RICARDO, F. M.: was born in Ireland in 1846. He came to America in 1849. Ricardo commenced stage life in 1868 with Kelly and Leon in New York, although he had previously been noted as a public singer, having been engaged for some time as the regular soprano of St. George's Church. His voice was particularly adapted to the burlesque prima donna business. He sang with a clear, sweet and perfectly trained tone of the most undoubted falsetto, and when rising to the higher notes was able to hold to them perfectly even and with purity, without being forced off into the customary shriek with which wench personators of less extensive vocal powers are obliged to conclude a roulade. While possessing hardly less of the grace and thorough familiarity with all the many little details of stage business, that is noticeable in other performers of his class who have had a more prolonged acquaintance with the footlights than himself, Ricardo's superior qualities as a singer gave him a stable advantage over most of his competitors that nothing could counteract.

RICE, THOMAS D.: "Jim Crow," was born in New York, May 20, 1808. He first learned the trade of a carver, but on attaining his majority, joined a theatrical association and then went to Kentucky, under the management of Noah Ludlow. He made his first appearance in Negro character at Ludlow's Amphitheatre, Louisville. He was in Mr. Ludlow's company as a member of the stock company, playing inferior characters, but he was an excellent imitator of the Negro in their peculiarities, singularities and eccentricities, and especially could he imitate the Negro in song. Accordingly, between the play and farce, Mr. Rice was often announced and put forward to sing a Negro song in character. On one of these occasions I heard and saw Mr. Rice in Negro character sing a Negro song. This song, as I remember, was called, "Kitty-co-dink-a-ho-dink! oh, oh, roley-boley. Good morning, ladies all." He first appeared in New York at the Park Theatre in "Jim Crow." After a most successful career in New York, Boston, Philadelphia, and other cities, he crossed the Atlantic, and appeared in 1836 at the Surrey Theatre, London. His career in England was a most extraordinary one. The "Jim Crow" entertainment was a rage. He managed to keep up the excitement by improvising new verses to his song and thus making it entirely new every evening. On June 18, 1837, he married Miss Gladstone, eldest daughter of Mr. Gladstone, formerly manager of the Surrey Theatre. Mr. and Mrs. Wood could not draw a house and Macready had to quit the field for Jim Crow. We find on one occasion, at Dublin, the Lord Lieutenant and suite were present, and $1,800 in the house, one clear third of which went to Mr. Rice. On his fourth night he had $1,400 in the house, and in Cork the receipts were $1,900 per night. At all these places, independent of jumping Jim Crow, he appeared as Ginger Blue, Caesar, and in several pieces of similar merit. When he returned from Europe, he was eagerly sought after by the managers and played as a star in all the theatres in the country. His favorite role was the "Fancy Negro," now nearly gone out, but he was equally good as the plantation hand. He opened with Wood's Minstrels, 561 and 563 Broadway, New York, August 4, 1858. About 1840 he was for awhile deprived of speech and the use of his limbs by an attack of paralysis. He composed a burlesque opera called "Bone Squash," and a Negro extravaganza on the plot of "Othello," both exceedingly entertaining and very successful. Mr. Rice was stricken with paralysis and suffered very much until the day of his death, which occurred in New York, September 19, 1860.

RICHARDS, WARREN: right name, Richard A. Warren, tenor singer, died in New York, June 15, 1876, and was buried in Calvary Cemetery.

ROSS, ALEX: died in St. Louis, Mo., May 19, 1866, from consumption.

RUMSEY, HIRAM S.: died in Newburgh, N.Y., of paralysis of the spine, September 9, 1871, aged 43 years, 2 months and 28 days. His remains were interred in St. George Cemetery, Newburgh. He lay ill at his father's residence in Newburgh a long time. He lay ill, for some time in the home known as Dr. Burdell's, Bond Street, New York. In November, 1864, he became paralyzed and unable to resume his profession. As a banjo player, in his day, he had no superior.

RYDER, WILLIAM: solo cornettist with the Moore & Burgess party, died in Brighton, England, on June 14, 1871, aged 24 years.

SANFORD, SAMUEL S.: was born in New York, January 1, 1821. He made his debut at 9 years of age at Dan Neunan's ballroom, located at what is now known as Eighth and Willow Streets, Philadelphia, as a singer. He traveled with his uncle, Hugh Lindsay, a celebrated clown, until 16 years of age. In 1840, he entered into the minstrel business. On July 4, 1863, he was married in Philadelphia to Miss Appoline M. Bond. Mr. Sanford was a liberal and kind-hearted gentleman and his purse was always open to the calls of the needy. In assisting others he had forgotten himself. He was industrious, persevering and generous. As a delineator of the "old darkie of the Southern plantation" there were few, if any, performers equal to him. He gave a very faithful portraiture of the contraband, both in manner of speaking and the peculiar characteristics of the Southern Negro. He died December 31, 1906, at his home in Brooklyn.

SAVORI, J. H.: retired from the profession several years ago and has been practicing medicine in Harlem under the name of Dr. Wheeler.

SEARCH, JACOB: "Old Jake," violinist, died in Philadelphia, February 12, 1874, age 66 years.

SEYMOUR, NELSE: died in New York February 2, 1875, at the age of 39 years and 8 months, having been born in Baltimore, Md., June 5, 1835. His death was the result of a complication of diseases from which he had long suffered. His real name was Thomas Nelson N. Sanderson, and he was a son of Col. Henry S; Sanderson, a prominent Democratic politician, who had held the offices of sheriff and city tax collector and was one of the original directors and for many years the treasurer of the Front Street Theatre in that city. It was at that theatre that Nelse Seymour made his first appearance in public as a volunteer clown in the circus ring. Shortly afterwards, he entered the minstrel profession and was connected with Myers & Madigan's Circus, also with Dan Rice's. He made his first appearance in public with cork on his face at Apollo Hall, Baltimore, Md., which was then managed by John T. Raymond and Fanny Forrest. He made his first appearance in New York August 25, 1862. He sailed for England June 12, 1869, under engagement to appear with Moore & Crocker's Minstrels in London. He made a hit among the Londoners but the climate did not agree with him and he was several times afflicted with hemorrhage of the lungs. After a sojourn there of a few months he returned to New York. He was billed to perform with Bryants' Minstrels Wednesday evening, January 27, 1875, in "Deaf in a Horn" and to impersonate the characters of the Policeman and King Kaliko in the closing pantomime of "Kuliko; or, Harlequin, King of the Sandwich Islands"; but he being too ill to fulfill his duties, his place in "Deaf in a Horn" was supplied by W. H. Brockway and one of the attaches of the theatre went on for the policeman and Mr. Seymour impersonated King Kaliko only. His illness increased so rapidly during the evening that at the close of the performance he was compelled to ask the aid of a brother performer to wash the cork from his face. He was conveyed in a carriage to his residence, where he remained until his spirit winged its flight. His remains were escorted from the residence of his mother to the church by one hundred and eighty-two members of Amity Lodge of F. and A. M. and by the New York Lodge, No. 1, of the B. P. O. Elks. Charles Backus, James Clute, John J. Tindale and Col. T. Allston Brown acted as pallbearers, upon behalf of the Masonic lodge; and Tony Pastor and Gus Williams of the New York Lodge of B. P. O. Elks; and Frank Moran and Robert Fraser of the Philadelphia lodge of that order, an behalf of the Elks. The remains were then conveyed to Evergreen Cemetery, East New York, followed by a long line of carriages; and the services at the grave were the most imposing of all. The cemetery was not reached until a quarter past 6 o'clock and, owing to the lateness of the hour and some misunderstanding, no one connected with the cemetery could be found. The office was closed and the grave-diggers had all gone home. For half an hour, all who had gone to the cemetery waited in the cold, biting wind while Tony Pastor went in search of the grave-digger, who arrived at a quarter of 7 o'clock, at which time it was dark. Candles were procured and by that light were the remains of Nelse Seymour committed to the earth.

SHADDUCK, BOB: violinist, died in St. Louis, Sept. 5, 1864.

SHARPLEY, SAM: died in Providence, R. I., January 1, 1875, after a long and painful illness of a combination of diseases, the principal of which were cancer of the stomach and ulceration of the bowels. His real name was Samuel Sharpe. He was born in Philadelphia, Pa., June 13, 1831. He first entered the minstrel profession at 16 years of age, and was on the road traveling with minstrel companies about 25 years.

SHEPPARD, BILLY: comedian and banjo performer, once a great favorite at Hooley's, died at Port Washington, N. Y., July 8, 1872, of consumption and was buried at Woodlawn Cemetery by the B. P. O. Elks of New York, Lodge No. 1.

SIMMONS, LEW: was run over by an auto truck at Reading, Pa., September 2, 1911.

SIMPSON, JOHN: died at his residence, 214 East Sixty-second Street, New York, December 6, 1878. His full Christian name was Jonathan, but by its being contracted for printing on show bills he came to be known as John, which name he subsequently retained as long as he was in business. In 1846 he was treasurer of Mitchell's Olympic Theatre, and left there to fulfill a similar position with E. P. Christy's Minstrels, 472 Broadway. For some time he occupied a like position at White's Varieties in the Bowery, and later he joined Bryant's Minstrels, 472 Broadway, and continued there as treasurer as long as the company had an existence in this city. After the death of Dan Bryant, April 10, 1875, the Opera House in Twenty-third Street was closed and Mr. Simpson retired to private life. He was of a very genial disposition and much liked by all with whom he came in contact.

SLITER, R. H.: died in Jackson, Mich., May 21, 1861. He danced three nights previous to his death and then complained of his right leg paining him. The following day he was confined to his bed and he requested the violinist of the troupe to play "Sounds from Home." He also requested Tommy Jefferson to play a favorite jig for him on the banjo. His body was conveyed to the city cemetery. The minstrels who had come from Adrian, Mich., to his funeral sang over his grave, "Let Me Kiss Him for His Mother." On hearing of his death, his mother proceeded to Jackson and had the body conveyed to Buffalo, N.Y., where the remains were deposited in Forest Lawn, June 5.

SMITH, AL: died of consumption, in Jersey City, N. J., January 31, 1876, aged 33 years. He was considered a good jig dancer.

SMITH, JOHN PEMBERTON: was born in Richmond, Va., August 3, 1832. He first appeared in minstrelsy as Master Smith in 1845. He joined a small party and played the jawbone, the bones and danced jigs with old Joe Sweeney. The party lasted about six months and John returned to Richmond and entered the office of the *Richmond Enquirer*, where he remained six years as a "typo." He then joined the Old Dominion Minstrels in 1850, under the name of John P. Weston, and played the bones. When the party disbanded, John remained in Suffolk and published a newspaper called *The District Republican*. He remained there four months; then joined Bill Parrow's Minstrels, playing the bones. He next organized the Smith & Hernandez Minstrels. He retired from the profession in 1855 and remained idle for about six months, after which he was employed in the Government Printing Office at Washington as proofreader, where he remained until 1858. John T. Ford then engaged him to manage the Washington Theatre for six months; after which, Ford sent him to Baltimore as business manager for the Front Street Theatre. He next took a trip of two weeks as far as Norfolk, Va., for the Buckley Bros.' Minstrels, then returned to Baltimore and joined George Christy's Minstrels and went through the South as advance agent. This was during the war when everything was pretty lively down there. Then he organized the Olympic Minstrels in Norfolk in 1864. He was manager of the Melodeon, Baltimore, for six months for Albert Lea. He joined the Raynor Christy Minstrels as agent in June, 1864. Next he made a trip through the East with the Bryant's Minstrels, and in 1865 became business manager for Artemus Ward. His next venture was a most desperate one; that was going through the South and West as agent for Belle Boyd. He reached Memphis, but found things getting too warm for him, so he returned to New York. He was manager of the Park Theatre, Brooklyn, for the season of 1872-73; was manager for Mrs. Conway of the Brooklyn Theatre for several seasons and up to her death; was two seasons manager for the Vokes Family; for three years he attended to all business engagements for Clara Morris; and in 1876 brought out "Uncle Tom's Cabin" with a great many original slaves (from Thompson Street) in the plantation scene. He made his debut as an actor at Albany, N. Y., in April, 1858, playing the Auctioneer in "Uncle Tom's Cabin." He died in New York, November 12, 1897.

SMITH, JOHN WASHINGTON: better known as "old Bob Ridley," died at South Yard, Australia, August 31, 1877, and was buried in St. Kilda Cemetery, Melbourne. He had been troubled with asthma for some time. As far back as 1838 he was singing and dancing the tragico-comico extravaganza of "Jim Along Josey," together with giving the Negro song of "Jim Brown," at the Lion Circus, Menagerie and Gymnastic Arena, Cincinnati, Ohio. Smith was known to familiars as "The Arkansas Traveler" and was the first person in America to make a decided feature of the song of "The Fine Oil English Gentleman." Jim Sanford and Smith were rivals in "Jim Along Josey." In the summer of 1841 he got back to the Bowery and he and his pupil, Piccaninny Coleman, were doing "Jim Along Josey" and kindred negroisms. They next went to England and in November of 1840 did their grotesque acts at the Surrey Theatre, London. They returned in 1841 and in the fall of 1842 they joined Master John Diamond and Billy Whitlock in negroisms at the Chatham Theatre, this city. In 1849 he was with Stone & McCollum and wrote the song-and-dance "Old Bob Ridley," which he first gave in New Orleans. He was also the first person to do it in New York and first with a minstrel band, which was at the Melodeon, this city, opposite the Old Bowery Theatre, in the fall of 1852. In 1854 he went to San Francisco. From San Francisco he went to the Sandwich Islands, which he left in 1857 for Australia, where he managed for Burton. In 1860, he left Australia and went to China, India, the Philippine Islands and Java. In 1865, he returned to Australia, whence he proceeded to London, where he became manager of the Collins & Brown "Christys," whom he took to Australia and played until 1865. His last tour was with Heller, which began at Bombay in October, 1871, whence he took him by rail across Central India, stopping at Jubbulpore, Allahabad, Dinapore, and Calcutta, where he played him from November to the middle of January, 1872, going thence to Ceylon, Hong Kong, Shanghai, Singapore, Batavia, Java, Soolo (residence of the Emperor), and Djola Karta, the Sultan's domain. In October, Heller went to England and Smith returned to Australia, where in the interim he had managed several troupes. About August 26, 1876, he arrived in San Francisco on a brief visit to the Pacific States.

SMITH, WILLIAM N.: the champion bone soloist, died in New York after a lingering illness on January 4, 1869. He was born in Albany, N.Y., and first went into the show business with a miscellaneous traveling troupe in 1841, performing in white face. He was the first man to give imitations of the snare drums with the bones, which he did in Baltimore while traveling with a variety troupe and performing in white face. He afterwards traveled all over the United States with circus companies, performing in the side shows with a minstrel band. He also appeared with Charley White at 119 Bowery, this city, where he became a great favorite. He continued with traveling companies until 1866, when an abscess formed in his right breast, which, after being operated upon, affected him in his right arm, drawing it up so that it was impossible for him to shake the bones any more. He went to the hospital, and while under the influence of ether the doctors forced his arm back, making it straight, but in doing so snapped some of the tendons, from which, up to his death, he suffered constant pain. He retired from the profession, and on the afternoon of April 18, 1867, took a benefit at Charley White's Music Hall (formerly Bryant's), this city. Shortly after this he had an operation performed on his right arm (it having become paralyzed), having a portion of the bone removed, but he received no benefit from this operation. He continued to suffer great pain from his arm. He then became doorkeeper at Tony Pastor's Opera House in the Bowery, up to four months previous to his death, when he took a violent cold, which so prostrated him that he was confined to his room. The writer saw him about six weeks prior to his death. His right arm hung by his side, perfectly helpless, and he had a terrible cough. He was also in destitute circumstances, and an appeal was made through the columns of the *Clipper* to the profession to send in their little for the benefit of his wife and child. He received half salary from Tony Pastor for four months and up to his death, during which four months he was not once attending to his duties as doorkeeper. Singular to state, not a dollar was otherwise contributed from a single professional. Mr. Smith was buried on the 7th, and his remains were interred in Greenwood. The following day ten dollars was received from Sam Hague, the well known Liverpool, England, manager. As a bone soloist he was the best ever heard in this country, having played for and won the championship, which he retained up to his death. In his coffin were placed his castanets.

STEELE, KARL: violoncellist, retired from public life in 1873 and returned to Germany, but becoming tired of inactivity, he returned to America, August 9, 1876, and soon after returned to the minstrel profession.

STONE, A. C.: while traveling with Burgess, Prendergast, Hughes, & Donniker's Minstrels, was attacked with cholera in Frankfort, Ky., November 10, 1866, and in two hours was dead. He was a good performer from end to middle business, clog dancing, singing or anything else.

STRAIGHT, CHARLES WESLEY: brother of Ned Straight, and at one time known in the profession as Charley West, died at Omaha, Neb., on March 14, 1870. He was in the business for 17 years and was a good musician, fine singer, both ends and interlocutor.

SULLIVAN, ED: of the Albino Minstrels, was married in Boston, July 2, 1866, to Agnes Kennedy.

SULLIVAN, J. F.: balladist, died in Boston, Mass., August 20, 1866, of bronchial disease of the throat, aged 25 years. His remains were taken to Lowell, his native place, and interred in the Catholic burying ground.

SWEENEY, DICK: banjoist, died in Washington, D. C., in the winter of 1854.

SWEENEY, JOE: died in Appomattox, Va., October 27, 1860, about 45 years of age. Who, in the Southside, Virginia, does not remember old Joe Sweeney and his banjo. During his time there were several popular performers on the banjo but none of them had his thorough conscientiousness in the matter of make-up, which undoubtedly enhanced the popularity of his really superior playing. Joe used to black not only his face, neck, hands, and arms, but his feet as well, and would come on the stage barefoot, carrying a rude old saw buck for a seat, the perfect personification of a "plantation nigger." Most of his playing, though, was done in a standing position, in which attitude he performed his famous "chimes," which were original with him. His brother, Dan Sweeney, was also a good banjo player but rather a copy of Joe, who was in many respects original. Old Joe was looked upon as a sort of demigod by the music-loving Negroes of the South. And for dancing the jig, the breakdown, the old Virginia reel, he was perfectly at home. Sometimes he moved with inimitable grace through the figures of the dance, and there was no one that could "cut the pigeon wing" like him.

SWEENEY, SAM: banjoist, died in Virginia during the war. He was courier for Jeb Stewart and a great favorite.

THAYER, AMBROSE A.: vocalist, died in Boston, June 10, 1863, from consumption, aged 20 and 6 months.

THAYER, AMIDON L.: better known as "Bije" Thayer, was one of the pioneers in the minstrel business and associated with some of the best troupes in the country. He died in Boston, Mass., February 20, 1864, aged 41 years. He retired from the profession some years previous and opened a restaurant in Boston on Tremont Street; and at the time of his death was proprietor of a similar establishment on State Street. He was interred in Mount Auburn.

THOMAS, WALLY: who had been middle man for Sharpley, died at Lowell, Mass., May 29, 1864, aged 26 years. His disease was consumption. He neither drank any spirituous liquors, smoked or chewed, and at the time of his death had amassed considerable property, owning several houses in his native city, Lowell. He was a good general performer, jig and clog dancer, end man, banjoist and drummer.

TURNER, MALVIN: well known as "Mob" Turner, died in New York on September 27, 1862, from the effects of a severe surgical operation which had been performed a few days prior to his death. He was a useful and reliable man in his line, was also a quiet, unassuming and intelligent person, and paid great devotion to his profession, without regard to position or fame.

TURNER, RICHARD J.: balladist of this company, died in Sykesville, Md., August 6, 1857. He was born in Baltimore, Md.

TURNER, ROBERT: died in St. Louis, Mo., on January 15, 1875, of smallpox, aged 32 years. He was leader of the brass band.

TURNER, W.: tenor and bone soloist, for many years with Christy's Minstrels, died at Kidderminster, England, on March 22, 1872.

UNSWORTH, JAMES: died in Liverpool, England, February 21, 1875, from a complication of diseases, among which were jaundice, dropsy and enlargement of the liver. He was born at Liverpool, England, July 2, 1835, and commenced his career in burnt corkdom at 14 years of age in Montreal with an amateur party. The next year he joined S. S. Sanford's Minstrels in Philadelphia. After that he appeared in every portion of the United States and Canada. He visited Europe with Eugene early in June, 1861. He settled in London, where he remained several years. He was induced to return to America by Dan Bryant. He was a good end man, a merry handler of the banjo, a good comic singer, quick at an impromptu repartee, and a successful performer in broad burlesque. The comic speech, the refrain of which was "or any other man" was originated by Billy Thomas but popularized by Unsworth. A very chaste and valuable monument is erected over the grave of Unsworth in Ford Cemetery, Liverpool. The monument bears the following appropriate inscription:

> Of wit as genial as of humor bright;
> The people's favorite and his friends' delight;
> A man in everything a man should be;
> And yet simplicity's own child was he.
> Who on the stage e'er heard that ready tongue,
> But, mirth-convulsed, on his account hung?
> Yet from that tongue no accent ever fell
> That virgin virtue might not dare to tell,
> Wit stands aghast, and Genius, pierced by grief,
> In vain to stricken Mirth turns for relief;
> Tears are shed, and prayers, too, fast arise,
> Round this lone grave where genial Unsworth lies.

VAUGHN, THOMAS: died in Zanesville, Ohio, September 3, 1875. He was one of the original members of E P. Christy's Minstrels. Mr. Vaughn was an excellent banjoist and a very popular performer. He was about 52 years of age and was the last surviving member of the original Christy minstrels, as well as one of the oldest banjoists of America. During the last few years of his life he suffered considerably from lack of pecuniary means. He was helpless, his constitution having been broken down through exposure while serving in the army during our Civil War, the 165th Regiment, N. Y. Volunteers (Second Duryea Zouaves). He was unable to work for some three years prior to his death and during that time he received some relief from troupes passing through Zanesville.

VON BONHORST, JULIUS A.: died in Reading, Pa., on February 15, 1869, after a brief illness of inflammation of the bowels. He had a brother, Charles, at one time a popular banjoist, and who originally performed with Dan Rice and the Pig Show. He retired from the profession and practiced dentistry in Pennsylvania. Von Bonhorst joined S. S. Sanford's Minstrels in 1851 as a banjoist and remained with him three years, when he married Miss Luther of Philadelphia clandestinely; and quite a fuss was made over the affair when it became known to the lady's family. He then retired from the profession and went into the mercantile business in Pittsburgh. One year sufficed and he again engaged with Sanford. He next took charge of a store in Alexandria, Va., and was afterwards removed to Reading, Pa., where he became clerk in the Revenue Department, his father-in-law being the collector there. In the meantime, his wife was sent to the insane asylum for lunacy, where she died. This worked so upon Von Bonhorst that he died as stated above. He was generous to a fault and as a banjoist was good.

WAGNER, CALVIN: was born in Mobile, Ala., July 4, 1840. He appeared before the public since he was 17 years of age.

WALSH, MICHAEL: was one of the best banjo players in the business. He died in Boston August 29, 1866, age 27 years. His remains were taken to Quincy.

WAMBOLD, DAVID S.: was born in Elizabethtown, N. J., in April 1836, and put on the burnt cork for the first time in 1849 with a company numbering four, and took a short tour through New England, visiting many of the principal towns and cities. In 1850 he visited Philadelphia for the first time, and in company with Johnson, the comic singer, and Charles Jenkins, an old Ethiopian performer, appeared at what was then called Winter Garden, located at 101 Chestnut Street. He remained here about eighteen months, after which he joined a party at Paterson; N. J., calling themselves the Thespians, and went on a short traveling tour with them. In 1853 he made his first appearance in New York at Hope Chapel, with W. Donaldson's Ethiops. Leaving here after a short reign, he became one of Charley White's school boys, and remained with him off and on for about two years. From Charley White's he bent his steps to the Dan Bryant and Ben Mallory party, traveling all through the Eastern country and bringing up finally in Philadelphia, where Jerry and Neil Bryant came into the company and Mallory stepped out. His next trip was with the Raynor and Pierce party, whom he joined in 1857 and traveled through the West and South-west. Returning to New York, he became a member of Wood and Christy's Minstrels, at 444 Broadway. He remained here some time and became a favorite as a ballad singer. On July 11, 1857, he sailed for Europe, as one of the principal members of the Raynor-Pierce-Christy party. Mr. Wambold remained with this company thirteen months. In 1859 he returned to the States and joined the Bryant Brothers, but remained only three months, when he took a short rest and then we next find him at Wood's Marble Hall; but only for a brief period, as he returned to his old love, the Bryants, continuing there eight months. He was married in Philadelphia, April 23, 1859, to Isabella Young; then later joined Lloyd's Minstrels, but he soon left them. He returned to Europe in June, 1861, and joined Brown and Templeton's African Minstrels, then traveling over the Continent. He remained with them nine months, when he re-joined the old Christy party and was with them fifteen months. After which, in company with his wife, he took a trip over the Continent on a pleasure tour, visiting France, Belgium, Prussia, Austria, Hungary, Italy, returning home through Tyrol, Bavaria, Baden-Baden, to Strasburg, returning to this country on June 30, 1863. And as soon as arrived, he was secured by Henry Wood for his troupe. Mr. Wambold, as a tenor singer, took rank with any in minstrelsy and was one of the best ballad singers in the profession. His voice, rich, earnest and tender, was used with great taste and feeling. Dave Wambold died November 10, 1889, in New York City.

WAMBOLD, JAMES: was married at the residence of Mrs. Matt Peel in Catskill, N.Y., in October, 1861, to Miss Hatton, sister of Mrs. Peel. They lived together but three weeks. The lady sued for and obtained the divorce on the fourth week in Buffalo.

WARDEN, E.: left the minstrel business in May, 1861, and gave Sunday concerts in London.

WARREN, MICKEY: a famous jig dancer, died at Bellevue Hospital, New York, May 14, 1875, aged 47 years. His early history is shrouded in mystery and the earliest record we can find of his public performances is that he was dancing at Charley White's Melodeon in the Bowery in 1849; and this may possibly have been his first appearance on the stage. He was connected as a star feature with Bryant's Minstrels for a number of seasons.

WELLS, FRANK: right name, Bernard F. Mundy, died in Brooklyn, N.Y., on April 25, 1874.

WELLS, SAM: died in Virginia City, August 30, 1864, aged 38 years. He was horseback riding and received an injury, from the effects of which he died. He was buried in Lone Mountain Cemetery.

WEST, LUKE: right name William Sheppard, died in Boston, Mass., May 26, 1854, of inflammation of the bowels. He was born in Philadelphia in 1826. In 1831, at the age of 5 years, the sight of his left eye was totally destroyed by a fork, held in his own hands, which had been diverted from its course by his brother, who accidentally forcibly hit his elbow. In 1832, he narrowly escaped death by drowning. Again he came near drowning, having been rescued by James Gown, a boat builder's apprentice in his native town. In 1835, while climbing an awning post, upon the top of which rested a bar with iron hooks used for hanging meat, just as he had reached the top and was resting his hands upon the bar, a companion caught hold of his feet, causing him to lose his hold and one of the hooks caught in the flesh of his wrist and tore his hand open to the end of the thumb. In 1840, he developed a talent for whistling, imitation of birds and instruments, and his services were secured by Samuel Johnson, who was giving entertainments with a troupe in Hoboken, N. J. He met with success and in 1848 he, with a few others, organized a band known as the Campbell Minstrels. On November 29, 1849, under his own name of William Sheppard, he joined A. P. Christy's Minstrels, remained with them eight months, and then rejoined his old company and associated himself in the management with Joseph Murphy and Matt Peel. His last appearance on the stage was May 23, 1854, in Boston.

WEST, WILLIAM H.: was born in Syracuse, N. Y., June 18, 1832, and first went into the business August 20, 1870. He married to Mrs. Harris of Baltimore on November 24, 1867, in New York.

WESTON, FRANK: left the business in December, 1864, and went to Havana, Ill., where he practiced medicine. He afterwards settled down in Cynthiana, Ky., and took his real name of Dr. Henshall.

WHITE, CHARLEY: was born in June, 1821. He first appeared in public in 1843 at Thalian Hall, 492 Grand Street, New York, as a performer on the accordion. He at once made his mark in the profession. In conjunction with Billy Whitlock, Tom Booth and Barney Williams, he opened with a minstrel organization at Vauxhall Garden, New York, in 1843. In 1844 he organized and played with The Kitchen Minstrels. He then went on a tour of the eastern and middle states. He afterwards associated with the Ethiopian Operatic Brothers, among whom was Barney

Williams. He played the tambourine on the end. He next joined the Sable Sisters and Ethiopian Minstrels. They included three lady vocalists. He was in various combinations up to 1846. He opened The Melodeon, 53 Bowery, New York, November 24, 1846. The prices of admission were 6¼ and 12 cents. He was burnt out twice but each time he rebuilt. With Eph Horn he occupied, April 2, 1851, the Coliseum, 448 Broadway, near Grand Street. He finally closed the Melodeon April 24, 1654. Among those who became famous in the minstrel world that appeared here were Master Juba, Neil Hall, Bill Smith, Clem Titus and Zeke Backus. Salaries at this place ranged from $6 to $12 a week. He next went to the Art Union Rooms, west side of Broadway (495-497), between Broome and Spring Streets, where he opened with his Serenaders and called the place the St. Nicholas Exhibition Rooms, on April 10, 1854. He opened White's Varieties, 17 and 19 Bowery, September 13, 1852. In the company were Corrister, Deaves, G. Rich, Rose Merrifield, Dan Emmett, John Diamond and Master Franks. He was next found at 49 Bowery, opposite the Old Bowery Theatre, which he opened August 7, 1854. No similar place ever introduced one-third of the comic material during its whole existence as this same establishment. Dan Emmett, Frank Stanton, Billy Coleman, John Murray, Picayune Butler, M. Turner, W. Roark, John T. Huntley, L. Donnelly, M. Lewis, G. White, W. N. Smith, Master Juba, Boston Rattler, William Donaldson, W. Quinn, J. Carroll, Tim Norton, Tom Briggs, Hi Rumsey, James and William Budworth, Dan Gardner, Joe Brown, Mike Kitchell, T. D. Rice, John Mulligan, Luke West, Johnny Pell, Sam Wells, Billy Newcomb, Charles Fox, Dave Wambold, Ned Deaves, Dan Bryant and E. Bowers were among those who appeared there at various times. In June, 1860, he opened old Washington Hall, 598 Broadway, three doors above Niblo's Garden, with a variety show, including Kate Partington, Emma Schell, Laura Le Claire (afterwards Mrs. Josh Hart). He then went to Bob Butler's, 444 Broadway, where he remained four years. He joined the company January 7, 1861. On May 20 he appeared in the burlesque of "Mazeppa," playing the title role. He was manager of Mechanics' Hall, June 26, 1866. Johnny Thompson, George Warren, M. Campbell, Charles Collins, Clinetop Sisters, Millie Young, Viro Ferrand, Lizzie Whelly, Julia Melville, Bob Hart, Frank Kerns, Wash Norton, Nelse Seymour, George R. Edeson and Fanny Forrest were his associates. Dave Braham was musical director. White retired from the management April 30, 1867. On August 27, 1867, in conjunction with Sam Sharpley, he opened the Theatre Comique. He then went to the hall formerly occupied by the San Francisco Minstrels, which he opened with a variety show August 12, 1870, and remained there until June, 1873. He then became associated with dramatic companies and played Uncle Tom, etc. He died at his home in New York January 4, 1891. By a close scrutiny of Negroes of all ages and characters, by studying their dialect, imitating their actions, gestures and carriage, by closely examining their tastes, peculiarities and humors, their friendships and hatreds, by noticing carefully the blending in their character of the deeply pathetic with the grotesquely and exuberantly droll, Mr. White became a master of his art and made himself one of the most useful and popular performers that ever put on burnt cork.

T. D. Rice esteemed Mr. White so highly that he left him all his manuscript material and E. P. Christy presented him with a silver pitcher.

WHITE, CHARLES H.: comedian of the Leavitt party, died at Springfield, Mass., on October 21, 1872, aged 23 years. His disease was quick consumption.

WHITE, COOL: was born in 1821. In 1838 he made his first appearance at the Walnut Street Theatre, Philadelphia, singing Ethiopian songs between the pieces, making his first appearance in the original song written by himself, entitled "Whose Dat Nigger Dar a Peeping?" From this time out he was considered quite a card and was eagerly sought for to perform on all benefits. In 1839 he played a star engagement at the Front Street Theatre, Baltimore, opening as Snowball (a dandy Negro servant) in a piece of his own writing, entitled "The Fall of Babylon, or, The Servant Turned Master." From this time until 1842 he played various engagements as the representative of dandy Negroes. In 1842 he created quite a furor at the Arch Street Theatre, Philadelphia, as Fancy Cool, in Silas S. Steele's great burlesque of "Philadelphia Assurance." In 1843 he organized the band of minstrels known as the Virginia Serenaders.Cool re-organized the Virginia Serenaders and gave performances in the large canvas of Raymond & Waring's Menagerie. Becoming dissatisfied with the style of traveling (on the top of cages, over rough roads), he left the menagerie at Wythe Court House, Va., joined Robinson & Eldred's Circus and traveled with them throughout the entire South. Returning North as far as Lynchburg, he there started another minstrel troupe, called the Sable Melodists. Cool next turned his attention to the drama, the war excitement proving too strong to make the minstrel profession a paying business at that time. He accordingly rented the Newark Theatre, in Newark N. J., and having secured his company, opened with the moral drama of "Uncle Tom." He next took the stage management of Dick Sliter's Empire Minstrels. He was a Shakespearean clown with Spalding & Rogers' Circus. He then organized Mason's Metropolitan Serenaders, then Dumbolton's Minstrels, and then S. S. Sanford's Troupe.Then he appeared with Griffin's Minstrels at 444 Broadway; next at Wood's Marble Building, 561 Broadway; then he was manager of George Christy's Minstrels; then Lloyd's Minstrels. Between 1860 and '70, he was stage manager and interlocutor at Hooley's Minstrels, Brooklyn. He went to Chicago with R. M. Hooley and was the founder and organizer of the Chicago Lodge, 3, of B. P. O. Elks. He died in Chicago on April 23, 1891.

WHITLOCK, WILLIAM M.: was born in New York in 1813 and was employed as compositor on a religious journal. In 1835 he made his debut at the Patriot House, in Chatham Square, New York, as Cuff in "Oh, Hush!" While traveling through the South with Whipple's Circus, he met Joe Sweeney at Lynchburg, Va. Up to that time Whitlock had never seen a banjo; but during his brief stay in Lynchburg, Sweeney made him one and taught him the tune "Sittin' on a Rail." From this time forth he made the banjo his study by day and by night. Every night during his journey South, when he was not playing, he would quietly steal off to some Negro hut to hear the darkies sing and see them dance, taking with him a jug of whiskey to make them all the merrier. Thus he got his accurate knowledge of the peculiarities of plantation and cornfield Negroes. Reaching this city on July 6, 1838, he at first performed with Dan Gardner in Hester Street and then went with Henry Rockwell, the circus manager, to the Richmond Hill Theatre. There, singing "The Raccoon Hunt," he played the banjo for the first time in public. Although in his autobiography he specifically sets up no such claim, yet he seems to have been the first person to play that instrument in this city. Billed as "Billy Whitlock, the Celebrated Ethiopian singer and original banjoist," he had the metropolitan field all to himself until 1839 when Joe Sweeney came to town. It was his custom to travel with circuses in the summer, and to work typesetting in the winter. In the winter of 1839-40, he quit the life of a "typo" and went traveling with P. T. Barnum, playing the banjo while Master Diamond danced. While in Philadelphia performing with Diamond, Whitlock practiced with "Ole Bull" Dick Myers, the violinist, and on their joint benefit night the two played the banjo and the fiddle together for the first time in public. Whitlock afterwards traveled with P. T. Barnum, again playing the banjo to the dancing of the new Master John Diamond (Frank Lynch). Shortly after this he was at Barnum's Museum, New York, in a minstrel band of which Barney Williams was a member. In 1844, Whitlock traveled with Barnum's Bonaparte Funeral Exhibition. Reaching Buffalo, N.Y., on their return, the party chartered a canal boat and traveled the entire length of the Erie Canal, exhibiting at every town on the route. Whitlock also traveled with the Bonaparte funeral as late as 1850. Whitlock brought out a Bryant on the museum stage as "Little Jerry." He taught Frank Lynch ("Master Diamond" the false) about all that he knew and it was from him that Tom Briggs acquired much of his superior knowledge of the banjo, of which instrument Whitlock was also a maker. In 1845, he constructed a miniature locomotive to run from the Hoboken Ferry to the Elysian Fields. The season closed before it was finished; but he afterwards inhibited it at the Bowery Circus, illustrating it by relating the well-known "Locomotive Story." The last time he traveled was in conjunction with Duke Morgan in 1855 with Dan Rice's Circus. In that year he took up his residence in Jersey City, N. J., having received an appointment in the drug department of the Custom House. This he held for four years, under the successive administrations of Presidents Pierce and Buchanan. Political influence caused his removal and he returned to the printing business, at which he worked until the breaking out of the Rebellion, when he became a volunteer. In 1862 he was paralyzed and lay for a long time in the York (Pa.) Hospital. He died at Long Branch, N. J., March 29, 1878. He had been off the stage about 22 years.

WILKES, GEORGE: right name George Miller, female impersonator with Emerson in the South, died in Memphis, Tenn., October 1, 1870, of neuralgia of the stomach.

WILLIAMSON, PETE: died in Philadelphia October 3, 1871.

WILSON, GEORGE: was born in London, England, September 28, 1844, and commenced in the "bigger" business in San Francisco in 1869 as a song and dance artist.

WILTERS, CHARLES: died in New York, January 31, 1878, from consumption. He first attracted marked attention with Newcomb & Arlington's Minstrels. Where they discovered him we do not know. It was with them that he first appeared in this city. His initial song and dance here was "The Water Nymph," which he followed in the succeeding week with "He's Standing on his Head."

WINSHIP, GEORGE C.: was born in New York March 7, 1833. He first put on burnt cork when 11 years of age and appeared at the old Bowery Circus, New York, as a jig dancer for the benefit of Dick Pelham (Pell). Afterwards he traveled as an end man, jig dancer and general performer. Since 1856, he has been identified with the variety theatres as performer and manager. Probably he is the oldest variety performer and manager living. While sitting upon the deck of a steamer conveying him to Boston on the night of July 30, 1868, he complained of feeling unwell and retired to bed. Upon arising the next morning he reeled and fell to the floor, when it was found that during the night he had been stricken with paralysis, rendering powerless his left side from head to foot.

WOODRUFF, TIM: died at his home in Cincinnati, Ohio, November 12, 1872. For many years he was a favorite comedian throughout the West and the country generally; and, as a representative of the slouchy plantation Negro, was hard to equal. He was born in Hamilton, Ohio, and was at his demise about 47 years of age. His first appearance on the stage was at the occasion of a fire company's benefit at Smith & Nixon's old hall, opposite the present Pike's Opera House in Cincinnati, March 15, 1842. He blacked up, gave the act known as "Spirit Rappings," and made a hit which determined his future career. His death was the result of hasty consumption, arising from a cold contracted while visiting the fairs of 1872. Poor Tim had the virtues and failings of his trade. There was none more generous to needy brethren in his days of prosperity, none that more strongly disdained a mean or unkind action towards any human being. Even in his latter days, when the world went not well with him financially, these traits distinguished him; and, in good or bad fortune, there was the stamp of the true gentleness ever upon him.

WRIGHTMAN, GEORGE: whose right name was George Wright, died at Bellevue Hospital, New York, September 28, 1866.

WYATT, ANDREW M.: solo violinist, died at Salem, Mass., on August 5, 1874, age 42 years.

"YOUNG AMERICA": See HUGHEY DOUGHERTY.

I returned to the *Palace* and immediately gave warning that I purposed leaving as soon as someone could be got to fill my place. It struck me as somewhat odd that it was six months from that date before I could get away. It has been explained to me since. The fact is, I received what, as a boy, I thought a good salary, but nothing like what I earned. It took two men afterwards to fill my place. I have been told since, that more than a year before that time, and prior to this last engagement, the late E. P. Christy had written for me from New York, but that the letter had been intercepted by those whose interest it then was that I should not know my own value in the "profession." I used to see that my name was larger than almost any other on the bills, but was led to believe that it was because I was a boy and not likely to excite the jealousy of the other members of the company. It may not be very soothing to my vanity, but, dwelling upon these things dispassionately, I have my honest doubts now whether I was not always a greater success as an advertisement than as a performer.

I was promised at New Orleans that if I would go over to Galveston, Texas, with the minstrel troupe, I should certainly be allowed to retire from public life. So we left the *Palace* and the *Raymond* at the levee of the former city and took passage in the regular steamship crossing the Gulf to Galveston. We performed there two or three weeks with great success. Few minstrels had then wandered that way, and thus it happened that my farewell appearance as a dancer was greeted with a crowded house. Except as a poor lecturer, I have never been on the stage since I left Galveston.

Still resolved to go to college at Cape Girardeau, I returned to New Orleans, and took passage to Cairo on the steamer *L. M. Kenett*. Barney Williams and his wife were on board during the tedious voyage; but I suppose they have long since forgotten all about the urchin who surprised and bored them with his minute knowledge of the early history of the country through which we passed. The river above Cairo, very much to my sorrow, was frozen over, for it was midwinter. There was no alternative for me but to proceed to Cape Girardeau by land—a long, difficult, and expensive journey in those times. After a great deal of trouble and some danger, I arrived at the gates of the college and proceeded directly to the room of the president. The kindly face that I remembered so well again beamed upon me, as I again stood before him and said that I had come to stay a year, at least, at his school. At his good-natured question as to how much money I had, I emptied my pocket of just thirty-five dollars in gold. That was the sum to which the unforeseen expenses of my long journey had reduced me. The president being aware that the river was frozen—so that I could not get away even if I had had money enough to go with—and having much greater discretionary power than the presidents of our Protestant colleges, told me that I might stay.

At the end of my year the river was again frozen and the good president was again prevailed upon to keep me till the close of that college term, which would be in the middle of the ensuing summer. So I was for sixteen months in all a student in Saint Vincent's College. Most of the students were the sons of French planters of Louisiana and the institution was more French than English. Things were ordered very much as they are in the religious houses of Europe. We slept in large dormitories, and ate in a refectory, someone reading aloud the while from an English or a French book. The college had its own tailors and shoemakers; and by the favor of the president, who seemed to take a great liking to me, my credit was made good for anything I wanted and I was provided for as well as the richest of them. The instructors were all priests and generally good men. I was never required to change my religion or to conform more than externally to their worship. The president, Father S. V. Ryan, has since met the recognition which his piety and abilities so justly deserved. Within the past year, if I have read the papers aright, he has been made Roman Catholic Bishop of Buffalo. I applied myself so zealously to study, that at the expiration of my sixteen months, I was nearly prepared to enter Kenyon College, in which I spent the next four years.

When I came to leave Saint Vincent's, I drew out a deposit which I had in a bank in Toledo, and gave it into the hands of the college treasurer, reserving for myself only what I thought would be enough to take me back to Ohio. As good luck would have it, the little steamer *Banjo*, a showboat belonging to Dr. Spalding, the manager of the *Floating Palace*, was advertised to be at Cape Girardeau the week in which I proposed to leave there. Seeing the names of some of my old comrades on the bills, I waited to meet them. They generously made me bring my trunk on board, and have a free ride to St. Louis, or, if I chose, to Alton, where I was to take the cars for Chicago. The remembrance of this trip up the river with these jovial, reckless souls has made it my duty always to defend my old associates when I hear the censure heaped on them by inconsiderate ignorance or blind prejudice.

And I can take my final leave of the show business and of show people in no better way, I think, than in relating an incident which occurred on this little steamer. On the afternoon before our arrival at Alton, as I was sitting on the deck by the side of one of the performers—Mr. Edwin Davis, who had been a member of our company on the Floating Palace—-he asked me to let him see my money, adding that I might have had imposed upon me some of the "wildcat" bills then afloat. Taking out all I had, I placed it in his hands. He counted it and scrutinized it thoroughly and, folding it up carefully, returned it to me with the remark that my bills were all good. I had no occasion to use my money till I came to pay my railway fare at Alton, when I discovered that my wealth had increased by nearly half. He had, indeed, been a better judge than myself of my necessities; for, with his generous addition, I had barely enough to take me to my destination.

I met Mr. Davis in New York years afterwards and offered him the sum he had added to mine, but could not prevail upon him to take it. And this is the way he stated his reason:

"No; it does not belong to me. Keep it till you see some poor fellow as much in need of it as you were then on the Mississippi and give it to him."

NEGRO MINSTRELSY
Its Starting Place Traced Back Over Sixty Years, Arranged and Compiled from the Best Authorities
By Charles White [*New York Clipper*, April 28, 1860]

Minstrelsy for the past seventeen years has been steadily improving, until we now see it firmly established among our standard amusements and sought after as much as the opera or drama; in fact, in some respects, far out-rivaling either in point of patronage. Although this species of entertainment is often discussed, and the merits of the different artists connected therewith criticized, yet the origin, or any pretension thereto, has never been clearly explained (except by the present writer some time since), for two very great reasons. First, because no individual ever interest himself so much as to seek or trace out the foundation or starting place; and secondly, if he had, his labors would have proved fruitless, for who can tell when and where the Negro first introduced the banjo (for it is from that instrument we begin to get at the notes of Ethiopian minstrelsy). Such being the case, it would be in vain to attempt to ascertain how long, when, and where the Negro, or African, first manufactured or introduced the gourd banjo, which instrument, no doubt, has been in existence nearly as long as that race of people. Consequently, it is impossible to get at its origin from that source. The point then is this: who first made pretensions to imitate the colored race or introduce their quaint and humorous character to the public? Some, I know, will doubt, and others will claim their knowledge in the matter as indisputable. Suffice it to say, that this subject will be picked all to atoms, and after the storm is over it will return to its present truthful shape again, as facts indelible. The writer does not go so far back for dates, or even assert anything in this brief description of minstrelsy, but what can be vouched for and identified as facts by actual printed documents of each and every assertion herein made, which documents have ever been preserved with great care until the present time; and now feeling desirous of giving a more general publicity to the same, he does so with no selfish motive or partiality, but with a view of enlightening the minds of the curious, and showing those in the profession the path which their predecessors have traveled, and what has been done towards the elevation of minstrelsy, which amusement, in the writer's estimation, will in a few years far eclipse all its former improvements, and become an indispensable entertainment, claiming for its support in vocal, instrumental, and physical force, the best talent in the theatrical line. For already has the minstrel introduced his merry afterpiece, with all its appropriate costume, scenery, and music; burlesques upon burlesques have since appeared in rapid succession; operas have also been introduced; and, in fact, artists of merit in former days now seek in vain for positions in minstrel companies.

Many suppose that negro minstrelsy originated about twenty-three or twenty-five years ago, or in the days of Barney Burns, Enam Dickinson, Tom Bleakly, George Washington Dixon, T. D. Rice, Leicester, John Smith, Joe Sweeney, &c., who all had their own peculiar style in singing and dancing, individually; some with the banjo, and some without it; others having for their principal attraction only some simple Negro melody, such as "Coal Black Rose," "Such a Getting Up Stairs," "Gumbo Chaff," "Sitting on a Rail," "Jim Crow," and one or two others of less popularity. I will now give a short description of a few prominent performers who succeeded the parties just alluded to and became vastly popular, particularly in this city. These were Dick Pelham, James Sandford, Frank Brower, and others, to whom I shall allude in the following order viz.: 1838---Jim Sandford played the Black Door Keeper or Ticket Taker, at the Franklin Theatre, Chatham Street, N.Y. For the next two or three years very many aspirants for colored fame made their debut with faces blacked. Prior to the organization of the first regular minstrel company, January, 1842, the following parties appeared in public---Charles Jenkins and G. W. Pelham, at American Museum, January, 1842; Frank Diamond, Whitlock, and Tom Booth, at Arcade Garden, 255 Bleecker Street, January, 1842; Dick Pelham, Master Chestnut, Dick Van Bremen, and Joe Sweeney at Bowery Amphitheatre, 37 Bowery, January, 1842; Frank Diamond and Whitlock, at Chatham Theatre, April, 1842; John Smith, T. Coleman, Chestnut and Hoffman, at Bowery Amphitheatre for Smith' benefit, June, 1842; John Diamond and Whitlock, at American Museum, December, 1842; Dan Emmett, Frank Brower, Master Pierce, Jimmy O'Connell, Frank Diamond and Mestayer (all dancers but Mestayer), Franklin Theatre (Dan Emmett and Master Pierce were performing the same time at the Bowery Amphitheatre), December 29, 1842; Dan Emmett and Frank Brower, at the Bowery Amphitheatre, where, and at which time the idea of a minstrel company was put in motion by the following persons, viz.: Dan Emmett., Frank Brower, Billy Whitlock, and Dick Pelham, who all immediately went into a thorough course of rehearsals at the boarding house of Emmett, No. 37 Catharine Street, kept by one Mrs. Brooks. They were all diligent in their labors and it did not take long to acquire the scanty versatility necessary in those days for a cork professor to delight his patrons. The idea was original; but I might deserve censure in applying it to any one of the number, and have therefore distributed the honor among the party. The cause of their organization was simply to make up a combination of Negro stuff for one night only, which was expressly for the benefit of Pelham, who at that time was dancing between the pieces at the Chatham Theatre.

Their rehearsals were sufficiently encouraging to satisfy them that they had indeed found a novelty. They styled themselves the Virginia Minstrels, made their debut at the above mentioned place (this was early in February, 1843), and were received with deafening plaudits! During the same week they played one night for the benefit of Mr. John Tryon, then manager of the Bowery Amphitheatre. Their performances here met with astonishing success, so much so that they were secured by Messrs. Welch and Rockwell, than managers of the Park Theatre, at which place they performed two weeks in conjunction with the great dancer, John Diamond. This was about the middle of February, 1843; and after this they proceeded to Boston, where they played six weeks with wonderful success. They then returned to New York and performed three nights for manager Simpson at the Park Theatre. Having now fairly introduced their novelty and expecting every day to meet with opposition here in Yankee land, they determined on a trip to England, where all idea of rivalry was out of the question, for a time at least.

Accordingly, with Mr. George B. Wooldridge at their head, they immediately embarked for Europe. Hence arose the various minstrel companies that are now in existence. On the arrival of the Virginia Minstrels in Europe, they immediately gave two concerts in Liverpool. From thence they proceeded to the Adelphi Theatre, London, at which place they performed six weeks in connection with Professor Anderson, the Great Wizard of the North. After this engagement, owing to some misunderstanding, Mr. Richard Pelham left the company. The balance organized in connection with Joe Sweeney, who had then just arrived in the country; and in this way they traveled through Ireland and Scotland for six months with success. The company then disbanded and Whitlock returned to America. The others soon followed him, with the exception of Pelham, who has remained in England up to the present time.

Another company arrived in Europe from Boston, known as the Ring and Parker Minstrels. They performed in Liverpool and Bolton, while the Virginia Minstrels were playing in London. One of the members of the company personated the character of "Lucy Long," which, evidently, must have been original with them. This rival party afterwards performed at the Garrick Street Theatre, London. They arrived in Liverpool in three or four weeks after the Virginia Minstrels, having organized in Boston at the time the Virginia Minstrels were playing there.

On the return of the Virginia Minstrels to America, they found, as they had anticipated, minstrel companies in abundance all over the country. Band after band was organized, almost every day, with various titles, and many of them passed away almost as suddenly as an April shower. A vast improvement, however, had been made in minstrel business, notwithstanding its short existence.

We now arrive at a period in our little history which is still free in the memory of all who were connected with this profession seventeen or eighteen years ago. I will now name the prominent companies only, that have been regularly organized and met with success since the commencement of Ethiopian minstrelsy up to the present time. It is necessary to mention, however, that in the year 1842 at Vauxhall Garden, New York, under the proprietorship of Mr. P. T. Barnum, the renowned John Diamond first created a great sensation; shortly after, however, owing to some difficulty, Mr. Barnum dispensed with the original John Diamond and secured another person in the same business by the name of Frank Lynch, who was placarded and styled the "Great Diamond." He was an extraordinary dancer, and afterwards became a very prominent member of his profession.

The originators and inventors of minstrelsy consisted of Dan Emmett, Frank Brower, Billy Whitlock and Richard Pelham, calling themselves the

Virginia Minstrels. The next company presenting themselves to the notice of the public was known as the Kentucky Minstrels, composed of Frank Lynch, T. G. Booth, H. Mestayer and Richardson. Some time after their organization, they disbanded; but reorganized under the same title and performed at Vauxhall Garden, etc., with the following persons: William Whitlock, T, G. Booth, Barney Williams, and C. White. The next company were the Ring and Parker Minstrels; and, next on the list, the Congo Minstrels, now known as Buckley's New Orleans Serenaders." They performed at the Chatham Theatre.

The Original Christy Minstrels were the next company, consisting of E. P. Christy, George N. Christy, L. Durand, and T. Vaughn. This company organized in Buffalo and traveled principally through the Southern and Western country. They first called themselves the Virginia Minstrels. Soon after their organization, Enam Dickinson and Zeke Bachus were added to the company; and they then assumed the title of Christy's Minstrels. They first appeared in this city at Palmo's Opera House (late Burton's Theatre), 1846. On their second appearance in New York, they performed at the Alhambra, Broadway near Prince Street; and from thence to the Society Library (now Appleton's Building), and afterwards at Mechanics Hall, 472 Broadway, at which place they permanently remained from March 1847 to July 1854.

During the short time that minstrelsy had been in operation, great improvement had been made in a company known as the Ethiopian Serenaders. They organized in Boston, came to New York, and performed with immense success at the Chatham Theatre. They consisted of Frank Germon, M. Stanwood, Tony Winnemore, Quinn, and others. Soon after they remodeled their band and sailed for Europe with Mr. J. Dumbolton as their agent. They then consisted of F. Germon, G. Harrington, M. Stanwood, G. Pelham, and W. White. This was the company that proved so successful at Palmo's Opera House. While in London, they performed at the St. James Theatre and so great was the demand to see them that they gave morning performances and were frequently solicited to give their entertainments at the private mansions of the highest nobility.

During the success of the Ethiopian Serenaders in Europe, they were called to Arundel Castle by special command of Her Majesty Queen Victoria. For this they each received a splendid crest ring as a token of her appreciation. Some time after their return to America, Mr. Dumbolton, the manager, made an addition to his band and crossed the Atlantic again, taking with him Mr. J. A. Wells and Jerry Bryant.

The next company of note organized in Philadelphia and styled themselves the Virginia Serenaders, consisting of James Sandford, Cool White, Richard Myers, Robert Edwards, &c., &c. They also performed at the Chatham Theatre in this city; also at Boston and all the principal towns and cities East. They were successful and created a great sensation wherever they appeared. Mr. G. B. Wooldridge at that time was their agent.

Next we have another very clever company known as the Harmoneans, consisting of L. V. Crosby, Frank Lynch, Pike, Powers, &c., &c. They organized in

Boston and traveled principally through the Eastern states with very great success for a long time.

We now arrive at the true position of White's Serenaders. They organized in 1846 and consisted of C. White, R. White, F. Stanton, W. Smith, H. Neil, and Master Juba. They performed at White's Melodeon, White's Varieties, and White's Opera House, all in the Bowery. They remained here, continually playing, for a space of eleven years---a longer active permanency than ever attained by any similar exhibition; during which time, and at which places, many of the present prominent performers graduated under the favorable auspices of Mr. White's establishments.

I shall now record the names of the Sable Harmonists, whom I certainly class as among the best. I am unable to name the exact time of their organization but am almost positive it was in the early part of 1846. They traveled principally through the Southern and Western country. The band consisted of Messrs. Plumer, Archer, J. Farrell, W. Roark, Nelson Kneas, J. Murphy, &c., &c. They performed for a short time at the Minerva Rooms, Broadway, in this city, November, 1847.

Now we come to the starting place of the Original Campbell Minstrels, who were brought together in June, 1847, by a gentleman named Mr. John Campbell, who at that time was the proprietor of a restaurant corner of Bayard Street and the Bowery, in this city. The company, all complete, consisted of W. B. Donaldson, Jerry Bryant, John Rea, James Carter, Harry Mestayer, and David Raymond. Shortly after its organization, Mr. Rea withdrew from the company and joined the Original Christy's Minstrels. Soon after, Mr. Donaldson resigned and the now deceased and much lamented Luke West took his place. They were playing at the American Museum at the time.

Next we come to a company known as the Sable Brothers, consisting of Messrs. Evans, Turpin, Cleveland, &c., &c. They performed at Convention Hall in Wooster Street and afterwards appeared at Barnum's American Museum. The time of their organization is not known but I am under the impression that they succeeded the Campbells.

From this point, my qualified friends will coincide with me in placing the remaining companies in rotation as follows: the "Nightingale Serenaders," formerly known as Kunkel's Minstrels; Sandford's Opera Troupe, still in operation; Sliter's Empire Minstrels, Washington Uterpians, Ordway's Aeolians, Pierce's Minstrels, at the Olympic; Fellows' Minstrels, Horn & White's Opera Troupe, Kimberly's Campbell Minstrels, Norris' Campbell Minstrels, New York Serenaders, California, 1850; Raynor's Serenaders, California, 1850, afterwards appeared in Australia, 1852; Murphy, West & Peel's Campbell Minstrels, 1852; Backus' Minstrels, California, 1853; George Christy's & Wood's Minstrels, at 444 Broadway, 1854; Perham's Burlesque Opera Troupe, 1854; Pierce and Raynor's Christy's Minstrels, now in Europe, 1856; Bryant's Minstrels, at Mechanics Hall, 472 Broadway, February 22, 1857; Rumsey & Newcomb's Campbell Minstrels, April 28, 1857; Morris Brothers, Pell & Huntley's Minstrels, 1857; Fox & Warden's Campbell Minstrels," now in Europe, 1859; Mrs. Matt. Peel's Campbell's Minstrels, 1859;

Hooley & Campbell's (late George Christy's) Minstrels, January 30, 1860; Converse's Campbell Minstrels, March 12, 1860.

Before concluding these remarks, I will again repeat that it is impossible at this late day to tell who first set the "ball rolling" in negro minstrel business. No one has any idea of its existence beyond the time above mentioned. I would, however, say that individual Negro business was done in character sixty-one years ago at the Federal Street Theatre, Boston. I have in my possession the actual newspaper which gives this information; and for the gratification of the profession particularly, will give a duplicate of the advertisement relative to the fact as it appeared in *Russell's Boston Gazette* dated December 30, 1799, which journal, at that time, was the largest in America. The following performance took place on the night in question: "Orinoko, or the Royal Slave" was the first piece and at the end of Act II, "Song of the Negro Boy in Character" by Mr. Grawpner; after which, a pantomime called "Gil Blas, or the Cave of the Robbers"; the whole to conclude with a Representation of A Spanish Fair. It is also underlined at the bottom of same bill that "the Theatre will be hung with mourning." This was the month and year that Washington died---hence the cause of mourning.The newspaper from which I gather these important facts is also in deep mourning for the same lamentable cause. Thus ends the explanation of negro minstrelsy up to the present time, 1860. I could make the subject somewhat more lengthy by introducing many outside particulars, but as my intention was merely to give a brief sketch of my profession, I trust those who peruse it will look at it as such only.

THE GOLDEN DAYS OF MINSTRELSY
By Frank Dumont [*New York Clipper*, December 19, 1914]

This is not a history of minstrelsy. In a short review of this kind it would not be possible to enumerate all the troupes or individuals comprising them to the present time. This is the musing of an old-timer, recalling the golden days of minstrelsy from 1843 to 1864. Between those years the Negro slave of the Southern States, toiling in the fields of cotton, cane or corn, created an interest and a sympathy. His songs and peculiar dances appealed to all classes and the white man began to imitate him in his mannerisms. His queer antics and style of vocalism sprang into popularity. His melodies were purely American, easily understood, and better suited to the American taste than the high flown Italian opera patronized, but really not understood, by the richer classes.

The songs were simple, reached the heart, and were of our own soil and its institutions. The instruments used by the slaves were very primitive. The banjo, bones, tambourine and violin. The banjo was borrowed from the guitar and the tambourine from Spanish sources---also the bones to imitate the castanets of the Spaniards and Mexicans. With these, the plantation hands regaled visitors to the planter's home or amused themselves in their cabins or in the open air in the moonlight.

The Negro composed his own words and melodies and the subjects were taken from everyday incidents or his humble surroundings. Later on, the white minstrels added to the stock of songs and good composers entered the field of minstrelsy and furnished songs that will never die, notably the compositions of Stephen C. Foster. The white performers were quick to note the melodies of the Negroes on the plantations, river fronts or levees, where darkies were employed as roustabouts and deck hands. One of the most popular Negro melodies came from the river darkies. It was called "Shoo Fly, Don't Bodder me." But this was after the war; and the firemen of New Orleans gave it its first popularity and then it found its way North.

Before 1843 each circus had one or two "Negro singers," as they then designated them. They performed on the banjo or violin, with bones or tambourine, and imitated the Negro in all his peculiarity of dance or shouting songs. Notably among these circus singers were Frank Brower, Dick Pelham, Billy Whitlock, old Dan Emmett, Wash Donaldson, George Washington Dixon, Ben Mallory and Joe Sweeney.

So, in fact, minstrelsy as we know it was born in the circus ring and first presented by circus "Negro singers." It remained for Frank Brower, Billy Whitlock and old Dan Emmett to join together in a benefit performance to be given to Dick Pelham in the Chatham Theatre, January 31, 1843. The four circus Negro singers appeared together for that event and created a sensation....

From 1843 to 1850 the minstrel bands multiplied rapidly under the following titles: Virginia Minstrels, Virginia Serenaders, Ethiopian Serenaders, Ethiopian Minstrels, Kitchen Minstrels, and Kentucky Minstrels. Many of them advertised they were the oldest bands. For instance, the Virginia Serenaders in Philadelphia claimed to have organized in 1840. They had with them: Jim Sanford, Eph Horn, Old Bull Myers, Ed. Deaves, Tony Winnemore and P. Solomons (accordion). There are no bills extant to prove the claim that they were before the public in 1840.

The Christy's claimed they were organized in 1842 but their earliest program is in August, 1843, and then they were called The Virginia Minstrels. The Buckleys, as the Congo Melodists, claimed to have organized in 1841 but their earliest bills are about 1843.

This latter troupe was composed of the Buckley Family (right name Burke), James, the father; Swaine Buckley, R. Bishop Buckley and little Fred Buckley, called Master Ole Bull Buckley. Ole Bull, the Norwegian violinist, was in America at the time and almost anyone who could perform upon a violin added the name of "Ole" to his name. The Buckleys were a grand troupe of skilled musicians and singers. One of their comedians was billed as S. Samuels, who afterwards adopted the name of Sanford, and then his name on the bills appears as S. Samuel Sanford. He gave many good songs and innovations to this company.

They were popular in the South and, after locating in New Orleans, they called themselves The New Orleans Serenaders. They located in various halls in New York and Boston. Sometimes in the Chinese Assembly Rooms, 539 Broadway, then in 444, and finally built a new opera house opposite Niblo's, at 585 Broadway but did not long remain there. They visited Europe several times, went to California in the "Days of '49," and performed in all the mining camps and along the Pacific Coast. Their last location was in Boston, during the Civil War; and in this location E. N. Catlin was their leader, Fred Buckley having died.

When the Virginia Minstrels, in 1843, sailed from Boston for England, they did not remain abroad very long; for early in 1844 they were back in America again, leaving Pelham in England, where he opened a public house (saloon).

In 1845, Barney Williams, Dan Rice, J. P. Carter, Howard and Jones appeared in Tryon's Bowery Circus, under the title of The Negro Band. In 1843 E P. Christy still called his troupe the Virginia Minstrels.

In 1844 Whitlock and Donaldson appeared in Barnum's Museum as the Kentucky Minstrels. The Great Western was one of the troupe. He was the father of Helen and Lucille Western. And, by the way, the first female minstrels were presented by the Western Sisters in their play of "The Three Fast Men," in which they presented a first part, March 9, 1857, at the Boston National Theatre.

Almost the same names appear on the bills of the Virginia Serenaders or Ethiopian Troupes or Virginia Minstrels up to 1849, such as Eph Horn, Jim Sanford, Ed Deaves, Ole Bull Myers, Tony Winnemore, J. Kavanagh, James Lynch, Charles Jenkins, Bill La Conta, J. Rudolph, Cool White, Bob Edwards,

George Kunkel, Kelly, H. S. Rumsey, Billy Birch, Jim Farrell, Frank Brower, E. M. Dickenson, F. Whittaker, William Horn, Nelson Kneass, F. Solomon. The first lady to "black up" and play with the minstrels is Mrs. Harriet Phillips with the Virginia Serenaders in May, 1848, in the burlesque of "The Bohemian Girl," in the Chestnut Street Theatre, Philadelphia.

As far back as 1840 Jim Sanford was singing "Jim Along Josey," and dancing "the Grapevine twist," with Ole Bull Myers playing the violin for him. Such songs as: "Old Dan Tucker," "Walk Along, John," "Old Tar Ribber," "Lucy Long," "Dance de Boatman Dance," "Virginny Rosebud," "Cudjo's Wild Coon Hunt," "Jenny, Get Your Hoe Cake Done," "Clar de Kitchen," "Sich a Getting Up Stairs," "Jump, Jim Crow," "Pickayune Butler," "Long Tailed Blue," "Dandy Jim ob Caroline" and "Old Zip Coon" were the popular darkie songs of that time. Old Daddy Rice (T. D. Rice) sang many of them, also. Daddy Rice's last appearance upon the stage was in the Art Union Concert Hall, 497 Broadway, in 1860. While performing in "The Mummy," he was taken ill and died September 19, 1860.

On October 7, 1844, an Ethiopian band appeared in the Bowery Circus--- Dan Emmett, Frank Brower, Evans and W. Donaldson. They claimed to be the only original and legitimate band of minstrels. After all, it is a question of the word "minstrels," for on June 15, 1842, at the Walnut Street Theatre, Philadelphia, five performers took part between the acts and called it on the bill "Negro Oddities, by Five of the Best Niggers in the World." This is given for the benefit of Master Diamond. The players are Jim Sanford, Master Diamond, Ole Bull Myers, Pickaninny Coleman and Master Chestnut, in a grand trial dance---"Lucy Long," by Jim Sanford, "Piney Woods Jig," by Master Diamond.

On June 18, 1842, the same party produced "Oh Hush," and added Fulton Myers to the troupe as Dinah Rose. They do not call themselves minstrels, but antedate Brower, Emmett, Whitlock and Pelham at the Chatham Theatre, January 31, 1843.

The Serenaders and Minstrels performed in the following places in Philadelphia: Temperance Hall, Third Street, near Green; Walnut Street Theatre; Arch Street Theatre; Old Chestnut Street Theatre; Peale's Chinese Museum; Barnum's Museum, corner Seventh and Chestnut Streets; Welch's National Circus; Melodeon Concert Hall; Franklin Institute; Southwark Hall; Jayne's Hall; Continental Theatre; Masonic Hall; Washington Hall; Long's Varieties; Olympic, near Sixth; and a hall next to the Arch Street Theatre.

In New York City the minstrels appeared in Society Library Rooms; Minerva Rooms; Pinteaux's Saloon, 307 Broadway; Barnum's Museum; Chatham Theatre; Bowery Theatre; Tryon's Circus; Hope Chapel; Perham's, 663 Broadway; Niblo's Saloon; Olympic, 442 Broadway; 444 and 472 Broadway; St. Nicholas Exhibition Rooms (under the St. Nicholas Hotel); Chinese Assembly Rooms; Stuyvesant Institute, opposite Bond Street; Novelty Hall, Centre and Pearl Streets; Convention Hall; Rutger's Institute; Franklin Theatre; Old Park Theatre; Bleecker

Building; Wood's, Broadway near Prince; 514 Broadway; Stadt Theatre and Onderdonk's Hall.

In 1846 the celebrated Ethiopian Serenaders, comprising: Harry Pell, Moody Stanwood, G. C. Germon, Harrington and White attracted a great deal of attention. They went to England and appeared before the queen and were very popular throughout the country. T. D. Rice (Daddy Rice) had paved the way for darkie songs and his singing of "Jump, Jim Crow" made a terrific hit in England. Rice's memory is still kept green by calling some cars down South "Jim Crow Cars." At one time Daddy Rice's wooden figure stood before many cigar stores. T. D. Rice was a wood carver and carved the first statue of himself---and hence the "Jim Crows," Indians and Highlanders displaced him to some extent.

About 1844 E. P. Christy formed a small band in Buffalo. They performed in a hall near the canal, kept by the widow Harrington. She had a son named George who, under E. P. Christy's tutelage, became one of the most talented and popular minstrels in this country. They first called themselves the Virginia Minstrels but early in 1847 assumed the title of Christy's Minstrels. Their first leader was R. M. Hooley, a noted violinist. His place was taken late in 1847 by Charles Abbott....

* * * * * * * * * *

These were the golden days sure enough. The troupes were small, comprising about seven or eight, including the agent, who traveled ahead, hired the halls and posted the bills, and the manager, who took the tickets at the door. Very often the end man formed one of the quartet. The salaries were moderate, traveling by stage coach or railways was cheap, and hardly any baggage to haul. The baggage often consisted of a few battered trunks, champagne baskets and carpet bags. The minstrels made their own wigs---principally of curled hair from mattresses or sofas. A few corks, burned at gas jets or incinerated in an old tin pail, furnished the make-up. Sometimes they "blacked up" with burnt paper.

The halls were bare of scenery, so each troupe carried curtains which they arranged at each side of the stage and dressed behind them. The footlights were of gas, camphene or kerosene lamps. Their wants were very few, and they performed to "packed houses," and the profits were enormous for those days. Minstrelsy was a craze, as there was no other entertainment to compete with it. All the jokes and songs were brought to town by them and for days afterwards were the topic of conversation. The halls of Albany, Troy, Syracuse, Rochester, Buffalo, Oswego, and, in fact, everywhere, had no scenery. You simply hired the bare hall.

Crowds of boys brought in the baggage and carried pails of water for the troupe, for which they receive free admission. While on the subject of baggage, it may be said that Charles H. Duprez introduced a few reforms. He furnished trunks of similar appearance and covered with zinc. This created quite a lot of comment as this baggage was hauled to and from the hall. Jealous rivals poked fun at this but they fell in line. This was just before the Civil War. Duprez also uniformed his troupe with high hats and coats with chinchilla material around the collars and cuffs. He was the first manager to introduce the brass band in conjunction with his troupe and consequently the parade from depot to hall. Later on he had a spotted coach dog that joined in the parade, receiving its share of attention. The brass band performed in front of the hall or upon its balcony. Nearly all the troupes had fine bands, though small in numbers. Everybody performed on some instrument, and the comedians had charge of the snare drum, cymbals or bass drum.

John Campbell, who kept a small hotel on the Bowery, corner of Bayard Street, organized the first Campbell's Minstrels late in 1846. Matt Peel, Luke West, Joseph D. Murphy, Jack Herman and several others were the members. From this troupe sprang all the "Original Campbell Minstrels," first under one manager, then another, with some of the members of the original party to give it a "Campbell" flavor.

In the late forties the programs were very simple, consisting of songs, solos on the banjo or violin, "Essence of Old Virginny," champion jigs, double polka, solo on a comb, jewsharp, snare drum, or kitchen bellows. The bill was divided into two parts. Part first, as "Dandy Negroes of the North," attired in black swallow-tail coats, with brass buttons; white vest, tight black pants with straps that passed under the shoes. This was supposed to be the refined part of the bill. Part second was called "Plantation Darkies of the South." They were attired as field hands, checked shirts, with large collars, striped pants and big shoes. This consisted of plantation songs, grotesque dancing, banjo songs, "Lucy Long," "Old Bob Ridley," "The Cachuca" dance, "Banjo Lesson," and wound up with a festival dance for the whole troupe, called a "walk around."

In 1849 Earl Pierce left Christy and with J. B. Fellows organized Pierce and Fellows' Minstrels, and opened in the Society Library Rooms. They removed to Mitchell's Olympic Theatre, 442 Broadway. Fellows had a building next door (444) re-constructed and, Pierce retiring, he opened 444 and called it Fellows' Opera House and Fellows Minstrels. In 1850, Eph Horn, Tom Briggs, Sam Wells, Luke West, J. B. Donniker, Jack Herman, Hi Rumsey, Billy Birch, and later the entire Buckley Family, appeared on their bills. Henry Wood succeeded J. B. Fellows in 1852. George Christy, who had a misunderstanding with E. P. Christy, joined forces with Henry Wood late in October, 1853, and the troupe was then called George Christy and Wood's Minstrels. In 1857, Henry Wood removed to a new opera house he had built on Broadway near Prince Street. Wood retired from business in this year. E. P. Christy retired from the field in 1854. The secession of George Christy had created havoc with his business. Although he had tried the best of performers to take George's place, the public simply adored him and bestowed their patronage upon him wherever he appeared.

Everything was a close imitation of the Negro, his dialect being one of the essential points necessary for a comedian to possess. Grimaces, contortions, shuffling walks, very comic and ragged garments, large shoes, small hats or battered high hats and old umbrellas, with queer looking carpet bags were absolutely part and parcel of the comedian's outfit. In the middle fifties he added grotesque female garments for a lecture on "Woman's Rights" or old military clothes to show the return from the Mexican War, which began in 1846. He also became an orator on the questions of the day as a stump speaker. This enabled the comedian to get off lots of local allusions. One of the funny sketches was "The Railroad Smash-up."

* * * * * * * * * *

In the early days of minstrelsy the "orchestra," or what few instruments were deemed an orchestra, performed upon the stage for the various acts and did not occupy the pit or orchestra space down front. The "Bryants" kept up this formula almost to the end of their stay at 472 Broadway. "Living Statuary," on a revolving platform, was presented in March, 1859, by Morris Brothers, Pell and Trowbridge in the Boston Museum. About this time P. S. Gilmore, who was celebrated as the conductor of Gilmore's Band, was with the Morris Brothers, Pell and Trowbridge, and on one bill he is performing a "Tambourine Solo." He was the author of many popular songs, also. Late in the fifties there was a steamboat called the *Banjo* with a troupe of minstrels to play the Mississippi River towns. Ben Cotton, Jim Woodruff, Frank Cordella and Joe Mairs were the principal members.

Charley White was a very prominent figure in the early days of minstrelsy and was the manager of White's Serenaders. He was located in two different places in the Bowery, 49 and 53. He introduced both Dan and Jerry Bryant to the public and the great dancing Negro boy, Juba, also the two Diamonds, as there were two Master John Diamonds. Master Marks (Dick Carroll) began his career there also. Old Dan Emmett and Dick Sweeny were members of his company.

The Sable Brothers and Sisters appeared in Convention Hall, Wooster Street, opposite the school, in 1847. The Virginia Serenaders were an institution in Philadelphia. In this company Eph Horn first appeared with Jim Sanford as his vis-a-vis on the end as bones. By the way, in the old days the bone player was the dandy coon of the troupe. He assumed the female character and appeared in the then famous "Lucy Long" specialty, or the "Cachuca" dance. Jerry Bryant was great in this delineation and so was George N. Christy. Both were fine as the dusky belle "Lucy Long," at the soiree.

Some troupes introduced a wench in the first part circle, and called this person "Miss Fanny." The best known and most popular one was undoubtedly "Master Floyd," Tom Moxley of Baltimore. He was the whole show down South when he traveled with Kunkel's Nightingale Minstrels. Everybody would ask for Master Floyd, and his "Lucy Long" was a great feature of the bill. With this troupe was: Harry Lehr, a fine comedian and William Penn Lehr.

Later on, Nelse Seymour was one of the Nightingales. John T. Ford, who managed the Holliday Street Theatre in Baltimore, Md., was the agent of this troupe. Late in the fifties Kunkel and Floyd left minstrelsy and managed the Richmond, Va., Theatre until the Civil War began. Ford, until his decease, managed the theatres in Baltimore. Kunkel's Nightingales were exceedingly popular down South and, in fact, was regarded as the great Southern troupe.

George Kunkel was the basso of the Virginia Serenaders, who were located in the old Chestnut Street Theatre, Chestnut Street, above Sixth, Philadelphia. In this troupe, Eph Horn, Jim Sanford, Cool White, Tony Winnemore and others were exceedingly popular. It must be recollected that about this time the slavery agitation placed the Southern slave prominently before the Northern public and his sighs for freedom and his lost love sold into slavery to other cotton states created a sympathy or romance and made minstrelsy a little more attractive as the "under dog" in the then gathering controversies fanned by agitators, North and South.

The Campbells had a large poster announcing the "Campbells are coming." A few camels were on this poster, also several large bells; and the legend above them the "Camp Bells" are coming. Luke West, Matt Peel and Joseph D. Murphy managed the best known Campbell Troupe. Luke West dying, left Matt Peel finally in possession of the trade mark. At one time W. W. Newcomb, Jack Herman, Max Zorer, Tom Briggs, Master T. J. Peel, Max Irwin, Mert Sexton, John Adams and Jack Huntley were of the Campbells. Matt Peel died in 1859 and Mrs. Matt Peel continued the business with J. H. Huntley as manager. For years they conducted a hotel at Catskill Landing and later at Mamaroneck, N.Y. Mrs. Matt Peel is still alive and a fine looking woman, active and lively as ever.

About 1845 J. P. Ordway organized Ordway's Aeolians in Boston. Ordway kept a music store and was quite a composer. His "Twinkling Stars Are Laughing Love" and "Home Again" are popular to this day. About 1850, Ordway leased the Old Province House, opposite the Old South Church on Washington Street, and, remodeling the interior, called it Ordway Hall. He sat behind the black faced circle and performed upon the piano. Johnny Pell, Warren White, Jack Huntley, the Morris Brothers, Al Jones, Edwin Kelly, Ambrose Thayer and others held forth until the Morris Brothers, Pell and Huntley began operations in 1857. Later, Huntley retired and J. T. Trowbridge became a partner.

This company also called themselves the Cow-bell-o-gians, burlesquing the Swiss bell ringers, who had created a furor throughout the country and especially in Boston. The minstrels performed tunes on the cowbells. After Pell's death the troupe became known as the Morris Brothers' Minstrels. It was with this troupe that Fred Wilson introduced the clog dance for the first time with a minstrel troupe. Dick Sands, Tim Hayes, Dick Carroll and Ben Goldsmith introduced the clog dance with the minstrel troupes, also.

For a long time, with the early troupes, the jig dancer was monarch of all he surveyed. He posed about attired in a velvet coat, flashy, flowing necktie, glazed cap, tight pants, patent leather shoes with old copper pennies fastened to the heels. He was the star of the troupe. If he signified his intention of quitting the show the entire troupe would almost upon their bended knees beg him to remain and not leave them to their fate. Without the champion jig dancer the minstrel show was a ship without a rudder.

Dick Sliter, John Diamond, Juba (colored boy), Jim Sanford, Billy Birch, Pete Lane, Dick Carroll, Mickey Warren, Hank the Mason, Tommy Peel, Joe Brown, Williams and a few others were the great jig dancers of the early troupes. The clog dancer finally displaced him and pulled him "off his pedestal."

Sam Sanford's Minstrels were located in Philadelphia in 1853, corner of Twelfth and Chestnut Streets. Here he was burned out and he took the Eleventh

Street Opera house, which then (1855) was called Cartee's Lyceum. He continued there until 1862, when Carncross and Dixey's Minstrels began their career. With a few changes of ownership the house finally passed under the control of Frank Dumont, who remained there until 1911; and then removed to the Museum, corner Ninth and Arch. This building was first intended to be a minstrel home for Carncross, Dixey and Simpson. After years of vicissitude it finally became the minstrel house it was first intended to be.

All the famous stars of minstrelsy appeared upon the stage of the old Eleventh Street Opera House during its great career. There was: George Christy, Cool White, Kelly and Leon, Billy Birch, Charley Backus, Dave Wambold, Archie Hughes, Sam Sanford, J. L. Carncross, E. F. Dixey, Ira Paine, Charles Campbell (Templeton), James W. Glenn, (alto singer), Jim and Bill Budworth, Unsworth and Eugene, Billy Manning, Frank Moran, Lew Simmons, E. N. Slocum, Byron Christy, Sam Wells, Eph Horn, John Mulligan, W. W. Newcomb, Bobby Newcomb, Gustave Bideaux, the Buffalo Boys, George Charles, John Dudley, Sam Sharpley, Ben Cotton, Dick Sliter, Signor Rafael Abecco, Francis Wilson, Carroll Johnson, George Powers, Carl Schwicardi (a noted basso), Charles Henry (a tenor), and in fact everybody and anybody noted in minstrelsy trod those historic boards. In later years from its stage graduated Weber and Fields, Eddie Foy, Chauncey Olcott, Lew Dockstader, Press Eldridge, Tom Lewis, John C. Rice and many others now famous and prosperous.

When the Civil War began in 1861 there were numerous troupes traveling, more or less successful. Rumsey and Newcomb's Minstrels, Duprez, Carle, Shorey and Green's Minstrels, who changed to Duprez and Green and later Duprez and Benedict. There was Sam Sharpley's Ironclads and Cal Wagner's Pontoons. There was Skiff and Gaylord's Minstrels, organized by Johnny Steele (Coal Oil Johnny), who spent thousands buying hotels, diamonds, race horses, etc., etc., but the troupe long survived the spendthrift that organized it. There was George Christy's Minstrels, Arlington, Donniker, Kelly and Leon's Minstrels.

Lloyd's Minstrels was organized by Lloyd, the map man. He took all the famous stars of minstrelsy and promised them huge salaries. Among those he engaged were: Billy Birch, Charley Fox, Dave Wambold, Gustave Bideaux, Cool White and a number of others. Philo A. Clark was the agent. When the members of the troupe called for their salaries, Lloyd sat at a table with a revolver and perhaps dared them to touch the money. He afterwards organized Lloyd & Bideaux's Minstrels but their career was short. Dan Bryant publicly horsewhipped Lloyd on Broadway. Another short lived troupe was Anderson's Minstrels of Boston, which started in as opposition to the Morris Brothers. The Clipper at the time predicted an early dissolution and the collapse came as predicted. The fancy salaries and the gathering of so many minstrel stars settled the venture.

In the middle fifties Perham's company were located at 663 Broadway. Perham tried the gift business to attract crowds. Those who did not draw prizes (and they were in the majority) denounced the swindle and Brother Perham's gift minstrels fell by the wayside. W. W. Newcomb tried the gift "enterprise" to revive his business while located in Wood's Theatre, Cincinnati, and he, too, met with disaster. Up to 1864 were the golden days of minstrelsy as a picture of Negro life in the South. With the end of the war or emancipation of the slaves, the Negro lost his pathetic or attractive position as an object of interest. The draft riots in New York were leveled at the Negro.

The slave songs and other bits of Negro life underwent a great change and minstrelsy had to be practically renovated on different lines; but it was still as amusing and the war songs and home ballads superseded the slave songs. We saw the Negro in a new light and important innovations were made in the way of special acts or more attention paid to the singing and instrumentations.

Duprez's company first introduced the four end-men, namely: Lew Benedict, Hughey Dougherty, Charley Reynolds and Charley Gleason. From the early troupes comprising four or five performers, the minstrel troupes gradually grew larger until some of them would announce in bold type on posters and bills "Ten star performers." And when a troupe announced "fourteen star performers" other managers would shake their heads and predict an early "burst up" or give them about two weeks to live. Once the slave or Negro of the South lost his "drawing powers" or attractive position, something had to be done to keep minstrelsy before the public just as entertaining as ever.

In 1859, the "variety" entertainment became quite popular in New York and halls formerly used by minstrel companies were leased for variety shows, notably 663 Broadway (Mozart Hall), where Perham's troupe had been located. This was called The Canterbury Music Hall. The Chinese Assembly Rooms, 539 Broadway, was also given over to variety entertainments. When 663 burned out, Fox and Curran took 585 Broadway (built by the Buckleys) and called it the New Canterbury. Most of the minstrel performers were drawn into this new form of entertainment. Then 444 became the American Music Hall. Here Charley White, Lew Simmons, Bob Hart, Harry Leslie, Tony Pastor, Billy Arlington and all the noted minstrels appeared. At the other houses were Tony Hernandez, Moffit and Bartholomeu, Andy Leavitt, Dan Gardner, Dick Sands, Mike McKenna. During the war the pretty waiter girls flourished in most of the variety places. Old timers will probably remember the Dew Drop In and the Art Union. It was while performing in the Art Union (1861) that Daddy Rice was taken ill and in a few days died, lamented by the whole minstrel profession.

Some grand troupes flourished after the war, on different lines, of course. The crude songs of the slaves had been laid aside for ballads of home and mother. New posters and ideas came forth. Troupes were augmented. Fortunes were made even after the Negro was no longer a trump card as in former years. Many troupes would meet on the New York Central Railroad, some coming in as others were going out of a town. Everybody had money and all were prospering. Several troupes were located at the same time in New York City: Wood's, Bryant's, San Francisco Minstrels, Sharpley & Cotton and, late in 1866, Kelly & Leon joined the throng.

From time to time dwarfs have appeared with the troupes and excited attention, notably Japanese Tommy, a colored dwarf, who was quite funny as a "prima donna," and in the "Essence of Old Virginny." Bryant's Minstrels had another dwarf, called "Little Mac."

After the war Jack Haverly began to loom up as a minstrel manager. He managed Cal Wagner's Minstrels for a while, then the first Haverly Minstrels. In later years he organized the "Forty, Count Them, Forty," went to England with them, and then began the gradual disintegration. Imitators had organized large troupes and the novelty was done as a big money maker. The old time troupes and most of the old timers have passed away and with them the real Negro burlesque and mannerisms with the broad dialect. Their mantle has not fallen on the shoulders of many of the present generation.

Fortunes are still gathered in by such clever men as Al. G. Field, Neil O'Brien, George Evans, Lew Dockstader, George Primrose, John W. Vogel, J. A. Coburn and Guy Brothers. These still uphold the banner of minstrelsy and do a land office business, especially in the South.

With closed eyes, musingly, I see the great procession of the early minstrels passing by, the great and famous men of those days, each and every one a grand artist in his line.

THREE YEARS AS A NEGRO MINSTREL
By Ralph Keeler [*New York Clipper*, August 1, 8, 15, 1874]

Negro minstrels were, I think, more highly esteemed at the time of which I am about to write than they are now; at least, I thought more of them then, both as individuals and as ministers to public amusement, than I ever have since. The first troupe of the kind I saw was the old Kunkels, and I can convey no idea of the pleasurable thrill I felt at the banjo-solo and the plantation jig. I resolved on the spot to be a negro minstrel. Mr. Ford, in whose theatre President Lincoln was assassinated, was, I believe, the agent of this company. I made known my ambition to that gentleman and to Mr. Kunkel himself and they promised, no doubt as the best means of getting rid of me, to take me with them the next year. Meantime I bought a banjo and had pennies screwed on the heels of my boots and practiced "Jordan" on the former, and the "Juba" dance with the latter, till my boardinghouse keeper gave me warning. I think there is scarcely a serious friend of mine acquainted with me at that period who does not remember me with sorrow and vexation. The racket that I made at all hours and in all places can be accounted for only by the youthful zeal with which I practiced and which I despair of describing in anything so cold as words.

I was then in my twelfth year and my own master. At the mature age of eleven I had run away from Buffalo, N. Y., where I had been placed at school, and traveled during six months all over the Western lakes, with one suit of clothes, a single shirt, and a cash capital of five copper cents. I was impelled by the same romantic instincts, I suppose, which at twenty prompted me to undertake the "barefooted" tour of Europe on the sum of one hundred and eighty dollars in United States currency. In which of these two adventurous enterprises I came nearer starving to death, it would be difficult now to say. I had no parents to grieve after me and knew little and cared less about the broad prairie in Ohio which was my patrimony and place of nativity. It was my relatives from whom I fled and to whom I never returned.

Towards the close of my eleventh year, I found myself possessor of a considerable sum of money in bank, which I had made out of my five coppers, after carrying them through all the hunger and squalor of my six months' wandering. I had these coppers, I remember, in one pocket---it was also the only pocket---of my ragged pantaloons, in the dusk of that summer evening when I escaped from the benevolent gentleman at Detroit, who purposed taking me to the House of Vagrancy. I had made my money by selling papers and books on the lake steamer *Northern Indiana*, commanded by the late Captain Pheatt. I mention this kindly old gentleman because he suffered a great deal from my early penchant to perform the clog-dance on the thin deck above his stateroom. It is unnecessary to repeat here the eager and emphatic remonstrances which the good captain would make when I had inadvertently seized the occasion of his "watch below" to shuffle him out of a sound sleep. Just before the steamer was laid up for the winter, I had taken my leave of her at Toledo, Ohio, where I was boarding and going to school on my earnings when I met Messrs. Ford and Kunkel. About the same time my landlady gave me warning to take myself and banjo and obstreperous feet out of her house. In the course of a month or two, I left school that I might have more time to devote to minstrelsy. I found another boarding house, however, where the plastering of the apartment below mine was proof against the coppers on my heels and the complicated shuffles of "Juba," and organized a band of boys into a minstrel troupe and appointed myself musical director, though I knew no more of music than of chemistry. I spent my money for instruments for the company and for furniture to deck the room in which we met for rehearsal. The musical instruments, however, were the least of the expense, since these consisted, if I well recollect, of the banjo before mentioned, three sets of bones, a tambourine, a triangle, and an accordion. With these, nevertheless, we succeeded in making it very unpleasant for some quiet-loving Teutons, who were accustomed to dream over their beer at a *Wirthschoft* in the same wooden building and, indeed, just under the apartment in which we rehearsed every evening.

On certain occasions, when I executed my "Juba" dance, or in company with others performed the Virginia Walk-around, these honest Germans would leave their beer and sometimes their hats and pipes behind them in terror and rush precipitately into the middle of the street. There they would stand and gaze in silent amazement up at the windows, or utter their surprise and wrath at the proceedings in the expressive speech of fatherland.

The host, a portly gentleman with a red nose, remonstrated with us about four times a week, to little purpose. The owner of the building also remonstrated, but we had rented the apartment and would not leave till our time was out. We were constrained, however, to forego our jig and walk-around. Still our music and singing, to which we were now confined, came near breaking up the poor retail Gambrinus of the saloon beneath. His "stem-guests" fell off one by one and sought a quieter neighborhood for their evening potations. It was only the bravest of them that could be prevailed upon to return for anything more than their hats and pipes, after having been driven into the street on any of our siege-nights.

The best praise I can give the young gentleman who played the accordion is, that he was worthy to be under such a musical director as myself. He could play only one tune from beginning to end and that was "The Gum-tree Canoe." Now, it happened that none of us could sing the song, which, as is well known, is of the slow, melancholy, sentimental order; so this single tune would have been of very little benefit to us, had we not, luckily, pressed it into the incongruous double service of opening overture and closing quickstep. The songs that we sang, or attempted to sing, were executed to the accompaniment of the three sets of bones, the tambourine, triangle and banjo, with an uncertain ghostly second on the accordion, which, being the same for all tunes and following no lead whatever, was of a sufficiently lugubrious and dismal nature, when it was not wholly drowned by the clangor of the other instruments.

My company, it must be confessed, had zeal, but little talent. I spent what was left of my summer's earnings before I could get them up to a point that would, in my judgment, warrant a hope of success, should we give the public exhibition for which my minstrels were clamorously ambitious. After many long months of fruitless trial, the rent for our room becoming due, our furniture and instruments were seized; the landlord turned us out of doors; the German beer-seller crossed himself thankfully; and I was as completely ruined as many a manager before me.

It may as well be owned that I had no natural aptness for the banjo, and was always an indifferent player; but for dancing I had, I am confident, such a remarkable gift as few have ever had. Up to this day, I did not think I ever have seen a step done by man or woman that I could not do as soon as I saw it---not saying, of course, how gracefully. I am not, however, so vain or proud of this gift as I used to be; and should hardly have written the foregoing sentence at all, had it not seemed necessary to a proper understanding of subsequent passages in this narrative.

I was still so small of stature, and yet capable of producing so much noise with the coppers in my heels, that, by the wholesale clerks and young bloods about town, I was considered in the light of a prodigy and made to shuffle my feet at almost all hours and in almost all localities. It was by this means, at some convivial resort, that I attracted the notice and admiration of a conductor on the Michigan Southern and Northern Indiana Railroad. He determined to have so much talent with him all the time and prevailed upon me to be his train-boy. Here, as on the lake, I had the exclusive privilege of selling books and papers to the passengers. The great railways were not then farmed by a single person or firm as now. I was my own agent and the regulator of my own prices and profits. Both of these latter I found it convenient to make large and was again the possessor of more money than I cared to spend. It was my business to carry water through the cars at stated intervals. On a day train I could afford to perform my duty with promptness, when I had sufficiently worried the passengers with my merchandise. But on a night train, which came to my lot just as often as a day train, I took a more lucrative and, I fear, less reputable means of quenching the thirst of travelers. There were no sleeping cars in those times, and, I believe, no water tanks in the passenger cars. My memory may fail me in this matter of the water tanks, but I am certain I never filled them, if there were any on our road. I don't know whether more people traveled then than now, but I remember the trains were exceedingly long ones in those hot summer nights and the people became terribly thirsty. And in this way I comforted them. Taking a barrel of water, a pailful of brown sugar, and a proper amount of a well-known acid, I concocted lemonade which I sold through the train for five cents a glass. When thirsty lips asked piteously for water, I would tell the sufferer with perfect truth that there was not a drop of pure water left on the train. I blush to write that I sometimes sold fifteen dollars' worth of this vile compound in a night. I was taught how to prepare it by a man who traveled with a circus and who assured me that all his ice-cold lemonade was concocted in the same way; and that, far from having killed anybody, it gave perfect satisfaction to the gentlemen and ladies from the country, who were his principal customers. The only excuse I have to offer for myself, now, is that I was not conscious then how great a villain I really was.

Towards the middle of the summer the cholera became so prevalent in the Western cities that I thought it prudent to retire from the active life of a train-boy and live quietly on my earnings. I settled myself, therefore, at a fashionable boarding-house in Toledo. Here the landlady, fearful of dust and anxious for the integrity of her carpet, made a remarkable compromise with me to the glory of aesthetics. Whenever there was a pressing request from the boarders for me to exercise my feet, she would bustle in with a large roll of oil-cloth and spread it uncomplainingly on the parlor floor, near the piano, to the music of which I danced. This was, I think, the first introduction of clogs as a drawing-room entertainment. I soon came to be invited out as a sort of cub-lion; and thus it happened that the rumor and dust of my accomplishments spread gradually through the city.

One evening I strolled into what is now called the St. Nicholas, and, stepping to the bar, which came just up to my juvenile shoulders, I demanded authoritatively of the bar-tender if he had any good pale brandy. He said he had. I told him in the same imperative tone to give me a ten-cent drink, "and none of his instant-death kind, either." This made somewhat of a sensation among the frequenters of that fashionable resort. They evidently mistook this brandy-bibbing as a swaggering habit of mine; whereas I was honestly prescribing for myself what had been recommended to me as the best preventive of cholera. Having swallowed and paid for the brandy, I was preparing to withdraw, when I heard this dialogue going on behind me:

"Who for pity's sake is that?"

"That? Why, that's just the boy you want. But can't he dance, though!"

Turning, I saw a couple of well-dressed men seated together at the end of the room. I had barely time to observe that one was a stranger to me, when the other called me to him and introduced me to Johnny Booker. Now, I had heard the songs, then popular "Meet Johnny Booker in the Bowling Green" and "Johnny Booker, Help Dis Nigger," and when I was aware that I was standing before the person to whose glory these lyrics had been written, I was very much abashed. I looked upon a great negro minstrel as unquestionably the greatest man on earth and it was some time before I could answer his questions intelligibly. In the course of a few minutes, however, I was conducted into a private room, where I was made to dance "Juba" to the time which the comedian himself gave me by means of his two hands and one foot, and which is technically called "patting." My performance, it seems, was satisfactory, for I was engaged on the spot. Mr. Booker was then waiting for the rest of his company to join him; and when they arrived, I was instituted jig-dancer to the troupe, with a weekly salary of five dollars and all my traveling expenses.

It is impossible to convey an idea of the gratified ambition with which I prepared for my first appearance on the stage. The great Napoleon, in the coronation robes which can be seen any day in the Tuileries, was not prouder or happier than I when I made my initial bow before the footlights in my small Canton-flannel knee-pants, cheap lace, gold tinsel, corked face, and woolly wig. I do not remember any embarrassment, for I was only doing in public what I had already done for the majority of the audience in private. If I had acquitted myself much worse than I really did, my debut would still, I am convinced, have been considered a success. So great, indeed, was the local pride of the good Toledans in their infant phenomenon, that, after the company had exhibited a week, my name---or rather the *nom de guerre* which I had assumed---was put up for a benefit. On that day I had the satisfaction of seeing hung across the street, on a large canvas, a watercolor representation of myself, with one arm and one leg elevated, in the act of performing "Juba" over the heads and carts and carriages of the passersby. At night the house was crowded and I was called out three times; but what afterward struck me as unaccountably odd was, that I received not one cent from the proceeds of that benefit. When my salary was paid me, at the end of the next week, I was assured that "this benefit business" was a mere trick of the trade, and I was forced to content myself with the fact that I had learned something in my new profession.

We now started on our travels, staying from one night to a week in a city, according to its size, stopping always at the best hotels, and leading the merriest of lives generally. I had the additional glory of being stared at as the youthful prodigy by day and of having more than my share of applause, accompanied sometimes with quarter-dollars, bestowed on me at night. There was in our troupe a remarkable character by the name of Frank Lynch, who played the tambourine and banjo. He and the celebrated Diamond had been in their youth among the first and greatest of dancers. Too portly now to endure sustained effort with his feet, he was yet an excellent instructor and I was constantly under his training.

Lynch and I were together in another troupe afterwards. I never knew him, in all the time of our association, to talk ten minutes without telling some story, and that always about something which had happened to him personally in the show business. In the long nights, when we had to wait for the cars or steamboats, he would sit down and, taking up one theme, would string all his stories on that, and that alone, for hours. His manner would make the merest commonplace amusing. We had been together a year or more, I think, when Barnum's autobiography came out. I shall never forget my comrade's indignation when he read that passage of the book which runs something in this way: "Here I picked up one Francis Lynch, an orphan vagabond," etc., etc. It was really dangerous after that for a man to own, in his presence, to having read the life of the great showman. Henceforth, Lynch omitted all his stories about the time when he and P. T. Barnum used to black their faces together.

Lynch professed to live in Boston, though he had not been there in fifteen years. During all this time, he had been earnestly trying to get back to his home. He would often spend money enough in a night to take him to Boston from almost any place in the broad Union, and back again, and then lament his folly for the next week. Once he left our company at Cleveland, Ohio, for the express purpose of going back to Boston. Unfortunately, a night intervened, and, in the middle of it, the whole Waddell House was aroused from its slumbers by poor Lynch in the last stage of intoxication, vociferating at the top of his lungs that he had been robbed of the money with which he was going back to Boston. By some means, he got hold of a lighted candle without a candlestick, and with this he purposed to search the house. The clerks and porters were called out of bed and, led by Lynch with his flickering taper, came in melancholy procession up the long stairs to the rooms occupied by our troupe. Lynch insisted that we should all be searched---a whim in which, under the circumstances, we thought it best to humor him. This having been done, without finding his lost treasure, he bolted the doors and proceeded to examine the surprised clerks and porters. Meeting with the same ill-success, he finally threw himself in despair upon his bed and wailed himself to sleep. The next morning he found all the money which he had not spent in the side-pocket of his overcoat, where he had carelessly thrust it himself. And his joy was so great at this, and his sorrow so lively when told that he had searched us all, that he insisted on spending what money was left to celebrate his good luck and the triumph of our honesty.

Lynch never got back to Boston. He died several years ago, somewhere out in the Far West. Since then it has transpired that Barnum was wrong in calling him an orphan, at least; for his father sought him a long time, before hearing of his death, to bestow upon the poor fellow a considerable fortune that had been left him by some relative.

Johnny Booker was the stage-manager of the company with which I left Toledo. Our first business manager and proprietor was a noble-hearted fellow, who has since distinguished himself as a colonel in the late war; but the managership changed hands after a while and we finally arrived at Pittsburgh. Here we played a week to poor houses; and, one morning, awoke to find that our manager had decamped without paying our hotel bills. When this became known, through the papers or in some other way, the landlord got out an attachment on our baggage. The troupe was disbanded, of course. When, therefore, I desired to take my trunk and go home, the hotel-keeper told me that I could do so as soon as I paid the bills of the whole company. This was appalling. After a great deal of wrangling the landlord was convinced at last that he could hold us responsible only for our individual indebtedness. Accordingly, Mr. Booker, Mr. Kneeland, a violinist, and myself were allowed to pay our bills and depart with our baggage.

I never learned exactly how the greater part of the company escaped, but it certainly could not have been by discharging their accounts; for they were generally of that reckless disposition which scorns to have any cash on hand or to remember where it has been deposited. The sentimental ballad-singer---the one who was the most careful of his scarves, the set of his attire, and the combing and curling of his hair, and who used to volunteer to stand at the door in the early part of the evening, and pass programs to the ladies as they came into the hall---this languishing fellow, I am sorry to say, was obliged to leave his trunks and the greater part of his wardrobe behind him in the hands of the inexorable landlord.

Frank Lynch had led this nomadic life so long that he never carried any trunk with him. He had already sacrificed too much, he averred, to the rapaciousness of hotel-keepers and the villainy of fly-by-night managers. He contented himself, therefore, with two champagne baskets, one of which, containing his stage wardrobe, always went directly to the hall where we were to play, while the other, containing his linen, went to the hotel, where, in company with the baggage of the whole troupe, it excited no suspicion. Whether or not Lynch left one of his champagne baskets with the Pittsburgh landlord, I cannot say. When I next heard of him he was at Cincinnati in search of an engagement.

The two gentlemen with whom I left Pittsburgh accompanied me to Toledo, where Mr. Booker set to work to get up another company. Lynch was accordingly sent for. Mr. Edwin Deaves, also a member of the former troupe---and now, by the way, a veteran scenic artist at San Francisco---was brought from some other place; and the Booker Troupe set out on its travels.

This company prided itself on its sobriety and gentlemanly conduct. It was the business of the four other members to keep poor Lynch straight, and if, in the endeavor, some of them occasionally fell themselves, it was put down to the reckless good-fellowship of the merry veteran, and hushed up as expeditiously as possible. There were so few of us that we could afford to go to smaller towns than the other troupe had ever visited. It was deemed a good advertisement, as well as in some metaphysical way conducive to the morale of the company, to dress as nearly alike as we could when off the stage. This had the effect, as will be readily understood, of pointing me out more prominently than ever as the juvenile prodigy, whose portrait and assumed name were plastered about over the walls of the towns and cities through which we took our triumphal march.

The first part of our performances we gave with white faces, and I had so improved my opportunities that I was now able to appear as the Scotch girl in plaid petticoats, who executes the inevitable Highland fling in such exhibitions. By practicing in my room through many tedious days, I learned to knock and spin and toss about the tambourine on the end of my forefinger; and, having rehearsed a budget of stale jokes, I was promoted to be one of the "end men" in the first-part of the Negro performances. Lynch, who could do anything, from a solo on the penny trumpet to an obligato on the double bass, was at the same time advanced to play the second violin, as this made more music and helped to fill up the stage. In addition to my jig, I now appeared in all sorts of *pas de deux*, took the principal lady part in Negro ballads, and danced "Lucy Long." I am told that I looked the wench admirably.

The Booker Troupe wandered all over the Western country, traveling at all hours of night and day and in all manner of conveyances, from the best to the worst. The life was so exciting and I was so young that I was probably as happy as an itinerant mortal can be in this world of belated railway trains, steamboat explosions and collisions, and runaway stage-horses.

We were on our way East from Chicago, exhibiting at the towns along the line of the Michigan Central Railroad, when Ephraim came to us. Ephraim was one of the most comical specimens of the Negro species. We were playing at Marshall, Michigan, when he introduced himself to our notice by bringing water into the dressing-room, blacking our boots, and in other ways making himself useful. He had the blackest face, largest mouth and whitest teeth imaginable. He said there was nothing in the world which he would like so well as to travel with a show. What could he do? Why, he could fetch water, black our boots and take care of our baggage. We assured him that we could not afford to have a servant travel with us. Ephraim rejoined that he did not want any pay; he just wanted to go with the show. We told him it was simply impossible; and Ephraim went away, as we thought, discouraged.

The next morning, as we were getting into the railway car, whom should we discover there before us but Ephraim, with his baggage under his arm---a glazed traveling bag of so attenuated an appearance that it could not possibly have had anything in it but its lining. To the question as to whither he was bound he replied:

"Why, bless you, I's goin' wid de show."

Again he was told that it could not be and made to get out of the car. This occurrence gave Mr. Lynch the theme for a long series of stories about people he had met, who were what he called "show-struck"; and with these narratives our time was beguiled till we reached the town at which we were to perform that night. As we walked out towards the baggage car, what was our surprise to see Ephraim there picking out and piling up our trunks and bestowing sundry loud and expressive epithets upon the baggage-master, who had let a property box fall upon the platform. I think we laughed louder now than we had at any of Mr. Lynch's stories. Ephraim deigned not to notice us or our mirth but, having picked out the baggage that went to the hall where we were to exhibit, he called a dray and rode away with it. He made himself of great use during our stay in that place, in return for which his slight hotel expenses were paid; but he was told positively that he could go no farther. We knew that he had no money, yet did not dare to give him any, lest he should be enabled to follow us to the next town. So, when we came to go away, we expressed our regrets to the ingenuous darkie, and once more bade him good-bye. He disappeared in the crowd and the train moved off. When we arrived at the next town, however, there again was Ephraim, at the baggage car, giving his stentorian commands about our trunks and properties and taking not the least notice of the surprise depicted on our faces.

The discharge and mysterious reappearance of Ephraim occurred in about the same manner at every town along the road, until we reached Detroit. We never could find out how he got from place to place on the cars; but where our baggage was, there was Ephraim also. We had to succumb. His persistency and faithfulness and perfect good nature carried the point; and he became a regular attaché of the Booker Troupe. The story of the fights and beatings that poor Ephraim sustained in his jealous care of our luggage would alone make a long chapter. He was always in fisticuffs with the Irish porters of the hotels. On one occasion, when remonstrated with for his excessive pugnacity, Ephraim explained himself in this way:

"For one slam of a trunk I gen'lly speaks to a man; for two slams I calls him a thief; and when it comes to three slams, den dere's gwine to be somebody knocked down. Now, you heared me!"

On our arrival at the hotel in Detroit, we observed that the porter was an Irishman, and were really surprised that he and Ephraim did not quarrel in handling the baggage---an anomaly which was satisfactorily explained to us afterwards by the fact that the porter had lately come to this country and was, moreover, only about half-witted. Now, Ephraim was in the habit of taking his meals in the kitchens and of sleeping in whatever attic was assigned him. On our first night in Detroit he had been sent into the servants' chamber, somewhere in the topmost part of the hotel. Ephraim ascended, disrobed himself, and with his usual recklessness got into the first of the many beds he saw in the large room. At twelve o'clock, when his watch was over, the Irish porter also proceeded to the same apartment with the purpose of retiring. Opening the door, he discovered by the dim gaslight something dark on the pillow of his own bed. This brought all his Old World superstition into play in a moment. Going as much nearer as he dared, he saw that it was a black head, and believing firmly that the devil was black, he was sure that the devil was in his bed. The affrighted porter gave an unearthly yelp, at which Ephraim started up in terror. Whereupon the Irishman seized one of the Negroes boots from the floor by the foot of the bed and fell to beating the supposed devil over the head with all his might. The attack was so sudden that Ephraim never thought of defense, but, springing to his feet, fled precipitately down the six flights of stairs, out into the middle of the street, crying "Watch, watch!" at the top of his voice. Here a policeman came along and took poor Ephraim off to the stationhouse just as he was and in spite of all his protestations of innocence. The next morning Mr. Booker carried his clothes to the unfortunate Negro, and brought him back to the hotel.

In the course of time the Booker Troupe was disbanded and Ephraim, as well as ourselves, was, in green-room parlance, out of an engagement. I never saw him or Lynch afterwards. I found myself, after some minor adventures, at Cincinnati, where the once notorious Mike Mitchell left the Campbell's Minstrels and took me with him into a company which he organized in that city, under the title of "The Mitchells."' We played for some time at the largest hall in Cincinnati, and traveled afterwards through a few of the neighboring states. This troupe, too, having gone to pieces, I was one of the volunteers at the grand complimentary benefit given to Mitchell at Cincinnati, with the proceeds of which he was sent out to California to join his friends Birch and Backus.

Mitchell, poor fellow, like Lynch and Sliter and so many of my old associates in the cork opera, has passed away, let us hope to a quieter stage, beyond the double-dealing of managers and the contumely of publicans. An old showman is, in truth, a being *sui generis*. You rarely meet one who will not tell you he has been twenty-two years in the show business. He always talks in hyperbole, uses adjectives for adverbs, and arranges all the minor incidents of his life, as well as his conversation, in the most dramatic forms. He is often a better friend to others than to himself; he is not naturally worse than the majority of men, but has more temptation. A good negro minstrel would in any other profession be an Admirable Crichton in respect to morals. While acknowledging with pride that I met in this calling some who deserve even such praise, it is due to the truth to state also that I have known many and many a poor fellow who was, in the language of Addison:

> Reduced, like Hannibal, to seek relief
> From court to court, and wander up and down,
> A vagabond in Afric.

The day after the farewell benefit of Mitchell, I was engaged by Dr. Spalding, the veteran manager, whose old quarrel with Dan Rice has made him famous to the lovers of the circus. He was then fitting out *The Floating Palace* for its voyage on the Western and Southern rivers. *The Floating Palace* was a great boat, built expressly for show purposes. It was towed from place to place by a steamer called the *James Raymond*. The *Palace* contained a museum, with all the usual concomitants of Invisible Ladies, stuffed giraffes, puppet-dancing, etc. The *Raymond* contained, besides the dining hall and state rooms of the employees, a concert saloon fitted up with great elegance and convenience and called "The Ridotto." In this latter I was engaged, in conjunction with "a full band of minstrels," to do my jig and wench dances. The two boats left Cincinnati with nearly a hundred souls on board, that being the necessary complement of the vast establishment. We were bound for Pittsburgh, where we were to give our first exhibition; purposing to stop afterwards, on our way down, at all the towns and landings along the Ohio. Everything went well on our way up the river till we came within about twenty miles of Wheeling, Va., when the *Raymond* stuck fast on a sand bar. It was thought best for the people to be transferred to the *Palace* so as to lighten the steamer and let her work off. When, accordingly, we had all huddled into the museum, our lines were cast off and our anchor let go; but we were carried half a mile down stream before the anchor caught. Here, all day, from the decks of the *Palace*, we could watch the futile efforts of the *Raymond* to get off the bar. The only provision for the inner man on board of our craft was a drinking saloon, which was of very little comfort to the numerous ladies of the party, to say the least. Towards night we became exceedingly hungry but no relief was sent us from the steamer. One Riesse, an obese bass singer, who was a terrible gourmand, and who had been for the last five hours raving about the decks in a pitiable manner, rushed suddenly out upon the guard, about eight o'clock, declaring that he saw a boatload of provisions coming from the *Raymond*. A shout of joy now went up from the famished people that shook the stuffed giraffes and wax-works in their glass cases. It was a boat, indeed; but it contained simply the captain, mate and pilot, who had come all that way after their evening bitters at the drinking saloon.

They expressed themselves very sorry for us and were confident that they could now get the steamer off the bar. This liquid stimulus was all that had been needed from the first. With this mild assurance for a foundation to our hopes of relief, they took their departure and we waited on and on through the long night. Riesse, the bass singer, never slept a wink or allowed many others to sleep, his hungry voice, like a loon's on some solitary lake, breaking in upon the stillness where and when it was least expected. Wrapped in the veritable cloak of the great Pacha Mohammed Ali, I drowsed through the latter part of the night, crouched down between the glass apartments of the waxen Tam O'Shanter and the Twelve Apostles. In the morning there were several more steamers on ground in the neighborhood, but no better prospect of the *Raymond's* getting off. We were finally taken off to her in small boats and allowed to break our long fast. Instead of rising, the river fell, and we were left almost a week on dry land. Our provisions giving out, it was thought best for the performers to be taken up to Wheeling by a little stern-wheeler that happened to come along. At that city we gave several exhibitions at Washington Hall. Proceeding thence down the river, on the stern-wheeler, to play in the towns along till we should be overtaken by the *Palace* and the *Raymond*, we passed those unfortunate boats, still laboring to free themselves, and were greeted with hearty cheers by the people on board. One night the river rose suddenly, and in a day or so we were overtaken by the whole establishment, at Marietta, Ohio. The proposed trip to Pittsburgh was abandoned. We commenced our voyage down the river, exhibiting in the afternoon and evening, and sometimes in the morning, at two, and often three, towns or landings in a day.

It needed not this excess of its labors to tire me with the showman's life. Several months before I had begun to doubt whether a great negro minstrel was a more enviable man than a great senator or author. As these doubts grew on me, I purchased some school books and betook myself to study every day, devouring, in the intervals of arithmetic and grammar, the contents of every work of biography and poetry that I could lay hands on. The novelty and excitement of this odd life, indeed, were wearing away. All audiences at last looked alike to me, as all lecture-goers do to Dr. Holmes. They laughed at the same places at the performance, applauded at the same place, and looked inane or interested at the same place, day after day, week after week, and month after month. I became gradually indifferent to their applause, or only noticed when it failed at the usual step or pantomime. Then succeeded a sort of contempt for audiences, and at last a positive hatred of them and myself. I noticed, or thought I noticed, that their faces wore the same vacant expression whether their eyes were staring at me or the stuffed giraffes or the dancing puppets of the museum.

I obtained my first view of the great Mississippi and of the practical working of Lynch law at the same time. The night of our advent at Cairo was lit up by the fires of an execution. A Negro, it seems, was the owner or lessee of an old wharf-boat, which had been moored to the levee of that town and which he had turned to the uses of a gambling-saloon. People who had been enticed into it had never been seen or heard of afterwards. The vigilance committee then governing Cairo had frequently endeavored to lay hold of the Negro and bring him to trial, but he had secret passages from one part of the wharf-boat to the other by which he always eluded his pursuers. Having no doubt that he was guilty of several murders, the vigilantes on the night of our arrival had come down to the levee two or three hundred strong, armed, equipped, and determined to make the wretch surrender. In answer to the summons, they received nothing but insults from the Negro, still out of sight and secure in one of his hiding places. At a given signal, the wharf-boat was set afire and cut adrift, and, as it floated out into the current, the vigilantes surrounded it in small boats, with their rifles ready and pointed to prevent the escape of their victim. When the wharf-boat was well into the stream the Negro appeared boldly at the place which, in the middle of all river craft of that kind, is left open for the reception and discharge of freight. And now a scene occurred, so sensationally dramatic, so easily adaptable to the stage of these latter days, that I would not dare to relate it for truth if I had not witnessed it with my own eyes. The Negro was not discovered till he had rolled a large keg of powder into the middle of the open space just mentioned. As he stood in the light of his burning craft, it could be seen by the people in the small boats in the river that he had a cocked musket with the muzzle plunged into the keg of powder. The Negro dared them to come on and take him, pouring upon them at the same time such horrible oaths and curses as have rarely come from the lips of man. The small boats kept at a proper distance now, their occupants caring only to prevent his escape into the water. As the flames grew thicker around him, there the Negro stood, floating down into the darkness that enveloped the majestic river, with his cocked musket still in the keg of powder and cursing and defying his executioners. He was game to the last. We heard the explosion down the stream and saw the wharf-boat sink. The next day I spoke with the leader of the band in the small boats---a short, wiry little man, with a piercing eye. He said that he had not the heart to shoot the "nigger" because he showed such pluck. He even confessed that, for the same reason, he felt almost sorry for the victim after the explosion had blown him into eternity.

We saw, indeed, a great deal of wild life in the country which we visited, for we steamed thousands of miles on the Western and Southern rivers. We went, for instance, the entire navigable lengths of the Cumberland and Tennessee. Our advertising agent had a little boat of his own, in which he preceded us. The *Palace* and *Raymond* would sometimes run their noses upon the banks of some of these rivers where there was not a habitation in view, and by the hour of exhibition the boats and shore would be thronged with people. In some places on the Mississippi, especially in Arkansas, men would come in with pistols sticking out of their coat pockets or with long Bowie knives protruding from the legs of their boots. The manager had provided for these savage people, for every member of the company was armed and, at a given signal, stood on the defensive. We had a giant for a doorkeeper, who was known in one evening to kick down stairs as many as five of these bushwhackers with drawn knives in their hands. There were two other persons, employed ostensibly as ushers, but really to fight the wild men of the rivers. These two gentlemen were members of the New York prize ring, one of whom, I believe, went to Englaad with Heenan at the time of the international "mill," and whose name I saw in a New York paper the other day as the trainer of a pugilistic celebrity of the present time. The honest fellows scorned to use anything but their fists in preserving order; and it is strange, considering the number of deadly weapons drawn on them, that they never received anything worse than a few scratches. Nor did they, indeed, ever leave their antagonists with anything worse than a broken head; except in a solitary case, which befell at a backwoods landing on the Upper Mississippi, where a person who had made an unprovoked attack on the boats was left for dead on the bank as we pushed out in the stream. We never heard whether he lived or died.

Besides these pugilists, we had in our company other celebrities---for instance, the amiable and gentlemanly David Reed, whose character song of "Sally, Come Up," made such a furor not long ago in New York and, I believe, throughout the country. His picture is to be seen at all the music stores. One other of our company has since had his name and exploits telegraphed to the remotest ends of the earth. I remember to have read of him myself in a little German newspaper on the banks of the Danube. This was Professor Lowe, the balloonist, late of the Army of the Potomac. I doubt very much whether the Professor had dipped very deeply into aeronautics at that time. He was an ingenious, odd sort of Yankee, with his long hair braided and hanging in two tails down his back. His wife, formerly a Paris *danseuse*, was my instructor in the Terpsichorean art. By the aid of a little whip, which she insisted was essential to success, she taught me to go through all the posturings and pirouettes of the operatic ballet girls. I was forced often to remonstrate against the ardor with which she applied her whip to a toe or finger of mine which would get perversely out of the line of beauty.

Professor Lowe and Madame, his wife, conducted the performance of "The Invisible Lady," a contrivance that may not be familiar to all my readers. A hollow brass ball, with four trumpets protruding from it, is suspended inside a hollow railing. Questions put by the bystanders are answered through a tube by a person in the apartment beneath. The imaginations of the spectators make the sounds seem to issue from the brass ball. It used to be amusing to stand by and listen to the answers of "The Invisible Lady," alias Madame Lowe, whose English was drolly mixed up with her own vernacular. But if the responses were sometimes unintelligible, this only added to the mystery and success of the brazen oracle.

The Professor was passionately fond of game. He was struck with the abundance of turkeys in one of the Southern states where we chanced to be and, throwing his gun across his shoulder, sallied forth to bring some of them down. He returned shortly with two large black birds, which he exhibited about the decks amid the grins and suppressed laughter of the crew. It was not till the Professor took his game into the kitchen to have it dressed for dinner that he was informed not only that his birds were not turkeys at all, but that he had been breaking one of the statutes of the state, which prohibits, under pecuniary penalty, the killing of turkey buzzards.

In his social relations, a performer, like many another great man or woman, is liable to mistakes of head and heart. The ladies of the profession are sometimes given to gossip and backbiting in as great a degree at least as are the gentlemen. Jealousy may be as rife on a Mississippi show-boat as in the ante-chamber of any court in Europe. I have known a *danseuse* to furnish boys with clandestine bouquets to throw on the stage when she appeared; not that she cared at all for the praise or blame of the audience, but that she did care to crush a cleverer rival. I have known men, whose names have made some noise in the world, to measure with straws the comparative size of the letters in which they were announced on a poster. In our company on board the *Palace* and the *Raymond*, we had strange contrasts in human nature. It would happen, for instance, that the man who could not sleep without snoring would be placed in the same state room with the man who could not sleep within hearing of the most distant snore. The man who could not eat pork was seated at the table just opposite the man who doted on it. We had one gentleman---the fleshy bass singer already mentioned---who spent all his leisure in catching mockingbirds; and another, who passed his spare hours in contriving new and undiscoverable ways of letting these birds escape from the cages. There were on board ladies who had seen more prosperous days, when they were the chief attractions at the theatres of London, Paris and New York (according to their own stories); other ladies who had never associated with such vulgar people before; other ladies who hoped they would die if they did not leave the company at the very next landing, but never left; and yet other ladies, I am rejoiced to add, who were lovely in nature and deed---kind mothers and faithful wives, whose strength of character and ready cheerfulness tended as far as possible to restore the social equilibrium.

In the course of the long association, grotesque friendships sprang up. The man who played the bass drum was the bosom companion of the man who had charge of the machine for making the gas which supplied the two boats. The pretty man of the establishment, he who played the chimes on the top of the museum and the piano in the concert room---at present a popular composer at St. Louis---this young gentleman who broke all the hearts of the country girls that came into the show, was the inseparable friend of the pilot---a great, gruff, warm-hearted fellow, who steered the *Raymond* from the corners of his eyes and swore terribly at the snags. The man who dusted down Tam O'Shanter and the Twelve Apostles in wax and had especial care of the stuffed birds, giraffes, and alligators, was on most intimate terms with the cook. The youngest of the ladies who hoped to die if they didn't go ashore at the next landing and never went (or died either, for that matter), well, she was, or pretended to be, desperately in love with the treasurer of the company, a thin, irascible old fellow, with a bald head. On the arrival of another *danseuse* in the company, the two dancers, who were before deadly enemies, became sworn friends and confidants, united in their jealousy and hatred of the newcomer. The lady who was loudest in proclaiming that she had never before associated with such low people as the performers on board of these boats seemed to enjoy herself most, and indeed spent most of her time, in the society of Bridget, the Irish laundry-woman of the establishment, who on one occasion, after excessive stimulus, came very near hanging herself overboard to dry, instead of a calico dress.

As a general thing, however, the ladies, performers, and crew of our boats were not so quarrelsome as I have seen a set of cabin passengers on a sea voyage between America and Europe, or especially on the three weeks' passage to or from California. When I consider that there were so many of us together in this narrow compass for nearly a year, it seems to me strange indeed that there was not more bad blood excited.

Madame Olinza was, I believe, the name of the Polish lady who walked on a tight-rope from the floor of one end of the museum up to the roof of the farthest gallery. This kind of perilous ascension and suspension was something new in the country then. It was before the time of Blondin, and Madame used to produce a great sensation. Now, it may be interesting to the general reader to learn that this tight-rope walker was one of the most exemplary, domestic little bodies imaginable. She and her husband had a large state room on the upper deck of the *Raymond*, and she was always there with her child when released from her public duties. One afternoon the nurse happened to bring the child into the museum when Madame Olinza was on the rope; and out of the vast audience, that little face was recognized by the fond mother and her attention so distracted that she lost her balance, dropped pole, and fell. Catching the rope with her hands, however, in time to break her fall, she escaped, fortunately, without the least injury; but ever after that her child was kept out of the audience while she was on the rope.

Going up the Mississippi from Cairo, we passed, one Sunday, the old French town of Cape Girardeau, Missouri, and its Roman Catholic college on the river bank. The boys were out on the lawn under the trees and I became as envious of their lot as I ever had been before of a man who worked on a steamboat or who danced "in the minstrels." I suddenly resolved that I would go to that college. We did not stop at Cape Girardeau till our return down the river some weeks afterwards. Then I went boldly up and sought an interview with the president of the institution. I found him to be a kindly mannered priest, who encouraged me in my ambition. He told me it would be well to save up more money than I then had and that he would do all he could for me.

I returned to the *Palace* and immediately gave warning that I purposed leaving as soon as someone could be got to fill my place. It struck me as somewhat odd that it was six months from that date before I could get away. It has been explained to me since. The fact is, I received what, as a boy, I thought a good salary, but nothing like what I earned. It took two men afterwards to fill my place. I have been told since, that more than a year before that time, and prior to this last engagement, the late E. P. Christy had written for me from New York, but that the letter had been intercepted by those whose interest it then was that I should not know my own value in the "profession." I used to see that my name was larger than almost any other on the bills, but was led to believe that it was because I was a boy and not likely to excite the jealousy of the other members of the company. It may not be very soothing to my vanity, but, dwelling upon these things dispassionately,

I have my honest doubts now whether I was not always a greater success as an advertisement than as a performer.

I was promised at New Orleans that if I would go over to Galveston, Texas, with the minstrel troupe, I should certainly be allowed to retire from public life. So we left the *Palace* and the *Raymond* at the levee of the former city and took passage in the regular steamship crossing the Gulf to Galveston. We performed there two or three weeks with great success. Few minstrels had then wandered that way, and thus it happened that my farewell appearance as a dancer was greeted with a crowded house. Except as a poor lecturer, I have never been on the stage since I left Galveston.

Still resolved to go to college at Cape Girardeau, I returned to New Orleans, and took passage to Cairo on the steamer *L. M. Kenett*. Barney Williams and his wife were on board during the tedious voyage; but I suppose they have long since forgotten all about the urchin who surprised and bored them with his minute knowledge of the early history of the country through which we passed. The river above Cairo, very much to my sorrow, was frozen over, for it was midwinter. There was no alternative for me but to proceed to Cape Girardeau by land---a long, difficult, and expensive journey in those times. After a great deal of trouble and some danger, I arrived at the gates of the college and proceeded directly to the room of the president. The kindly face that I remembered so well again beamed upon me, as I again stood before him and said that I had come to stay a year, at least, at his school. At his good-natured question as to how much money I had, I emptied my pocket of just thirty-five dollars in gold. That was the sum to which the unforeseen expenses of my long journey had reduced me. The president being aware that the river was frozen---so that I could not get away even if I had had money enough to go with---and having much greater discretionary power than the presidents of our Protestant colleges, told me that I might stay.

At the end of my year the river was again frozen and the good president was again prevailed upon to keep me till the close of that college term, which would be in the middle of the ensuing summer. So I was for sixteen months in all a student in Saint Vincent's College. Most of the students were the sons of French planters of Louisiana and the institution was more French than English. Things were ordered very much as they are in the religious houses of Europe. We slept in large dormitories, and ate in a refectory, someone reading aloud the while from an English or a French book. The college had its own tailors and shoemakers; and by the favor of the president, who seemed to take a great liking to me, my credit was made good for anything I wanted and I was provided for as well as the richest of them. The instructors were all priests and generally good men. I was never required to change my religion or to conform more than externally to their worship. The president, Father S. V. Ryan, has since met the recognition which his piety and abilities so justly deserved. Within the past year, if I have read the papers aright, he has been made Roman Catholic Bishop of Buffalo. I applied myself so zealously to study, that at the expiration of my sixteen months, I was nearly prepared to enter Kenyon College, in which I spent the next four years.

When I came to leave Saint Vincent's, I drew out a deposit which I had in a bank in Toledo, and gave it into the hands of the college treasurer, reserving for myself only what I thought would be enough to take me back to Ohio. As good luck would have it, the little steamer *Banjo*, a showboat belonging to Dr. Spalding, the manager of the *Floating Palace*, was advertised to be at Cape Girardeau the week in which I proposed to leave there. Seeing the names of some of my old comrades on the bills, I waited to meet them. They generously made me bring my trunk on board, and have a free ride to St. Louis, or, if I chose, to Alton, where I was to take the cars for Chicago. The remembrance of this trip up the river with these jovial, reckless souls has made it my duty always to defend my old associates when I hear the censure heaped on them by inconsiderate ignorance or blind prejudice.

And I can take my final leave of the show business and of show people in no better way, I think, than in relating an incident which occurred on this little steamer. On the afternoon before our arrival at Alton, as I was sitting on the deck by the side of one of the performers---Mr. Edwin Davis, who had been a member of our company on the Floating Palace---he asked me to let him see my money, adding that I might have had imposed upon me some of the "wildcat" bills then afloat. Taking out all I had, I placed it in his hands. He counted it and scrutinized it thoroughly and, folding it up carefully, returned it to me with the remark that my bills were all good. I had no occasion to use my money till I came to pay my railway fare at Alton, when I discovered that my wealth had increased by nearly half. He had, indeed, been a better judge than myself of my necessities; for, with his generous addition, I had barely enough to take me to my destination.

I met Mr. Davis in New York years afterwards and offered him the sum he had added to mine, but could not prevail upon him to take it. And this is the way he stated his reason:

"No; it does not belong to me. Keep it till you see some poor fellow as much in need of it as you were then on the Mississippi and give it to him."

Tony Pastor

THE YOUNGER GENERATION IN MINSTRELSY
AND REMINISCENCES OF THE PAST
By Frank Dumont [*New York Clipper*, March 27, 1915]

Much space has been given to the old timers of minstrelsy, but were it not for the younger generation and the new blood from time to time injected into it, minstrelsy would have perished long ago. Many clever ideas and innovations were brought into it by the young and ambitious element. This began almost as soon as the older performers retired or passed away. The old timers in minstrelsy were a "close corporation" and did not welcome the young aspirant with much warmth. On the contrary, they frowned upon all innovations and were contented to stand pat.

Minstrelsy was not quite twenty years old when the Civil War began, and had been inaugurated by men in middle life. These, of course, could not hold out against time or innovations. Young singers, musicians, dancers, and comedians were knocking at the doors for admission and, as troupes were being enlarged, their services were welcome and timely. The banjo playing of the old-timer was something that would not be tolerated at present. It was banging and twanging and plunketty plunk, used probably for plantation songs of a hilarious or noisy order. The banjos were almost devoid of the fine tone of later years.

The first of the fine banjos were made by the Dobson Bros., who were also expert players. There was Charley, George and Frank, who were also teachers of that instrument. Charley played the banjo in the orchestra of Wallack's Theatre, Thirteenth Street, corner of Broadway, early in the Civil War days, in an overture depicting camp life in our army. Jimmy Clark made some fine banjos, so did a Mr. Farnham, of Troy, N.Y. Frank B. Converse, an excellent banjoist, turned out some fine instruments also. From the rattling banjo playing, descriptive of a "coal cart and an express wagon racing," came the more artistic playing of marches, waltzes and difficult selections. An idea may be gained of the banjo solo of early times when Billy Arlington used to take a common broom and use it as a banjo for his solo turn. He it was who first introduced feathers or rope for whiskers; deep-seated pantaloons, small hats, and boys' jackets and vests. He was a clever all around comedian.

I have Sam Devere's banjos, including the fine presentation instrument once the property of Horace Weston, the colored banjoist.Harry Stanwood performed difficult music on his banjo, and so did Billy Carter and Jim Roome. One of the greatest of players was George Powers of the firm of Johnson and Powers; but E. M. Hall, in his time, was the greatest of them all. Edwin French was a close second. Then there was Lew Brimmer who played the "Chimes" on his banjo and a march, called "The Seventh Regiment Coming Down Broadway." There were also "Pickayune" Butler, Billy West, Andy Collum, Sam Sharpley, Frank Moran, Dick Little and others of the early sixties.

Hi Rumsey performed upon his banjo while standing up, and was called "The Lion Banjoist." Dick Sweeney and Joe Sweeney were the earliest banjo players in minstrelsy. Among the very earliest comedians can be named the Original Four Virginia Minstrels, Frank Brower, Dan Emmett, R. W. Pelham, and Billy Whitlock. Then the Power Brothers, John and James; Earl Pierce, Matt Peel, George Christy, Ben Mallory, Jerry Bryant, Moody Stanwood, W. White, Frank Pell, Frank Germon, W. Harrington and S. C. Howard. Some of these were with Major Dumbolton's "Ethiopian Serenaders," who went to England in 1844.

Then came old Bob Sheppard, Eph Horn, Jim Sanford, Bill Laconta, George Kunkel, Mick Campbell, Billy Birch, Johnny Pell, Frank Moran, Sam Sanford, Swayne Buckley, George Christy, E. P. Christy, Lansing Durand, W. Porter, William B. Donaldson, Tom Briggs, Sam Wells, Edwin Deaves, Pop Jones, Billy Lom, and Charley Morris, Neil Bryant, Charley Reynolds, John Carle, J. G. H. Shorey, Pony Moore, Charley Backus, Joe Murphy, Ben Cotton, E. F. Dixey, Harry Lehr, Johnny Duly, Cool White and a few others that brings this list to the middle fifties. Then we have Tony Hernandez, John Mulligan, Max Irwin, J. H. Budworth, and W. S. Budworth, George Thatcher, W. W. Newcomb, Nick Bowers, G. W. H. Griffin, Marshall S. Pike, Master Floyd, and Ned Davis. Among the very earliest vocalists were: Nelson Kneass, Jack Herman, Max Zorer, Tom Christian, T. B. Prendergast, Ambrose Thayer, Warren White, John R. Hector, S. P. Ball, J. Lynch, William P. Collins, J. H. Rainer, and J. W. Raynor, J. P. Trowbridge, Doctor Ordway, Edwin Kelly, Sig. Gustave Bideaux, Sig. R. Abecco, Chas. F. Shattuck, J. R. Thomas, J. A. Basquin, Charles Henry, Charles Campbell (Templeton) and James Carroll.

On some early bills of the Buckleys will be seen the name of S. Samuels. This comedian was known later as S. S. Sanford, he having attached the name of Sanford to it. He was a very capable man, and was the manager of S. S. Sanford's Minstrels in the old Eleventh Street Opera House from 1855 to 1862. Just a few years before the Civil War we find the names of the following singers on the bills: Sher Campbell, J. L. Carncross, Dave Wambold, Edwin Holmes, Jules Stratton, M. Ainsley Scott, Jack Hilton, George Washington Dixon, Rollin Howard, etc.

At one time the early minstrels affected beards or chin whiskers. These were worn by Frank Brower, S. S. Sanford, Sam Sharpley, Charles Henry, Cool White, Dave Wambold, R. M. Hooley, E. P. Christy, Johnny Booker, William H. Bernard, Sam Wells, Sam Gardner, Hank White and a few others. Then the style changed to the long thick mustaches that dropped down below the jaws. Billy Morris was the first to thus appear. Then came Cool Burgess, Nick Bowers, Charles H. Duprez, Edwin Holmes, G. W. H. Griffin, Frank Cilly, C. C. Templeton, William P. Spaulding, Mocking Bird Green, Ike Withers, Edwin Kelly, Hugh Hamill and E. M. Kayne. Charley Reynolds had a long strip on his chin, and he could make it wiggle to and fro. Archie Hughes also had a chin piece. Cool

Burgess and a few others later tried side whiskers. Even Hughey Dougherty returned from South Africa with reddish side whiskers, but the boys "guyed" him until he had them removed.

An act that was quite popular for many years was "Old Bob Ridley," and the representative of the aged colored individual. He needed a crooked cane and a red bandana handkerchief to mop the perspiration from the top of his bald head. Among the earliest was Eph Horn, in the "Power of Music;" then Ben Cotton, as Old Uncle Snow; J. P. Trowbridge, as the old Sexton. John Mulligan, Lon Morris and Bob Hart were fine old darkies. Then "Old Black Joe" found a representative in Marsh Adams, Billy Sweatnam, Sam Devere, Johnny Ray, Harry Bloodgood, Milt Barlow, Frank Cushman, Old Charley Howard, Harry Woodson, Lew Baker, George Thatcher, Golden and Hughes, Ralph Wray and Walter Bray.

The opening chorus of the troupes were: "Down the River, Down the Ohio," "Joy, Joy, Freedom To-day," "Dinah's Wedding," etc. The Buckleys introduced "Operatic Choruses" from the different operas. The Buckleys built the Opera House at 585 Broadway, but it did not long remain in their possession. White faces and female vocalists did not suit the minstrel patrons, and they vacated the place. At one era all the titles and songs in minstrelsy were of girls and sweethearts. They were praised an loved in the first verse, but then all died in the second verse. I dare say they could not stand the excessive praise and love-making. You will find this to be the theme in the following songs: "Nellie Was a Lady," "Carrie Lee," "Rosa Lee," "Kitty Wells," "Hazel Dell," "Belle Brandon," "Ellen Bayne," "Nettie Moore," "Kitty Clyde," "Rosalie, the Prairie Flower," "Gentle Annie," "Lottie Lee," "Sadie Ray," "Jenny With the Light Brown Hair," and a dozen others in the same strain. In recent years the authors picked all the mountains and rivers as subjects for songs. During the Civil War the songs were of the battlefield, home and mother, or dying for the flag. "When This Cruel War is Over," "Marching Through Georgia" have outlived those stirring days. "Dixie," the product of minstrelsy, lives as one of our national songs, and belongs to the entire country.

It would be impossible to mention the names of all the new talent coming into minstrelsy between 1860 and 1870. Many of the troupes were short lived, and many good amateur companies finally drifted into it and became part and parcel of the regular organized troupes. Very often troupes changed titles and re-appeared under other names, with a different "angel," but always with the same membership. "Whitmore & Clark's Minstrels" were very popular for years in the Eastern States. It was with this company that the first triple clog dance was introduced by Stiles, Phelps and Johnny Armstrong. Years afterwards Primrose, Goodyear and Whiting introduced a triple clog dance, also.

Late in the sixties and early in the seventies, I find Jerry Cohan (father of our George) with the Morris Bros. Minstrels and La Rue's Carnival Minstrels. He is flourishing as an "end man" and doing the "Dublin Dancing Master" in the olio, or second part. Joe Norrie's name appears on bills of Sam Sharpley's Minstrels, also Frank Campbell. These names are mentioned to show the leaven working its way forward, and adding new vim and strength to minstrelsy. Such artists as M.

Ainsley Scott, Gustave Bideaux, J. Brandisi, Edwin Kelly and Gonsalvo Bishop had become known in the late fifties.

Once in a while some little oddity appeared, such as "Japanese Tommy" or "Little Mac," and added to the attraction. George Christy had been very clever and introduced some clever things on the minstrel stage, such as "Granny and Her Son." The son was a stuffed figure in front of him. He was very popular as "Lucy Long," and was the first to present the bloomer girl. This was a freakish sort of a Doctor Mary Walker dress, and created a sensation when worn by a Mrs. Bloomer. The wits seized upon it for ridiculous pictures and verses, and Christy imperson- ated the "Advanced" woman of that day, which we now call "Suffragette." Cool White, Eph Horn and W. W. Newcomb delivered speeches, called "Woman's Rights."

The minstrel boys were among those pioneers, the men of '49 and spring of '50, who swarmed to the California gold mines. They went around the horn or across the Isthmus of Panama. All the well known names of the popular minstrels of the Eastern States are to be found upon the early programs of the San Francisco halls or hastily built theatres, such as the "Jenny Lind," managed by Tom Maguire, the pioneer manager of the Pacific Coast, and the "Forest Theatre." The name of Birch, Backus, Joe Murphy, William White (Bernard), Sam Wells, Charles Henry, Sher Campbell, Edwin Deaves, Charles Shattuck, Neil Bryant, George H. Coes, Frank Moran and a host of others who flocked to the new Eldorado.

In 1854 E. P. Christy took his entire company to the Coast. Early in the Civil War days "Lotta," appeared with the minstrels. Her banjo playing, dancing, mimicking and grotesque humor were acquired from the minstrels, of course. She was a grand drawing card in the East in later years. Young talent went into the ranks of the California troupes. The names of Johnny De Angelis (father of Jeff) appears, also Fred Sprung, Johnny Mack, Tommy Bree, Tim Darling, William H. Barker, Tom Raleigh, Frank Hussey. The minstrel troupes would not he complete without alluding to Billy Emerson, who located there for many seasons in the eighties. From 'Frisco came that talented comedian and stage producer, George Marion, who was an end man with Lew Dockstader's Minstrels. Great names like Unsworth and Eugene now appear, also Master Adams, Tommy Gettings, T. J. Peel, George Charles, Charley Gardner, "Hop Lite Lou," A. J. Talbott, George Gray, George Guy Sr., Louis Nevers, William P. Collins, and M. B. Leavitt, who is now a theatrical magnate, but was a clever minstrel comedian in the early sixties. Leavitt was the first to organize a female minstrel troupe, and called it "Madam Rentz's Female Minstrels." From this sprang all the burlesque shows in which females predominated.

The San Francisco Minstrels, headed by Birch, Wambold, Bernard and Backus, located at 585 Broadway in April, 1865, and became great favorites and successful in that once "Jonah" house. They removed uptown in the early '70s, and after awhile moved again to Twenty-ninth Street, corner of Broadway, from the place on Twenty-eighth Street, called St. James Hall (same block of the Gilsey estate). Here Beaumont Reed, Carl Rudolph, H. W. Frillman, William Dwyer and young singers, dancers and comedians began to bud and blossom into popularity.

Francis Wilson and his partner, Mackin, performed in songs and dances for a few seasons. "Ricardo" gained popularity here, so did Johnson and Powers, Bobby Newcomb, Add Ryman, Bob Hart, Joe Norrie and a host of others.

In 1866 Ben Cotton's Minstrels had succeeded Cotton & Murphy's Minstrels. They presented Jake Budd, Frank Campbell, C. H. Atkinson and Joe Norrie. Jake Tannenbaum was the musical director. Mr. Tannenbaum is now a celebrated theatrical manager down South, especially well known in Mobile, Ala.

Early in the Civil War, General Ben Butler coined a new word for the minstrels, which proved both funny and of interest. To all the Negro refugees who were flocking to Fortress Monroe, having escaped from their masters, he applied the term, "Contrabands of War." The papers took up the phrase, and in fact everybody talked about it, and the word "Contraband" crept into our conversation. The minstrels were quick to attach the word to songs, nigger acts and speeches. "The Happy Contraband," "Contraband From Dixie," "Contraband's Lament," "Contraband Children," "Contraband's Adventures" and "Contraband Brothers" appeared on all programs, and furnished subjects for all kinds of songs and dances.

Another phrase used even at the present time relates to the same era. The term, "Hamfatter." This was taken from a popular song called "The Ham Fat Man." This is the chorus:

> Ham fat--Ham fat,
> Zig-a-Zaw-Zan.
> Ham fat--Ham fat
> Smoking in de pan.
> Get you to the kitchen
> Quickly as you can.
> Rootchie--Kootchie--Kootchie
> I'm de Ham fat man.

Almost any new applicant when asked, "What do you sing and dance?" would reply, "I can do the Ham Fat Man." And hence was called a "Ham Fatter." "The Contraband's Adventures" related how a band of "abolitionists" took a colored brother to make him the equal of the white man. How they washed him, scraped him and nearly skinned him, to make him white, but failed. The concluding lines of the chorus tell the sad tale of the attempt:

> Dey rubbed and dey scrubbed,
> Oh! dey kept at it all dat night,
> And dey found next day
> Dat de job--it wouldn't pay,
> Kase dey nebber could wash a nigger white.

It need hardly be said that this was greeted by yells from democratic listeners in those troubled times.

232

The expression "In the Soup" is taken from the minstrels, and is of vintage of 1860, possibly earlier. When the minstrel comedian flung his battered hat, torn umbrella, or old carpet bag into the entrances he would say, "Put them in the soup." If one comedian would say to the other one, "Where's my hat?" the reply would be "In the soup."

Another incident much used in farce comedies was the individual thrown through a window and returning all "torn up," clothing in rags, his face streaked with red paint and chalk, and, in fact, mangled almost to death. It is not a clever new idea of the farce comedy writer. It was used before the Civil War in "Skylight Adventures" and also in "Beasley's Dog," as any old timer will tell you.

In presenting a partial list of some of the minstrel troupes, with the names of members, a history of minstrelsy is not contemplated. It would consume too much space, and this article is intended to present the new faces and names of the younger element coming into the field. In the list of the companies, new names appear in addition to the older professionals, but it will be noticed they are gradually forcing the older ones aside. Here and there familiar names continue to appear for a few years, then the younger element are much in evidence. By glancing over a collection of old minstrel bills this will be clearly shown. For instance, when the San Francisco Minstrels opened No. 585 Broadway in April, 1865, they introduced several names new to the theatregoers of New York. Cooper and Fields were young clog dancers, Ira Paine was a new singer, who later in life became the champion rifle shot of America. William Henry Rice had left Cotton & Murphy's Minstrels to join this new company. William Henry Rice had formerly been known as William H. Lewis. He was a grand burlesque actor, and became very popular with the "Friscoes."

Whitmore & Clark's Minstrels had the following young talent in 1866: Andy Wyatt, Johnny Armstrong, Thomas Maynard, Hank White, G. M. Clark, Boyle Brothers, J. B. Porter, etc., etc.

The minstrel world was stirred up considerably when a powerful confederation was formed by John Dingess, and called Burgess, Hughes, Prendergast & Donniker's Minstrels. This was the longest title yet assumed by any troupe, although in the early '50s a troupe with a long title had toured for a short time. It was called "Shorey, Carle, Duprez & Green's Minstrels." It was shortly condensed to Shorey, Duprez & Green. Then Duprez & Green, and finally Duprez & Benedict. But "Burgess, Hughes, Prendergast & Donniker" (or later La Rue) was the longest titled troupe ever announced on modern billboards or walls.

They had in their company Paul Berger, O. P. Sweet, Frank Bowles, Dion De Marbelle, Henry French, C. S. Fredericks, A. C. Stone, J. Saxton, Dave Thompson and an orchestra, presided over by John Donniker. This musician was an excellent "solo violinist," and performed also upon a peculiar instrument called the "melophone." Very few performers ever mastered this instrument. Fred and Swayne Buckley were fine players on it, so was William H. Smith. Ned Catlin possessed one of them and I have another. These are probably the only ones in existence at the present time. Of the above confederation, Donniker dropped out, and D. C. La Rue's name appears in his place as the proprietor. The names change until it becomes "Burgess & La Rue's Minstrels," then finally, "La Rue's Carnival Minstrels," and the name of H. W. Eagan appears on the bills, also Brandisi, Fredericks, Charles Church, S. S. Purdy, "Utica Boys," Kanane and West, Ned Kneeland, etc.

In 1868 another stir was created by the organizing of Emerson, Allen & Manning's Minstrels. They had in their company a great many "lured or borrowed" from La Rue's Minstrels. They had Dr. Hanmer, C. S. Fredericks, E. S. Rosenthal, Charles Wheaton, Kelly and Holly, Master Eddie, Frank Bowles, C. A. Boyd, leader, and Willie Guy, and later Stevie Rogers. They opened at Tony Pastor's Opera House, No. 201 Bowery, June 30, 1868. They remained but two weeks.

At one time Sandy Spencer was one of the best known men in New York City. He kept a saloon near the Theatre Comique, 514 Broadway---in a basement. This place was always crowded with theatrical people. Sandy ran afoul of the Sunday excise law and a Judge sent him to the county jail for one month. A minstrel wit who heard of it penned the following lines and fastened it to Sandy's door: "Thirty days hath September, April, June and Sandy Spencer."

In the old days, a gambler by the name of Dupree Dodge was well known to the circus, minstrel and theatrical fraternity. He was what might be called an old river "skin" gambler, depending upon marked cards for a sure thing. These cards were marked in a peculiar manner among the ornamental scrolls of the backs of the pasteboards. In the hands of a confederate or a victim Old Dodge could always tell what the person held in his "hand." It seems that Dodge retired and opened an oyster saloon. Charley Backus called to see how the ex-gambler was getting along. He found Dodge in a small store, behind a counter, with just one bushel of oysters dumped upon it. Then entered a customer who called for a half dozen of Shrewsbury oysters. Dodge took and opened the oysters from the only pile on the counter. Another customer came in and called for Blue Points. Dodge took them from the same pile of oysters. Another entered and asked for Saddle Rocks, the old gambler took them from the same lot. Charley Backus could not stand it any longer, but blurted out. "Gee, old man! You can still tell them by the backs, can't you?"

The march of the theatres and the places of amusement uptown in New York City was led by the minstrels. They were the first to "move up." In 1866, George Christy opened his New Opera House on Twenty-fourth Street, near Broadway, rear of Fifth Avenue Hotel, as it then stood. George Christy advertised on all his bills: "The Only Place of Amusement Above Fourteenth Street," and so it was. July 20, 1867, Horace Chase opened a Minstrel Opera House on the Southwest corner of Thirty-fourth Street and Eighth Avenue. He fitted up the second floor of the storage house with a stage and some scenery. It was a flat floor and had no gallery. The performances were given by "Chase's Minstrels," consisting of: Hughey Dougherty, S. S. Purdy, C. C. Templeton, George H. Coes, J. W. Hilton, Charley Church, Dave Reed, J. W. Clark, Charley Fox, John Sivori, W. L. Hobbs, Hi Melville, etc. They did not last three months.

George Christy's Twenty-fourth Street Opera House was later called "The Madison Square Theatre." In front of this place a shooting scrape took place after a matinee performance, in which Kelly, Leon and Sam Sharpley were implicated. Sam Sharpley's brother Tom was killed and Kelly wounded. He was tried and acquitted. The row began over the engagement of Delehanty and Hengler by these rival minstrel managers. These dancers were popular, and much sought after. Sam Sharpley accused Kelly and Leon of enticing them from a contract engagement, and hence the ill feeling and shooting affair. Both troupes suffered by the unpleasant notoriety and hastened their closing in this city.

Jerry Cohan (father of "our George") was in minstrelsy in 1867-68. He was an end man and comedian with the Morris Brothers Minstrels, of Boston. He introduced Irish dialect in his jokes and songs. He portrayed "The Dancing Professor," "The Irish Dancing Master" and "Paddy Miles' Boy." He wrote many comic and sentimental songs. He was for a season with La Rue's Carnival Minstrels. He was always ambitious and adding novel items to his line of business. He was for a time with Howarth's Panorama of Ireland, as Barney, the guide. Then he drifted back into minstrelsy and later to the vaudevilles of that day. The night of Jerry's wedding, in Providence, R. I., Dumont invited Jerry and his bride to witness the show. Not knowing the pair were united in marriage, the boys on the stage guyed them as they would a love stricken pair from the country.

Billy Emerson was the first man to ever present the "Hebrew" on the stage in dialect. He did it in an act called "The Old Clothes Dealer," wherein he tried to sell a coat that did not fit, etc. This act is on the bill of the above troupe June 30, 1868. Dave Wambold was the very first black face Dutchman ever seen on the minstrel stage. He did this act with the Bryants in 1858-59. Johnny Allen withdrew from the Emerson, Allen & Manning Company. It was then called Emerson & Manning, and about 1872-73, Manning's Minstrels.

Newcomb's Minstrels for 1868 had "Chang" the Chinese Giant, Carroll (Jim) Johnson, Dave Wilson, Harry Robinson, C. C. Palmer, Myron Calice, J. T. Gulick, Charles Hudson, J. R. Dudley, C. W. Millard, N. D. Roberts, manager. In 1869, Morris Bros. Minstrels announced that during the "Peace Jubilee" they will perform in two different theatres at the same time (in Boston). This is in their New Opera House, opposite the Coliseum, and their old place opposite the old South Church.

Some of the clever clog and song and dance teams were: Hogan and Hughes, Fox and Ward, Cooper and Fields, Kanane and West, Carroll and Childs, Pankhurst and Collins, Henri Stuart, Johnson and Pendy, Cogill and Cooper, Jake and Willie Budd, the Guy Bros., Harris and Carroll, McKee and Rogers, Quilter and Goldrick, Utica Boys, Empire Boys, Buffalo Boys, Kerns and Thompson, and the great Delehanty and Hengler, Bobby Newcomb and Billy Emerson. Fred Wilson had introduced the clog dance on the minstrel stage several years before the Civil War. Then came Dick Sands, Tim Hayes, Mort Williams, and several very clever wooden shoe dancers as they called it then. Some later announced it as a "See-Ell-Oh-Gee" dance. Luke Schoolcraft's first venture was in Dutch songs and dances until several hits as a "blackface" performer landed him in the minstrel ranks. There were several "Young Americans" in the early days. Hughey Dougherty was the most famous, and has outlived them all. At the present writing Hughey resides in Philadelphia, resting upon his laurels.

In 1870, Duprez & Benedict's Minstrels went to San Francisco, being the first organized troupe to go over the Pacific Railroad, then just completed for through traffic. They were the first to present "four end men," Benedict, Dougherty, Gleason and Reynolds. With this troupe were: Warren Richards, D. S. Vernon, Fred B. Naylor, Frank Dumont, Fox and Ward, Gonsalvo Bishop, and a full brass band and orchestra. Duprez was the first manager to introduce a brass band in conjunction with the minstrel troupe, and made a street parade. Other managers ridiculed this innovation, but they soon fell in and did likewise. Haverly was not the first to parade "Forty, Count Them, Forty." Duprez paraded about "sixty" persons, mostly musicians, when Duprez & Benedict's Minstrels performed in the Chestnut Street Theatre, Philadelphia, in the early seventies. He was the first to have the semblance of a uniform for a street parade. It was a dark broadcloth cape lined with red, the ends turned back. This with black pants and silk hats at least gave the parade a neat effect for those early times and attracted attention.

And while on the subject of correction, let me say that "Fox and Ward" are absolutely the oldest "Blackface" team on the American stage and are still in harness. Again, "Dixie" was not sung on the stage of Bryant's Minstrels for the first time as chronicled; neither did Old Dan Emmett write it especially for the Bryants. Emmett sang "Dixie" some years previous down South and never denied it. Al G. Field is my informant and he positively knows.

Dumont was the first to sing "Silver Threads Among the Gold," for whom it was written by H. P. Danks. He also first introduced "When You and I Were Young, Maggie" as the Duprez & Benedict's Minstrels programs, dated, will show and the still living members of that celebrated troupe remember well.

While Duprez & Benedict's Company was en route to the Coast, the troupe was reported to be attacked by the Indians, some killed and scalped and a few wounded. This was rumored to have happened near Elko, Nevada. I sent the report to The N. Y. Herald, which published it, creating a great sensation, until it could be "contradicted." Meanwhile, Charley Reynold's brother-in-law journeyed from Lowell, Mass., to Salt Lake City, Utah, to get his body and bring it East. Charley loved the red wine; and when brother-in-law came, he was paralyzed. The joke was that Charley had to pay his brother-in-law's fare back East, as he had arrived in Salt Lake broke. Charley hunted for the author of the hoax and had he discovered the culprit there would have been blood on the face of the moon. Of course I remained under cover, Dougherty being the only one who knew about it but he kept the secret until the storm blew over.

A few of the superstitions handed down from the old days still survive, although we do not generally admit it. For instance, no one wished to occupy room 13. In many hotels or dressing rooms the number is omitted. It was very unlucky to open an umbrella in a theatre. It was considered unlucky to walk under a ladder. I have seen an entire troupe, band and all, while parading on the sidewalk, suddenly come to a ladder. The entire troupe would circle out into the muddy street around the ladder and onto the sidewalk again. If you bragged of your health or any anticipated pleasure, you had to "knock wood." The most dreaded person was a "Jonah"; old timers firmly believed in them. Woe to the musician who joined the show and displayed a yellow clarinet. Bad business would overtake the show and the "Jonah" had to be gotten rid of. A cross-eyed man, a peculiar hat or an ancient carpet bag was a "Jonah." Some poor devils had the reputation of being one and were always blamed for poor business and accordingly had to be dismissed. If you saw a wagon loaded with barrels, it was a good sign. You would have a good house that night. It was seven years bad luck to break a looking-glass in the old time "Opry House."

A minstrel company in hard luck (with a "Jonah" somewhere) came to a town to remain "one night only." Just as the doors opened for the night show, a most violent storm of wind and rain broke loose. The rain fell in a deluge. The minstrels all made up, peered through a hole in the curtain and saw one lonesome man in the parquet. The manager stepped before the curtain to address this man.

He said: "My dear sir, you have ventured out in this terrific storm and you deserve to see a good show. We will not cut the program, but play it as if a thousand persons had assembled to see it."

"All right," said the lone man. "Hurry it up, for I'm the janitor and want to lock up and go home."

November 16, 1884, Thatcher, Primrose & West had: McNish, Banks Winter, Chauncey Olcott, Frank Howard (author of many popular songs), Billy Rice, Harry M. Morse, Harry Talbert, John Daly, Willie Girard, Burt Sherrard, Will Raymond, Charles Noble (basso), George Edwards, Sam Weston, T. Ward, George Turner, W. Wood, J. P. O'Keefe, with Charles F. Warner as musical director. Almost the same time Haverly's Mastodons announced: Carroll Johnson, Hughey Dougherty, Joe Garland, J. W. Meyers, Billy Richardson, Bobby Newcomb, Walter Hawkins, George Powers, Paul Vernon, the Three Gorman Brothers, Harry J. Armstrong, Dan Thompson, John S. Robinson, Seamon and Girard, W. H. Bishop and Charley Young.

McNish, Johnson & Slavin's Minstrels created quite a stir in the minstrel world when they launched their enterprise in 1885. They had some startling novelties with their show and jumped into instantaneous popularity and success. They had then the youngest manager in minstrelsy, W. S. Cleveland. It was his first opportunity in that capacity and he stirred up everything and everybody. Cleveland is now the head of a vaudeville agency and the producer of high class acts. After the above venture he piloted the Cleveland & Haverly Minstrels and then his own company. He imported the Cragg Family of acrobats and they created a big sensation. He had a company of minstrel stars, the names of which are to be found in the Haverly or Emerson Companies. To return to the McNish, Johnson & Slavin troupe, here are the names of that confederation: Billy McAllister, George W. Powers, Bob Slavin, Frank E. McNish, Carroll Johnson, Frank Howard, Harry M.

Morse, John Davis, W. W. Black, Raymond Shaw, George Hassell, Martin Hogan, Ernest Sinclair, William F. Holmes, Joseph Garland, Fox Samuels, Marcus Doyle, Willie Pickert, John Daly, Johnny Keegan, William Henry Rice, Henry Carmody, Larry McEvoy, Harry Long, John and Bob Morrissey, Mike Talbott, Dan Quinlan, master of transportation. Frank Bowles led the band and William Skuse was musical director; John Cressville, solo cornet. In the olio they had Nelsonia, a fine juggler; Fox and Van Auken, horizontal bar performers; the Selbini Family (five in number). They also had Charley Mitchel, the English Champion, and William Muldoon, Champion Wrestler of the World, in classic statue representation. Mr. Muldoon is the proprietor of a sanitarium in White Plains, N. Y. Charley Mitchell is in England. McNish is still popular in vaudeville, and Carroll Johnson now and then appears as a director or for his own amusement and is still sought after.

Frank Howard, one of the most popular composers and singers, was a feature with the minstrel troupes who were fortunate enough to secure his services. "When the Robins Nest Again," "Only a Pansy Blossom," "Sweet Alpine Roses," "I'll Await, My Love" were his best known ballads. He died at the home of his childhood, Greeley, Ia., December 4, 1914. Like many another he broke into the minstrel business with Happy Cal Wagner and then sang with the best troupes in the burnt cork line, including Barlow, Wilson, Primrose & West, McNish, Johnson & Slavin, and Cleveland's Minstrels, writing new songs at frequent intervals. In ten years, from 1880 to 1890, his compositions netted him over $250,000. Then he married and settled down on a stock farm; but misfortune followed all his operations, lightning struck his stock barn in Dakota and killed sixty head of fine horses, and fourteen head of registered Jersey cattle, and he quit country life, and for a number of years managed a theatre at Jacksonville, Ill. Later he toured with several dramatic companies, singing his favorite ballads with much of his former skill and sweetness between the acts as a feature.

In 1884 the Standard Minstrels, in San Francisco, Cal., had: Carroll Johnson, Al. Holland, Franz Wetter, Charley Reed, W. J. Morant, Harry Wyatt, William Henry Rice, John Robinson, Tommy Bree, Hooley Thompson, Keegan and Wilson.

C. W. Vreeland's Minstrels announced: George Hassall, soprano; Bassett and Cole, Arthur Deming, Harry Long, Hugh Franey, Billy Fries, Kennedy and Vonder, and George Dunbar.

Gorton's New Orleans Minstrels (1906) had Jake Welby, Sam Lee, Arthur Fulton, Fred Long, A. D. Roland, Welby and Pearl, C. T. Bell and R. J. Howland.

Careful research gives the first song and dance as "Jump Jim Crow" as sung by Daddy Rice. He sang verses and danced a few grotesque steps between them. Of course this would come under the heading of Negro dancing. Master Diamond and Juba, the colored boy, also danced but their efforts were in the form of jigs. Later these jigs were danced under the titles of "Champion Jig," "Rattlesnake Jig," "Smoke House Jig," "Grape Vine Twist" and "Virginny Breakdowns."

There is no doubt that darkies danced upon the levees along the rivers, and in the absence of music they "patted" for the dancers, singing something like:

> Forty horses in a stable,
> Forty niggers round a table.
> Juba dis and Juba dat,
> Juba 'round de kidney fat.

Darkies, as a rule, made their own poetry to suit the occasion and composed on the spur of the moment. From those crude dances came "Old Dan Tucker," "Old Bob Ridley," "Billy Barlow," and "Old Aunt Sally." Eph Horn danced the "Locomotive Darkie"; Frank Bower, "Happy Uncle Tom"; Ben Cotton, "Old Uncle Snow"; and Bob Hart, "Old King Crow." All of these pave the way for "Hop Lite Loo," "Ham Fat Man" and songs in use just before the Civil War on the same lines. Several verses with extravagant steps which were also part and parcel of the "Essence of Ole Virginny," "Essence of Moko," "Mississippi Fling," etc., etc.

* * * * * * * * * *

In 1839, T. D. Rice was performing at the Royal Pavilion, London, and appearing in the dramas when a nigger part was to be performed. His name appears in the drama of "Tom Tiller and Jack Mizen," as Gustavus Alolphus Pompey.

After Rumsey & Newcomb's Minstrels had performed in England, they crossed over to the continent and appeared in Germany. Their entertainment created quite a stir and pleased exceedingly. Unsworth and Eugene captivated them; but when the Germans found out that the troupe were composed of white men, "blacked up" and not the Simon pure article of Negroes, they were furious. They denounced the minstrels as swindlers and attempting to palm off as real darkies. The storm could not be allayed and, like the Arab, the Jolly Minstrels "folded up their tents" and skipped by the light of the moon back to a land where audiences are not so inquisitive and aggressive.

In the early seventies, Jack Haverly begins to loom up. His troupe has Charley Reynolds, Charley Pettingill, Sig. Brandisi, Gustave Bideaux, O. P. Sweet, Otis H. Carter and others. Later he becomes the manager of Cal Wagner's Minstrels, with Canfield and Booker, Cal Wagner, Sam Price, Lew Hallett, George Wilson, Milt Barlow, C. C. Templeton, and Harry Robinson, who is billed for the first time as the "Man With the Silver Horns." From this company springs the Barlow-Wilson, Primrose & West Company. Then the division of the partners. Then Thatcher, Primrose & West, and the separating of these companies also.

In 1870, Arlington's Minstrels had Saxton, Lumbard, Charles Sutton, "Fostelle," Ike Withers, Johnny Booker, Dick Gorman, and "Chang," the Chinese giant.

The Buckley's (1870) had Pete Lee, Hogan and Hughes, Joe Norrie, J. H. Murphy, Basquin Waterman, Cummings and Turner, and were located at the corner of Summer and Chauncey Streets, Boston, Mass.

In 1871, Hart, Ryman & Barney's Minstrels had Harry Norman, D. S. Vernon, Harry Saynor, Sam Ricky, and Master Barney, John Jennings and Add Weaver.

In 1872 the Morris Brothers announce Barnardo, Charles Sutton, J. C. Campbell, Barlow Brothers, Frank Campbell, J. W. McPhall, E. W. Prescott, Edwin Holmes, Sig. Lavalee.

While the name of Edwin Holmes is before me I am reminded that once if any minstrel boy made a funny blunder or mis-step a cry of "Holmes" would greet him from his comrades. This word is now and then used even by the younger element. This is its origin: Edwin Holmes, while a good fellow and capital singer, was singularly unfortunate. He blundered into everything. He upset pails of water in the dressing rooms, stepped on his high hat, and hundreds of mishaps befell him. Each time a crash or a noise betokened a trivial accident everybody would roar "Holmes." Once he was placed to guard a paper trap in the stage used for a skating scene and was warned to keep everybody away from it. When the scene was disclosed Holmes was nowhere to be seen. After the curtain fell on the climax, Holmes was discovered under the stage in a semi-conscious condition. He had himself fallen through the paper trap which he had been notified to guard others against.

There is a story that Holmes, disgusted, retired from the minstrel business and bought a milk route in Boston. The first day he went out the horse took fright and ran away. The milk cans were thrown out of the wagon, and horse and wagon ran over a boy, then became a wreck against a lamp post. This broke up Holmes in the milk business and he returned to minstrels, a penitent, but still able to furnish laughter to his comrades.

In the early seventies, Gustave Frohman piloted Callender's Georgia Minstrels to fame and prosperity. To Charles Frohman's clever business qualities and energy can be attributed the success of Haverly's Mastodon Minstrels. Thus it will be seen that clever men like the Frohmans were identified with minstrelsy and placed their marks of business methods upon the troupes with which they were connected.

This reminds me that Chauncey Olcott, Eddie Foy, John C. Rice, Tom Lewis, Press Eldridge, William P. Sweatnam, Weber and Fields, Little Sam Chip, and many bright lights of the present time were with the minstrels of the Eleventh Street Opera House, Philadelphia.

Haverly's Mastodon Minstrels---"Forty, Count Them, Forty"---created a tremendous sensation. All the other troupes had to expand or be wiped out. This brought a flood of young talent into minstrelsy---singers, dancers and comedians. Here is a partial list: Lew Spencer, James Fox, Pete Mack, Three Gorman Brothers, Three Crimmins Brothers, Frank Cushman, the Only Leon, H. M. Morse, Billy Arnold, Edwin Harley, Joseph M. Woods, E. M. Hall, Tom Sadler, Dan Thompson, Bob Hooley, E. M. Kayne, Eddie Collyer, Frank Casey, John Rice and almost everyone of any consequence was snapped up. Haverly at this time controlled theatres in almost every city of the Union and was rated the greatest manager America had ever seen. His tour to England began the undoing of all this, and his remaining days in late years were passed in a small museum in Brooklyn. Most of his staff of those prosperous days are theatrical magnates at present.

Later, the Mastodons announced Adams and Lee, O. H. Carter, Johnny Booker, Billy Rice, George Roe, Barry Maxwell, Harry Kennedy and the Arnold Brothers. Haverly's success induced Billy Emerson and R. M. Hooley to come into the field with their Megetharian Minstrels. The troupes were now digging up the fossilized remains of huge elephants, mastodons, mammoths and megetharians for titles to represent something huge and massive. Again the young talent had a chance to make good.

The following names appear with Emerson's company: James A. Barney, E. M. Hall, Luke Schoolcraft, Arthur Cook, H. W. Frillman, Carl, Will and Rit Rankin, Harry Robinson, Seamon Summers and the Girard Brothers, Gibson and Binney, Walsh and King, Burt Haverly and Gibbs, Park and Donnavan, Lyons and Healey, Kelly and O'Brien, John Oberist and V. Rigby.

I am reminded that the minstrels had a millionaire in their ranks. Not exactly a millionaire, but he bore his name. This was a singer named George W. Rockefeller.

Hi Henry discovered a great deal of young and genuine talent while he toured with his company. Other minstrel managers took good care to "annex" all the good ones developed by Hi Henry. In 1873, Kelly and Leon had Charles Lester, Sam Holdsworth, Dave Wilson, Frank Converse, H. T. Mudge, John Latour, Cool White, George Guy, Edwin Stanley, W. D. Corrister and Little Jake, a dwarf comedian.

Skiff and Gaylord's Minstrels, organized by Coal Oil Johnny, presented at one time the Albino Minstrels. They attired in white, wore white wigs and whitened their faces. The end men represented clowns. Bideaux, George Primrose, Goodyear Whiting, Lew Gaylord, Harry Talbott, John Lang and J. T. Gulick were with the Albinos; which, however, did not last long but returned to burnt cork. Later they had John Purcell, Con T. Murphy, Kelly and Holly, Joe Maiers, Ricardo, J. H. Carle, Mackin and Wilson, R. T. Tyrell, Andy McKee, Stiles Phelps, and Armstrong, Jim Gaynor, Johnny Howard, John Barsby, and the Masterson Brothers.

Simmons & Slocum's Minstrels, 1872 to 1874, presented many new faces and clever young performers. There was: Billy Manning, William Henry Rice, Primrose and West, William Hamilton, Shattuck, J. H. Stout, Matt Wheeler, Fred Walz, J. J. Kelly, Charles Stevens, Justin Robinson, Billy Sweatnam, J. L. Woolsey, William Dwyer, Welch and Rice, Charley Reed, George Thatcher, James G. Russell (the ventriloquist), Alexander Davis, and others. Quite another stir was made by Harry Robinson about this time. He called himself "the man with the silver horns," and he announced that he would not have any bills or posters on the walls. His war cry was "no paper on the walls." He antagonized all the billposters and those affiliated with them. For a season he triumphed, but had to fall in, same as the rest. He had with him Alf Miles, Billy McAllister, John E. Henshaw (now a noted comedian), Billy Ginevan, J. T. Simpson, George and Millie Guy, Johnny Shay, Tom Sadler and some fine young singers. John F. Henshaw is billed to sing and dance "Old Black Joe," and do a song and dance with Ginevan.

In 1878, Thatcher, Primrose & West announced Ed Marble, Lew H. Hawkins, Ben Collins, George Powers, John Daly, Eddie Marks, Hi Tom Ward, Fred Matthews, George Lewis, J. H. Davis, Bob McIntyre, Fred Oakland, Harry Constantine, Master Edward, Clipper Quartette, F. T. Ward, George Campbell, Bob McIntyre and Al Hart. Mr. Hart is now a very popular comedian in musical comedies. There was also Mack Mentor, Fred Herting, Eddie Macey and the proprietors.

About the same time, George Wilson announced Shattuck, Will Walling, W. E. Nankeville, John Davis, Tommy Donnelly, Fulton Brothers, Andy Rankin, Dan Quinlan, William Henry Rice. In 1890, Wilson had Ramsa and Arno, Hi Tom Ward, John T. Keegan, Howe and Wall, Fulton Brothers, Dan Quinlan, J. D. Daniels as manager, and William Rowe in a pedestal clog dance.

While on the subject it would be well to mention the greatest dancer and producer of dancing tableaux and novel groupings, Barney Fagan. He was a genuine "find" to minstrelsy and his methods are copied to this day in all dancing numbers. He was especially attentive to the young element and made great dancers of them.

In 1880 the San Francisco Minstrels had: Arthur Cook, W. F. Bishop, T. B. Dixon, Frank Dumont, Harry Wyatt, H. W. Frillman, Arthur Moreland, Johnson and Powers, George Thatcher, Edwin French, Harry Kennedy, Ricardo, Charles Gibbons, Carl Rudolph, etc., etc.; W. S. Mullaly, leader.

On the bills of different troupes, the names of the following appear: E. D. Gooding, Buck Shaffer, Bob Slaven, R. Jean Buckley, Dick Ralph, Ned Davis, Ned Turner. Emerson and the Big Four Minstrels (1879-80) had: Harry Stanwood, James and Barney Kine, Harry Armstrong, Theodore Jackson, Charles Heywood, Edwin Stanley, Weston Brothers, Sam and Morris, and the proprietors. This company introduced a banjo quintet by Stanwood, Kine Brothers and Weston Brothers. It was a novelty and was a big success. Burt Sheppard and Fred Walz joined this troupe also.

Barlow & Wilson Co. announced in 1884: E. M. Hall, Crawford and McKisson, Hughey Dougherty, Griffin and Marks, George Gale, Stanley Vernon, J. M. Woods, the Great McNish, Ed Talbert, Sam Bradbury. And for a while Dumont directed the company until the bill ran smooth. (The reader will note the new names and the young element in the above company.) In 1884, at the Standard Theatre, San Francisco, Cal., were: Carroll Johnson, Al Holland, Charley Reed, Franz Vetter, W. J. Morant, Hooley, Thompson, Keegan and Wilson, William Henry Rice, Harry Wyatt, John Robinson and Tommy Bree. Singers with phenomenal voices about this time were: Stanley Gray, Dick Jose, J. M. Woods, Charles Heywood and T. B. Dixon.

In 1888, I. W. Baird's Minstrels had Billy McAllister; Bryant and Sharpley's musical act; Billy Melville; Major Gorman, military drill expert; Fred Russell; Bartell; Brassell; Thomas Prosho; Conway; and Gardner.

C. W. Vreeland's Minstrels had: George Hassell, a remarkable soprano vocalist; Bassett and Cole; Arthur Deming; Harry Long; Hugh Franey; Billy Fries; Kennedy and Vonder; and George Dunbar.

In the eighties, Jack Aberle was induced to put out a minstrel show, as his name sounded much like Jack Haverly. In this company were: Billy Bryant, Bobby Newcomb, Joe Norcross, Dave Reed, Alf Holland, Joseph A. Kelly, Watson and Levanion, Three Crimmins Brothers, Foster and Hughes, Saunders, Morosco, Burke, Wright, and George W. Wood. The show did not travel very far in the East, as Aberle soon lost faith in it after counting the puny receipts.

Some of the phenomenal voices in minstrelsy were possessed by the following young talent: Rolin Dana, H. S. Thompson, Robert T. Tyrell, Banks Winter (White Wings), Charles F. Shattuck, Frank Howard, Carl Rudolph, William Dwyer, George Gale, Carl Rankin, William H. Frillman, Stanley Grey, Rayman Moore, Julius P. Witmark (a Madrigal boy singer with the San Francisco Minstrels, now of the firm of Witmark & Sons, music publishers), J. M. Woods, Dick Jose, T. B. Dixon, James G. Russell, Will Oakland, Edwin Harley, Beaumont Read, Leo Fagan, Fred Jarvis, Arthur Russell, the Great Millner, Fred Malcolm, William H. Windom and W. H. Nankeville. George B. Frothingham, the basso, of the Bostonians, who died about the middle of January, 1915, was for several seasons at the Eleventh Street Opera House, Philadelphia, before joining the operatic forces. Gus Williams, who died about the same date, often blacked up in his younger days or was added to some minstrel company as an extra attraction.

Al G. Field's Minstrels were organized in 1886, and gave their first performance at Marion, Ohio, October 6, 1886. It met with instant success and popularity and has been the leading troupe ever since. When the office of Klaw & Erlanger was called up and asked to name the best theatrical trade mark, the answer came, "The Al G. Field Greater Minstrels," and there is a reason for this. Al. G. Field had presented a new show every season, full of novelties, special acts, costumes and new scenery. He never fails to present an entertaining and amusing performance and is ever concocting new episodes of fun to add to his grand show. Even while spending a vacation on his farm (Maple Villa Farm), fourteen miles from Columbus, Ohio, surrounded by everything to make the farmer's heart glad, he is plotting and planning something out of the ordinary to place in his entertainment. That he succeeds is amply proved by the capacity business enjoyed everywhere by this great popular troupe, made so by his hard work and unremitting attention to all details. Al G. Field is the importer and owner of the great coach stallion, "Epernay," from France. It is the finest one in America and, as the war will prevent importations, in will become valuable indeed.

Here is a partial list of the graduates of the Al G. Field's Minstrels, furnished by Mr. Field himself to the writer: "Billy Van made his first appearance with my show and was here several seasons. Jimmy Wall did his first monologue with my company, also worked in a musical act, first as Howe and Wall, then as Howe, Wall and McLeod." Harry Shunk began his minstrel experience with this show. Billy S. (Single) Clifford began his career with this show, first as a drummer in the band, then as a song and dance man, and then as a comedian. Bernard Granville began his career with this show, in the bugle corps and as a song book seller, graduating into one of the brightest end men and neatest dancers in the country. Doc Quigley, one of the most versatile minstrel men of any age, began his career with this show. In fact, he was never with any other minstrels than the Al G. Field Minstrels, where he was a reigning favorite along the route for more than twenty years. Among his first minstrel engagements, Arthur Rigby was with the Al G. Field Minstrels. Harry Bulger began his stage career with the Al G. Field Minstrels as a drummer in the band, and a song and dance man, afterwards a comedian. The Diamond Brothers, Lawrence, Lew and Matt, began their minstrel careers with this company. John Russell was introduced to the minstrel stage by the Al G. Field Minstrels. West "Bud" Avey and Joe Coffman gained their minstrel experience here. Of the noted minstrel singers, Will L. Collins began his stage career with the Al G. Field Minstrels as tenor soloist. Collins is now Signor Toliona, of the Metropolitan Opera Company. Reese Prosser, another minstrel singer of note, began his career with this show, as did Jack Richards, Birch Logan and Harry Frillman. Charles Graham, the song writer, composer of "The Picture That Was Turned Toward the Wall," "Two Little Girls in Blue," etc., composed his most successful songs while a member of the Al G. Field Minstrels. Mr. Graham was the first stage manager of the company. He made his first appearance in minstrelsy with this company, as did also Gus White, Charley Greer, Eddie Harley, Charles Wilbur, Ed Munger, Ed Brown and Mr. Eldredge. Nearly all of these singers have made their marks in opera since graduating from the minstrel stage.

For the past few seasons the principal comedian has been Bert Swor. He has created characters new to the minstrel stage and is a most realistic impersonator of the real Southern darkie as he is. There is also West "Bud" Avey, with the comedy legs [who] is some dancer, as all critics express it. Eddie Uhrig is a fine dancer also. Boni Mack is an impersonator of colored belles. Joe Coffman is a real comedian, young and energetic. Jack Kennedy, a quaint fellow, is very funny. Ed Hughes and William Argall are a pair of fine vocalists. Herbert J. Leake, Billy Busch (band leader), Thomas E. Roper (director of the orchestra), Jack Richards, Denny O'Neil, John Morland, Adam Kessner, Sherman Dearn, Herbert Willison, Murphy and Terrill, Harry L. Frillman (solo basso), Harry Shunk, Frank Brown, William Wachsman, Charles L. Smith, Thomas Dent, Paul La Londe (vocal director for more than twenty years), Henri Neiser (animal impersonator), Frank Miller, Charles Markert, Edward Fisher, J. Lester Habercorn, John Carrmell, Ralph R. Scott, Harry W. Young, Birch Logan, J. W. Pickens, George Denton and Daniel Ryan. Eddie Conard is the manager and Al G. Field, the grand engineer of the throttle of this wonderful and speedy minstrel engine with H. W. Bedwards as advance agent.

In 1908, when Cohan & Harris ventured into the minstrel field, they created a tremendous stir. They had an immense company of the foremost talent to be found in America. Julian Eltinge was the great feature in a bill of startling novelties. George "Honey Boy" Evans, Eddie Leonard, Frank Morrell, John King, Vaughn Comfort and a grand singing and instrumental contingent comprised the troupe. The next season the company was called "The Honey Boy Evans Minstrels," with George Evans as the card. For a while Jim Corbett "blacked up" and appeared as the interlocutor. John L. Sullivan had done the same thing years previous in the Lester & Allen & John L. Sullivan's Minstrels. With Evans were Comfort and King, Sam Lee, Eddie Cupero, Le Roy White, John P. Rogers, Tommy Hyde, Eddie Barton, Arthur Rigby, William H. Thompson, Paul Van Dyke, Jim Doherty, James Meehan, Harold McIntyre, Willie Newsome, Eldon Durand, Charley Ufer, Billy Cawley, Dan Shea, etc.

Since writing the above, I regret to chronicle that death has claimed Mr. Evans. For the past two years, George Evans had been in poor health, suffering from a stomach trouble, but the George Evans "Honey Boy" Minstrels successfully toured the country, in spite of the fact that illness forced Mr. Evans to miss a number of performances from time to time. He died March 5 in Baltimore, Md.

The first McIntyre and Heath Minstrel Company was organized in Atlanta, Ga., December 18, 1878, and toured the South with John Steele, McIntyre and Heath, proprietors; Sugarfoot Smith, manager; Dick Turner, banjoist; Jim Librand, comedian. They had eighteen performers, mostly of the young element.

The second minstrel company was organized in St. Louis, Mo., in 1880, Matt Leland, Billy Monroe and McIntyre and Heath, proprietors; Senator Ed Wilson, end; Charley King, banjo and end man; the Great Rosselle, female impersonator; Adonis and Nun (Adonis was Johnny World), George Nun, of the Nun Bros., song and dance men; San Francisco Quartette: John Hall Greaves, first tenor; Charley Ukon, second tenor; Tom Ross, baritone; Frank Meader, bass.

The third company was in 1881, McIntyre and Heath and Jack Nugent, in Omaha, Neb.; George Costello, advance agent; Alf Barker, end man; Sam Yeager, leader of band; Blackford and Bye, musical act and end men; Latchow Bros., banjoists and clog dancers; Cummings and Clark, song and dance men; Lyons and Grayhill, song, dance and clog; Col. Bim Hall, second advance; Charley Herman, bass; Charley Lawrence, tenor; Nat Halstead, second tenor. On November 8 of the same year, Nugent sold his interest to Charlie Belmont, who purchased a sleeping car, the *Pontiac* which was the first car used by an organized minstrels to live in on the road.

The next McIntyre & Heath's Minstrels was in 1885 and 1886 with W. J. Gilmore, of Philadelphia, Ed Rosenbaum, managers; James Armstrong, treasurer; E. M. Kane, stage manager. Harry J. Armstrong and Lew Benedict, McIntyre and Heath on the ends; De Witt and Kerwin, musical team; Barlow Bros., Lewis and Stone, song and dance men; Davy Christy, tenor; Delhower and Guyer, contortionists; Jack Fielding, solo tenor; Graham, shadowgrapher; Clipper Quartette: George

Gale, first tenor; George Campbell, second tenor; Frank (Pop) Ward, baritone; F. A. Howard, bass.

McIntyre & Heath, Primrose & West's Minstrels, 1886-87, Henry J. Sayers, manager, opened in Youngstown, Ohio, in July. On the end: Harry J. Armstrong, Milt G. Barlow, Hi Tom Ward and McIntyre and Heath; George Stout, stage manager; Four Emperors of Music, Howard and Jack Burgess, added features; Markey and Hughes, song and dance; Prof. Gleason performing dogs; Talbot, Russell and Seeley.

McIntyre & Heath Minstrels, 1887-88, organized in Kenosha, Wis.: Al. Martin, proprietor; John Vogel, manager; George Osterstock, treasurer; J. L. Summers, stage manager; Billy Buckley, Milt G. Barlow, McIntyre and Heath, on ends; Old Hickory Quartette---Horace Rushby, tenor; Prof. Bushnell, performing dogs; Beatty and Bentley; Healy Bros.; Byron and Hogan; Lew Wells; Clifford and Hicky; the great "Stuart," female impersonator; Jule, the human bat (ceiling walker); and Prof. Abt, stereopticon views.

McIntyre & Heath's Southern Minstrels, in 1878, included: McIntyre and Heath, Senator Ed Wilson, Aldens and Nunn, the Great "Roselle," San Francisco Quartette; Fred Thatcher, first tenor; John Wilson, second tenor; Tom Ross, first bass; Frank Meader, second bass.

Richards & Pringle's Georgia Minstrels began operations in 1866, being founded by Mr. Spragueland, and four years later taken over by Orrin E. Richards and Charles W. Pringle. This would make this organization the oldest minstrel troupe still in existence. When the change of management took place, the title of Richards & Pringle was added to Georgia Minstrels and it has remained ever since. Still with the company is a tenor soloist, John A. Watts, now in his seventy-fifth year, a performer who has been connected with this company for twenty-eight years. Both Mr. Pringle and Mr. Richards have passed to the Great Beyond but their fame goes marching on. Sidney Kirkpatrick, dubbed the Black Billy West, has been interlocutor of this organization twelve years. Clarence Powell, leading comedian, has been with the company fourteen years. William Israel, double bass and tuba player, has been here ten years. David C. Smith, a brother-in-law of Billy Kersands and an able comedian, has been here six years. Billy Kersands was with this organization for many years before starting his own company. E. H. Dudley, well remembered with Gus Hill's Smart Set, first won recognition with this company. Fred W. Simpson, the greatest colored trombone player in the world, known from coast to coast as the Black Pryor, has had charge of the band for fifteen years, but owing to illness is temporarily absent. Two young comedians with this company who are rapidly winning recognition are Manzie Campbell and Chicken Reel Beaman. The company is now under the management of J. J. Holland and E. C. Filkins. They are very popular in the West and are at present on the Pacific Coast.

About six years ago Lew Dockstader's Minstrels went on tour under the management of Jim Decker. It was the last tour under that title. In the company were Neil O'Brien, Al Jolson, Eddie Mazier, Happy Naulty, Pete Detzell, Eddie Cupero and some fine singers and dancers engaged personally by Lew Dockstader.

They opened in Binghamton, N. Y. and created a furor by their up-to-date, lively performance. After the second performance, Decker made many "improvements" in the show. He discarded the fine first part costumes for the black coats, white vests and black pants worn since 1846. He introduced the "Jockey Clog Dance" and the "Cane Dance," which other troupes had cast out years previous. The show closed before the Christmas holidays and ventured out again after New Year's week. The show had been so renovated that in a few weeks it went into cold storage. Prize fighters are not the only men that can't "come back." No blame whatever could be attached to Lew Dockstader, as his entire company can testify. The members of his troupe scattered to the Honey Boy Evans Company and Neil O'Brien's new troupe. Neil is not only a fine and popular comedian but is progressive, energetic and capable, with a real manager like Oscar F. Hodge to aid him. They seek young talent at all times; and bear in mind that this is 1915.

This season (1915) the Guy Brothers Greater Minstrels, under the management of George R. Guy, has the following company: Charles Guy, Edwin Guy, Harry Toledo, Charles Cameron, Eddie Miller, Berlin and Urban, Bob McLaughlin, Steve McCarthy, Francis Blake, Rollin Webster, Harry Prince, Ansel and Hill, Billy Rush, Paridi Papanti, Ray Dion, Ed Wort, B. Proctor, Joe Wolfe, E. Volk, F. Nichols, J. Buckner, Charles Donahue, P. Hilligan, Andy Spoffard, Dean Lea and Clyde Ford. Bob McLaughlin is a young and ambitious comedian, rapidly forging to the front.

Neil O'Brien's company comprised the following names since he began under that title: Eddie Mazier, Harry Van Possen (monologist), Black Face Eddie Ross (banjoist), Pete Detzell, Major Casper Nowak, Less Copland, Happy Naulty, John King and Eddie Leonard. The bass singers are: David Morris (the greatest since Frillman), Al Fontaine and Fred Hodges. The interlocutors were: William H. Hallett, Leslie Berry and Walter Wolff. Orchestra leaders were Eddie Cupero and Frank Fuhrer, an excellent musician. The female impersonators: George Peduzzie and Walter Lindsay. The following vocalists: James Barardi, Master Georgie Hagan, Jack McShane, Joe McAnallan, Ward Barton, Winnie Williams, William Curran, Charles Wright, Jonathan Haw, Harry Ellis, William Oakland and Manuel Romaine, each and everyone a superb singer and popular. The dancers in past seasons were all young fellows: Du Ball Bros., Harry, Fred and Willie; Joe Marriott, Eddie Simms, Eddie Thurman, Ben Evans, Charles Ward, James Quinn, James Doyle, Harold Dixon, Jack Girard, Harold McIntyre, Jack Cochran, George Martin.

The dancers with Neil O'Brien this season are: Pete Detzell, producer; Charley Strong, William Doran, George Faust, Joe Mullen, James Monahan, Steve Werher, Lew Bligh, John Brennan, Charles Hodges, Joe Marinette and Eddie Dowling. Oscar F. Hodge is Neil O'Brien's manager and is the youngest manager in minstrelsy. He has had ample experience with the best of companies, including Lew Dockstader's Minstrels. He is now guiding Neil O'Brien to fame and prosperity.

On July 15, 1905, the De Rue Brothers organized a fine minstrel company and have been touring annually ever since. They had some of the best young element in their employ, many of whom have made their mark. Billy and Bobby De Rue are the principal comedians and have kept the show up to the standard. Both are skilled musicians. Bobby conducts a fine brass band and is considered a first class cornet soloist. They have had with them Walter Gassens; Happy Jack Lambert; Carl W. Ritter, an eccentric dancer of great merit, and who possesses a real coon dialect; Low Vanis; Joe Hill; Harry Young; George Adams; Jerry Le Roy; Fred Hill; Louis Tracey. The past two seasons, a double voiced vocalist, Arthur Russell, has been very prominent and rated as the most talented female impersonator in minstrelsy. William Sadler is an excellent tenor from Fort Jervis, N. Y. Russell Windenor is a grand basso; the Great "Millnor" is a clever impersonator; Walter K. Hearn, tenor; Willie Bawn, musical moke; the Fox Bros., two clever dancers; H. P. Savin have been leading members of De Rue Bros.' Minstrels in the past five years.

J. A. Coburn's Minstrels are very popular in the Southern and Western states. Manager Coburn's company comprises many of the younger element. The following is this season's roster: J. A. Coburn, owner and manager; Clayton L. Mix, business manager; Ted Galbraith, agent; Charles Gano, director and producer; Guy V. Risher, musical director; Fred Stowe, band director; Lester Lucas, interlocutor and basso; Joe McGuire, baritone; Claude Manvers, tenor; Donald Wilson, alto; Justin McCarthy, tenor; William Church, tenor; Shelby Baber, tenor; Archie Milton, tenor; Charles Scott, stage carpenter; Dan Kelly, properties; Joe Stirk, electrician; Nick Glynn, Tom Post, Charlie Vermont, Carl Hellman, Ollie Dillworth, Edward Powers, John Arnold, Carl Cameron, Evart Gavin, H. B. McBee, William Cover, Albert Morgan, Henry Whitman, William Porter.

Ralph Wray, of Los Angeles, Cal., and Billie S. Garvie, of Hartford, Conn., send me a few additional names of young talent who became well known: Frank Lawton, Eddie Horan, John Scott O'Hara, John Rooney, Fred Black, Sam Johnson, Joe Kelly. Sam Johnson is now in the hotel business in Willimantie, Conn. Joe Hooper, with Guy Bros.' Minstrels; Harry Boyd, Billy Beard, Andy McKee, Swor and Mack, and Billy Clark, of Grand Rapids. Al Fostell sends the following names of young minstrel talent: Sam and Wash Drane, Happy Reilly, Mike Dowd, Ad Hoyt, Greg Patti, Frank Golden, Hines, Lemar and Marron, Held and Cameron, F. E. Hughes, Jack Kennedy, Murphy and Terrill.

Lew Dockstader and George Primrose re-united for a tour season of 1913-14. The Six Brown Brothers were the musical feature of this combination. George Primrose, for the season of 1914-15, took George Wilson for a partner and then toured under the title of George Primrose and George Wilson's Minstrels. They had a good company in which the younger element predominated. They closed unexpectedly in Monmouth, Ill., January 7, 1915. They had with them: Earl Burgess, manager; comedians George Primrose, George Wilson, Happy Jack Lambert, Eddie Coe, Johnnie Bliss, Billy Sandy, F. Y. Grimley, Ray Hartigan, Jack Wier, Joe Hill,

Dick Barton, Harry Horton, Steve Fenton, Harry Greve; vocalists Lawrence J. Williamson, Fred C. Holmes, William G. Hayne, Harry F. Sievers, O. Sidney, Thomas Alton, Walter Remington, H. W. Robinson, Cal Douglas, L. M. Flaherty, Ed Neary, Newton Jones, Franklin, Carlyle and Walter Lawser.

From time to time articles or histories of minstrelsy have appeared in publications. These are mostly extracts or taken bodily from Charley White's "History of Minstrelsy," published by the *New York Clipper* in 1859, and Col. T. Allston Brown's "History of Minstrelsy," written also for the *New York Clipper*, which are notable. Both of these authors knew the early minstrels personally; saw them perform, and received from their own lips the story of their early careers. Naturally their histories are reliable and accurate and furnish all that a reader on the subject may need. Col. Brown is the only living authority on minstrelsy or the American stage.

John W. Vogel is one of the minstrel kings and began his show career in March, 1882, with Sells Brothers' Circus. He joined Thatcher, Primrose & West's Minstrels in November, 1882, at Cleveland, Ohio. One of the bitterest fights ever known was between Barlow & Wilson Minstrels and Thatcher, Primrose & West's Minstrels---the latter playing at the Euclid Avenue Opera House and the former at the Park Theatre.

Abe Erlanger assisted Vogel to bill Cleveland at that time. He has been identified with the following attractions in a managerial capacity since: Primrose & West's Minstrels; Primrose & Docksteder's Minstrels; McIntyre & Heath's Minstrels; McNish, Ramza & Arno's Minstrels; McNish, Johnson & Slovin's Minstrels; Dominick Murray's "Right's Right" Co.; Harry Bloodaood's "Happy Thought or Rose" Co.; George S. Knight's "Over the Garden Wall"; Al G. Field's Minstrels; the Original Adam Forepaugh's Circus; manager Fifteenth Street Theatre, Denver, Colo.; Thearle & Cooper's "Siege of Sebastopool"; Cliffside Park, Huntington, W. Va.; (lessee) "Darkest America"; John W. Vogel's Afro-American Mastodon Minstrels; John W. Vogel's (all white) Big City Minstrels, now in its twentieth year. He has several fine farms in Fairfield County, Ohio, on which there are a number of oil and gas wells. He is owner of the Gem Cigarette Roller and interested in numerous other business enterprises.

With Vogel's Minstrels this season, there are: Edwin De Coursey, James Conroy, Lew Denny, Al and Don Palmer, Ted Godfrey, Arthur Crawford, Tom Miller, Billie Mack, Harley Morton, Fred Miller, William Rowe, Ed Ewald, Jack O'Malley, Clyde Chain, Raymond Henry, Albert Petty, Carl S. Graves, F. S. Nagle, John Goodrich, George C. La Furroo, George C. Nunn, James S. Finning, Harry Baker, Newton Garner, George Van, "Zella" (the frog impersonator), Mack (the musical artist), Fred L. Day and Lee Mitchell, all splendid comedians, singers and dancers.

* * * * * * * * *

The old Eleventh Street Opera House, Philadelphia, was, prior to 1854, Dr. Wylie's Church. Sam Cartee leased it and opened it with a troupe he called

Julian's Serenaders and Opera Troupe. In fact, nearly all the troupes called themselves Burlesque Opera Troupes, in addition to the title of Minstrels. Ben Cotton
and E. F. Dixey were the comedians. Early in 1855, S. S. Sanford assumed the
lease and called it Sanford's Opera House. He remained there until 1862, when
Carncross & Dixey began their career as a permanent institution. Carncross remained there until 1896, when Dumont assumed the management and remained
there until four years ago. The neighborhood had become a mercantile district,
without traffic after dark. Dumont looked around and selected the old Museum,
corner of Ninth and Arch Streets, and moved into it, thus continuing Dumont's
Minstrels. The building had been erected by Carncross, Dixey and Simpson for the
new home of Carncross & Dixey's Minstrels, but they fluked at the last moment
and Simpson had to assume control. For years it had a varied experience, dramatic,
vaudeville, freaks, curiosities, etc., under various titles. Simpson lost the building
and after years of litigation again became its owner.

Four years ago it became what it had originally been built for---that is,
minstrel purposes. It became "Dumont's," and has been successful and flourishing.
It is the only located troup*e in the world and in the only city in America supporting its own minstrel company. Dumont has the proud distinction of not only being
the oldest minstrel manager still in active life but the proprietor of the only located
minstrel opera house in the world.

The following young talent became identified with Dumont's Minstrels in
Philadelphia and have achieved popularity: Vic Richards, Alf Gibson, J. M.
Woods, J. M. Kane, James McCool, Charley Dooin (a baseball favorite), Gilbert C.
Losee, Walter Johnson, Fred Jarvis (a phenomenal soprano), Fox and Ward (the
oldest black face team), John E. Murphy, Charley Turner, Jordan and White,
Evans and White, Happy Naulty, Leo Fagen, J. A. Dempsey, Vaughn Comfort,
Edwin Goldrick, with eighteen years' service. Most of the members have been here
for years: Tom Waters (the pianologist), Major Casper Nowak, Tom O'Brien,
Eddie Akin, Carroll Johnson, George Wilson, Dan McGarrigan, Bennie Franklin,
Harry Hoster, George Bradley, Ted Kahnar, Matt Wheeler, Billy Bowers, Jerry
Cunningham, Harry C. Shunk, Arthur Yule, John Haney, Patterson and Titus,
Eddie Cassady (and a clever fellow he is). Then there is Will Lawrence; and a
rising young comedian progressing rapidly called Charley Boyden, whom Dumont
has entrusted special comedy parts; John Lemuels, a character "coon" from the
South; Joe Perry, Earl and Will Dixon. R. P. Lilly, the musical director, has been
with Dumont for twenty-eight years.

As I write these lines, Joe Norcross and Sam Holdsworth, the two oldest
minstrel vocalists still in harness and performing in town this week, are looking
over my shoulder. And Joe says: "Put us down for a couple of kids, for we're just
starting in all over again." The staff has been connected here for many years also;
Howard M. Evans as business manager, John E. Besslin as treasurer.

With this final list of young names, it is fitting and proper to bring this
article to a close, having shown the great strides, changes and innovations created
by the Younger Generation in Minstrelsy.

George L. Fox

SOME CORK AND SAWDUST "THINKS" OF THE PAST
By Kit Clarke [New York Clipper, February 17, 1912]

An article recently printed in the *Clipper*, written by Edward Le Roy Rice, revived pleasant memories of my minstrel days and nights, and started my thinking machine into activity, resuscitating many delightful incidents and associations of the vanished "good old days of yore."

In my opinion the ancient and honorable pastime of negro minstrelsy met its severest blow---I might almost say crushing blow---when the late J. H. Haverly placed on the market his Mastodon Minstrels, and this not alone from a business point of view, but artistically as well. From the instant the curtain rose upon this organization, the bell tolled the requiem for our old time favorite, and the characteristics of the plantation Negro, the quaint antics of the river roustabout, and the unique genius of the darkie swell, went glimmering "down the corridors of time."

In place of these time honored, popular and enjoyable features, there came into the spotlight "Forty, Count 'em, Forty," embracing sixty or seventy people, exhibiting "mammoth" songs and dances, huge squads of electrically lighted acrobats in gaily caparisoned drills and marches, sumptuous silken draperies, gorgeous transformation scenes and daily parades, that rivaled an Oriental Durbar in clamor and display. If "Old Bill Jones" had been on earth at that time he would have reared up on his hind feet and openly declared that anybody who could possibly discover even a remote resemblance to negro minstrelsy in this entire production was a cowboy, a horse thief, and a two-story ding-bat liar, by gosh! And while the black face spectacular invasion---mixed occasionally with a small assortment of white face---was not negro minstrelsy by some sixty thousand miles, it appeared to be exactly what the public wanted and was willing to pay for, and this public got it and a lot more of it in copious doses.

When other energetic and ambitious managers heard the noise and observed the consequent amazing financial results, they promptly adopted the advanced spectacular proposition, and zoological dictionaries were searched with microscopes in digging up long and hard names to bestow upon new and big bunches of burnt cork crusaders. Among them came the "Megatherium" Minstrels, which "Dick" Hooley and "Billy" Emerson pushed out, and which sunk money in massive lumps, and the "Gigantean" Minstrels, which M. B. Leavitt organized, and when he became tired of the adventure, the wrong side of the ledger exhibited a loss of something close to one hundred thousand cold American dollars. In three or four years these exaggerated minstrels petered out and old time negro minstrelsy went with them---completely erased from the public mind, never again to attain its former welcome and general popularity.

Two hundred dollars daily was a rather heavy expense for an old time minstrel company to assume, and it is only requisite to compare this figure with the daily expenses of the spectacular shows to discover another "severe blow" to the old art far more effective than its desertion by a few performers for white face drama.

In January, 1865, I leased Bryan Hall, on Clark Street, Chicago, for a season of twelve weeks, and organized and played a company of twenty-two people under the name of the Empire Minstrels, with a salary list of much less than five hundred dollars weekly. There was nothing spectacular about this show or its expenses, but just a plain, old time negro minstrel company, with the "coon" element predominating, yet in the twelve weeks I cleared several thousand dollars, closing only because I was under contract to go in advance of the Adam Forepaugh's Show.

How long a period would a similar company exist in New York at present, and in this era of circus minstrelsy? Yet with this company there appeared for stated periods: Eph Horn, Sher Campbell, Sam Sharpley, Ben Cotton, Billy Manning, Johnny Allen and Unsworth and Eugene.

And it was here that Billy Emerson, Johnny Allen and Billy Manning organized and started Emerson, Allen and Manning's Minstrels, one of the most popular organizations of its kind ever placed before the public. This was, indeed, a splendid minstrel company, and met with great prosperity and this very great prosperity caused its final dissolution, which began in internal dissensions between the owners and ended in fisticuffs and separation. This "agreement to disagree," however, was not phenomenal, since it really appears as if the minstrel boys of ability, from that day to this, were all equally well developed in the art of "slugging." And no minstrel company was ever organized, in which performers were owners, that failed sooner or later to develop prolific internal dissensions that often resulted in first class fights and finally in separation.

From the Mastodons there graduated Barlow, Wilson, Primrose & West's Minstrels, which, because of disagreements, caused separations and reorganizations until no less than six different companies followed in quick succession, and all met with considerable success until family fights "busted" them. For such results there were, of course, many reasons; but I think the principal cause was an overdose of sudden, brain-affecting prosperity---something that few men, even ordinary men in other walks of life, find it difficult to assimilate with equanimity.

Because a number of talented black face comedians left minstrelsy to gain additional fame and dollars in drama, most assuredly redounded to the credit of the old art, since it conclusively proved that the actors on the minstrel stage were men of no ordinary ability. I have always thought there was a wide difference between the negro minstrel, the delineator of the quaint Negro character, and the black face comedian, exemplifier of "every old thing" to win a big laugh or "kill 'em dead"; and nearly all of the corkonians of the past, present and probably future, come under the latter definition. Some of these, too, are really fine performers, talented, artistic, humorous and most original, while the fact still remains that the coat of cork often leads to great success when the identical exhibit done in white face would probably be pushed down into the cellar.

Much publicity has been given to the names of many who moved from minstrelsy into the dramatic firmament; yet there is one name I have never seen printed in this connection---the name of one of our most illustrious actors. Indeed, I believe he was the most versatile and accomplished actor the American stage has ever known, a man who could act Sir Giles tonight, Hamlet tomorrow, Richelieu the next, and follow these with a black face song and dance or an "essence" that had but a single rival---Cool Burgess. I refer to E. L. Davenport, whose memory among many old departed friends is the best of all to me.

It would appear that anybody who covers his face with cork at once becomes a negro minstrel; but I cannot see it that away, since few, if any, ever pretend to imitate the colored race. Even Sweatnam, one of the most original and talented black face artists that ever lived, is not a negro minstrel, and Thatcher, Dockstader, George Wilson or George Evans, with scores of others, calling themselves such, are simply eccentric comedians. Billy Emerson's strongest effort was a rollicking Irish song, "Moriarity," and Carroll Johnson made an immense hit with Kennedy's Irish Song, "I Owe Ten Dollars to O'Grady," while Sweatnam's end song and greatest hit was celestial to the last degree, "Little Ah Sid"---a gem of the very first water, but quite some distance from anything of a Negro character.

An exhibit of Irish, Hebrew, Italian, Chinese and other foreign characters in black face make-up has helped some in putting negro minstrelsy into its little bed, and even in "vodvill" the true Negro is mighty scarce. Where, oh where, can we find the prototype of Billy Manning in his inimitable "Mrs. Dittmus' Party?" Where will we find another "Boy, Go 'Way from Dat Dar Muel," of McAndrews?

I think that more substantial talent was embraced in the Leavitt show than in any similar company ever organized, which, *en passant*, embraced several of the talented people named by Mr. Rice in his *Clipper* article. Among these were three famous quartettes---the musical group of Woods, Beasley and the Weston Brothers; the great acrobatic song and dance team of Leaman, Somers and the Girard Brothers, known as "The Grotesque Four," doubtless the strongest act of its kind ever seen upon the stage; and that constellation of true negro minstrel talent, called "The Old-time Quartette," who gave an exact reproduction of the "Virginia Serenaders," the original of all minstrel presentations.

In this act appeared one of the veritable founders of minstrelsy, Dan Emmett, who organized and rehearsed the act, which, besides himself, included Sam Sanford, Dave Reed and Archie Hughes. As I watched this act night after night, for I was the manager of the company, its unique quality, its absolute originality, its artistic versatility and its general excellence impressed me greatly; and I thought then, and still believe, that its associations and superb production made it by far the most interesting act the minstrel stage has ever seen, or ever will see.

Yet fine as was this act it never "caught on" with the public, for even then "old time" minstrelsy had gone glimmering. Only upon a single occasion did the act win large applause and this occurred in Atlanta, Ga., while even then the applause went out for Dan Emmett. The house was crowded, and as the curtain rose upon the Virginia Serenaders an enthusiast in the balcony shouted in a great big voice:

"Three cheers for the author of Dixie!"

Although it happened many years ago, I seem yet to hear the tumult, the volcanic noise of that vocal tornado, and can imagine as I saw him then, Emmett standing and bowing low while his hand grasped the back of his chair for support. After the show that night, Emmett and myself consulted about the act, seeking a reason for the light impression it usually made, when he suggested that its present form be dropped and in its place to introduce the entire company in a huge "walk around," just as it was done at Bryant's Minstrels, presenting "I Wish I Was in Dixie," with the author as the leading character, and with an appropriate moonlight cotton plantation scene as a background. This idea was promptly accepted; but was never completed for the interesting reason that a few days later Mr. Leavitt visited the show and "fired" me unceremoniously with the emphatic assertion that I was not worth a "continental ------." This little *pas de seul* forever terminated my association with that energetic gentleman, my position being assumed by J. H. Surridge, and I sailed for New York.

Hardly had I landed in the metropolis when a messenger brought me a letter saying that J. H. Haverly desired to have me call upon him at the Fifth Avenue Theatre, to which I gave no attention. The following morning Bob Filkins came to me and said "the governor" wanted me to come right up and see him on a matter of large importance; but I told Bob, who was a prince among good fellows, that "the governor" had mechanics at his service who could put in plain typewriting what intelligence he desired to convey. My reason for this was that but recently I had "bucked" the Haverly show and had "lambasted" it as hard as I knew how; and I did not care to have a "gabfest" with another minstrel king so quickly after the Leavitt matinee.

The following morning a carriage landed at my door and Mr. Haverly was before me and offered me an exceedingly liberal business proposition, after which he asked why I had left Mr. Leavitt. I replied that Mr. Leavitt had "fired" me in cold blood and said to me right out loud that I was not worth a "continental ------."

"That's a mighty good reason," said Mr. Haverly, and on the following afternoon, at Harrisburg, Pa., I became manager of Haverly's Mastodon Minstrels, superseding Joe Mack.

Negro minstrelsy has been forgotten, is not understood, while black face comedians, and a vast number who think themselves such, have flooded "vodville" with alleged acts and wild-eyed eccentricities to such an extent that interest in cork has been pretty well eliminated. Even the few traveling minstrel troupes that are still in existence venture an entire week in New York with no little timidity. I am glad to acknowledge that I always was, and always will be, fond of minstrelsy; and indeed it is about the only kind of an entertainment that, in these times, can induce me to leave my home at night. When George Evans brings his actors to the "City of Churches," in which I am permitted to live, I never fail to go back on the stage, sit on a real working trunk, and proceed to enjoy a talk with a minstrel, as well as the familiar sight of burnt cork and its fragrance. I think it stimulates the circulation of the blood and has an excellent effect upon my system, for the man who has once lived upon this "health food" never forgets its stimulating qualities; and although more than a quarter of a century has flown since I dropped the reins, I confess that whenever I hear the strains of a brass band I want to get out and lead the parade. Tom Moore was just about right when he sang:

> You may break, you may shatter the vase if you will,
> But the scent of the roses will cling to it still.

I recall the important fact that once upon a time I wrote a burlesque for production in black face, my topic being national in theme, the Credit Mobilier scandal, which destroyed the aspirations of James G. Blaine for the presidency. It was a magnificent example of literacy ability, this burlesque of mine, full of action, witticisms, topical hits and songs, and loaded with sarcastic "jabs" at politics and politicians. I sent the manuscript to Charley Backus, who read it, submitted it to Birch, Wambold and Bernard, and then returned it to me with but a single word of comment---"Funk."

Did I toss the dainty thing into the fire? No, sir. Did I rip it up? No, sir. Did I store it away for future ages to enjoy? Nein, Mein Herr. I mailed it to my friend, Pony Moore, in London, who, by return mail, thanked me very much and assured me he would give it consideration. About fifteen years later, while Pony and myself were enjoying a pleasant hour at Gatti's, I happened to remark:

"Say, Pony, do you remember that fine burlesque I sent you, and which you said you would consider?"

"Of course I do, and very well indeed," he replied.

"Well, what became of it?"

"I'm considering it yet."

The wall of my library holds a large and handsome crayon portrait of myself, made when I was a "corking" good looking young fellow, and every time I see it I am reminded of an incident which occurred in St. Louis. On the day the Mastodons opened at the Olympic Theatre, photographs of the company in a group and myself alone were made by Fox, a well known photographer of that city. Seven months later, when we again appeared in St. Louis, I was leisurely strolling along Fourth Street when my eye caught sight of a greatly enlarged crayon portrait of myself in the window of Fox. It was superbly made, and I stepped inside and inquired the price. A beautiful little girl, some ten or twelve years of age, said she thought it was not for sale, as her papa had taken great care in making it; but she would inquire, and went upstairs for this purpose. I seized the advantage of the moment, lifted the picture from the window and carried it outside. Just as I stepped into the place the child came down stairs and said emphatically that it was not for sale at any price. I bid her good-bye, had the picture carefully boxed and shipped to my home. That night Mr. Fox came to the theatre in a towering rage, accused me of stealing the picture, threatening everything he could devise from a "punch in the

256

jaw" to imprisonment for life. In all my experience I have never seen a man so thoroughly angry, so ferociously threatening; and yet, in half an hour the matter was amicably settled by paying him fifty dollars. The beautiful little girl mentioned is now known as Della Fox.

About the best "send off" that ever decorated my manly form emanated from this same good old St. Louis, and occurred while I was manager of Haverly's Mastodon Minstrels. A coterie of friends were assembled in the smoking room of the Planters Hotel when a letter was brought to me; and at once recognizing the writing of the address, and oblivious to my surroundings, I kissed the envelope. Just then a dozen hoots and guffaws broke out, and Charley Spaulding said:

"Now, look here, Kit, that won't do. Too spooney for anything. Confess now, your wife didn't write that letter?"

"No, she didn't," I replied. "It's from my best girl."

We all sat down and chatted a bit, when Pat Short said: "It s no use, Kit, you've got to read that letter to us. We want to know all about her."

"So you shall," I answered. "There it is," and I gave the precious missive to Spaulding to read.

"I guess not," said Spaulding. "We like to chaff a little, but I hope we are gentlemen. The young lady would hardly care to have her letter read by this crowd."

"But I insist upon it," I declared, "there's nothing to be ashamed of, barring the spelling, that is a trifle shaky, I admit. Read it, Charley."

Thus urged, Spaulding opened the letter and read it. There were only a few words. First he laughed, then swallowed suspiciously, and as he finished, threw it upon the table and rubbed the back of his hand across his eyes as if troubled with dimness of vision.

"Pshaw!" he exclaimed, "if I had a love letter like that----" and then he was silent.

"Fair play," cried one of the party.

"I'll read it to you, boys," said Spaulding, "and I think you'll agree with me that it is a model love letter.

And this is what he read: "Mi OWEN deer Pa Pa---I say mi prairs every nite and WEN i kiss yure pikshure i ask god to bless you. good bi Pa-Pa youre best girl, Elma."

Among those present was Tom Garrett, dramatic critic of the *Republican*, who decorated this incident with laces, frills and jewels of language until it filled a column, and it promptly went the rounds of the American press, headed "Kit Clark's Best Girl," while instantaneous and universal fame became mine. It was an affecting incident, to be sure, but was marred by a trifling error; because at that time I had no daughter named Elma. In fact I had no daughter of any name, was not married, and of course received no such letter, while Spaulding and Short were not in the party, and, as a climax, no such party had ever assembled. Garrett had invented the entire outfit; but it was a fine legend, anyway, went on its journey just the same, and I saw it in scores of newspapers.

The entire existence of the circus agent in those days might be correctly described in a single word, "hustle" and don't stop for a minute; and if any competition shows up, go at it with big guns. Yellow quarter-sheets in vast quantities flooded the land, and the grade and quantity of general and personal abuse those contained were invariably red hot and always sizzling. I still preserve two examples of such that are perhaps the most disreputable specimens of printed and openly circulated personal vilification, scandalous abuse and shameful adjectives that have ever been distributed. And they were written by W. W. Durand and Andrew Haight, both past masters of the art, in an effort to "down" our show. I went after these gentlemen and when I got through they and their show were wrecked and the two were in jail at Rock Island, Ill., where, after allowing them a few days to cool off, they were released and advised to "go and sin no more."

But the admonition was a failure, for not long afterwards they, with George W. De Haven, organized a "fly-by-night" affair, called the "Great Eastern," etc., etc., a very inferior little show with a huge and impressive title; and meeting the Forepaugh Show in Indiana, they again began a campaign of dirty yellow literature. Once more instructions came to me to chase them and never let up. I did so and followed them for weeks until they were swamped at Ogdensburg, N. Y., and skipped into Canada, where they were execution-proof. And yet, the crowd, outside of these villainous methods, were a mighty fine lot of men; but they cut out an immense amount of hard work for the opposition agent and just made him "hump" every minute, day and night.

I was agent for the Forepaugh Show until the Autumn of 1870, when I made a verbal agreement with W. C. Coup to go in advance of the newly organized Barnum Show on its inaugural tour in 1871. In November of that year, at the printing office of Clary & Reilly, No. 10 Spruce Street, New York, I met John O'Brien, a circus owner from Philadelphia; and during a quiet conversation I made an insignificant remark that reflected upon the illiteracy of Mr. Forepaugh. O'Brien returned to Philadelphia, met Forepaugh, magnified my remarks to such an extent that Adam sat down and wrote me a letter, which, for villainous abuse, I have never seen equaled. I still preserve this wonderful literary effort, and refer to it occasionally when I require a stimulant, since a reading does me far more good than half a dozen hot "sodas." Eliminating a splendid array of cuss words and vile phrases, the letter reads something like this:

> You confounded, low-lived, rotten, lying cur, I hear you are going 'round New York talking scandalous about me. Now, you ---- dirty, lying whelp, if I ever hear of such a thing again, you ----- petty loafer, I will come over there and club the dirty life out of you. (Signed) Adam Forepaugh. "P. S: If you want a situation I will give you $125 a week and your expenses the year round.

This offer was accepted by telegraph, as it was more salary than I had ever been paid before; and I remained with Adam Forepaugh seven years longer.

In 1884 Haverly's Mastodon Minstrels returned from England to the happy land of Klaw and Shubert. Aboard the ship, between stacks of chips, nausea and deck-chairs, I maintained a series of continuous thinking matinees; and after much mental argument reached the decision that it was about time, after twenty-five years of marauding, to bring my criminal career to an harmonious conclusion. This determination induced me to select a nice girl and marry her and then settle down in the peaceful lanes of commerce.

To give up the active and nervous career of the wandering showman for the quiet, grinding details of a commercial career was a more difficult task than I had conceived; but I always had a mania for "sticking," and eventually became acquainted with "time" and "terms," Bradstreet and Dunn, and above all, the certain reward of carefully negotiated discounts, short margins and speedy returns. Since then I have been happily interested in the career of an assortment of "kids," and once in a while lay back in my easy chair and ruminate over the past, and invariably conclude that if I could again live through the former years I would certainly choose the same career. They were good years to me, filled with happiness, romance, pleasure, friends, good health and hard work, and these are the greatest blessings that can come to a human being.

THE RISE AND FALL OF NEGRO MINSTRELSY
By Brander Matthews [*Scribner's Magazine*, June, 1915]

Of all the varied and manifold kinds of theatrical entertainment negro minstrelsy is the one which is absolutely native to these States and which could not have come into existence anywhere else in the civilized world. Here in America alone has the transplanted African been brought into intimate contact with the transplanted European. Other nations may have disputed our claim to the invention of the steamboat and the telegraph, but negro minstrelsy is as indisputably due to American inventiveness as the telephone itself. Here in the United States it had its humble beginnings; here it expanded and flourished for many years; from here it was exported to Great Britain, where it established itself for many seasons; from here it made sporadic excursions into France and into Germany; and here at last it has fallen into a decline and a decay which seem to doom it to a speedy extinction. Its life was little longer than that vouchsafed to man, threescore years and ten, for it was born in the fifth decade of the nineteenth century and in the second decade of the twentieth it lingers superfluous on the stage with none to do it reverence.

Time was when the negro minstrels held possession of three or four theatres in the single city of New York and when a dozen or more troupes were traveling from town to town; and now they have long ago surrendered their last hall in the metropolis and only two or three companies wind their lonely way from theatre to theatre throughout the United States. The few surviving practitioners of the art are reduced to the presentation of brief interludes in the all-devouring variety shows or to the impersonation of sparse Negro characters in occasional comedies. The Skidmore Guards who paraded so gaily at Harrigan and Hart's are disbanded now these many years; Johnny Wild, of joyous memory, is no more; and Sweatnam, bereft of his fellows in sable drollery, is seen only in a chance comedy like "Excuse Me" or the "County Chairman." George Christy and Dan Emmett and Dan Bryant have gone and left only fading memories of their breezy songs, their nimble dances, and their flippant quips. Edwin Forrest and Edwin Booth blacked up more than once, Joseph Jefferson and Barney Williams besmeared themselves with burnt cork on occasion; but it is not by these darker episodes in their artistic careers that they are now recalled, and the leading actors of today think scorn of negro minstrelsy whenever they deign to give it a thought. And yet it must be noted frankly that when Lambs wanted to raise money for their new clubhouse they did not disdain the art of the negro minstrel; and more than two score of them went forth to conquer willingly disguised in the uniform blackness assumed long ago by George Christy and Dan Bryant.

It is to be hoped that some devoted historian will come forward before it is too late and tell us the history of this very special form of theatrical art, the only indigenous to our soil. Indeed, now that our American universities are paying attention to the drama, what more alluring theme for the dissertation demanded of all candidates for the doctorate of Philosophy than an inquiry into the rise and fall of negro minstrelsy? In the late Laurence Hutton's conscientious and entertaining volume on the *Curiosities of the American Stage* there is a chapter in which the subject is treated historically, although the chronicler wasted much of his precious space in considering the succession of sable characters in the regular drama--- Shakespeare's *Othello*, Southerne's *Oroonoko*, Bickerstaff's *Mungo*, Boucicault's *Pete* (in the "Octoroon"), *Uncle Tom*, *Topsy*, *Eliza*, and their companions (in the undying dramatization of Mrs. Stowe's story). These were all parts in plays wherein white characters were prominent. The first performer of a song and dance, that is, of a sketch in which the darky performer was sufficient unto himself and was deprived of any support from persons of another complexion, seems to have been "Jim Crow" Rice--the title of whose lively lyric survives in the name bestowed upon the cars reserved for colored folk on certain Southern railroads. Rice found his pattern in an old Negro who did a peculiar step after he had sung to a tune of his own contriving:

> Wheel about, turn about, do jus' so;
> An' ebery time I turn about, I jump Jim Crow.

Rice carried Jim Crow to England and he made a specialty of dandy darkies. But he was not the discoverer of negro-minstrelsy, as we know it, although he blazed the trail for it. Indeed, it was quite probably due to the influence of Rice and his darky dandies that the negro minstrels confined their efforts to the imitation of the town Negro rather than of the plantation Negro, the field hand of the Uncle Remus type. Rice first impersonated Jim Crow in the late twenties, and it was in the middle of the thirties that he went to England. And it was in the early forties that Dan Emmett, Frank Brower, Billy Whitlock, and Dick Pelham happened to meet by accident in a New York boarding-house and amused themselves with songs accompanied by the banjo, the tambourine, and the bones. Pleased by the result of their exercises, they appeared together at a benefit; and negro minstrelsy was born. At first there was no differentiation into interlocutors and end men; they all took an equal share in the more or less improvised dialogue; they sang and they played and they danced the "Essence of Old Virginny."

Probably Emmett began early to provide new tunes for them. He was the composer of "Old Dan Tucker" and the "Boatman's Dance," of "Walk Along, John" and "Early in the Morning"; and one walk-around which be devised in the late fifties for Bryant's Minstrels, "Dixie," was introduced by Mrs. John Wood into a burlesque which she was playing in New Orleans just before the outbreak of the Civil War. The sentiment and the tune took the fancy of the ardent Louisianians and they carried it with them into the Confederate army, where it soon established itself as the war song of the South. And then when Richmond had fallen at last,

Lincoln ordered the bands of the victorious army to play "Dixie," with the wise explanation that as we had captured the Southern capital we had also captured the Southern song. And "Dixie," which had begun life so humbly as a walk-around in a minstrel show in New York, bids fair to survive indefinitely as the musical testimony to the fact that the cruel war is over and that these States are now one nation.

It was only a year or two after the quartet of Emmett, Brower, Whitlock and Pelham had shown the possibilities of the new form of amusement that troupes of negro minstrels began to supply an entire evening's amusement. The regulation "first part" was devised with its row of vocalists, instrumentalists, and comedians. The dignified interlocutor took his place in the middle of the semicircle and uttered the time-honored phrase: "Gentlemen, be seated. We will commence with the overture."

Bones captured the chair at one end and Tambo preempted that on the other; and they began their wordy skirmish with the middle-man, in which that pompous presiding officer always got the worst of it. This device for immediate and boisterous laughter, this putting down of the middle-man by the end-man, the negro minstrels appear to have borrowed from the circus, where the clown is also permitted always to discomfit the stiff and stately ringmaster.

But although the minstrels may have taken over this effective trick from the circus, with which some of the earlier performers had had intimate relations, the trick itself is of remote antiquity. The side-splitting colloquy of the end-man with the middle-man may be exactly like the interchange of merry jests between the clown and the ringmaster, yet it is far older than the modern circus. It existed in Paris, for example, in the sixteenth century, when the quack-doctor was accompanied by his jack-pudding. Many of the dialogues heard on the Pont-Neuf between Mondor and Tabarin have been preserved; and their method is precisely that of the dialogues ringmaster and clown, interlocutor and end-man, even to the persistent repetition of the question which contains the catch. "Mister," Tabarin would begin, "can you tell which is the more generous, a man or a woman?" And the quack-doctor would solemnly reply: "Ah, Tabarin, that is a question which has been greatly debated by the philosophers of antiquity, and they have been unable to decide which is truly the more generous, a man or a woman."

Then Tabarin would briskly retort, "Never mind the old philosophers. I can tell you."

And with great contempt the ponderous quack-doctor would return, "What, Tabarin, do you mean to say that you can tell which is the more generous, a man or a woman?"

Tabarin promptly responds that he can.

"Then," asks Mondor, "pray do so. Which is the more generous, a man or a woman?"

And thereupon, to the great disgust of Mondor, Tabarin would proffer his ribald explanation. Unfortunately the explanation he gave is frankly too ribald to be given here, for nowadays we are more squeamish than the idlers who gathered around the quack-doctor's platform in Paris three or four centuries ago. The dialogues of Mondor and Tabarin were brief enough, but they often made up for their brevity in their breadth.

This kind of catch-question was known in England under Elizabeth as "selling a bargain"; and it is not infrequent in the plays of the time. It will be found more, than once in earlier plays of Shakespeare; for example, when his "clowns" (as the low comedy characters were then called) were allowed to run on at their own sweet will. Not a little of the dialogue of the two Dromios is closely akin in its method to interchange of question and answer between the interlocutor and the end-man. We may be sure this method of evoking laughter was employed also by the improvising comedians of the Italian comedy of masks, with which negro minstrelsy has other points of resemblance. It must have been popular in the rude middle ages; and now that negro minstrelsy is disappearing, and now that our circuses have burgeoned into three rings under a tent too vast for any merely verbal repartees, it has not departed from among us for it still survives as the staple of the so-called "side-walk conversationalists" who swap personalities in our superabundant variety shows.

We do not know with historic certainty how soon the first part crystallized into the form which has long been traditional---the opening overture, the catch-questioning of end-man and middle-man, the comic songs of Bones and Tambo in turn, the sentimental ballads by the silver-throated vocalists, and the final walk-around. The rest of the evening's entertainment never took on any definite framework, although the final item on the program was likely to be a piece of some length, often a burlesque of a serious drama then popular, and this little play "enlisted the whole strength of the company." Between the stately first part and the more pretentious final sketch the minstrels presented a variety of acts in which the several members exhibited their specialties. A clog-dance was always in order, although the mechanical precision of this form of saltatorial exercise was wholly foreign to the characteristics of the actual Negroes whom the minstrels were supposed to be representing. A stump-speech was certain of a warm reception, although this again departed from the true Negro tradition and indeed often degenerated into frank burlesque, wholly unrelated to the realities of life. Sketches, like those which Rice had earlier composed for his own acting, were likely to have a little closer relationship to the genuine darky.

Yet here again the negro minstrel was not avid of overt originality. He was willing to find his profit in the past and to translate into Negro dialect any farce, however ancient, which might contain comic situations or humorous, characters that could be twisted to suit his immediate purpose. He seized upon the ingenious plots of certain of the pantomimes brought to America from France half a century ago by the Ravels. And on occasion he went unwittingly still farther afield for his prey. There is in print, in a collection of so-called "Ethiopian Drama," an amusing sketch entitled the "Great Mutton Trial"; and the remote source of this is to be sought in the oldest and best farce which has survived in French literature. "Maître Pierre Pathelin" is now acted occasionally by the Comédie-Française in Paris in a version which preserves its original flavor; but in the eighteenth century an adaptation, made by Brueys and Palaprat, and called "L'Avocat Pathelin," was popular. It is this later perversion which served as the basis of an English farce, entitled the "Village Lawyer"; and the "Great Mutton Trial" is simply the "Village Lawyer" transmogrified to suit the bolder and more robust methods of the negro minstrels.

And here we may discover the real reason why negro minstrelsy failed to establish itself. It neglected its opportunity to devote itself primarily to its own peculiar field---the humorous reproduction of the sayings and doings of the colored man in the United States. To represent the Negro in his comic aspects and in his sentimental moods was what the minstrels pretended to do; but the pretense was often only a hollow mockery. Even the musical instruments they affected, the banjo and the bones, were not as characteristic of the field-hand or even of the town darky as the violin. Indeed, the bones cannot be considered as in any way special to the Negro; they were familiar to Shakespeare's Bottom, who declares, "I have a reasonable good ear in music; let us have the tongs and the bones." And the wise recorder of the words and deeds of Uncle Remus declared that he had never listened to the staccato picking of a banjo in the Negro quarters of any plantation.

"I have seen the Negro at work," so Harris once asserted, "and I have seen him at play; I have attended his cornshuckings, his dances, and his frolics; I have heard him give the wonderful melody of his songs to the winds; I have heard him give barbaric airs to the quills (that is to say, to the Pan's pipes); I have heard him scrape jubilantly on the fiddle; I have seen him blow wildly on the bugle and beat enthusiastically on the triangle; but I have never heard him play on the banjo." Mr. George W. Cable thereupon came forward with his evidence to the effect that although the banjo was to be found occasionally on a plantation it was far less frequently seen than the violin. It will be noted that Harris was speaking of the Georgian Negro and that Mr. Cable was talking about the Negro in Louisiana; and perhaps the true habitat of the banjo is to be found further north and nearer to the border States. At any rate, there is a footnote to one of Thomas Jefferson's "Notes on Virginia," published in 1784, which informs us that the instrument proper to the slave of the Old Dominion is "the banjar, which they brought hither from Africa, and which is the origin of the guitar, its chords being precisely the four lower chords of the guitar."

Now and again some one negro minstrel did make a serious study of a Negro type; such a performer was J. W. McAndrew, the "Watermelon Man." But the most of them were content to be comic without any effort to catch the special comicality of the darky; and some times they strayed so completely from the path as to indulge in songs in an Irish brogue or in a dislocated German dialect. Now, nothing could well be conceived more incongruously inartistic than a white man blacked up into the semblance of a Negro and then impertinently caroling an impudent Irish lyric. Yet the general neglect of the opportunities for a more accurate presentation of Negro characteristics is to be seen in the strange fact that the minstrels failed to perceive the possible popularity of rag-time tunes and failed also to put the cake-walk on the stage. Even at the height of its vogue in the sixties negro minstrelsy did not copy its own field and did not try to raise therein the varied flowers of which they had the seed.

Instead of cultivating the tempting possibilities which lay before them and devoting themselves to a loving delineation of the colored people who make up a tenth of our population, they turned aside to the spectacular elaboration of their original entertainment. The clog-dance became more intricate and more mechanical and thereby still more remote from the buck-and-wing dancing of the real Negro. The first-part was presented with accompaniments of Oriental magnificence of variegated glitter. The chorus was enlarged; the musicians were multiplied; the end-men operated in relays; and at last the bass drum which towered aloft over Haverly's Mastodon Minstrels bore the boastful legend: "40. Count Them. 40." And when the suspicious spectator obeyed this command he discovered to his surprise that the vaunt was more than made good, since he had a full view of at least half a dozen performers in addition to the promised two score.

At the apex of his inflated prosperity Haverly invaded Germany with his mastodonic organization; and one result of his visit was probably still further to confuse the Teutonic misinformation about the American type, which seems often to be a curious composite photograph of the red men of Cooper, the black men of Mrs. Stowe, and the white men of Mark Twain and Bret Harte. And it was reported at the time that another and more immediate result of this rash foray beyond the boundaries of the English-speaking race was that Haverly was for a while in danger of arrest by the police for a fraudulent attempt to deceive the German public, because be was pretending to present a company of negro minstrels, whereas his performers were actually white men. It should be recorded that while the vogue lasted there did come into existence sundry troupes of minstrels whose members were all of them actually colored men, although they conformed to the convention set by those whom they were imitating and conscientiously disguised themselves with burnt cork to achieve the sable uniformity temporarily attained by the ordinary negro minstrels.

Perhaps the most obvious parallel of the blacking up of veritable colored men to follow the example of the white men who pretended to imitate the Negro is to be found in the original performance of "As You Like It," when the shaven boy actor who impersonated Rosalind disguised himself a lad, and then had to pretend to Orlando that he was a girl.

For the decline and fall of negro minstrelsy it is easy to find more than one sufficient explanation. First of all, it may have been due to its failure to devote itself lovingly to the representation of the many peculiarities of the darker people. Second, it is possible that negro minstrelsy had an inherent and inevitable disqualification for enduring popularity, in that it was exclusively masculine and necessarily deprived of the potent attractiveness exerted by the members of the more fascinating sex. And in the third place, its program was limited and monotonous; and therefore negro minstrelsy could not long withstand the competition of the music hall, of the variety show, and of the comic musical pieces, which satisfied more amply the same tastes of the public for broad fun commingled with song and dance.

Whatever the exact cause may be, there is no denying that negro minstrelsy is on the verge of extinction, however much we may bewail the fact. It failed to accomplish its true purpose; and it is disappearing, leaving behind it little that is worthy of preservation except a few of its songs. This at least it has to its credit, that it gave Stephen Collins Foster the chance to produce his simple melodies. Perhaps we might even venture to assert that the existence of negro minstrelsy is justified by a single one of these songs—by "Old Folks at Home," which has a wailing melancholy and an unaffected pathos lacking in the earlier and more saccharine "Home, Sweet Home," based on an old Sicilian tune.
After Foster came Root and Work; and "My Old Kentucky Home" was succeeded by "Tramp, Tramp, Tramp, the Boys Are Marching." and by "Marching Through Georgia"—which last lyric now shares its popularity only with "Dixie" as a musical relic of the Civil War.

It would be pleasant to know whether it was one of Foster's songs and which one it may have been that once touched the tender heart of Thackeray. "I heard a humorous balladist not long ago," the novelist recorded, "a minstrel with wool on his head and an ultra-Ethiopian complexion, who performed a Negro ballad that I confess moistened these spectacles in a most unexpected manner. I have gazed at thousands of tragedy--queens dying on the stage and expiring in appropriate blank verse, and I never wanted to wipe them. They have looked up, be it said, at many scores of clergymen without being dimmed, and behold! a vagabond with a corked face and a banjo sings a little song, strikes a wild note, which sets the heart thrilling with happy piety."

www.ingramcontent.com/pod-product-compliance
Lightning Source LLC
Chambersburg PA
CBHW060255100426
42742CB00011B/1753